Planet Ladder

Planet Ladder

Volume 4

Written and Illustrated by
Yuri Narushima

Los Angeles . Tokyo

Translator - Nan Rymer
English Adaption - Kristen Bailey Murphy
Associate Editor - Jodi Bryson
Retouch and Lettering - Yoffy
Cover Layout and Graphic Designer - Anna Kernbaum

Senior Editor - Julie Taylor
Production Managers - Jennifer Miller and Jennifer Wagner
Art Director - Matthew Alford
VP of Production & Manufacturing - Ron Klamert
President & C.O.O. - John Parker
Publisher - Stuart Levy

Email: editor@TOKYOPOP.com
Come visit us online at www.TOKYOPOP.com

A **TOKYOPOP** Manga
TOKYOPOP® is an imprint of Mixx Entertainment Inc.
5900 Wilshire Blvd. Suite 2000, Los Angeles, CA 90036

ISBN: 1-59182-063-4

First TOKYOPOP® printing: December 2002

10 9 8 7 6 5 4 3 2 1
Printed in the USA

Table of Contents

キャラクター紹介
Character Introduction

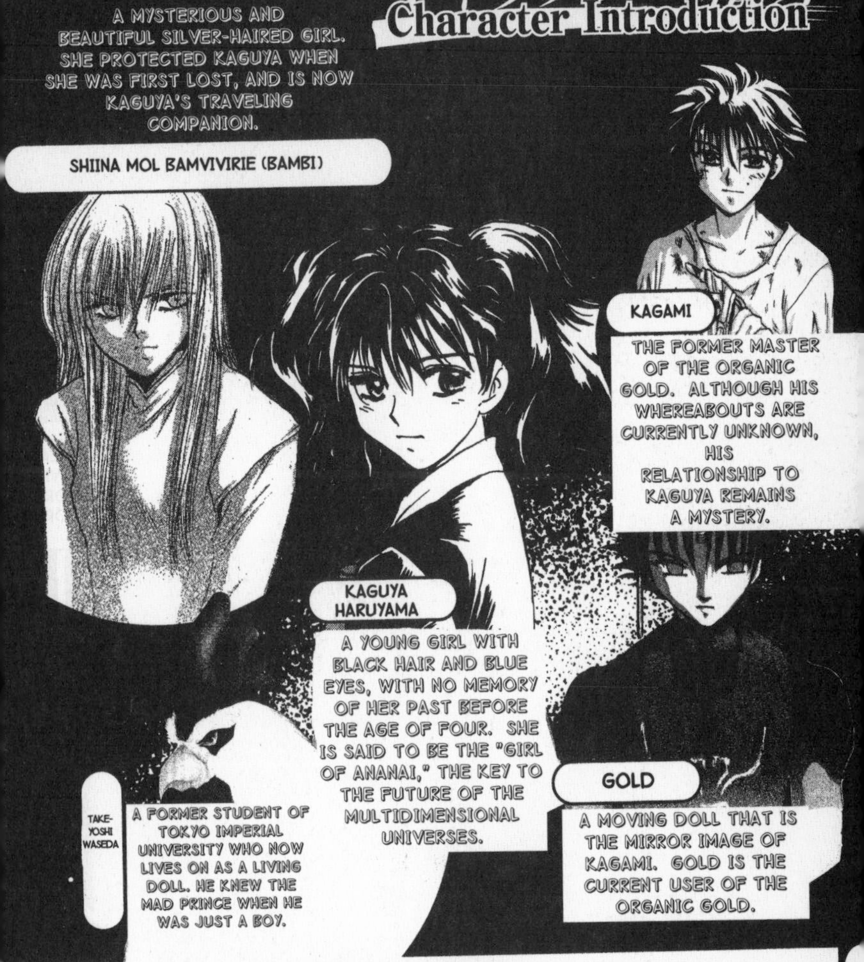
A MYSTERIOUS AND BEAUTIFUL SILVER-HAIRED GIRL. SHE PROTECTED KAGUYA WHEN SHE WAS FIRST LOST, AND IS NOW KAGUYA'S TRAVELING COMPANION.
SHIINA MOL BAMVIVIRIE (BAMBI)
KAGAMI
THE FORMER MASTER OF THE ORGANIC GOLD. ALTHOUGH HIS WHEREABOUTS ARE CURRENTLY UNKNOWN, HIS RELATIONSHIP TO KAGUYA REMAINS A MYSTERY.
KAGUYA HARUYAMA
A YOUNG GIRL WITH BLACK HAIR AND BLUE EYES, WITH NO MEMORY OF HER PAST BEFORE THE AGE OF FOUR. SHE IS SAID TO BE THE "GIRL OF ANANAI," THE KEY TO THE FUTURE OF THE MULTIDIMENSIONAL UNIVERSES.
GOLD
A MOVING DOLL THAT IS THE MIRROR IMAGE OF KAGAMI. GOLD IS THE CURRENT USER OF THE ORGANIC GOLD.
TAKE-YOSHI WASEDA
A FORMER STUDENT OF TOKYO IMPERIAL UNIVERSITY WHO NOW LIVES ON AS A LIVING DOLL. HE KNEW THE MAD PRINCE WHEN HE WAS JUST A BOY.

THE STORY UNTIL NOW...

AFTER STUMBLING INTO A FOREIGN WORLD, KAGUYA FINDS HER LIFE SAVED BY A BEAUTIFUL SILVER-HAIRED GIRL NAMED BAMBI. FROM BAMBI, KAGUYA LEARNS THAT SHE IS ON ANOTHER EARTH CALLED THE FOURTH WORLD, OR "TELENE," A WHOLLY SEPARATE WORLD FROM HER OWN "EARTH." SOUGHT BY MANY AS THE "GIRL OF ANANAI," KAGUYA, TOGETHER WITH BAMBI AND GOLD, SETS OUT ON A JOURNEY TO THE CITY WHERE THEY HOPE TO FIND THE COLLAPSER, A DEVICE THAT ENABLES FREE TRAVEL WITHIN THE UNIVERSES. DURING THEIR TRAVELS THROUGH THE WILDERNESS OF TELENE, KAGUYA MEETS UP WITH WASEDA, A SOUL THAT EXISTS IN THE BODY OF A GIANT ROOSTER. WASEDA REVEALS HIMSELF TO BE A JAPANESE NATIONAL WHO HAD COME TO THE SECOND WORLD, ASU, THROUGH A RIP IN THE DIMENSIONAL FABRIC OF THE UNIVERSE. ALONG WITH THIS REVELATION, WASEDA ALSO RELATES HIS MEMORIES OF SEEU'S CHILDHOOD, THE SECRETS SURROUNDING THE DEMISE OF THE SECOND WORLD, AND HOW HE HIMSELF CAME TO EXIST IN THE BODY OF A LIVING DOLL–A DOLL THAT WALKS AND TALKS AND POSESSES A HUMAN SOUL. HEARING WASEDA'S SAD BUT MOVING TALE, KAGUYA DECIDES TO USE HERSELF AS THE GREATEST LURE OF ALL SO THAT SHE MIGHT DIRECTLY FACE THE EMPEROR OF THE SEVENTH WORLD, GEO, AND GAIN THE CHANCE TO CHANGE THE INESCAPABLE AND RUINOUS FATE OF THE MULTIDIMENSIONAL UNIVERSE.

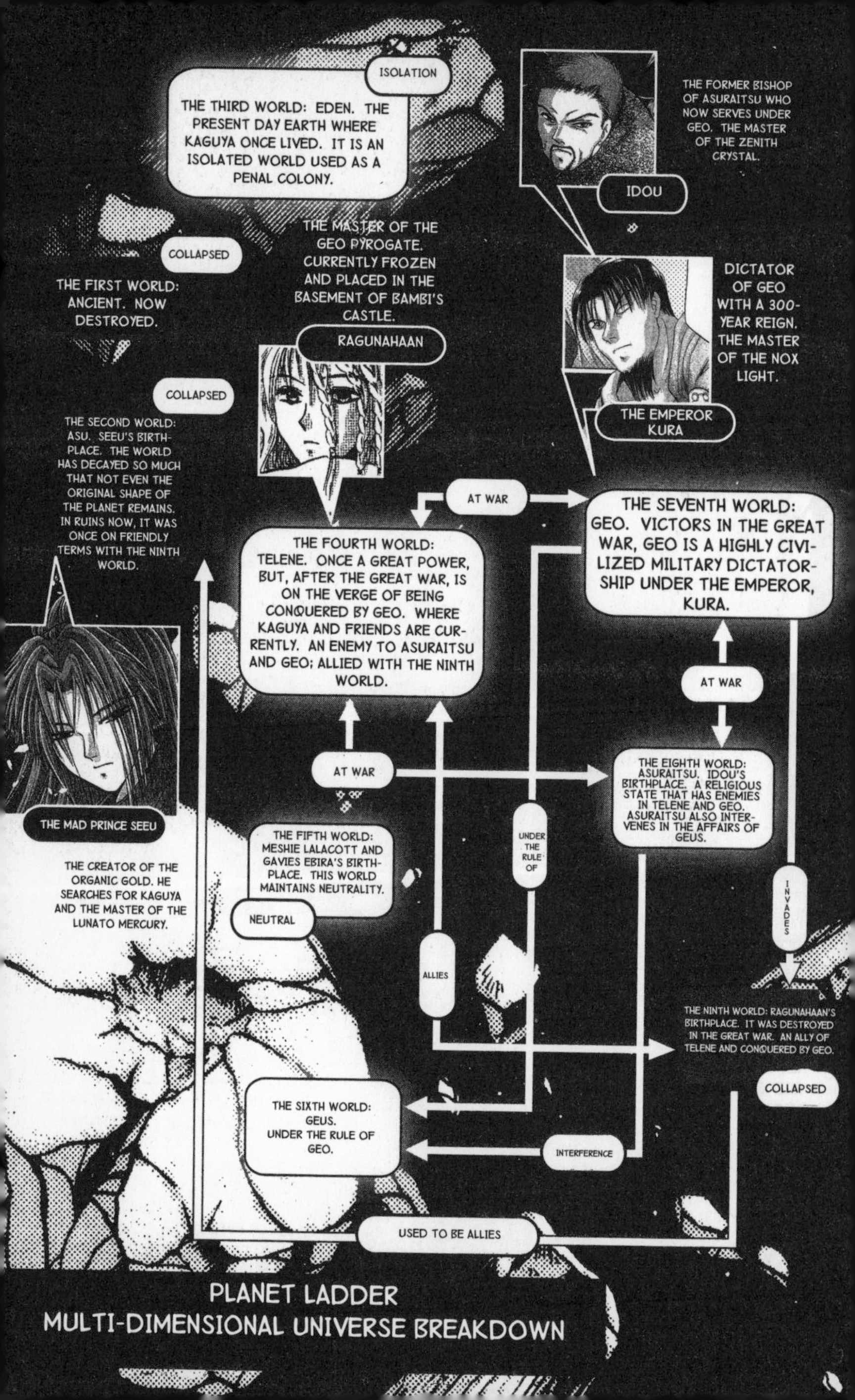
ISOLATION
THE THIRD WORLD: EDEN. THE PRESENT DAY EARTH WHERE KAGUYA ONCE LIVED. IT IS AN ISOLATED WORLD USED AS A PENAL COLONY.
THE FORMER BISHOP OF ASURAITSU WHO NOW SERVES UNDER GEO. THE MASTER OF THE ZENITH CRYSTAL.
IDOU
COLLAPSED
THE FIRST WORLD: ANCIENT. NOW DESTROYED.
THE MASTER OF THE GEO PYROGATE. CURRENTLY FROZEN AND PLACED IN THE BASEMENT OF BAMBI'S CASTLE.
RAGUNAHAAN
DICTATOR OF GEO WITH A 300-YEAR REIGN. THE MASTER OF THE NOX LIGHT.
THE EMPEROR KURA
COLLAPSED
THE SECOND WORLD: ASU. SEEU'S BIRTHPLACE. THE WORLD HAS DECAYED SO MUCH THAT NOT EVEN THE ORIGINAL SHAPE OF THE PLANET REMAINS. IN RUINS NOW, IT WAS ONCE ON FRIENDLY TERMS WITH THE NINTH WORLD.
AT WAR
THE SEVENTH WORLD: GEO. VICTORS IN THE GREAT WAR, GEO IS A HIGHLY CIVILIZED MILITARY DICTATORSHIP UNDER THE EMPEROR, KURA.
THE FOURTH WORLD: TELENE. ONCE A GREAT POWER, BUT, AFTER THE GREAT WAR, IS ON THE VERGE OF BEING CONQUERED BY GEO. WHERE KAGUYA AND FRIENDS ARE CURRENTLY. AN ENEMY TO ASURAITSU AND GEO; ALLIED WITH THE NINTH WORLD.
THE MAD PRINCE SEEU
AT WAR
AT WAR
THE EIGHTH WORLD: ASURAITSU. IDOU'S BIRTHPLACE. A RELIGIOUS STATE THAT HAS ENEMIES IN TELENE AND GEO. ASURAITSU ALSO INTERVENES IN THE AFFAIRS OF GEUS.
THE CREATOR OF THE ORGANIC GOLD. HE SEARCHES FOR KAGUYA AND THE MASTER OF THE LUNATO MERCURY.
THE FIFTH WORLD: MESHIE LALACOTT AND GAVIES EBIRA'S BIRTHPLACE. THIS WORLD MAINTAINS NEUTRALITY.
NEUTRAL
UNDER THE RULE OF
INVADES
ALLIES
THE NINTH WORLD: RAGUNAHAAN'S BIRTHPLACE. IT WAS DESTROYED IN THE GREAT WAR. AN ALLY OF TELENE AND CONQUERED BY GEO.
COLLAPSED
THE SIXTH WORLD: GEUS. UNDER THE RULE OF GEO.
INTERFERENCE
USED TO BE ALLIES

PLANET LADDER
MULTI-DIMENSIONAL UNIVERSE BREAKDOWN

Thoughts on Y2K:

PLANET LADDER.
I'M A PUZZLE, A
PRINCESS, AND AN
ANANAI, AS WELL.

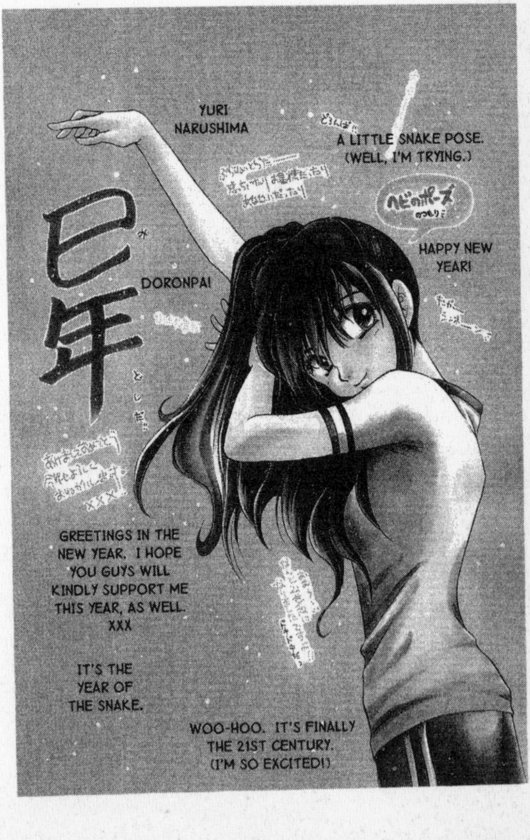
YURI
NARUSHIMA
A LITTLE SNAKE POSE.
(WELL, I'M TRYING.)
ヘビのポーズ
巳年
DORONPA!
HAPPY NEW
YEAR!
GREETINGS IN THE
NEW YEAR. I HOPE
YOU GUYS WILL
KINDLY SUPPORT ME
THIS YEAR, AS WELL.
XXX
IT'S THE
YEAR OF
THE SNAKE.
WOO-HOO. IT'S FINALLY
THE 21ST CENTURY.
(I'M SO EXCITED!)

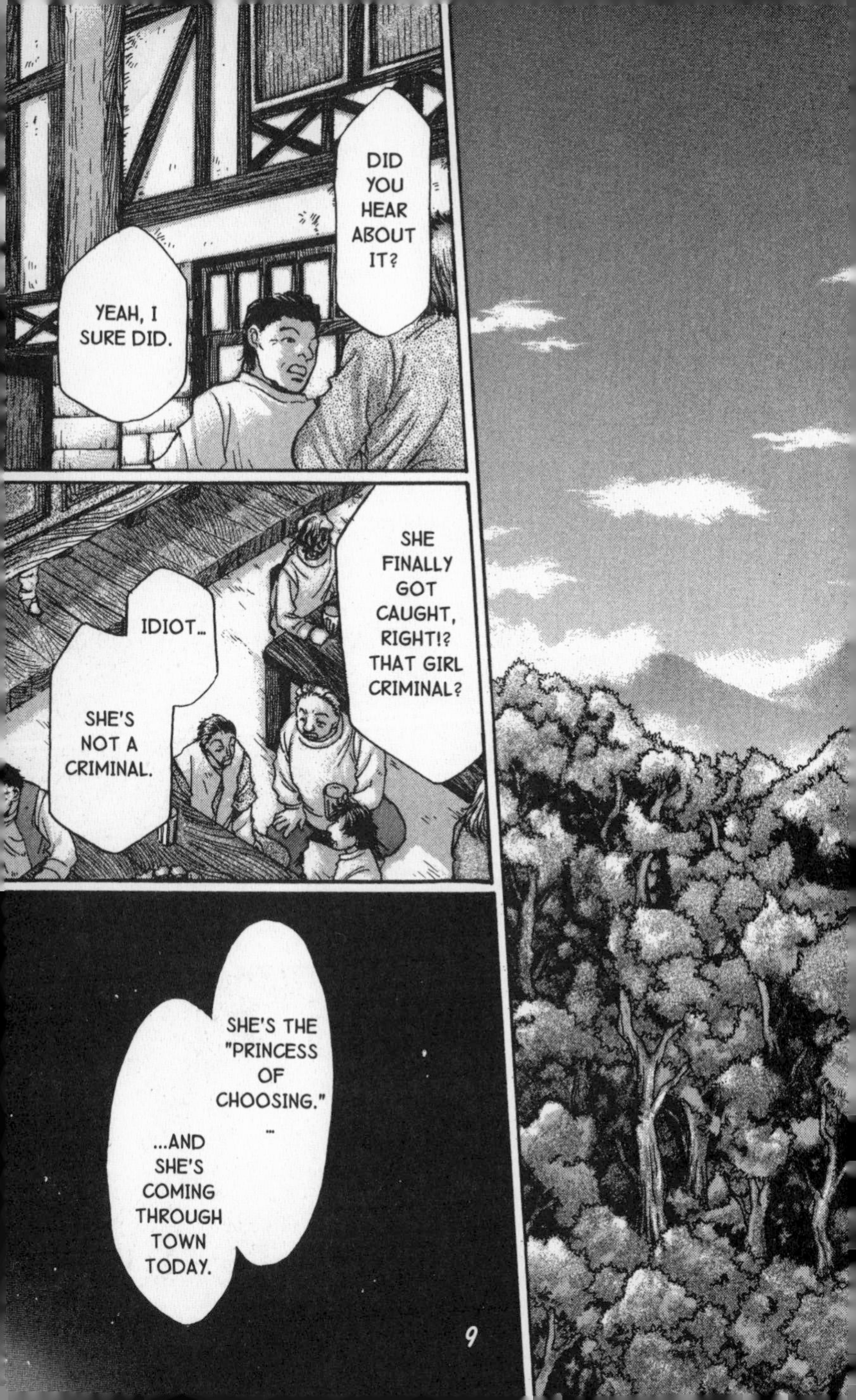
DID YOU HEAR ABOUT IT?
YEAH, I SURE DID.
SHE FINALLY GOT CAUGHT, RIGHT!? THAT GIRL CRIMINAL?
IDIOT...
SHE'S NOT A CRIMINAL.
SHE'S THE "PRINCESS OF CHOOSING." ...
...AND SHE'S COMING THROUGH TOWN TODAY.

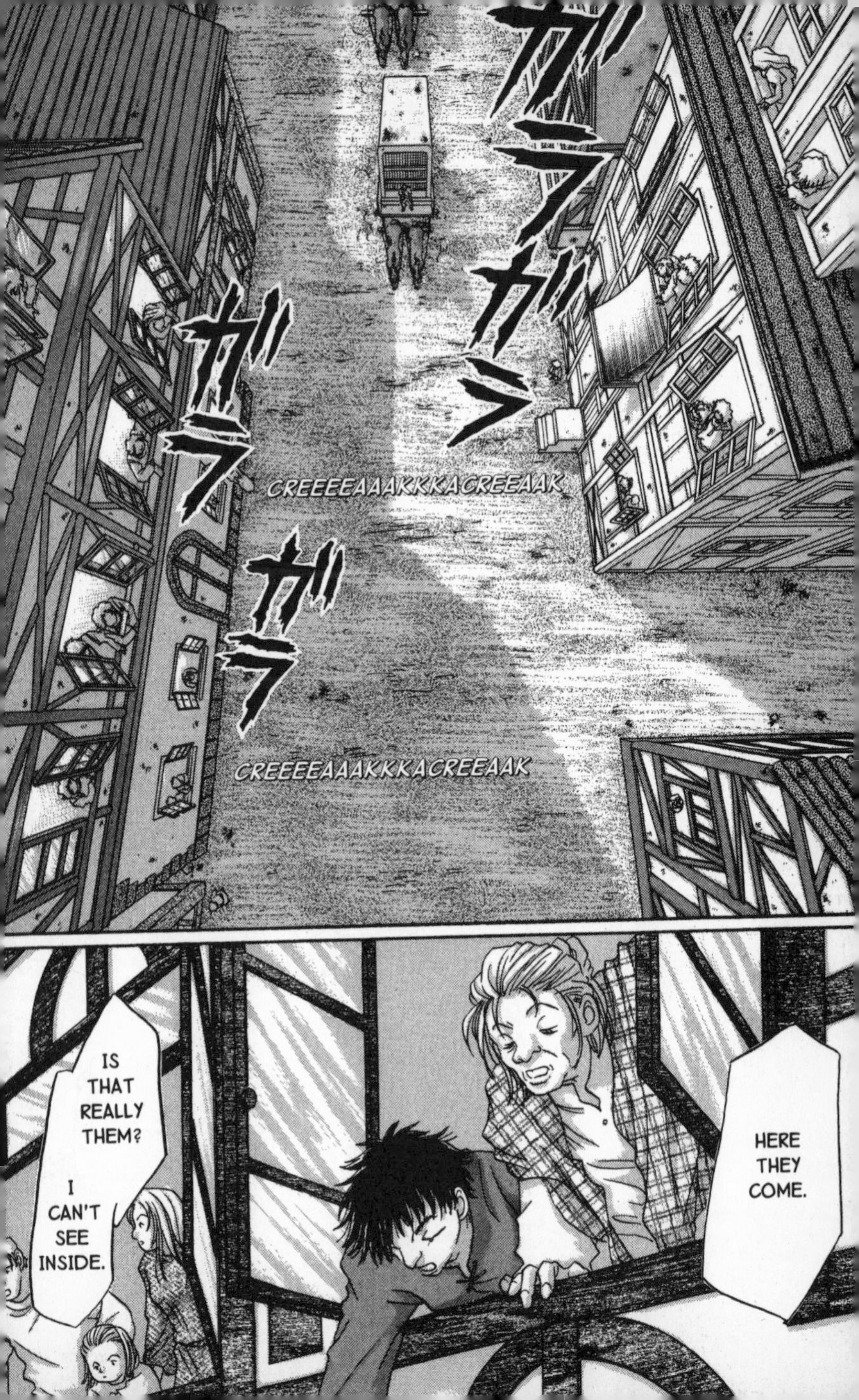
CREEEEAAAKKKACREEAAK
CREEEEAAAKKKACREEAAK
HERE THEY COME.
IS THAT REALLY THEM?
I CAN'T SEE INSIDE.

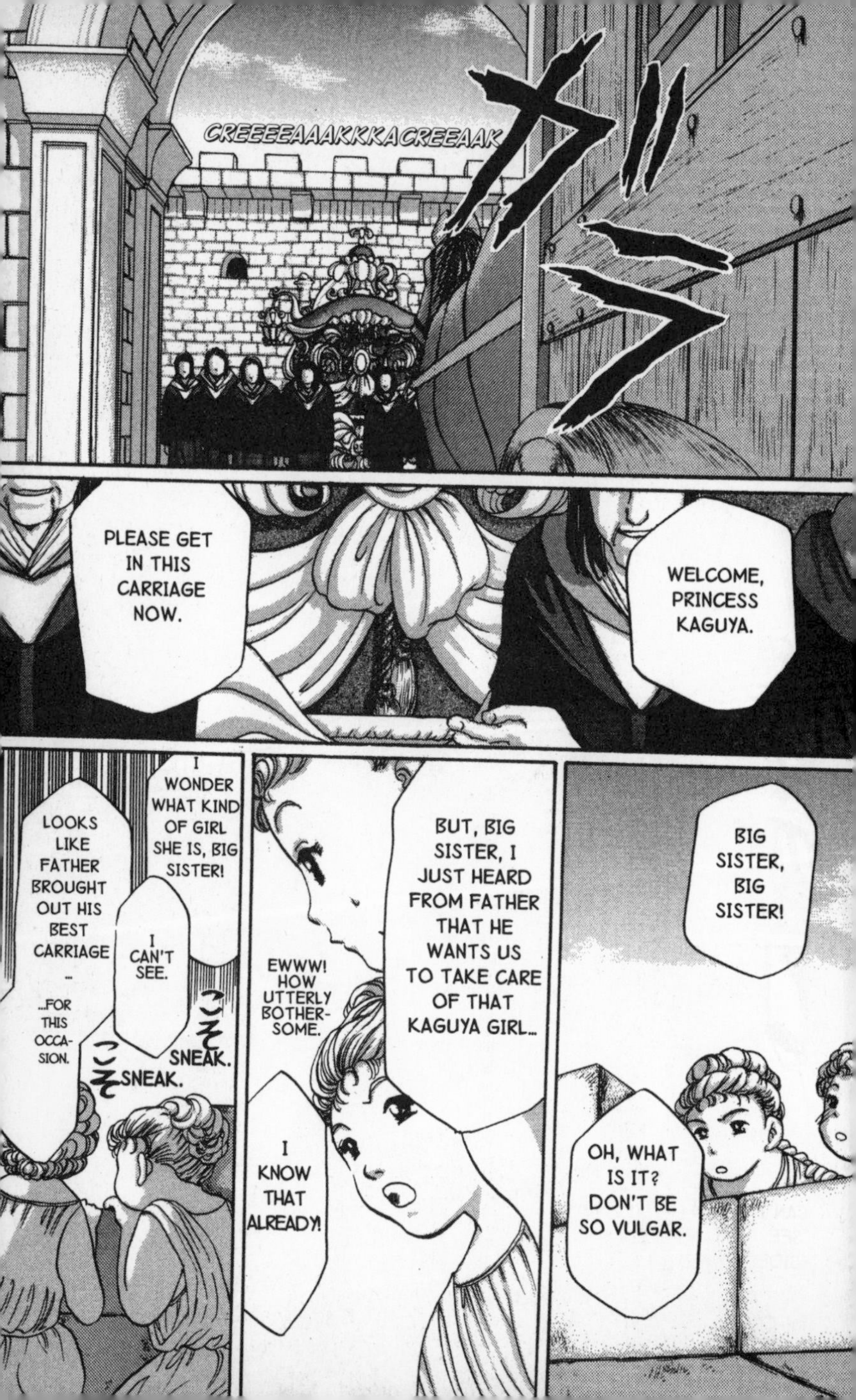
CREEEEAAAKKKACREEAAK
WELCOME, PRINCESS KAGUYA.
PLEASE GET IN THIS CARRIAGE NOW.
BIG SISTER, BIG SISTER!
OH, WHAT IS IT? DON'T BE SO VULGAR.
BUT, BIG SISTER, I JUST HEARD FROM FATHER THAT HE WANTS US TO TAKE CARE OF THAT KAGUYA GIRL...
EWWW! HOW UTTERLY BOTHER-SOME.
I KNOW THAT ALREADY!
I WONDER WHAT KIND OF GIRL SHE IS, BIG SISTER!
LOOKS LIKE FATHER BROUGHT OUT HIS BEST CARRIAGE...
...FOR THIS OCCA-SION.
I CAN'T SEE.
SNEAK.
SNEAK.

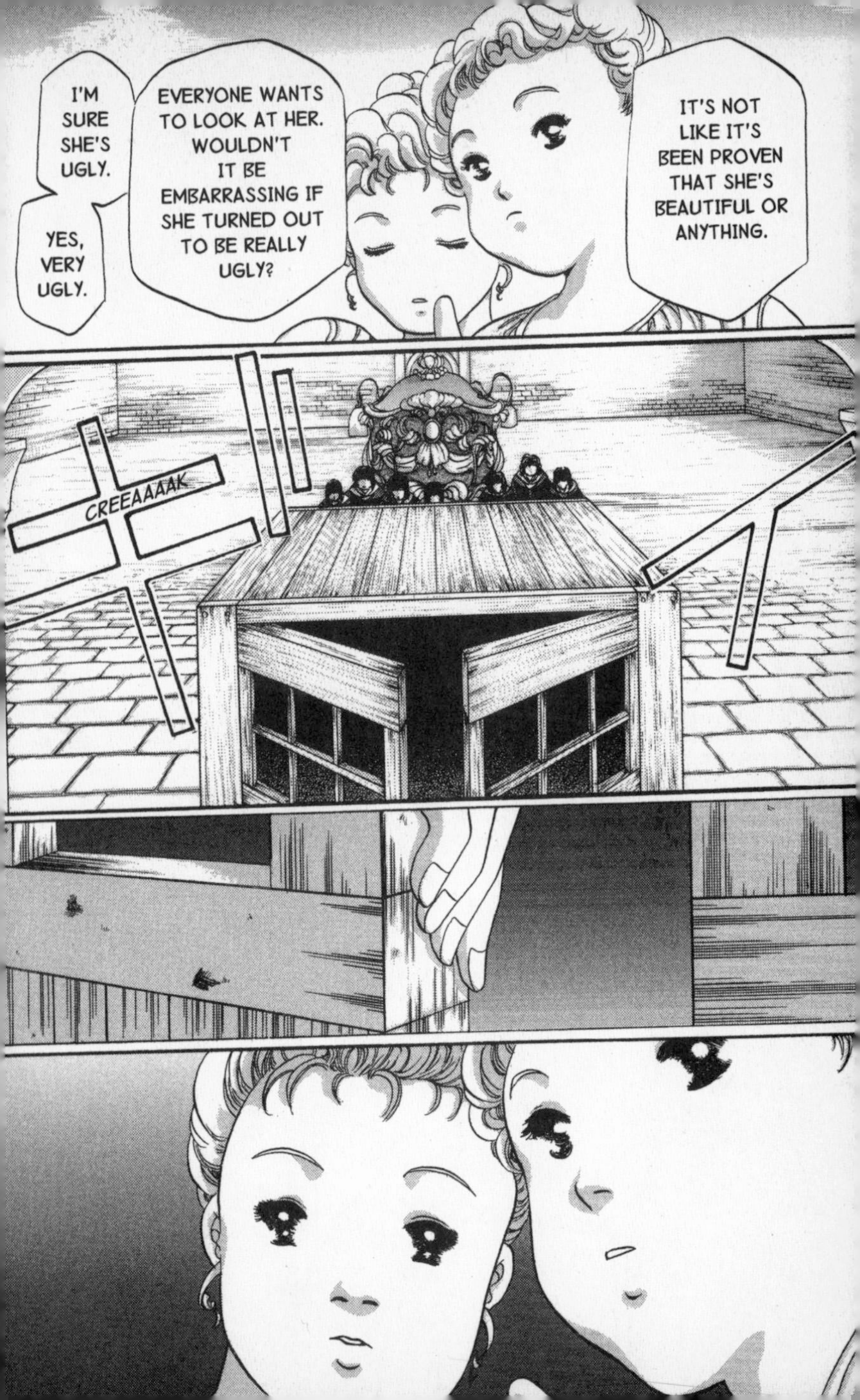
IT'S NOT LIKE IT'S BEEN PROVEN THAT SHE'S BEAUTIFUL OR ANYTHING.
EVERYONE WANTS TO LOOK AT HER. WOULDN'T IT BE EMBARRASSING IF SHE TURNED OUT TO BE REALLY UGLY?
I'M SURE SHE'S UGLY.
YES, VERY UGLY.
CREEAAAAK

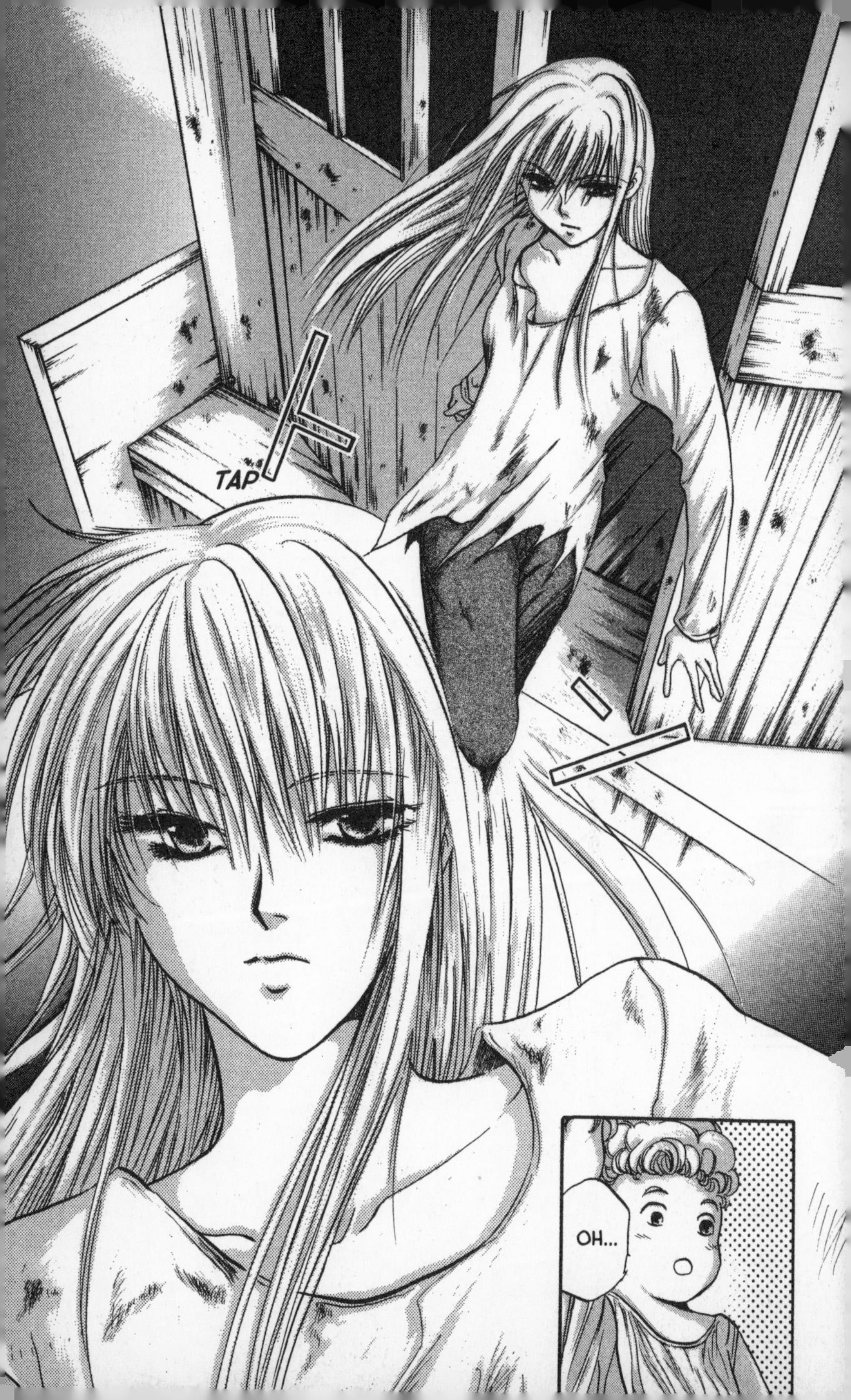
TAP
OH...

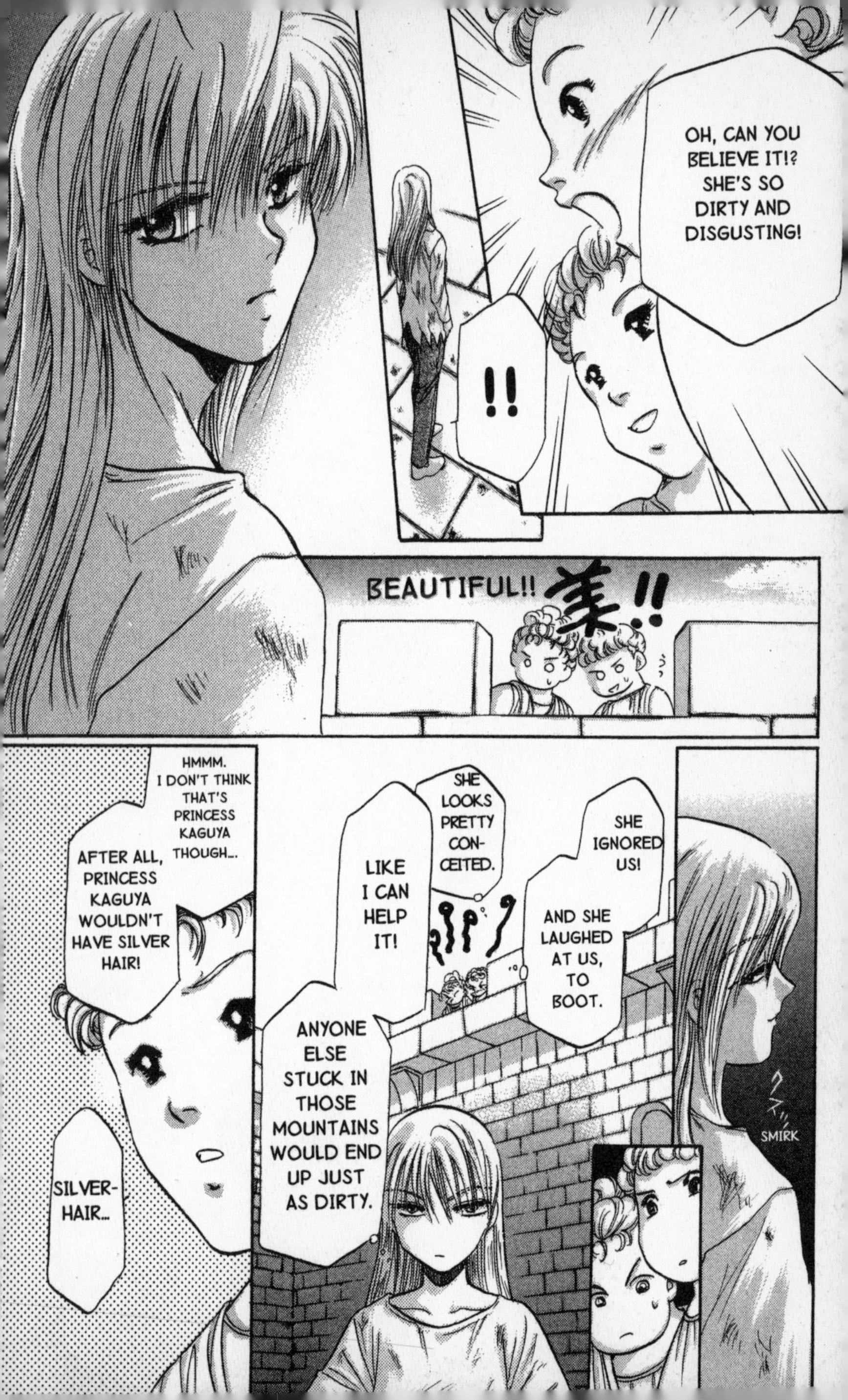
OH, CAN YOU BELIEVE IT!? SHE'S SO DIRTY AND DISGUSTING!
!!
BEAUTIFUL!! 美!!
SHE IGNORED US!
AND SHE LAUGHED AT US, TO BOOT.
SHE LOOKS PRETTY CON-CEITED.
SMIRK
LIKE I CAN HELP IT!
ANYONE ELSE STUCK IN THOSE MOUNTAINS WOULD END UP JUST AS DIRTY.
HMMM. I DON'T THINK THAT'S PRINCESS KAGUYA THOUGH....
AFTER ALL, PRINCESS KAGUYA WOULDN'T HAVE SILVER HAIR!
SILVER-HAIR...

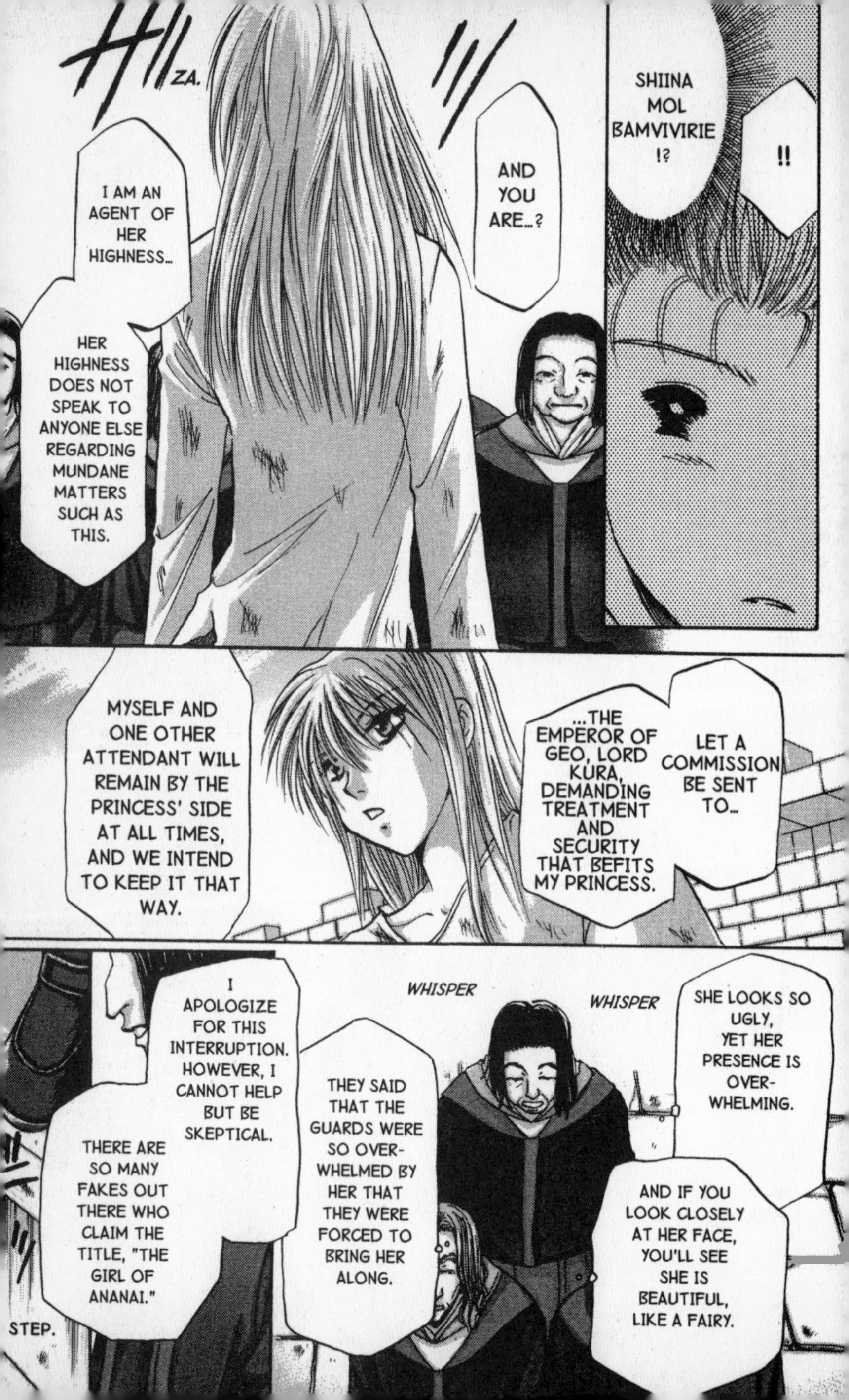

!!
SHIINA MOL BAMVIVIRIE !?
ZA.
AND YOU ARE...?
I AM AN AGENT OF HER HIGHNESS...
HER HIGHNESS DOES NOT SPEAK TO ANYONE ELSE REGARDING MUNDANE MATTERS SUCH AS THIS.
LET A COMMISSION BE SENT TO...
...THE EMPEROR OF GEO, LORD KURA, DEMANDING TREATMENT AND SECURITY THAT BEFITS MY PRINCESS.
MYSELF AND ONE OTHER ATTENDANT WILL REMAIN BY THE PRINCESS' SIDE AT ALL TIMES, AND WE INTEND TO KEEP IT THAT WAY.
SHE LOOKS SO UGLY, YET HER PRESENCE IS OVER-WHELMING.
WHISPER
WHISPER
AND IF YOU LOOK CLOSELY AT HER FACE, YOU'LL SEE SHE IS BEAUTIFUL, LIKE A FAIRY.
THEY SAID THAT THE GUARDS WERE SO OVER-WHELMED BY HER THAT THEY WERE FORCED TO BRING HER ALONG.
I APOLOGIZE FOR THIS INTERRUPTION. HOWEVER, I CANNOT HELP BUT BE SKEPTICAL.
THERE ARE SO MANY FAKES OUT THERE WHO CLAIM THE TITLE, "THE GIRL OF ANANAI."
STEP.

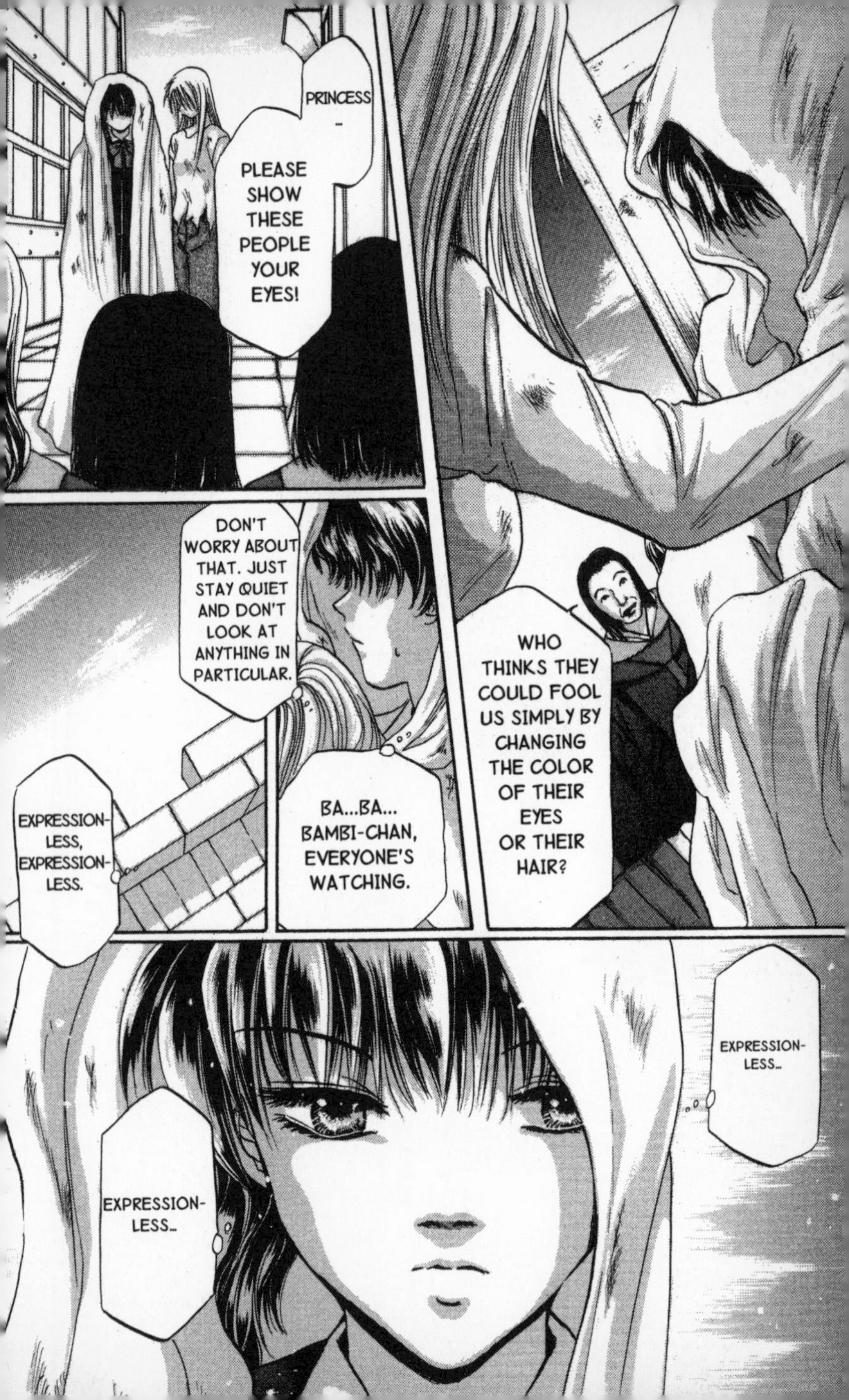
PRINCESS...
PLEASE SHOW THESE PEOPLE YOUR EYES!
WHO THINKS THEY COULD FOOL US SIMPLY BY CHANGING THE COLOR OF THEIR EYES OR THEIR HAIR?
DON'T WORRY ABOUT THAT. JUST STAY QUIET AND DON'T LOOK AT ANYTHING IN PARTICULAR.
BA...BA... BAMBI-CHAN, EVERYONE'S WATCHING.
EXPRESSION-LESS, EXPRESSION-LESS.
EXPRESSION-LESS..
EXPRESSION-LESS..

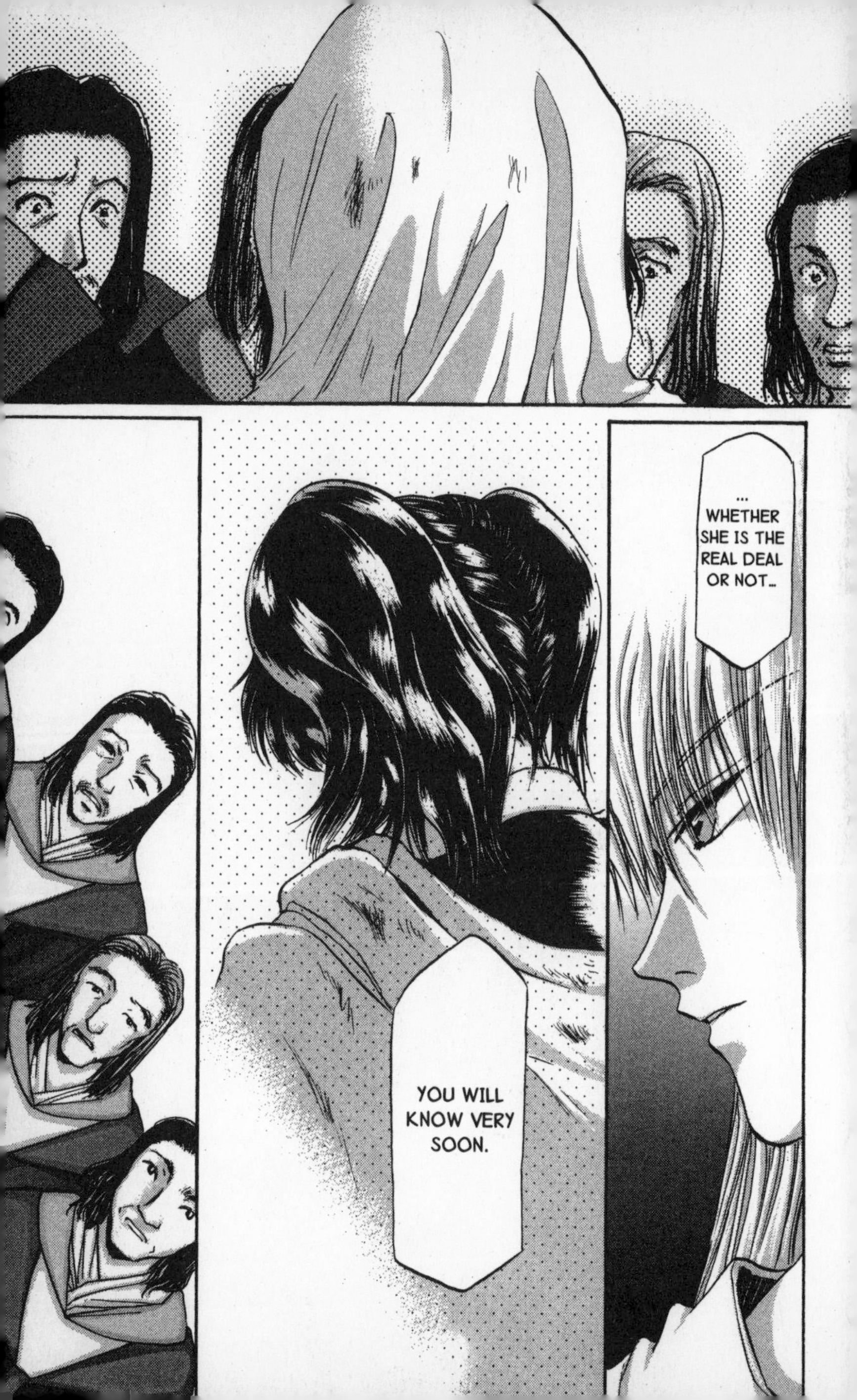
...WHETHER SHE IS THE REAL DEAL OR NOT...
YOU WILL KNOW VERY SOON.

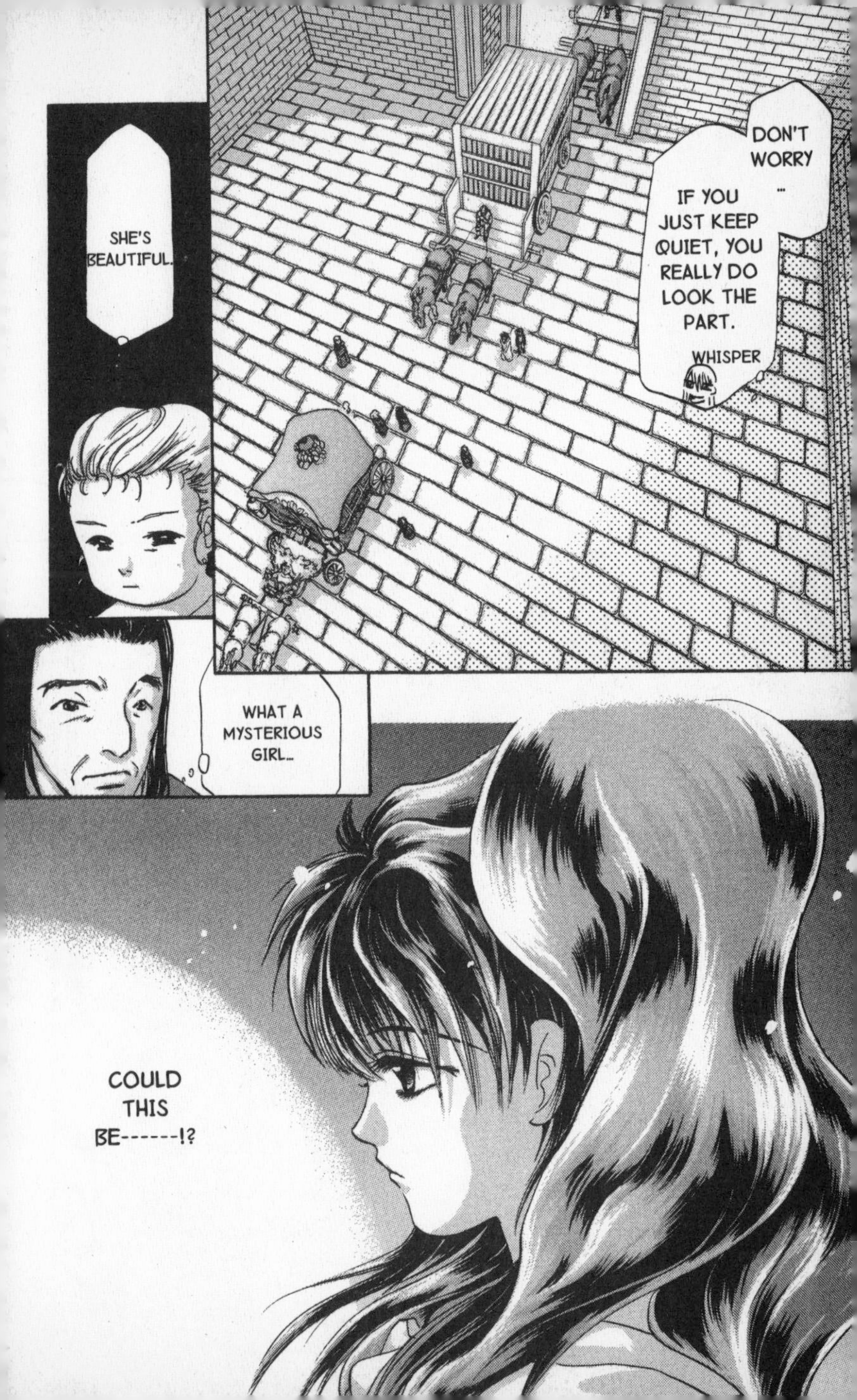
DON'T WORRY ...
IF YOU JUST KEEP QUIET, YOU REALLY DO LOOK THE PART.
WHISPER
SHE'S BEAUTIFUL.
WHAT A MYSTERIOUS GIRL...
COULD THIS BE------!?

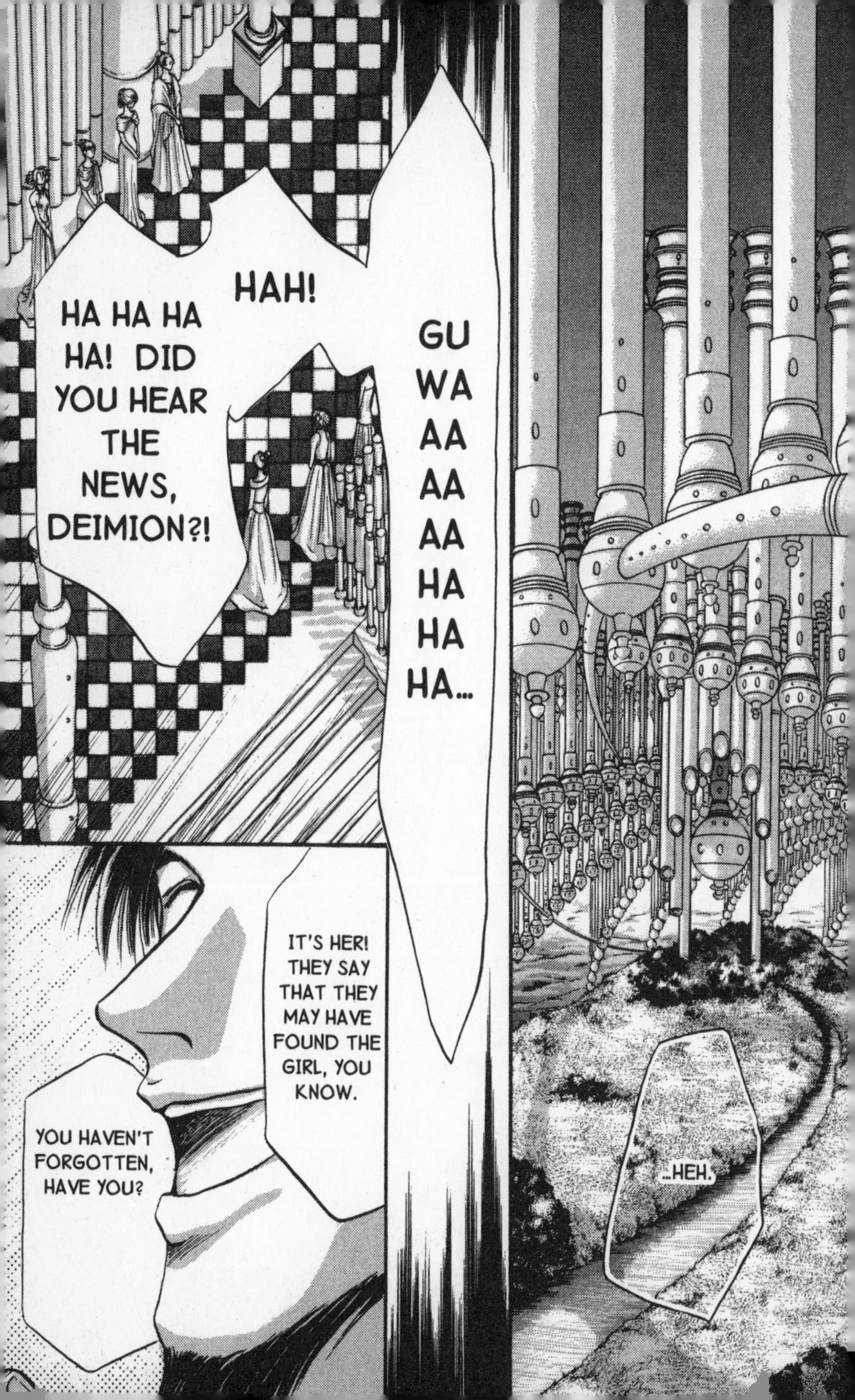
...HEH.
GU WA AA AA AA HA HA HA...
HAH!
HA HA HA HA! DID YOU HEAR THE NEWS, DEIMION?!
IT'S HER! THEY SAY THAT THEY MAY HAVE FOUND THE GIRL, YOU KNOW.
YOU HAVEN'T FORGOTTEN, HAVE YOU?

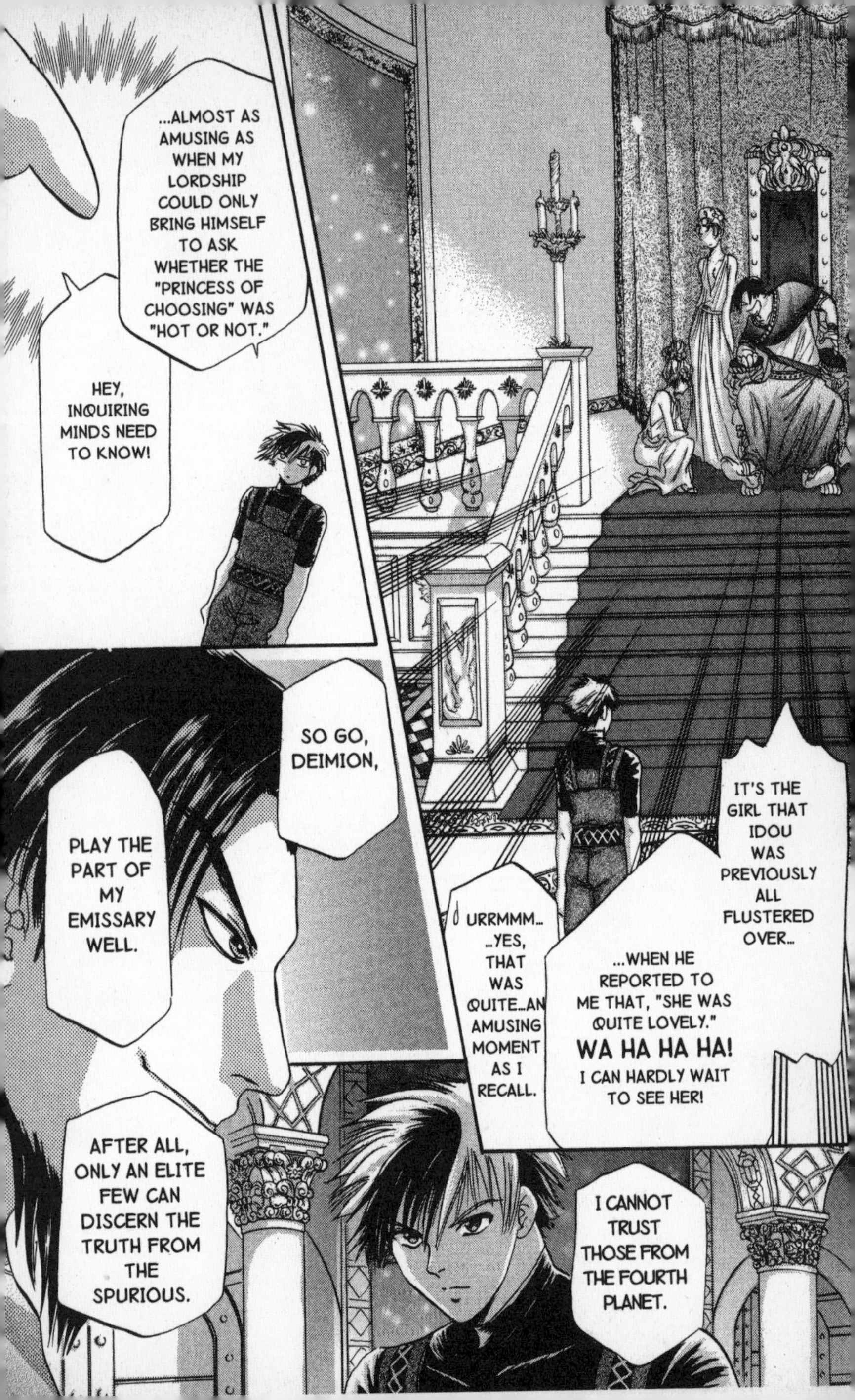

IT'S THE GIRL THAT IDOU WAS PREVIOUSLY ALL FLUSTERED OVER...
...WHEN HE REPORTED TO ME THAT, "SHE WAS QUITE LOVELY." WA HA HA HA! I CAN HARDLY WAIT TO SEE HER!
URRMMM... ...YES, THAT WAS QUITE...AN AMUSING MOMENT AS I RECALL.
...ALMOST AS AMUSING AS WHEN MY LORDSHIP COULD ONLY BRING HIMSELF TO ASK WHETHER THE "PRINCESS OF CHOOSING" WAS "HOT OR NOT."
HEY, INQUIRING MINDS NEED TO KNOW!
I CANNOT TRUST THOSE FROM THE FOURTH PLANET.
SO GO, DEIMION,
PLAY THE PART OF MY EMISSARY WELL.
AFTER ALL, ONLY AN ELITE FEW CAN DISCERN THE TRUTH FROM THE SPURIOUS.

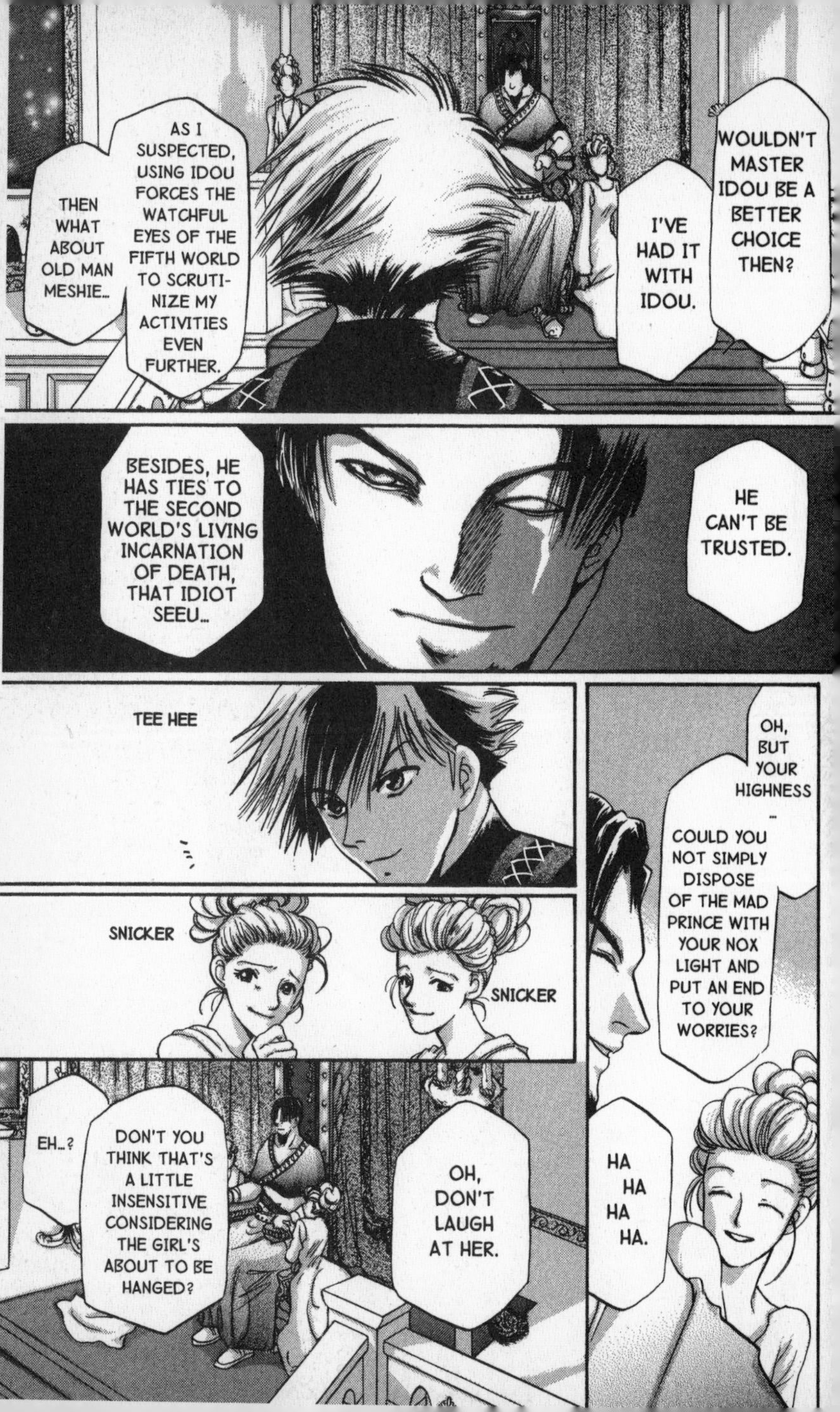
WOULDN'T MASTER IDOU BE A BETTER CHOICE THEN?
I'VE HAD IT WITH IDOU.
AS I SUSPECTED, USING IDOU FORCES THE WATCHFUL EYES OF THE FIFTH WORLD TO SCRUTI-NIZE MY ACTIVITIES EVEN FURTHER.
THEN WHAT ABOUT OLD MAN MESHIE...
HE CAN'T BE TRUSTED.
BESIDES, HE HAS TIES TO THE SECOND WORLD'S LIVING INCARNATION OF DEATH, THAT IDIOT SEEU...
OH, BUT YOUR HIGHNESS... COULD YOU NOT SIMPLY DISPOSE OF THE MAD PRINCE WITH YOUR NOX LIGHT AND PUT AN END TO YOUR WORRIES?
TEE HEE
SNICKER
SNICKER
HA HA HA HA.
OH, DON'T LAUGH AT HER.
DON'T YOU THINK THAT'S A LITTLE INSENSITIVE CONSIDERING THE GIRL'S ABOUT TO BE HANGED?
EH...?

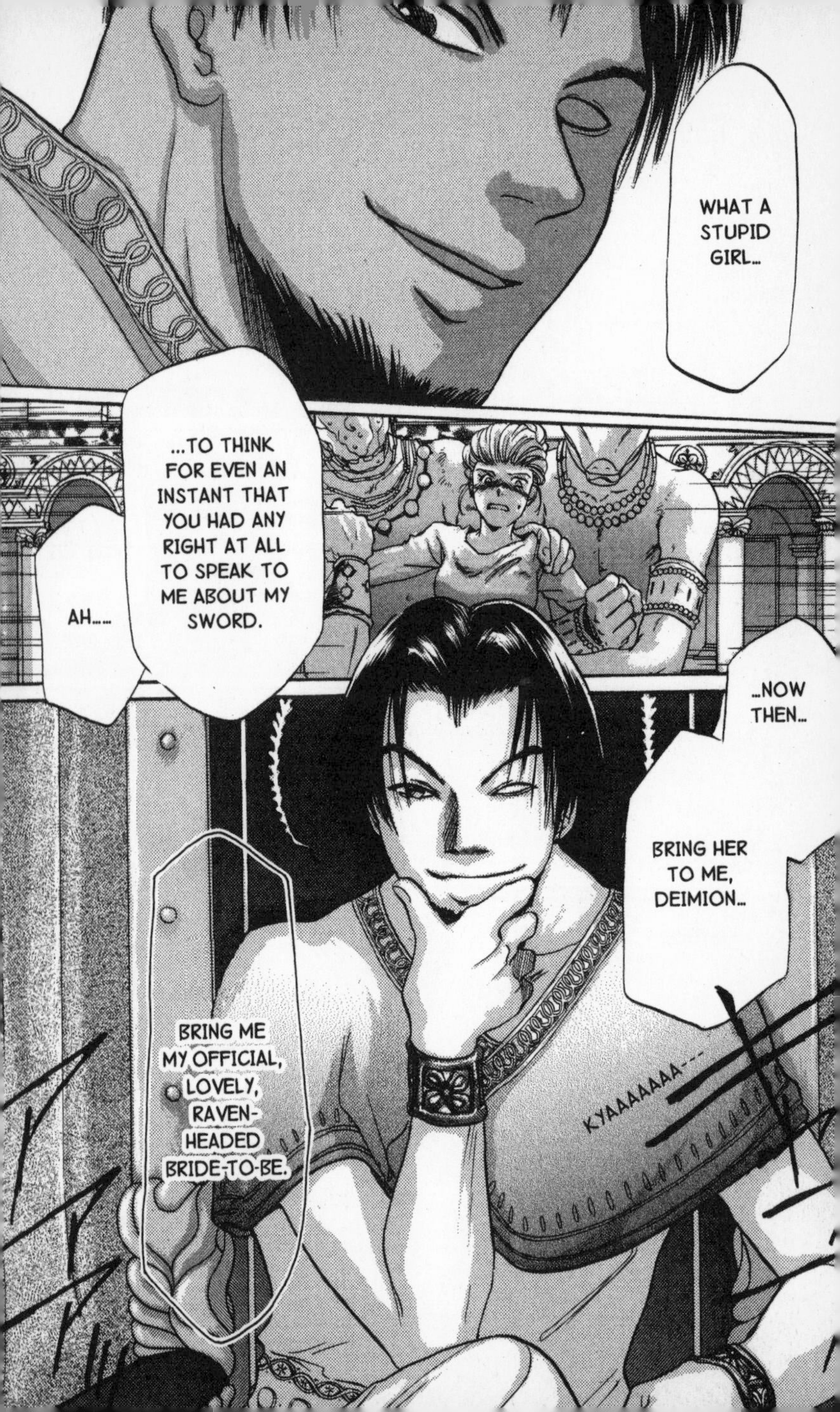
WHAT A STUPID GIRL...
...TO THINK FOR EVEN AN INSTANT THAT YOU HAD ANY RIGHT AT ALL TO SPEAK TO ME ABOUT MY SWORD.
AH.....
...NOW THEN...
BRING HER TO ME, DEIMION...
KYAAAAAAA---
BRING ME MY OFFICIAL, LOVELY, RAVEN-HEADED BRIDE-TO-BE.

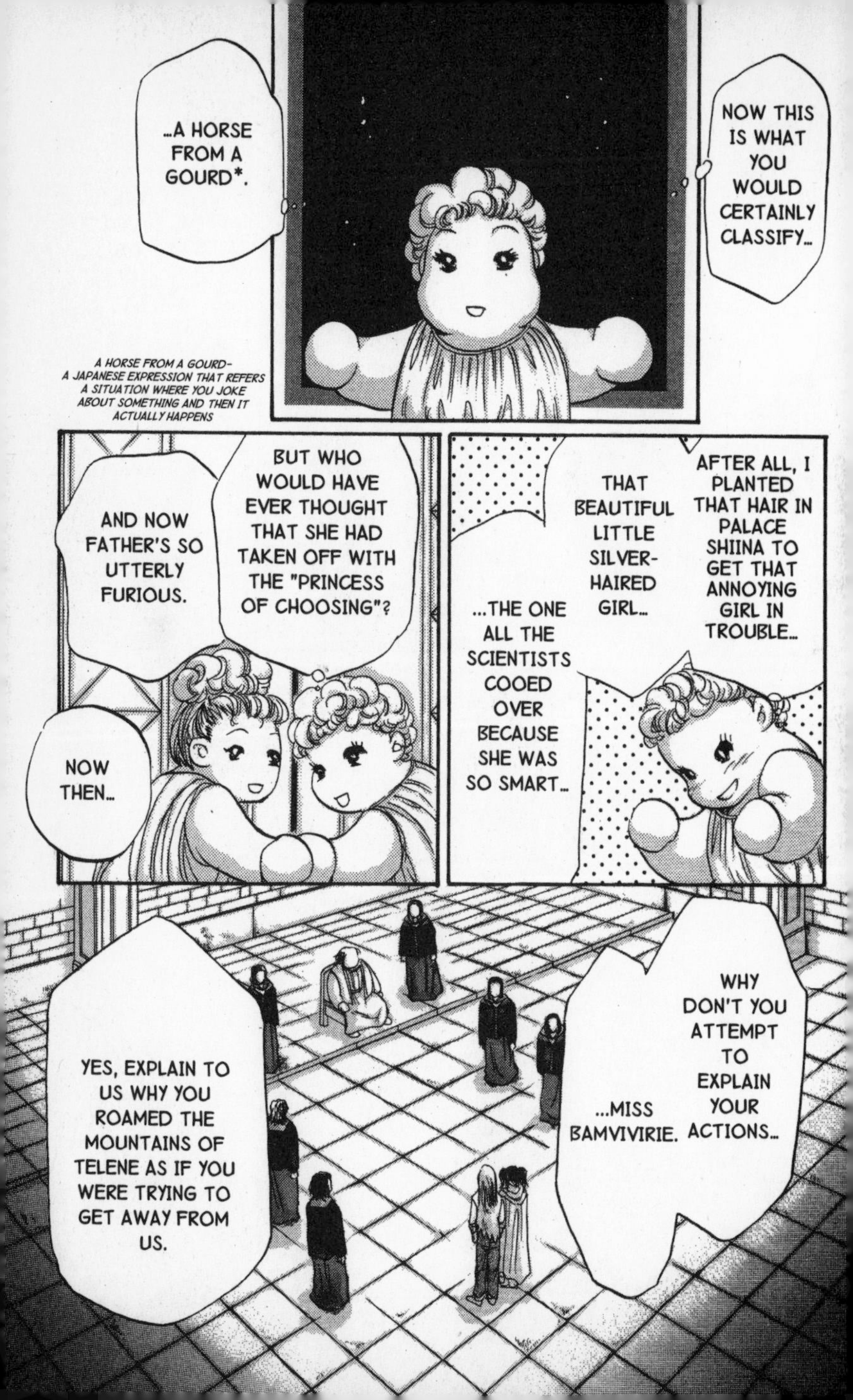
NOW THIS IS WHAT YOU WOULD CERTAINLY CLASSIFY...
...A HORSE FROM A GOURD*.
AFTER ALL, I PLANTED THAT HAIR IN PALACE SHIINA TO GET THAT ANNOYING GIRL IN TROUBLE...
THAT BEAUTIFUL LITTLE SILVER-HAIRED GIRL...
...THE ONE ALL THE SCIENTISTS COOED OVER BECAUSE SHE WAS SO SMART...
BUT WHO WOULD HAVE EVER THOUGHT THAT SHE HAD TAKEN OFF WITH THE "PRINCESS OF CHOOSING"?
AND NOW FATHER'S SO UTTERLY FURIOUS.
NOW THEN...
WHY DON'T YOU ATTEMPT TO EXPLAIN YOUR ACTIONS...
...MISS BAMVIVIRIE.
YES, EXPLAIN TO US WHY YOU ROAMED THE MOUNTAINS OF TELENE AS IF YOU WERE TRYING TO GET AWAY FROM US.

A HORSE FROM A GOURD- A JAPANESE EXPRESSION THAT REFERS A SITUATION WHERE YOU JOKE ABOUT SOMETHING AND THEN IT ACTUALLY HAPPENS

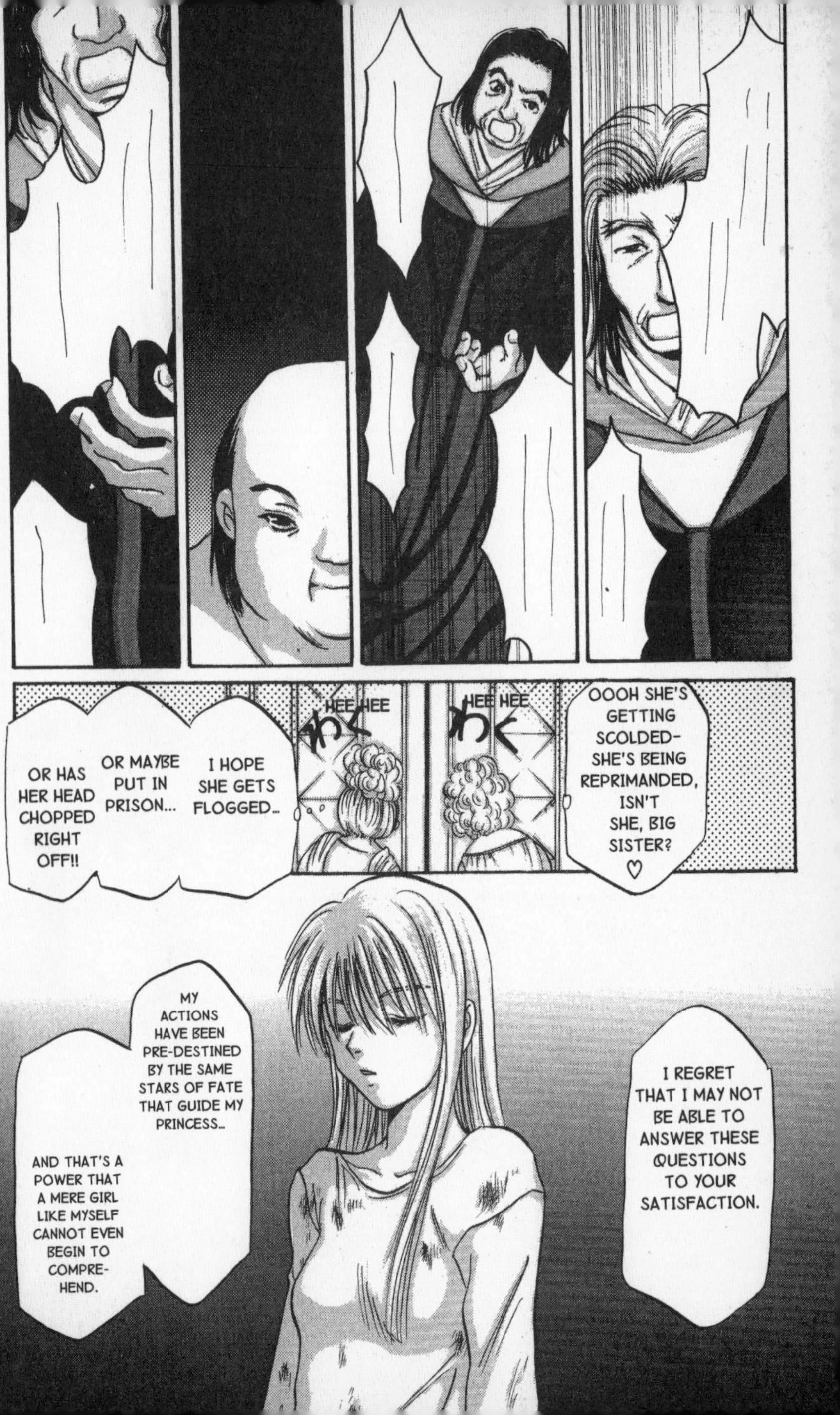
OOOH SHE'S GETTING SCOLDED- SHE'S BEING REPRIMANDED, ISN'T SHE, BIG SISTER? ♡
HEE HEE
HEE HEE
I HOPE SHE GETS FLOGGED...
OR MAYBE PUT IN PRISON...
OR HAS HER HEAD CHOPPED RIGHT OFF!!
I REGRET THAT I MAY NOT BE ABLE TO ANSWER THESE QUESTIONS TO YOUR SATISFACTION.
MY ACTIONS HAVE BEEN PRE-DESTINED BY THE SAME STARS OF FATE THAT GUIDE MY PRINCESS...
AND THAT'S A POWER THAT A MERE GIRL LIKE MYSELF CANNOT EVEN BEGIN TO COMPRE-HEND.

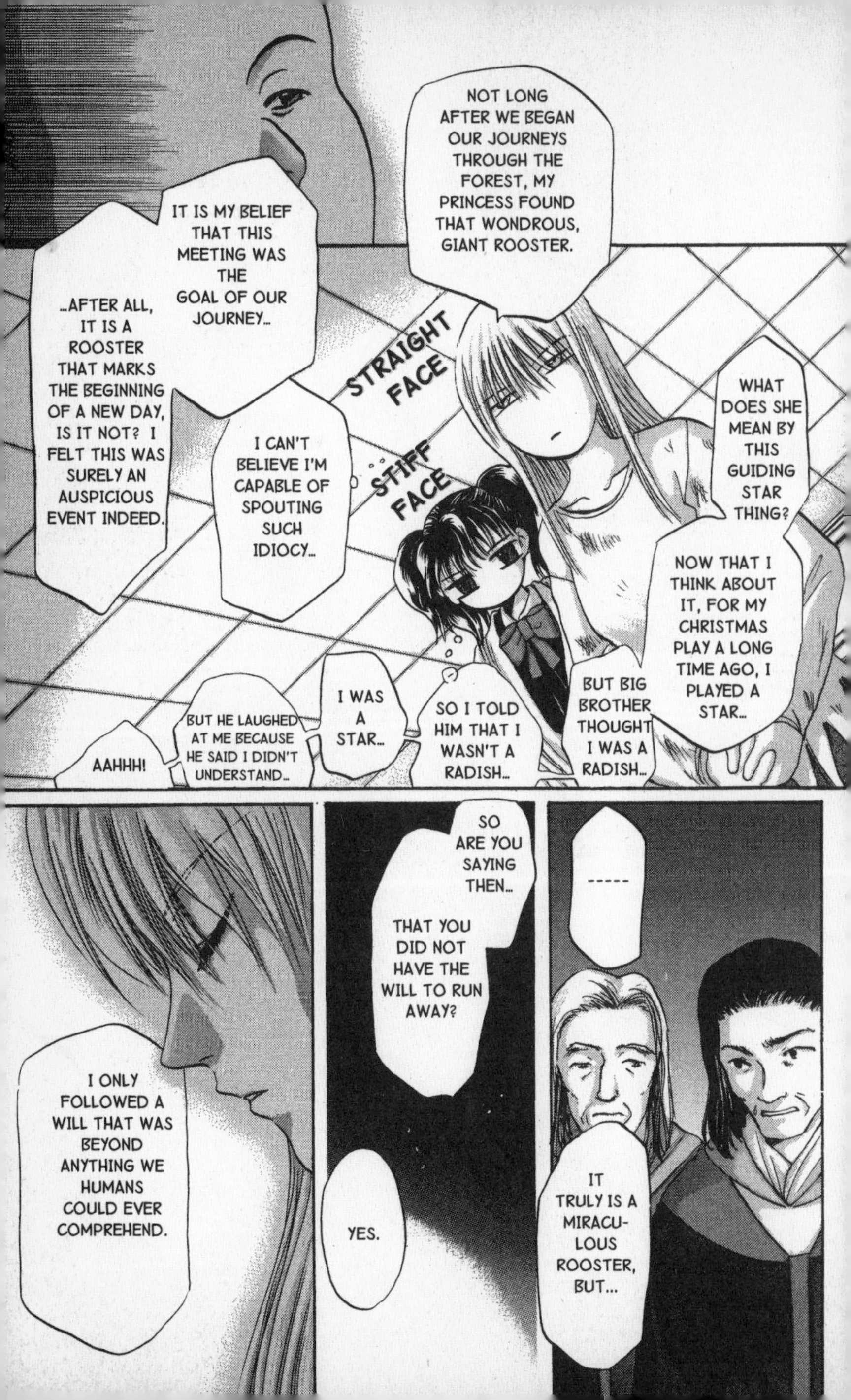
NOT LONG AFTER WE BEGAN OUR JOURNEYS THROUGH THE FOREST, MY PRINCESS FOUND THAT WONDROUS, GIANT ROOSTER.
IT IS MY BELIEF THAT THIS MEETING WAS THE GOAL OF OUR JOURNEY...
...AFTER ALL, IT IS A ROOSTER THAT MARKS THE BEGINNING OF A NEW DAY, IS IT NOT? I FELT THIS WAS SURELY AN AUSPICIOUS EVENT INDEED.
STRAIGHT FACE
I CAN'T BELIEVE I'M CAPABLE OF SPOUTING SUCH IDIOCY...
STIFF FACE
WHAT DOES SHE MEAN BY THIS GUIDING STAR THING?
NOW THAT I THINK ABOUT IT, FOR MY CHRISTMAS PLAY A LONG TIME AGO, I PLAYED A STAR...
BUT BIG BROTHER THOUGHT I WAS A RADISH...
SO I TOLD HIM THAT I WASN'T A RADISH...
I WAS A STAR...
BUT HE LAUGHED AT ME BECAUSE HE SAID I DIDN'T UNDERSTAND...
AAHHH!

IT TRULY IS A MIRACULOUS ROOSTER, BUT...
SO ARE YOU SAYING THEN...
THAT YOU DID NOT HAVE THE WILL TO RUN AWAY?
YES.
I ONLY FOLLOWED A WILL THAT WAS BEYOND ANYTHING WE HUMANS COULD EVER COMPREHEND.

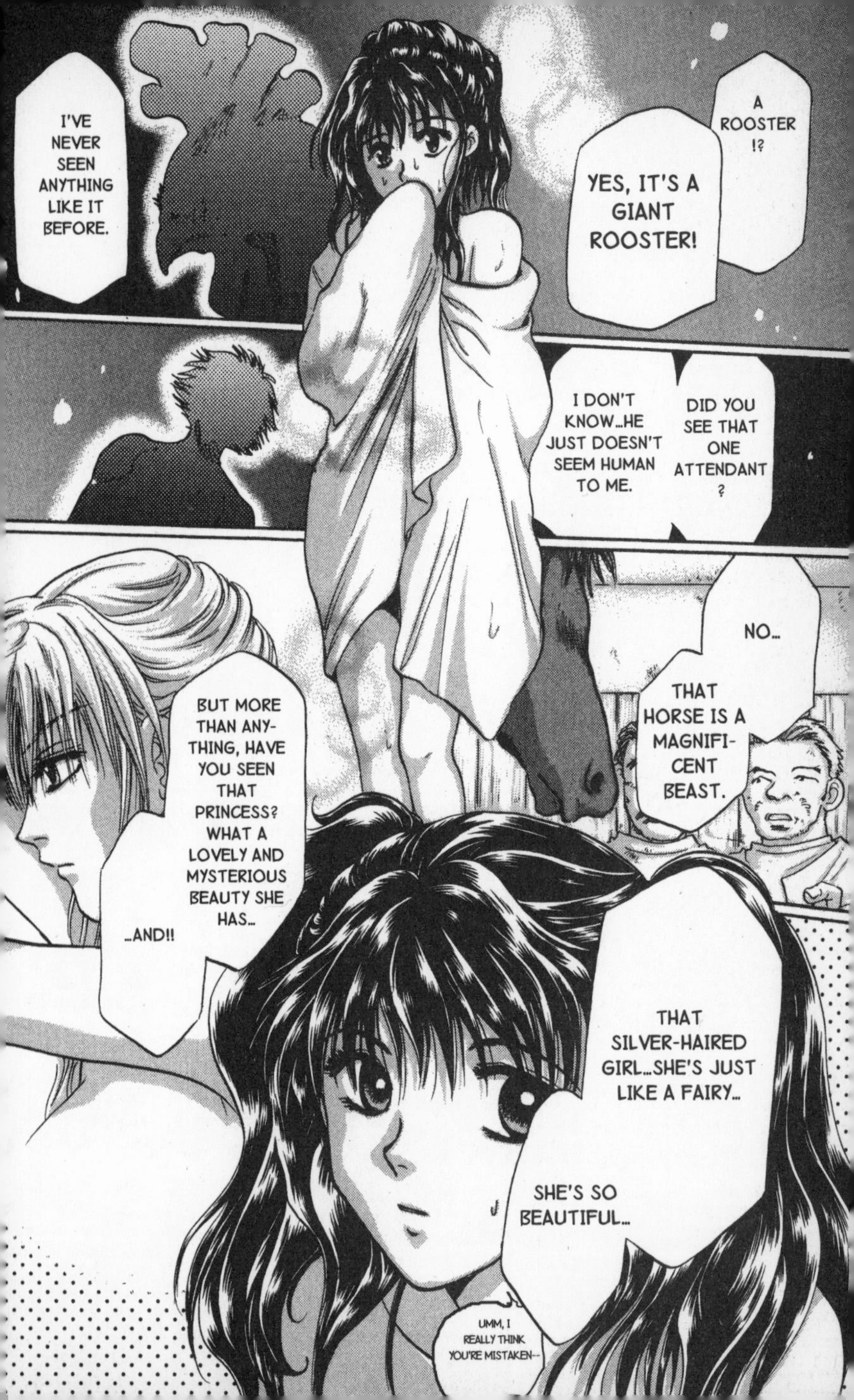
A ROOSTER !?
YES, IT'S A GIANT ROOSTER!
I'VE NEVER SEEN ANYTHING LIKE IT BEFORE.
DID YOU SEE THAT ONE ATTENDANT ?
I DON'T KNOW...HE JUST DOESN'T SEEM HUMAN TO ME.
NO...
THAT HORSE IS A MAGNIFI- CENT BEAST.
BUT MORE THAN ANY- THING, HAVE YOU SEEN THAT PRINCESS? WHAT A LOVELY AND MYSTERIOUS BEAUTY SHE HAS...
...AND!!
THAT SILVER-HAIRED GIRL...SHE'S JUST LIKE A FAIRY...
SHE'S SO BEAUTIFUL...
UMM, I REALLY THINK YOU'RE MISTAKEN--

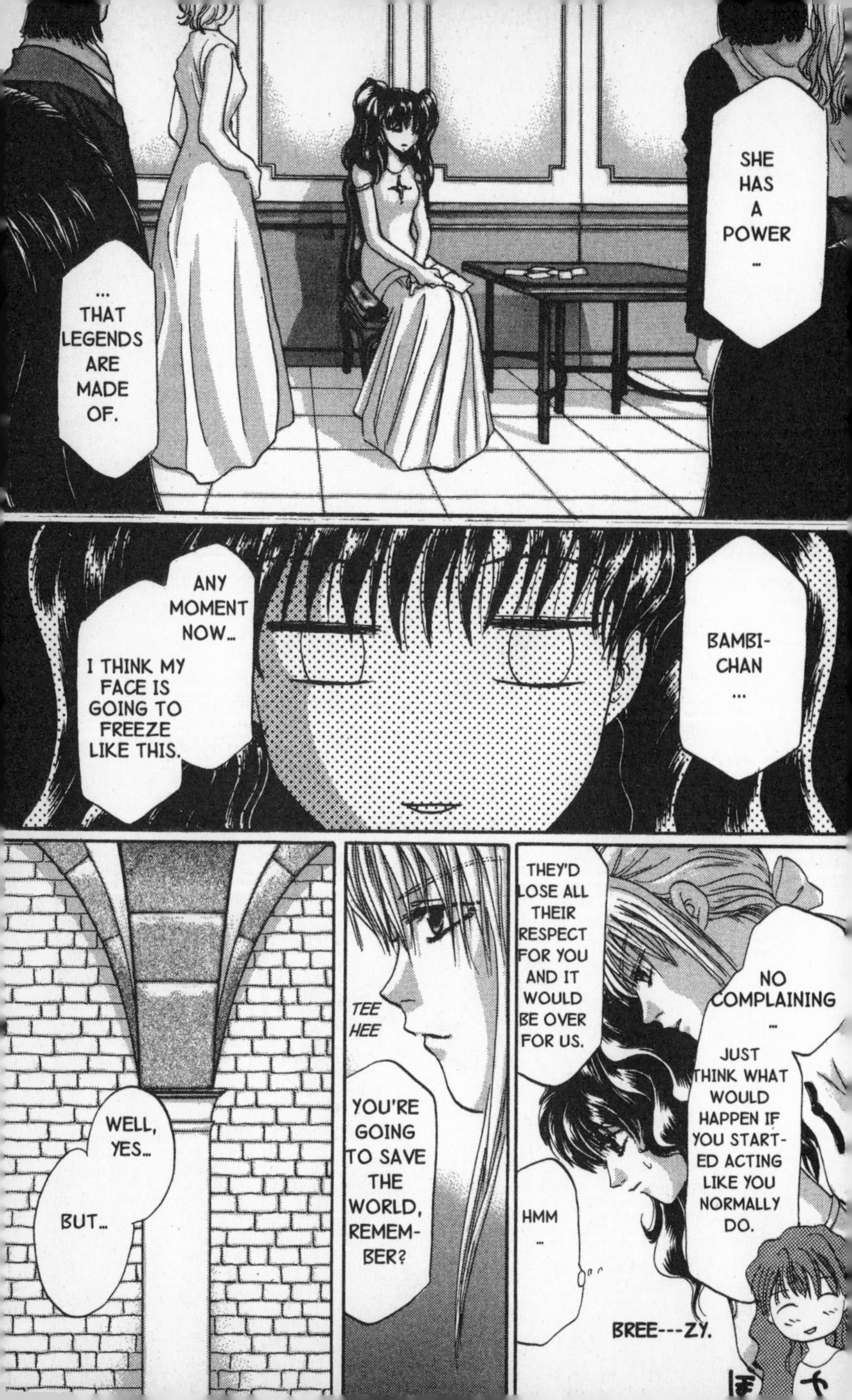
SHE HAS A POWER ...
... THAT LEGENDS ARE MADE OF.
BAMBI-CHAN ...
ANY MOMENT NOW...
I THINK MY FACE IS GOING TO FREEZE LIKE THIS.
NO COMPLAINING ...
JUST THINK WHAT WOULD HAPPEN IF YOU START-ED ACTING LIKE YOU NORMALLY DO.
THEY'D LOSE ALL THEIR RESPECT FOR YOU AND IT WOULD BE OVER FOR US.
HMM ...
BREE---ZY.
TEE HEE
YOU'RE GOING TO SAVE THE WORLD, REMEM-BER?
WELL, YES...
BUT...

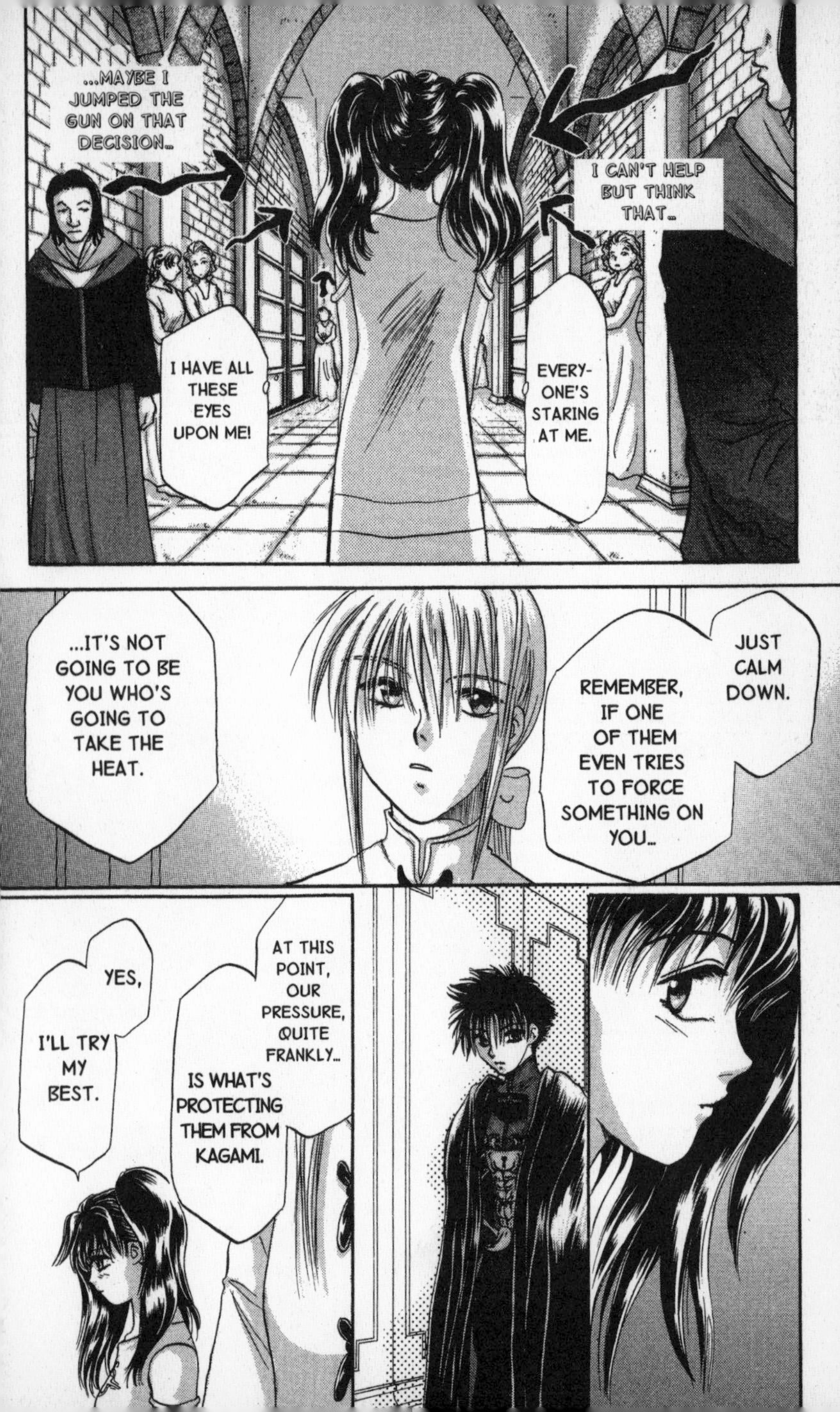
I CAN'T HELP BUT THINK THAT...
...MAYBE I JUMPED THE GUN ON THAT DECISION...
EVERY-ONE'S STARING AT ME.
I HAVE ALL THESE EYES UPON ME!
JUST CALM DOWN.
REMEMBER, IF ONE OF THEM EVEN TRIES TO FORCE SOMETHING ON YOU...
...IT'S NOT GOING TO BE YOU WHO'S GOING TO TAKE THE HEAT.
AT THIS POINT, OUR PRESSURE, QUITE FRANKLY...
IS WHAT'S PROTECTING THEM FROM KAGAMI.
YES,
I'LL TRY MY BEST.

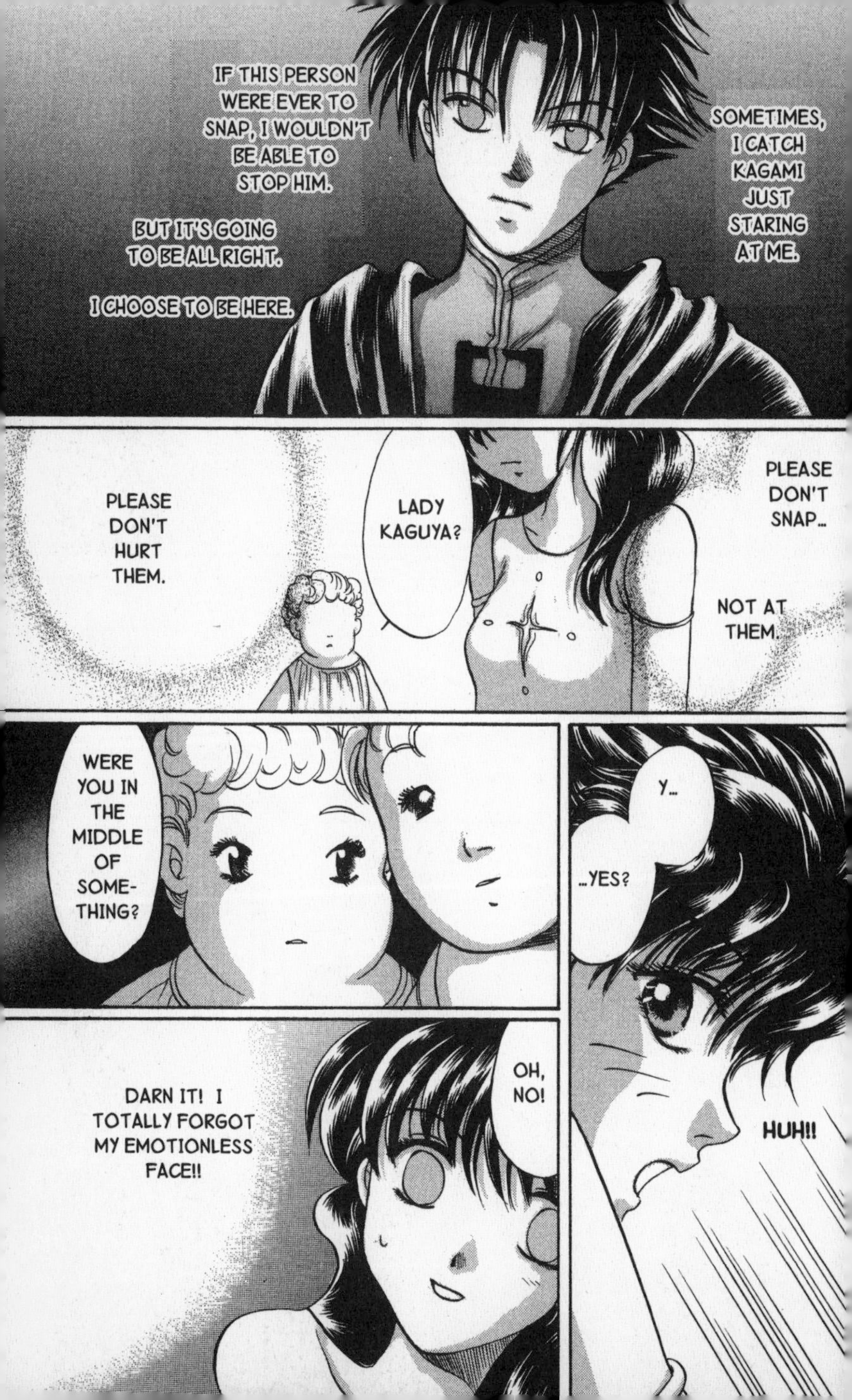
SOMETIMES, I CATCH KAGAMI JUST STARING AT ME.
IF THIS PERSON WERE EVER TO SNAP, I WOULDN'T BE ABLE TO STOP HIM.
BUT IT'S GOING TO BE ALL RIGHT.
I CHOOSE TO BE HERE.
PLEASE DON'T SNAP...
NOT AT THEM.
LADY KAGUYA?
PLEASE DON'T HURT THEM.
Y...
...YES?
HUH!!
WERE YOU IN THE MIDDLE OF SOME-THING?
OH, NO!
DARN IT! I TOTALLY FORGOT MY EMOTIONLESS FACE!!

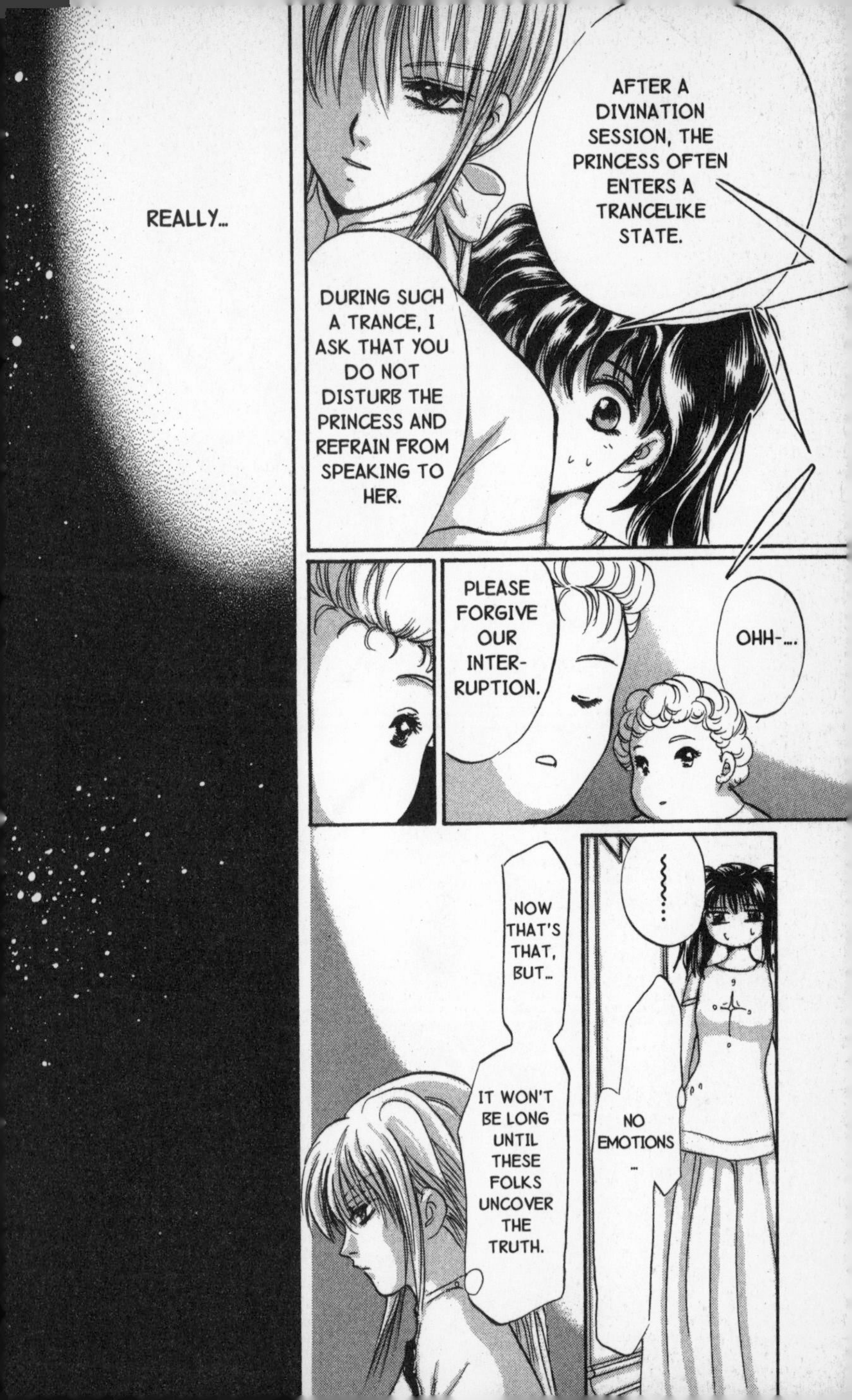
AFTER A DIVINATION SESSION, THE PRINCESS OFTEN ENTERS A TRANCELIKE STATE.
DURING SUCH A TRANCE, I ASK THAT YOU DO NOT DISTURB THE PRINCESS AND REFRAIN FROM SPEAKING TO HER.
OHH-....
PLEASE FORGIVE OUR INTER-RUPTION.
......
NO EMOTIONS ...
NOW THAT'S THAT, BUT...
IT WON'T BE LONG UNTIL THESE FOLKS UNCOVER THE TRUTH.
REALLY...

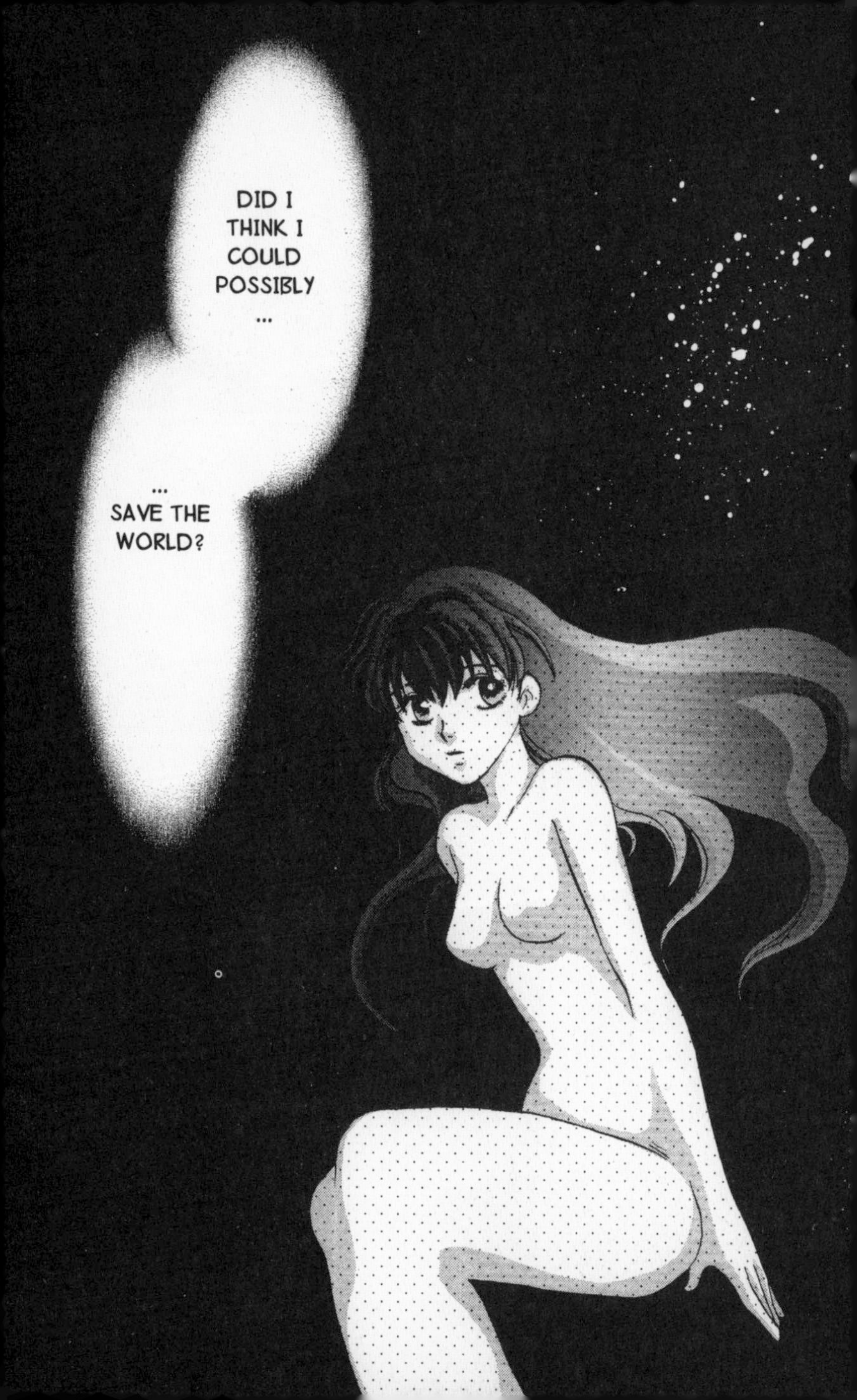
DID I THINK I COULD POSSIBLY ...
... SAVE THE WORLD?

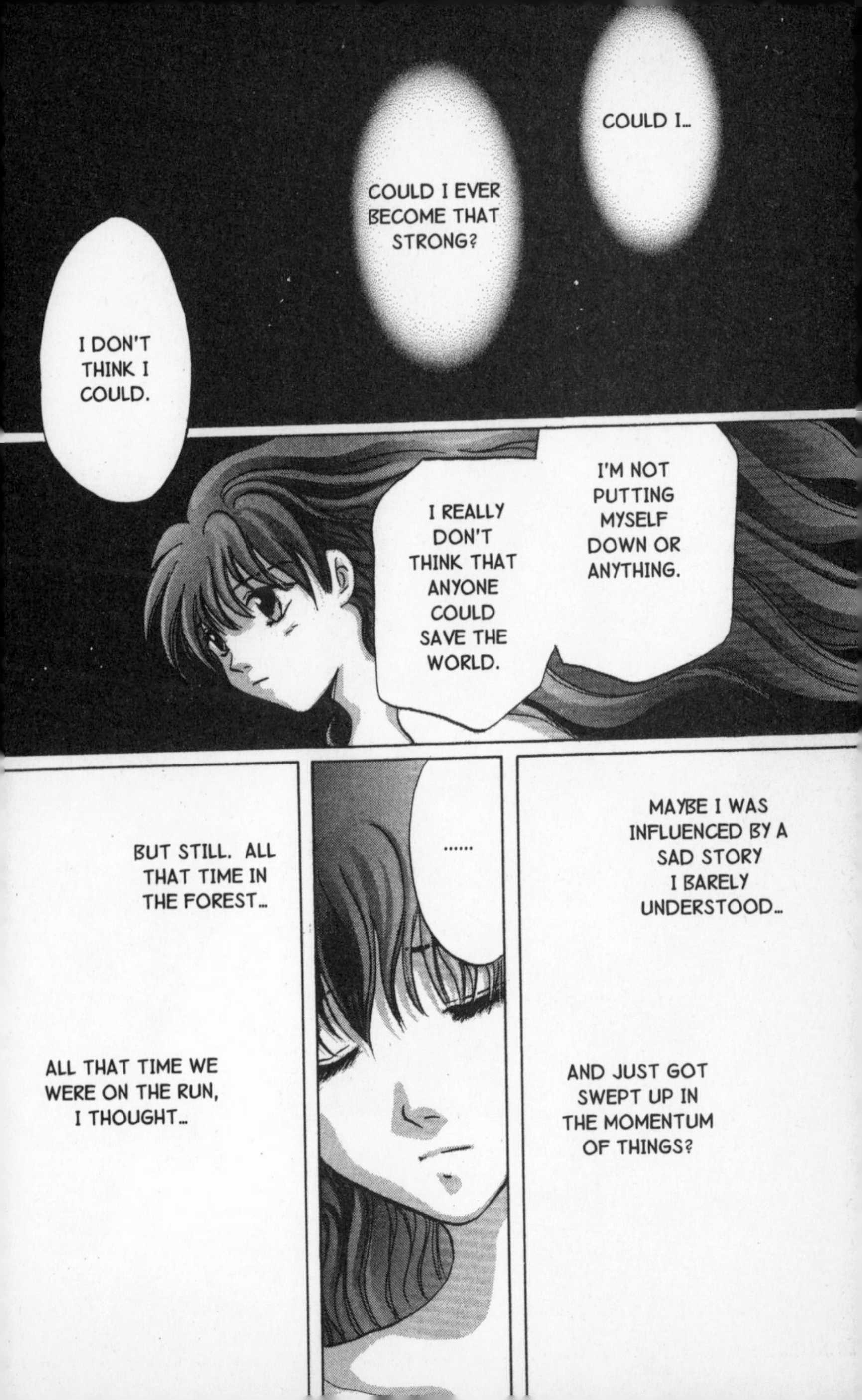
COULD I...
COULD I EVER BECOME THAT STRONG?
I DON'T THINK I COULD.
I'M NOT PUTTING MYSELF DOWN OR ANYTHING.
I REALLY DON'T THINK THAT ANYONE COULD SAVE THE WORLD.
MAYBE I WAS INFLUENCED BY A SAD STORY I BARELY UNDERSTOOD...
AND JUST GOT SWEPT UP IN THE MOMENTUM OF THINGS?
......
BUT STILL. ALL THAT TIME IN THE FOREST...
ALL THAT TIME WE WERE ON THE RUN, I THOUGHT...

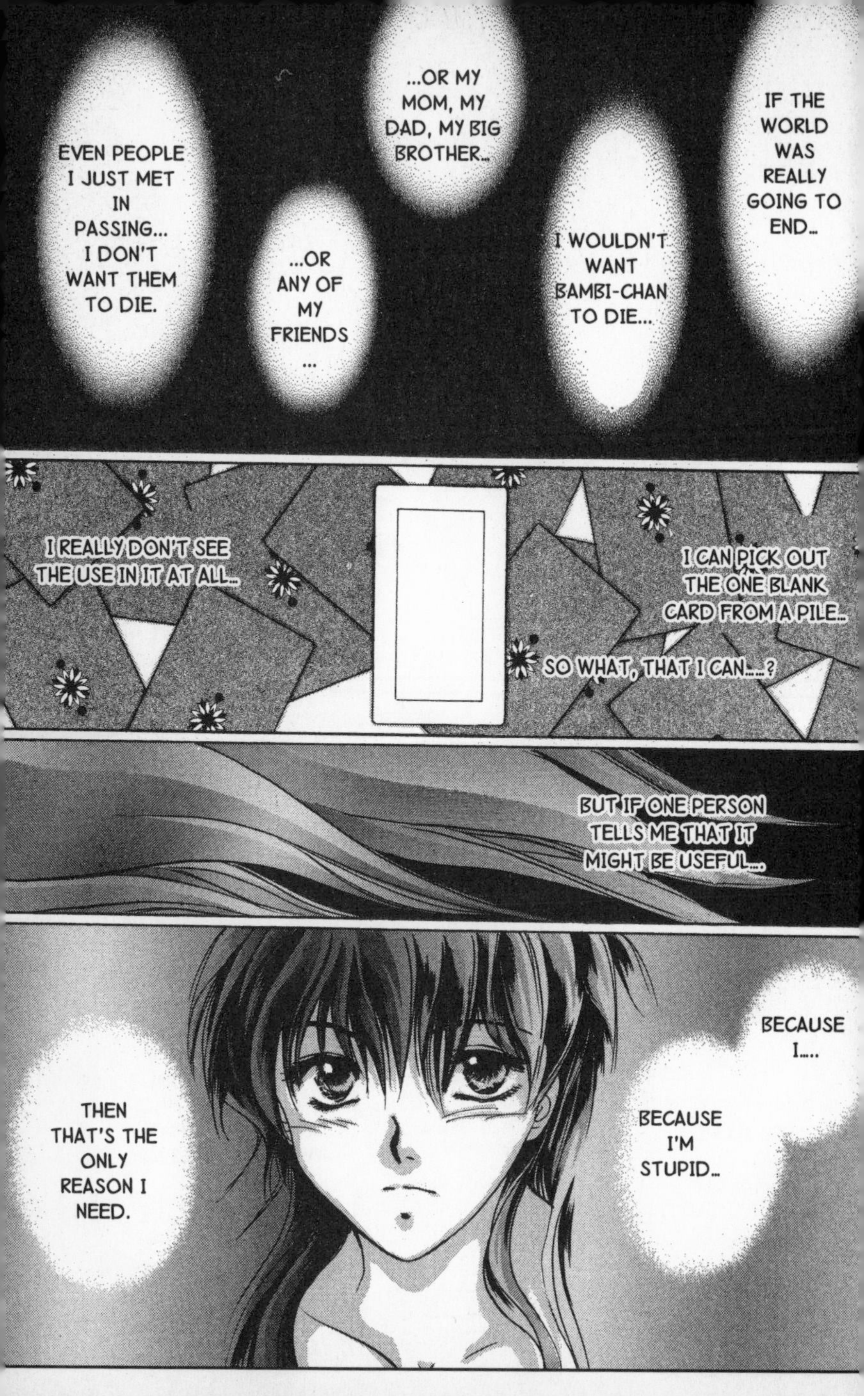
IF THE WORLD WAS REALLY GOING TO END...
I WOULDN'T WANT BAMBI-CHAN TO DIE...
...OR MY MOM, MY DAD, MY BIG BROTHER...
...OR ANY OF MY FRIENDS ...
EVEN PEOPLE I JUST MET IN PASSING... I DON'T WANT THEM TO DIE.
I CAN PICK OUT THE ONE BLANK CARD FROM A PILE..
SO WHAT, THAT I CAN.....?
I REALLY DON'T SEE THE USE IN IT AT ALL..
BUT IF ONE PERSON TELLS ME THAT IT MIGHT BE USEFUL....
BECAUSE I.....
BECAUSE I'M STUPID...
THEN THAT'S THE ONLY REASON I NEED.

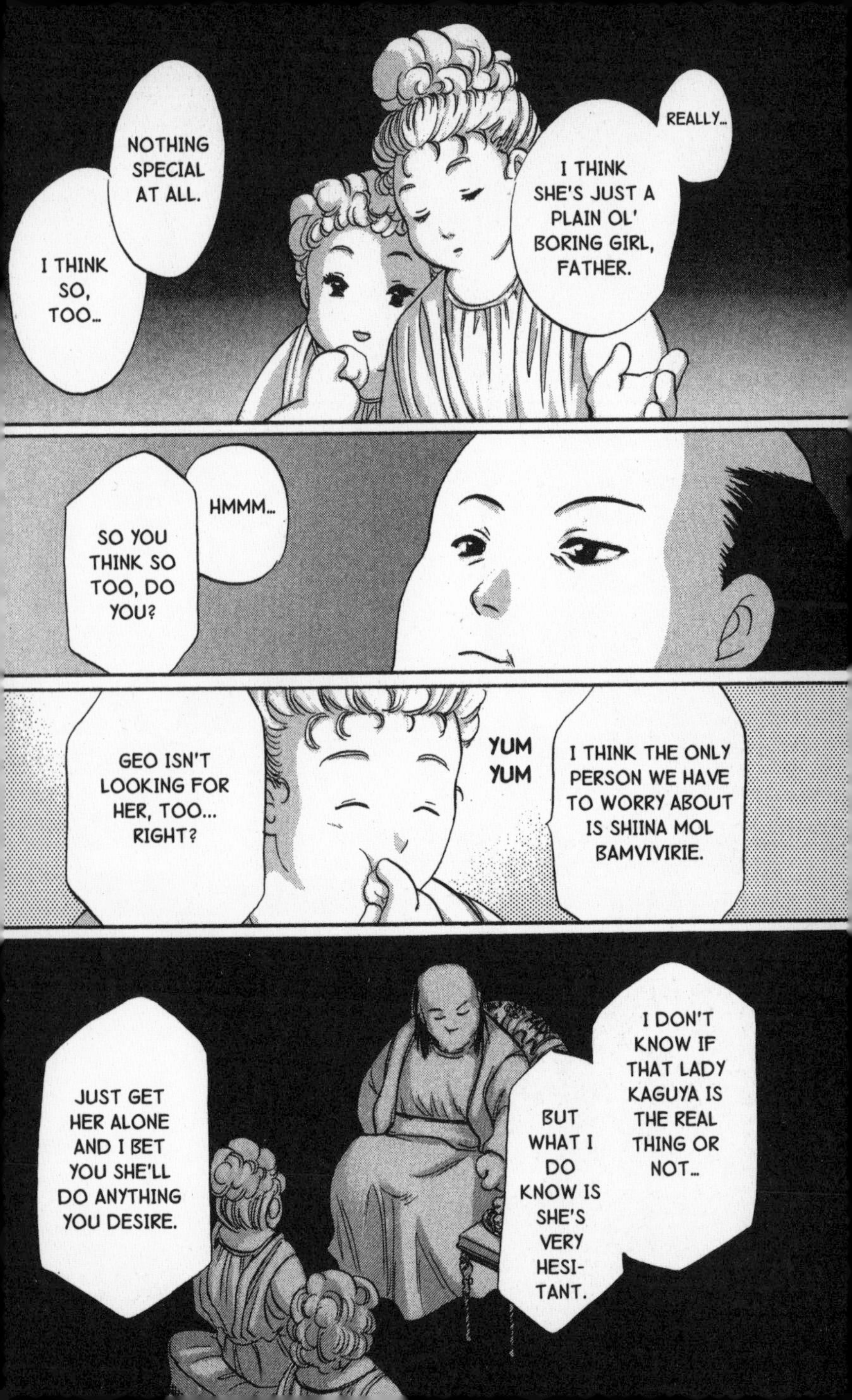
REALLY...
I THINK SHE'S JUST A PLAIN OL' BORING GIRL, FATHER.
NOTHING SPECIAL AT ALL.
I THINK SO, TOO...
HMMM...
SO YOU THINK SO TOO, DO YOU?
I THINK THE ONLY PERSON WE HAVE TO WORRY ABOUT IS SHIINA MOL BAMVIVIRIE.
YUM YUM
GEO ISN'T LOOKING FOR HER, TOO... RIGHT?
I DON'T KNOW IF THAT LADY KAGUYA IS THE REAL THING OR NOT...
BUT WHAT I DO KNOW IS SHE'S VERY HESI-TANT.
JUST GET HER ALONE AND I BET YOU SHE'LL DO ANYTHING YOU DESIRE.

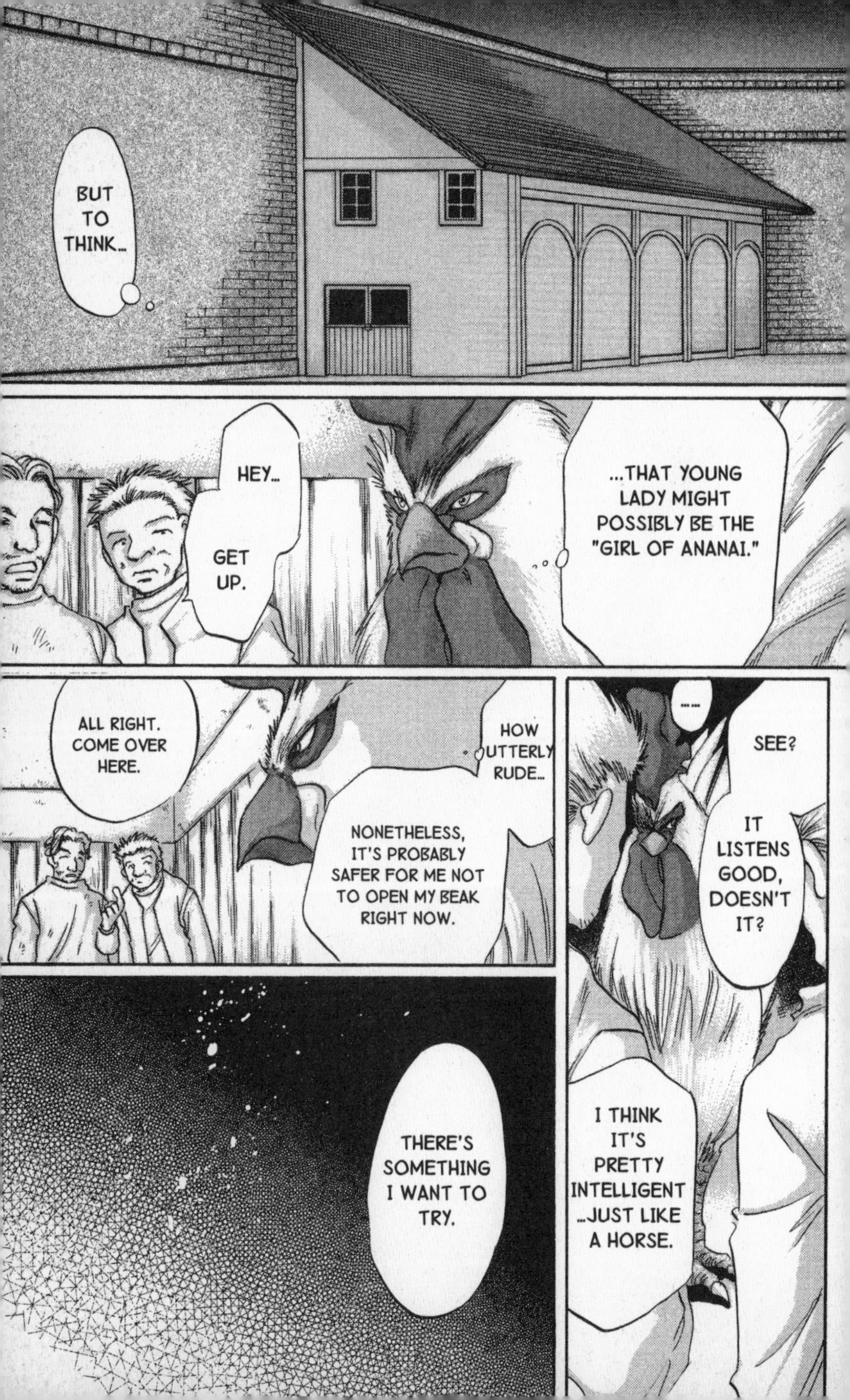
BUT TO THINK...
...THAT YOUNG LADY MIGHT POSSIBLY BE THE "GIRL OF ANANAI."
HEY... GET UP.
......
SEE?
IT LISTENS GOOD, DOESN'T IT?
I THINK IT'S PRETTY INTELLIGENT ...JUST LIKE A HORSE.
ALL RIGHT. COME OVER HERE.
HOW UTTERLY RUDE...
NONETHELESS, IT'S PROBABLY SAFER FOR ME NOT TO OPEN MY BEAK RIGHT NOW.
THERE'S SOMETHING I WANT TO TRY.

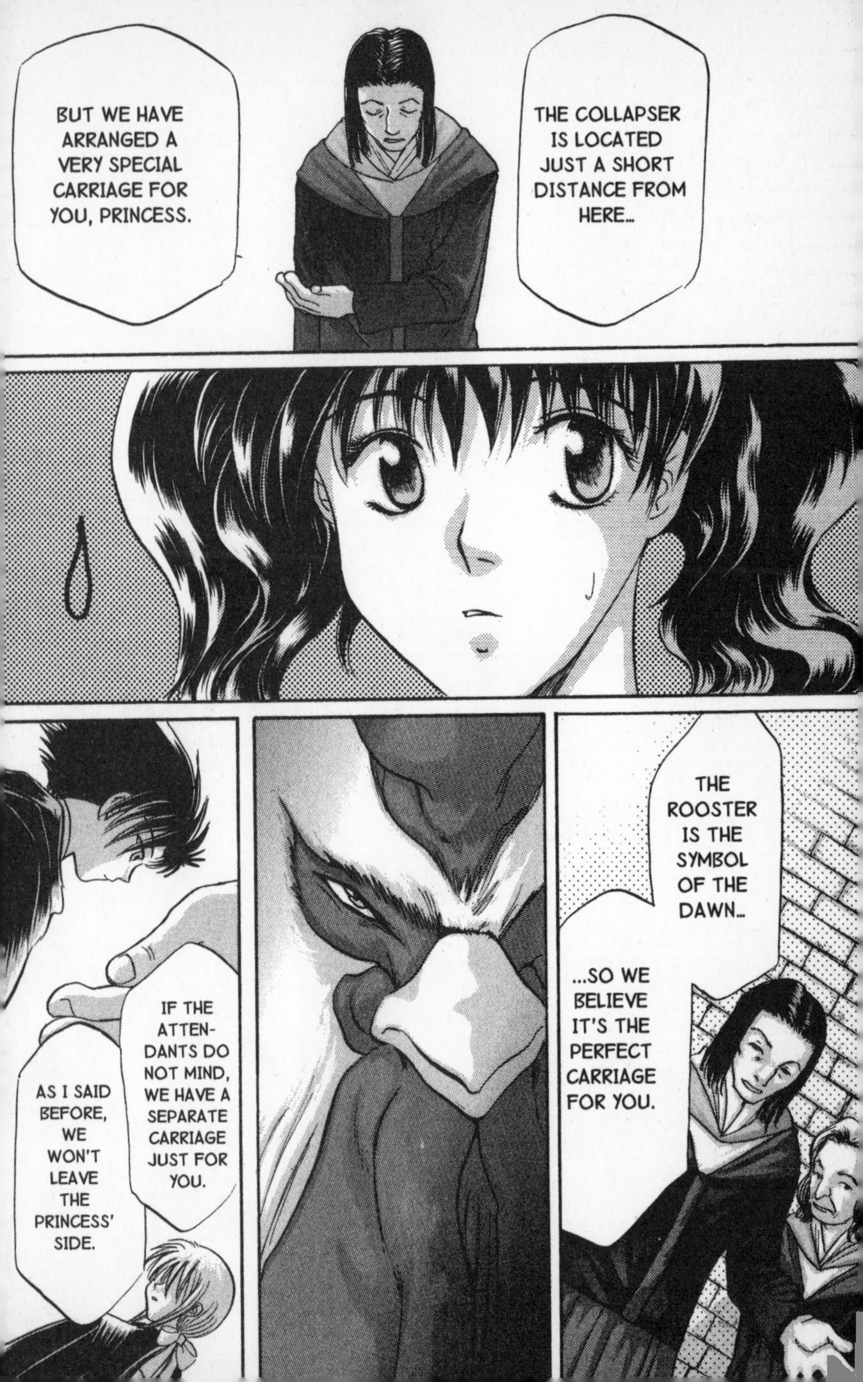
THE COLLAPSER IS LOCATED JUST A SHORT DISTANCE FROM HERE...
BUT WE HAVE ARRANGED A VERY SPECIAL CARRIAGE FOR YOU, PRINCESS.
THE ROOSTER IS THE SYMBOL OF THE DAWN...
...SO WE BELIEVE IT'S THE PERFECT CARRIAGE FOR YOU.
IF THE ATTEN-DANTS DO NOT MIND, WE HAVE A SEPARATE CARRIAGE JUST FOR YOU.
AS I SAID BEFORE, WE WON'T LEAVE THE PRINCESS' SIDE.

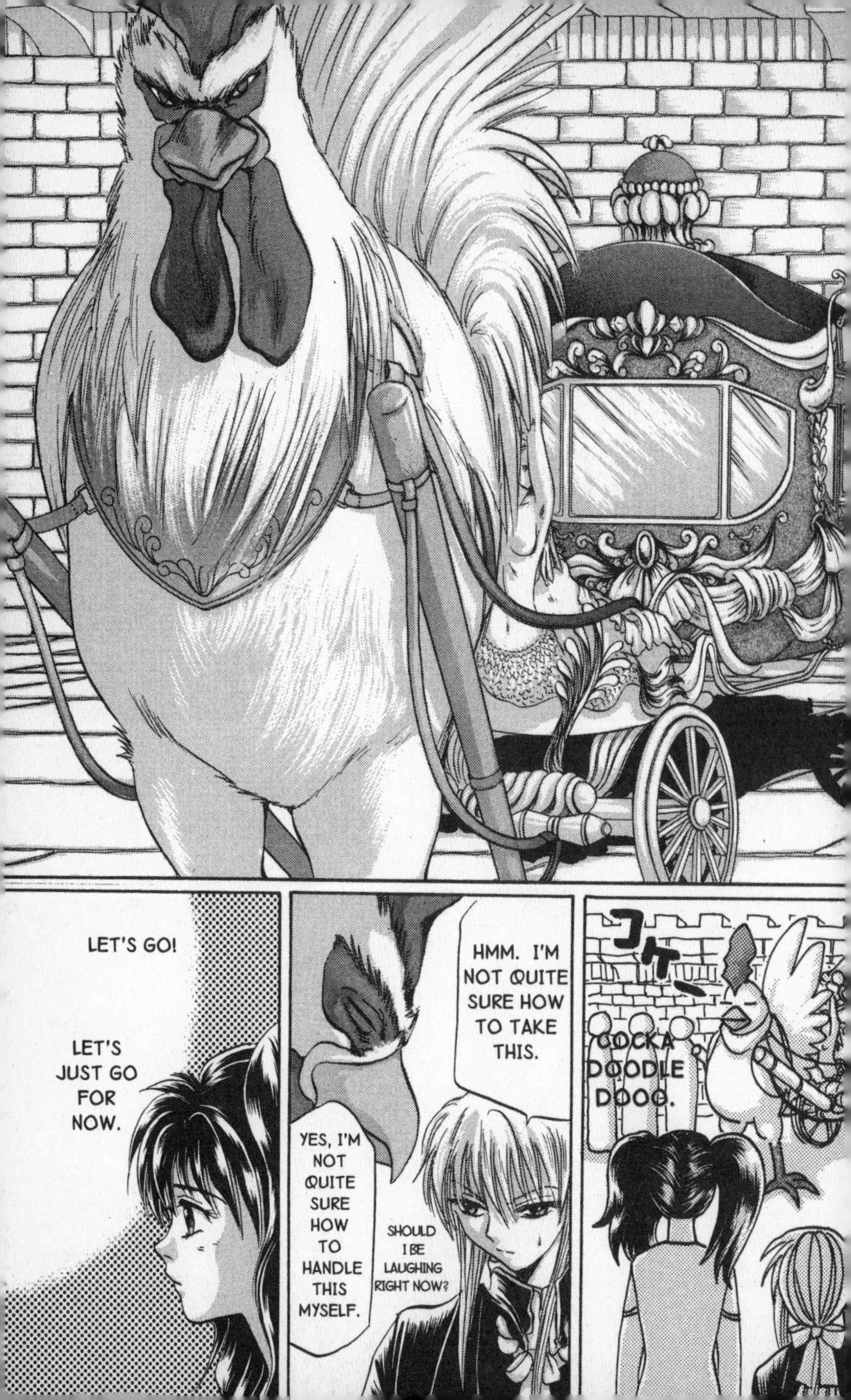
コケ
COCKA DOODLE DOOO.
HMM. I'M NOT QUITE SURE HOW TO TAKE THIS.
YES, I'M NOT QUITE SURE HOW TO HANDLE THIS MYSELF.
SHOULD I BE LAUGHING RIGHT NOW?
LET'S GO!
LET'S JUST GO FOR NOW.

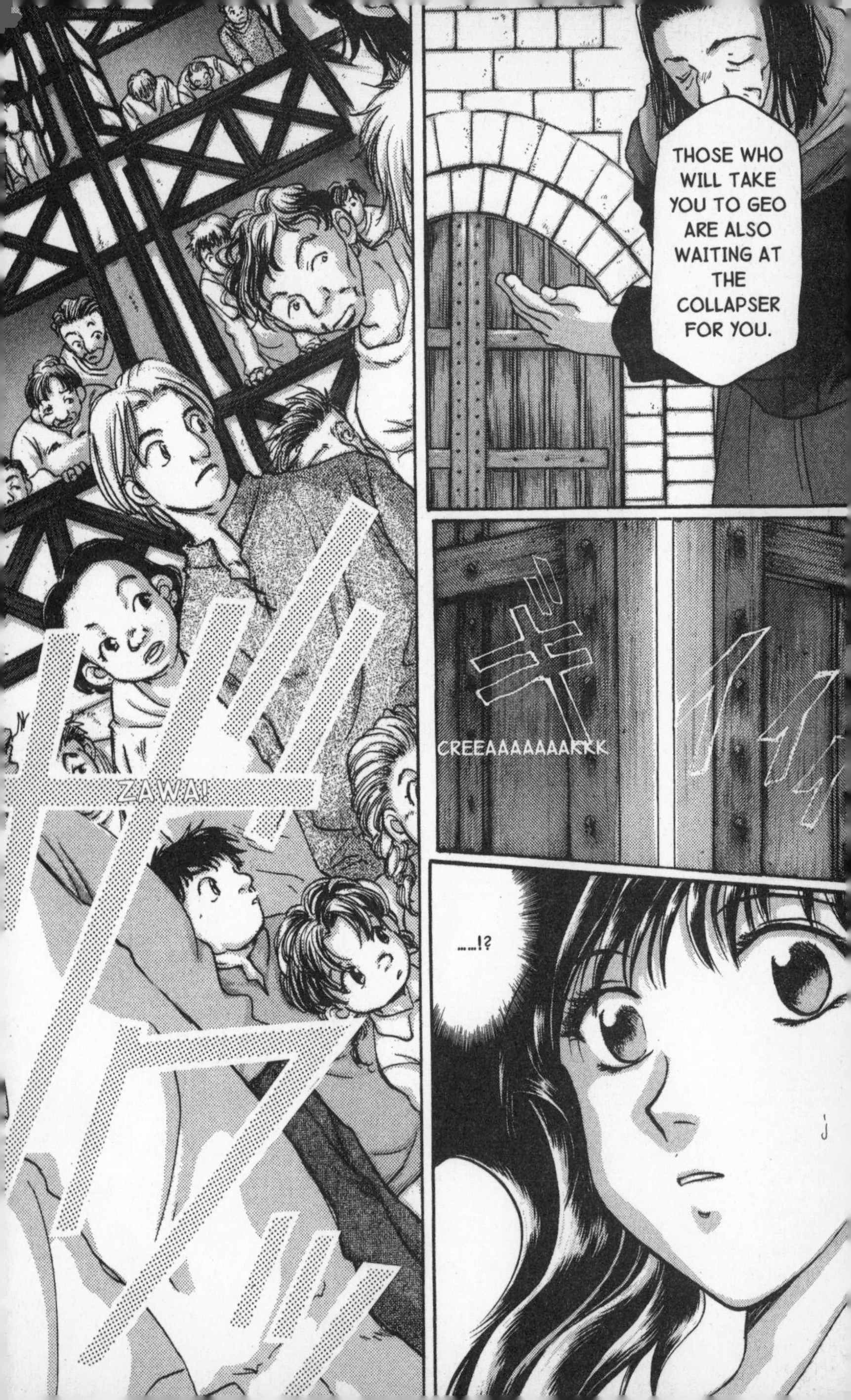
THOSE WHO WILL TAKE YOU TO GEO ARE ALSO WAITING AT THE COLLAPSER FOR YOU.
ギ
CREEAAAAAAAKKK
......!?
ZAWA!

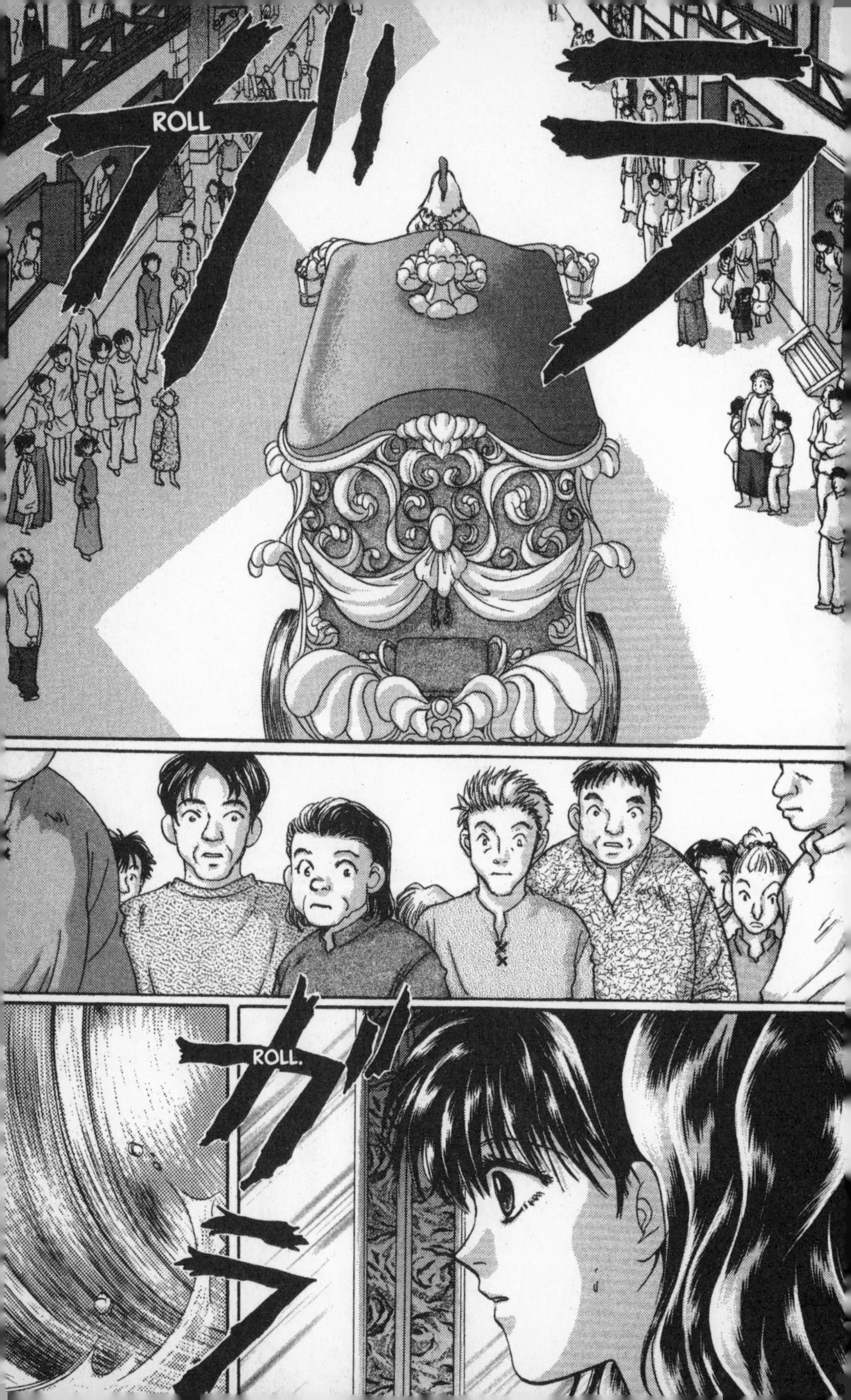
ROLL
ROLL.

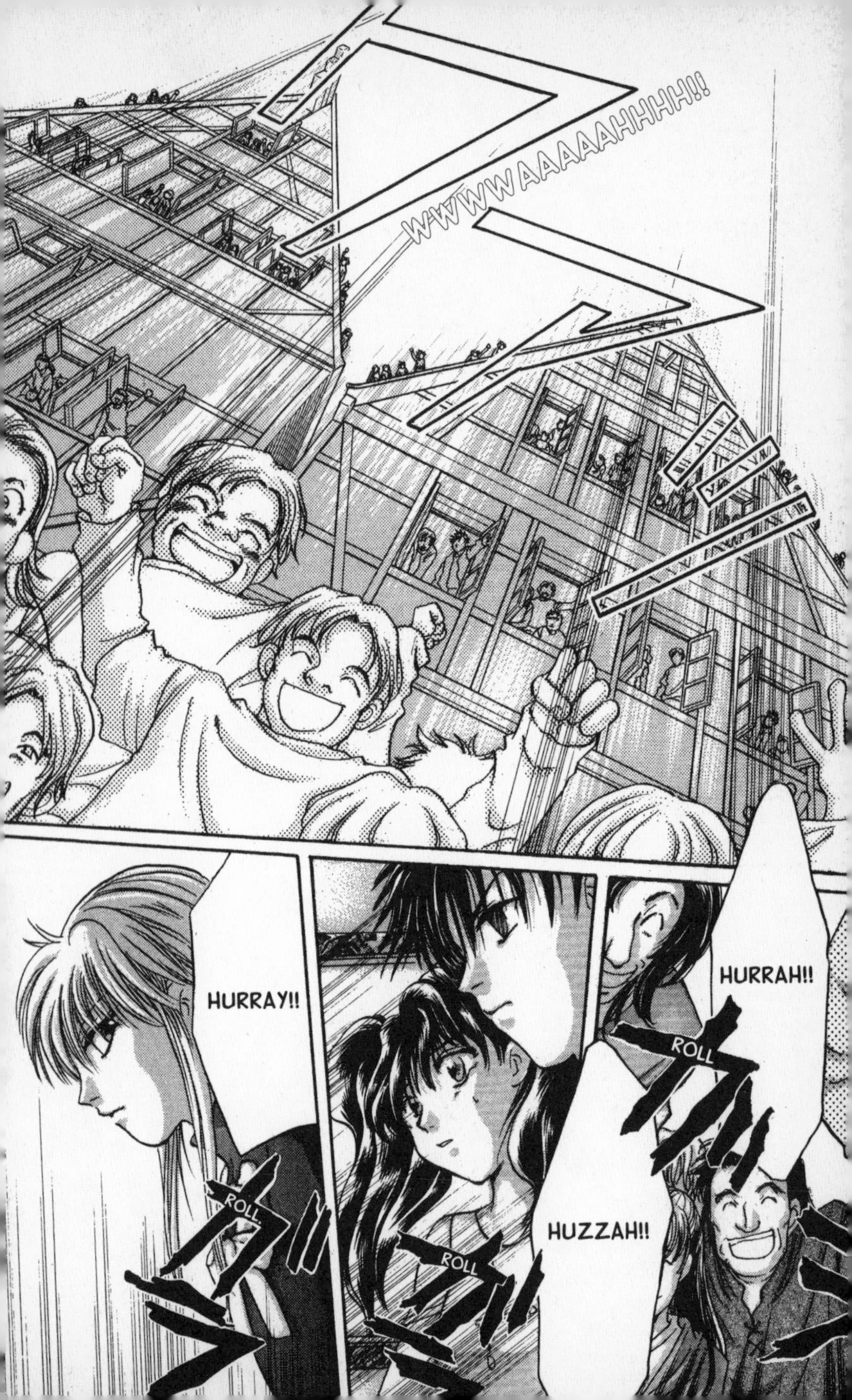
WWWWAAAAAHHHHH!!
HURRAH!!
ROLL
HUZZAH!!
ROLL
HURRAY!!
ROLL

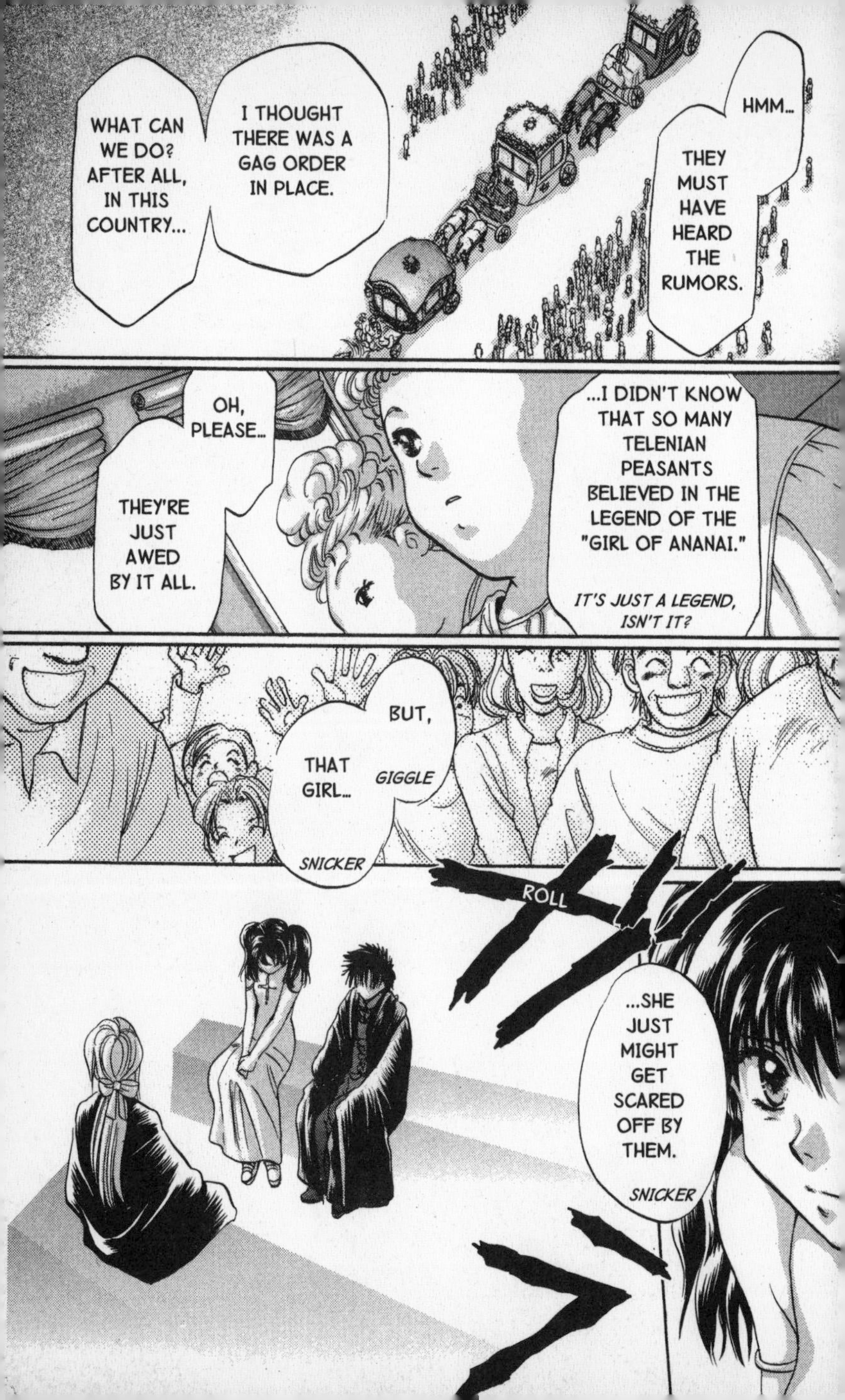
HMM...
THEY MUST HAVE HEARD THE RUMORS.
I THOUGHT THERE WAS A GAG ORDER IN PLACE.
WHAT CAN WE DO? AFTER ALL, IN THIS COUNTRY...
...I DIDN'T KNOW THAT SO MANY TELENIAN PEASANTS BELIEVED IN THE LEGEND OF THE "GIRL OF ANANAI."
IT'S JUST A LEGEND, ISN'T IT?
OH, PLEASE...
THEY'RE JUST AWED BY IT ALL.
BUT,
THAT GIRL...
GIGGLE
SNICKER
ROLL
...SHE JUST MIGHT GET SCARED OFF BY THEM.
SNICKER

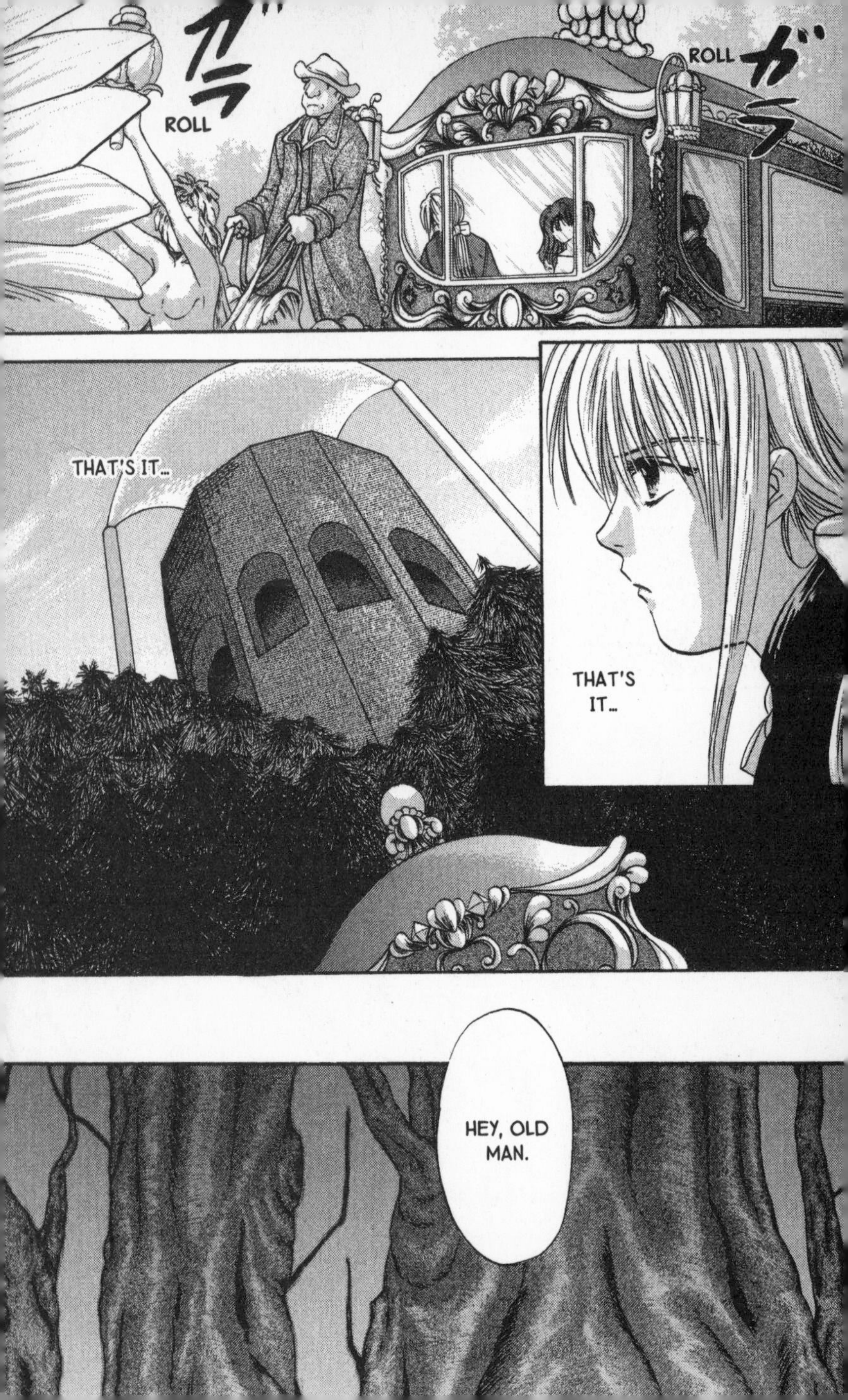

ROLL
ガラ
ガラ
ROLL
THAT'S IT...
THAT'S IT...
HEY, OLD MAN.

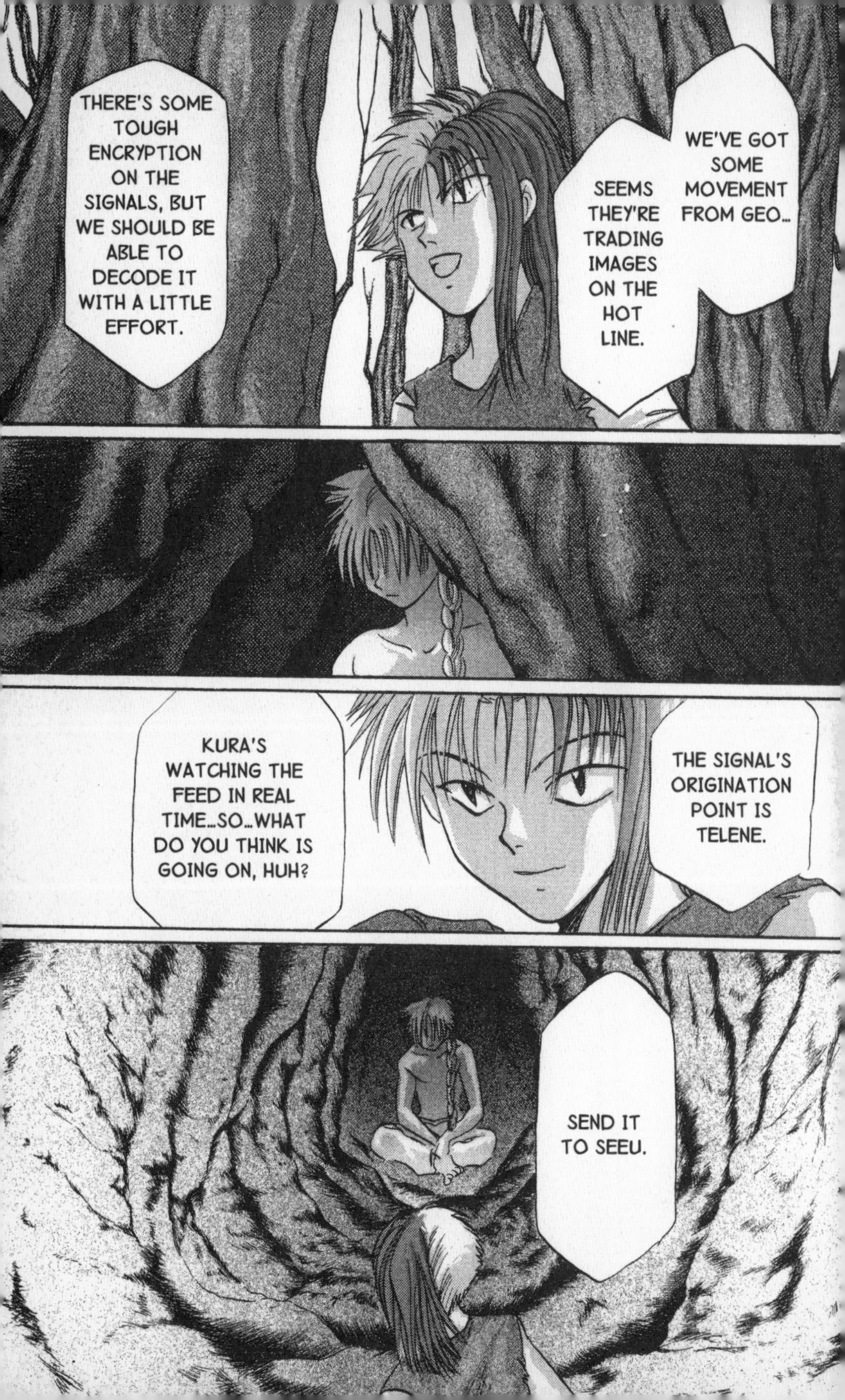
WE'VE GOT SOME MOVEMENT FROM GEO...
SEEMS THEY'RE TRADING IMAGES ON THE HOT LINE.
THERE'S SOME TOUGH ENCRYPTION ON THE SIGNALS, BUT WE SHOULD BE ABLE TO DECODE IT WITH A LITTLE EFFORT.
THE SIGNAL'S ORIGINATION POINT IS TELENE.
KURA'S WATCHING THE FEED IN REAL TIME...SO...WHAT DO YOU THINK IS GOING ON, HUH?
SEND IT TO SEEU.

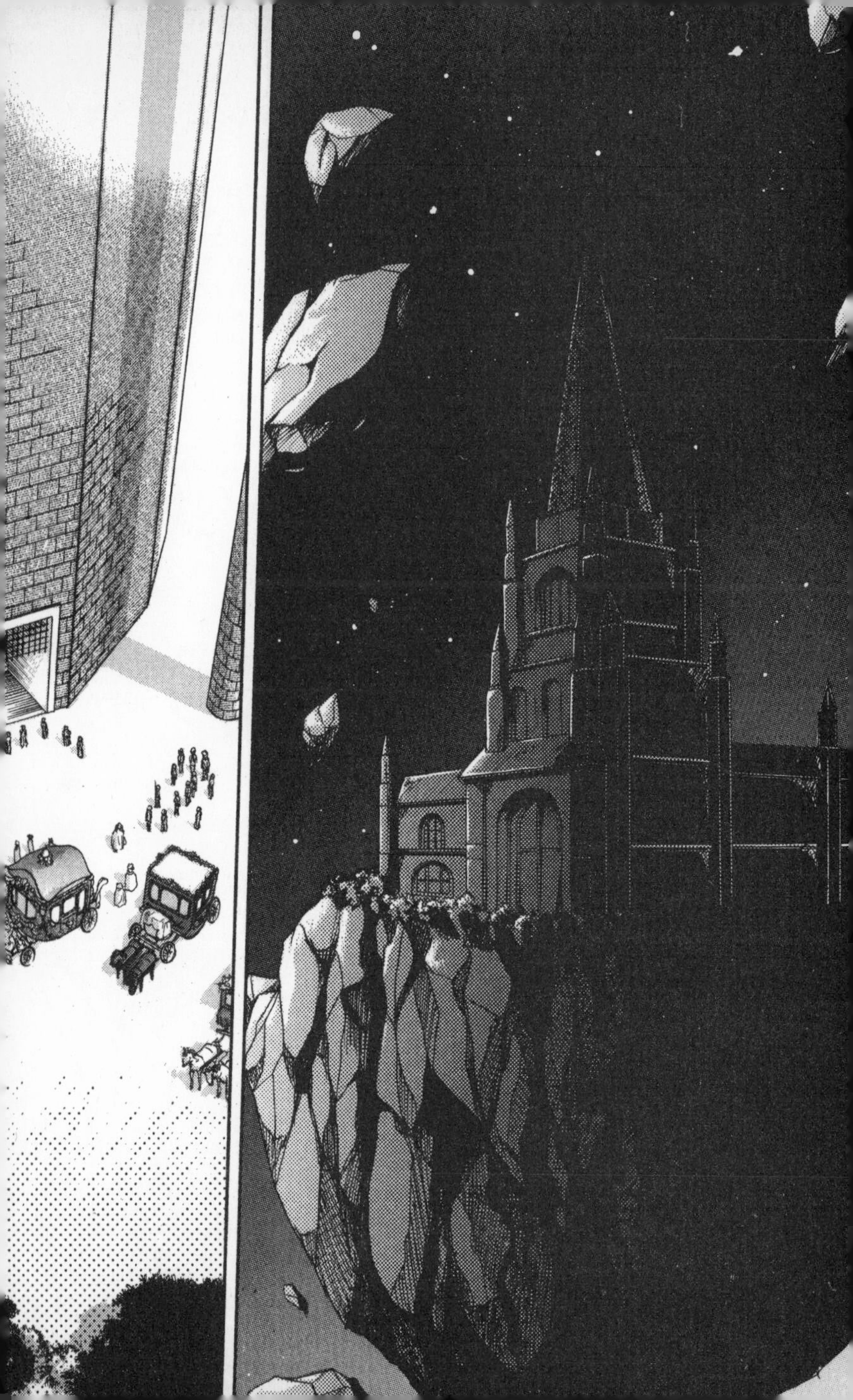

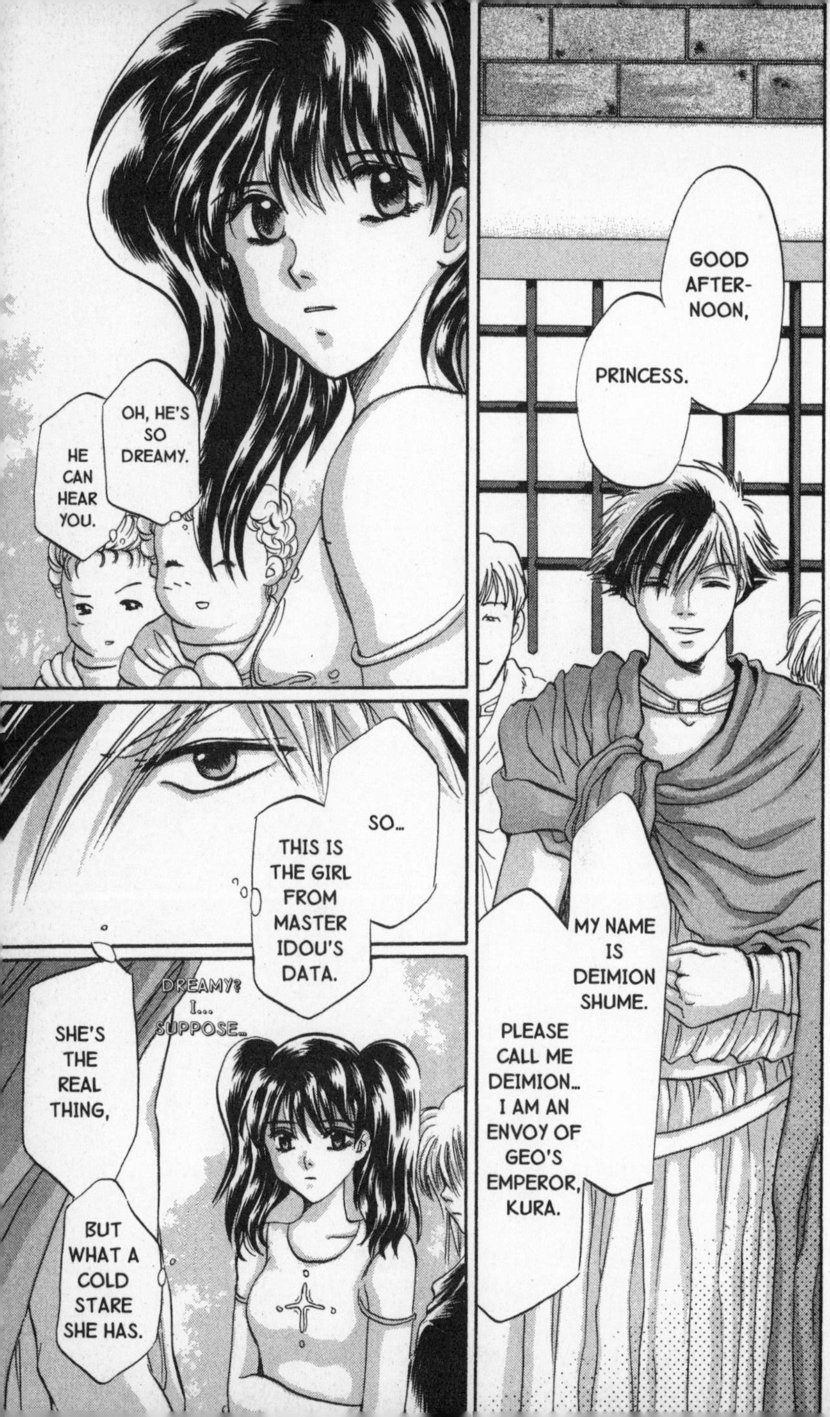
GOOD AFTER-NOON,
PRINCESS.
MY NAME IS DEIMION SHUME.
PLEASE CALL ME DEIMION... I AM AN ENVOY OF GEO'S EMPEROR, KURA.
OH, HE'S SO DREAMY.
HE CAN HEAR YOU.
SO...
THIS IS THE GIRL FROM MASTER IDOU'S DATA.
DREAMY? I... SUPPOSE...
SHE'S THE REAL THING,
BUT WHAT A COLD STARE SHE HAS.

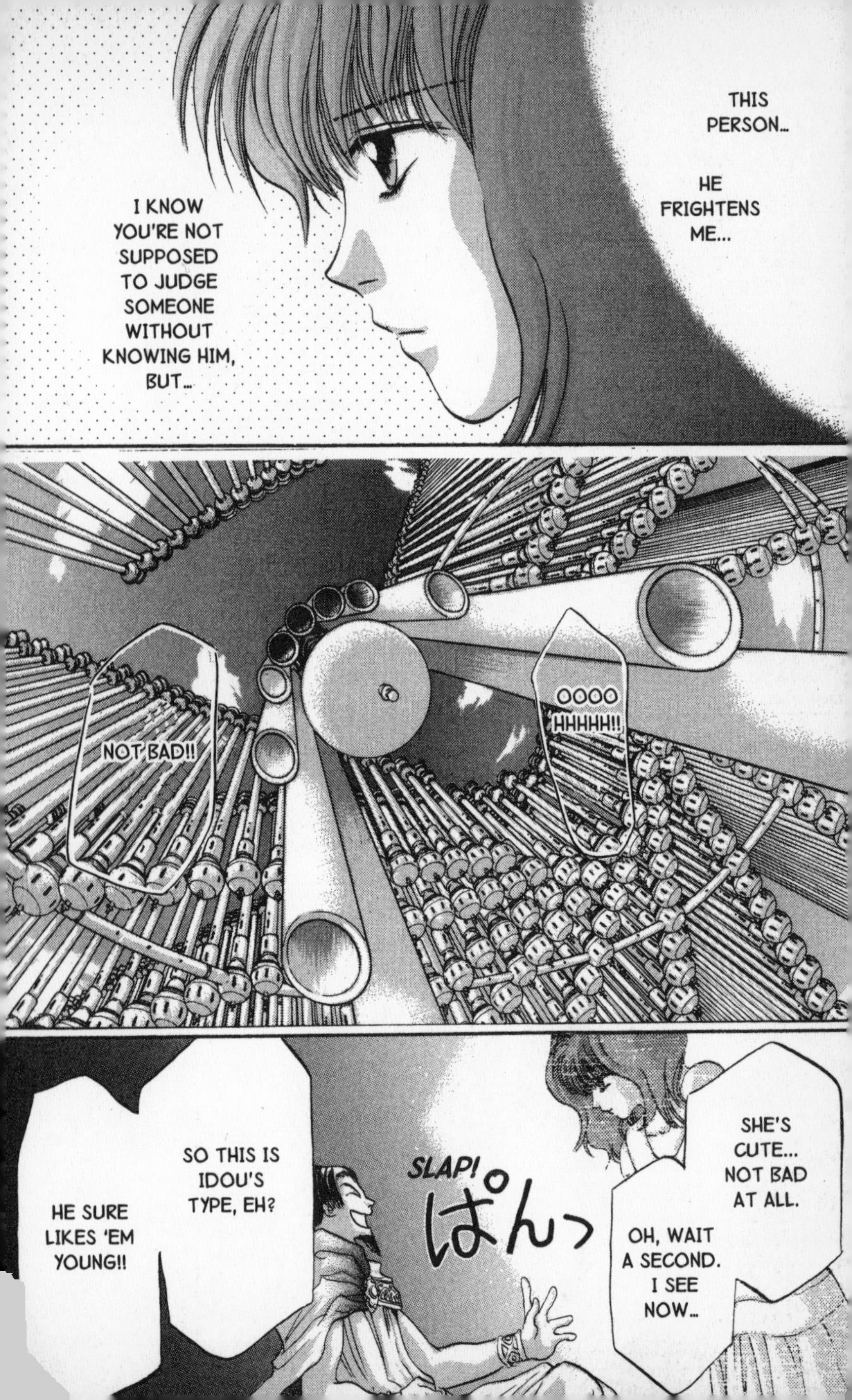
THIS PERSON...
HE FRIGHTENS ME...
I KNOW YOU'RE NOT SUPPOSED TO JUDGE SOMEONE WITHOUT KNOWING HIM, BUT...
OOOO HHHHH!!
NOT BAD!!
SHE'S CUTE... NOT BAD AT ALL.
OH, WAIT A SECOND. I SEE NOW...
SLAP!
ぱんっ
SO THIS IS IDOU'S TYPE, EH?
HE SURE LIKES 'EM YOUNG!!

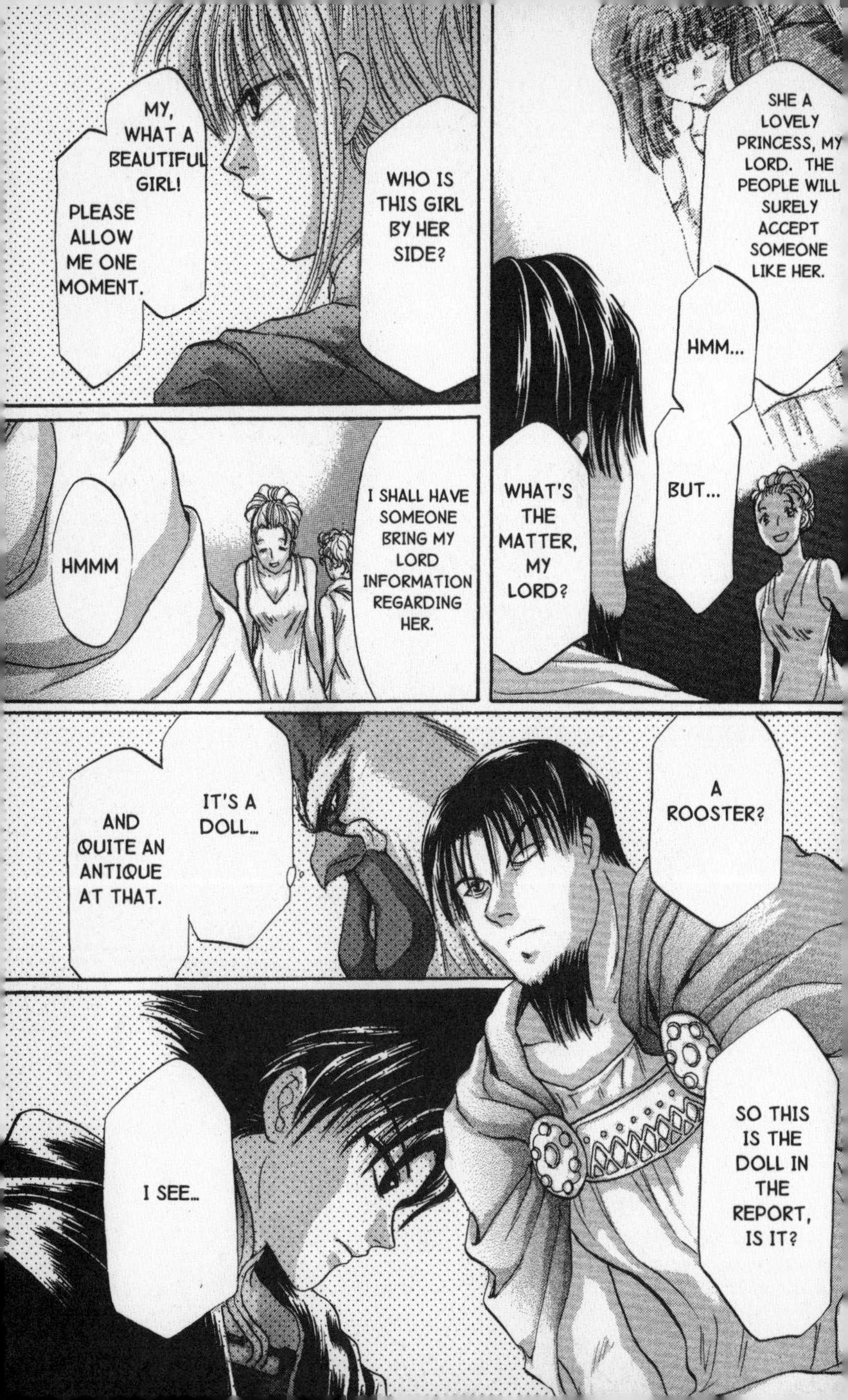
SHE A LOVELY PRINCESS, MY LORD. THE PEOPLE WILL SURELY ACCEPT SOMEONE LIKE HER.
HMM...
BUT...
WHAT'S THE MATTER, MY LORD?
WHO IS THIS GIRL BY HER SIDE?
MY, WHAT A BEAUTIFUL GIRL!
PLEASE ALLOW ME ONE MOMENT.
I SHALL HAVE SOMEONE BRING MY LORD INFORMATION REGARDING HER.
HMMM
A ROOSTER?
IT'S A DOLL...
AND QUITE AN ANTIQUE AT THAT.
SO THIS IS THE DOLL IN THE REPORT, IS IT?
I SEE...

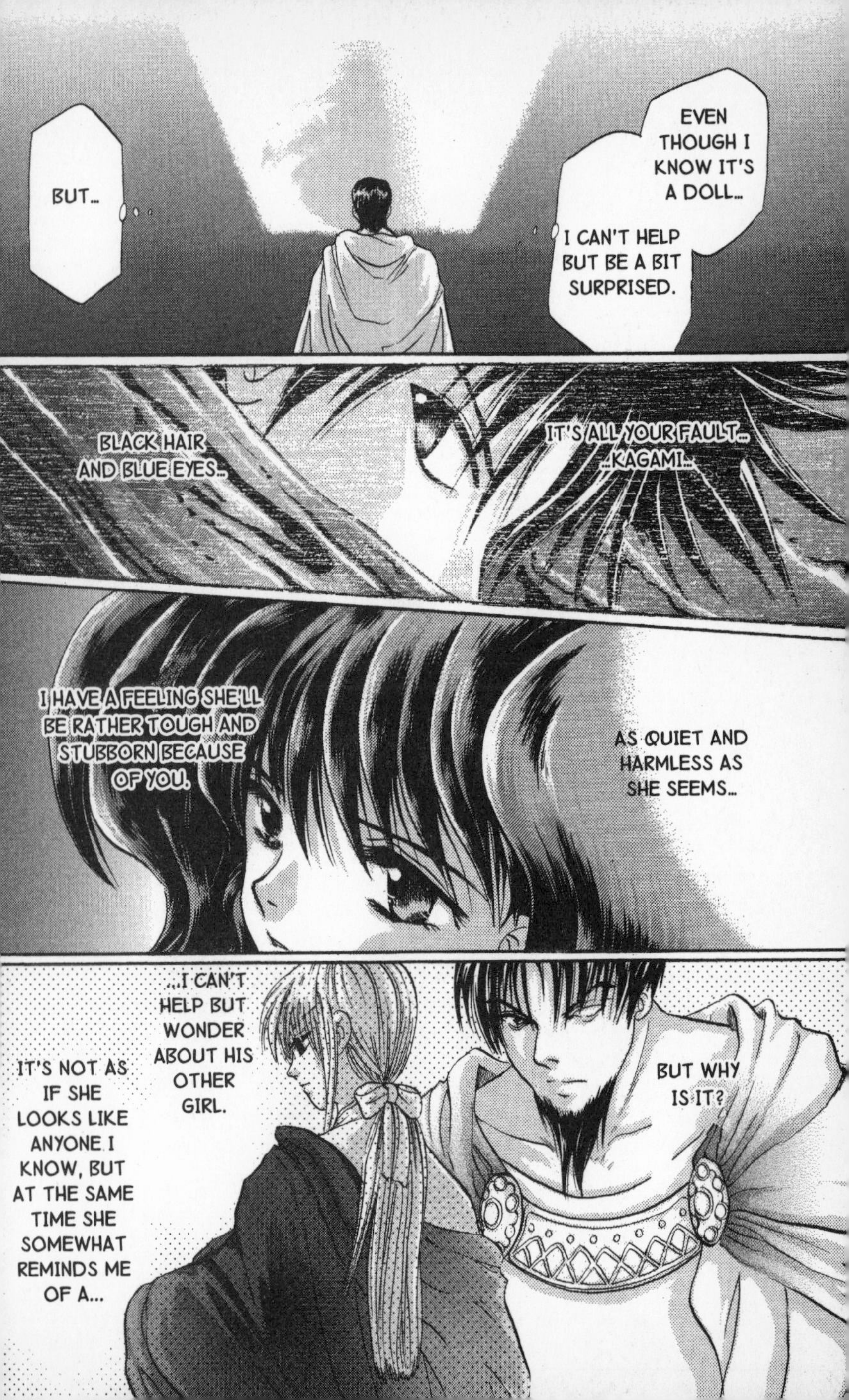
EVEN THOUGH I KNOW IT'S A DOLL...
I CAN'T HELP BUT BE A BIT SURPRISED.
BUT...
IT'S ALL YOUR FAULT... ...KAGAMI...
BLACK HAIR AND BLUE EYES...
AS QUIET AND HARMLESS AS SHE SEEMS...
I HAVE A FEELING SHE'LL BE RATHER TOUGH AND STUBBORN BECAUSE OF YOU.
BUT WHY IS IT?
...I CAN'T HELP BUT WONDER ABOUT HIS OTHER GIRL.
IT'S NOT AS IF SHE LOOKS LIKE ANYONE I KNOW, BUT AT THE SAME TIME SHE SOMEWHAT REMINDS ME OF A...

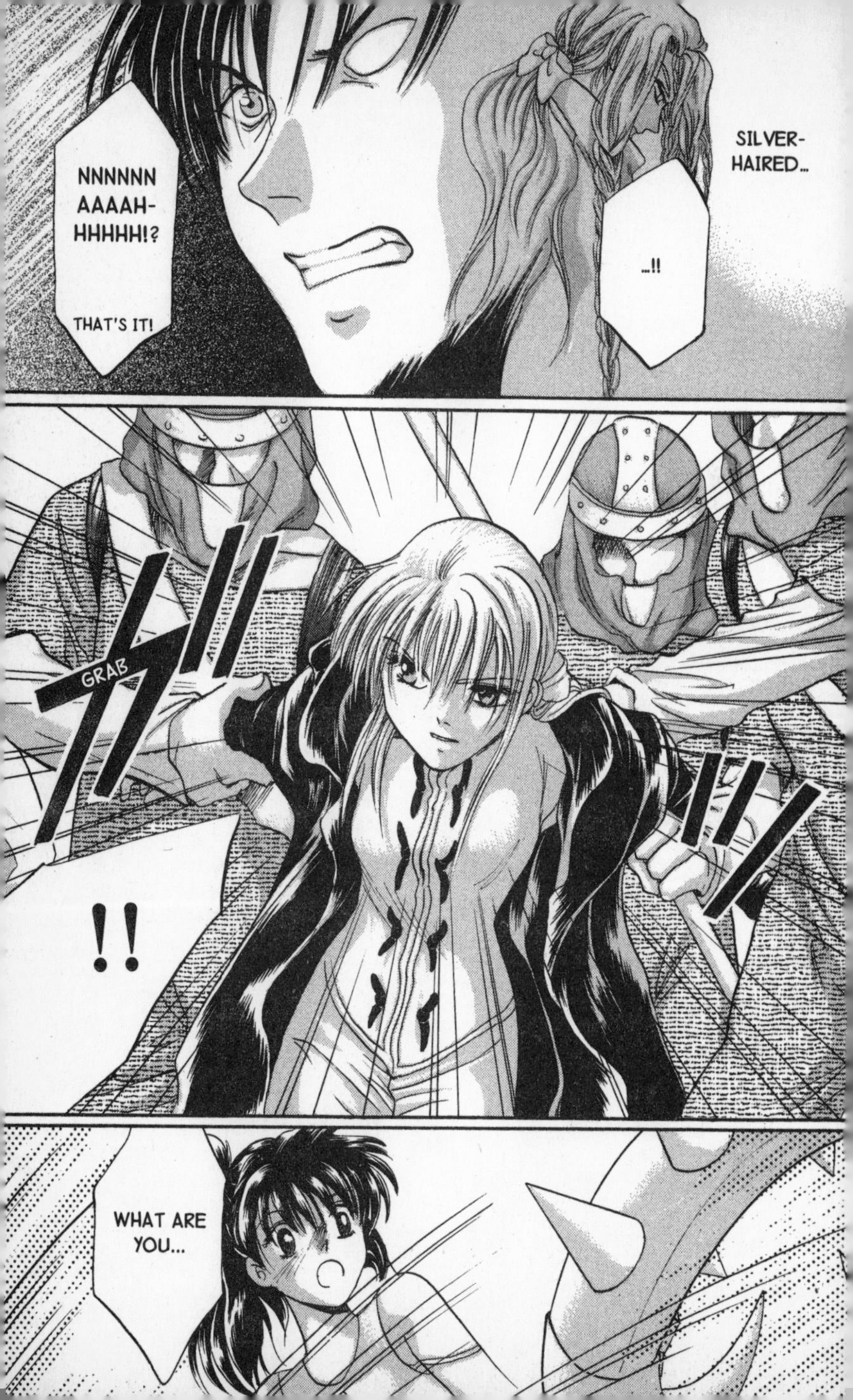
SILVER-HAIRED...
...!!
NNNNNN AAAAH-HHHHH!?
THAT'S IT!
GRAB
!!
WHAT ARE YOU...

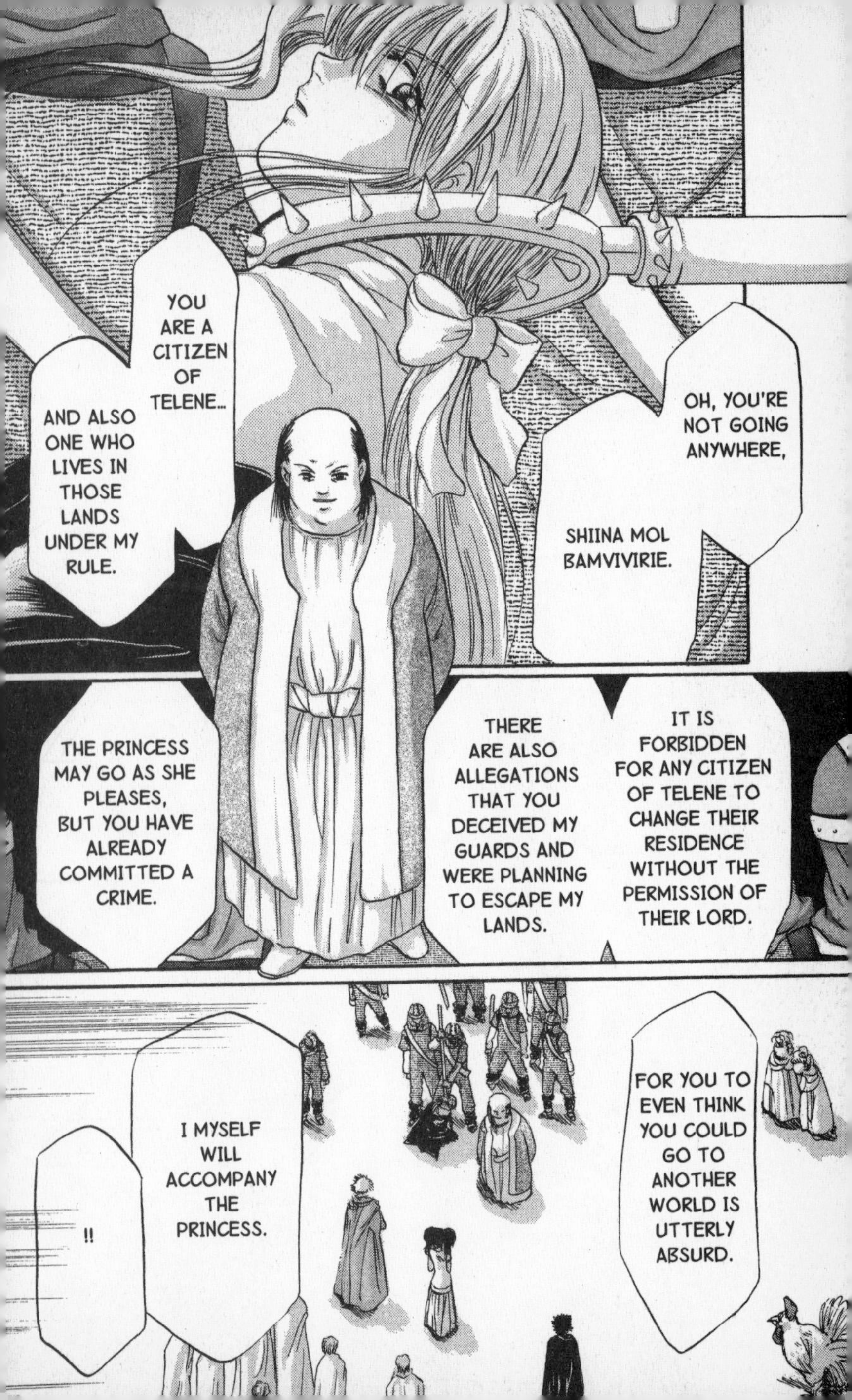
OH, YOU'RE NOT GOING ANYWHERE,
SHIINA MOL BAMVIVIRIE.
YOU ARE A CITIZEN OF TELENE...
AND ALSO ONE WHO LIVES IN THOSE LANDS UNDER MY RULE.
IT IS FORBIDDEN FOR ANY CITIZEN OF TELENE TO CHANGE THEIR RESIDENCE WITHOUT THE PERMISSION OF THEIR LORD.
THERE ARE ALSO ALLEGATIONS THAT YOU DECEIVED MY GUARDS AND WERE PLANNING TO ESCAPE MY LANDS.
THE PRINCESS MAY GO AS SHE PLEASES, BUT YOU HAVE ALREADY COMMITTED A CRIME.
FOR YOU TO EVEN THINK YOU COULD GO TO ANOTHER WORLD IS UTTERLY ABSURD.
I MYSELF WILL ACCOMPANY THE PRINCESS.
!!

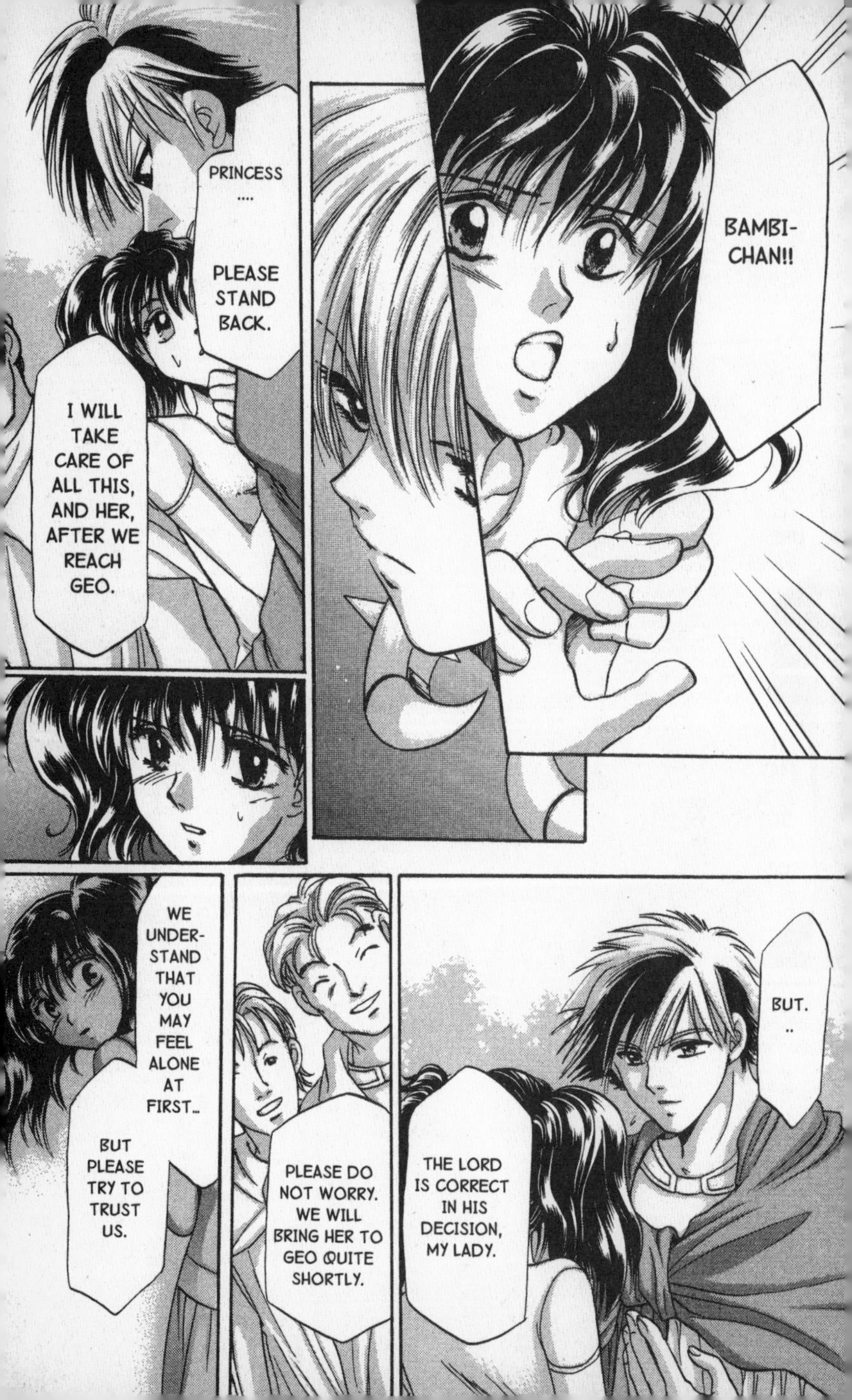
BAMBI-CHAN!!
PRINCESS .... PLEASE STAND BACK.
I WILL TAKE CARE OF ALL THIS, AND HER, AFTER WE REACH GEO.
BUT. ..
THE LORD IS CORRECT IN HIS DECISION, MY LADY.
PLEASE DO NOT WORRY. WE WILL BRING HER TO GEO QUITE SHORTLY.
WE UNDERSTAND THAT YOU MAY FEEL ALONE AT FIRST...
BUT PLEASE TRY TO TRUST US.

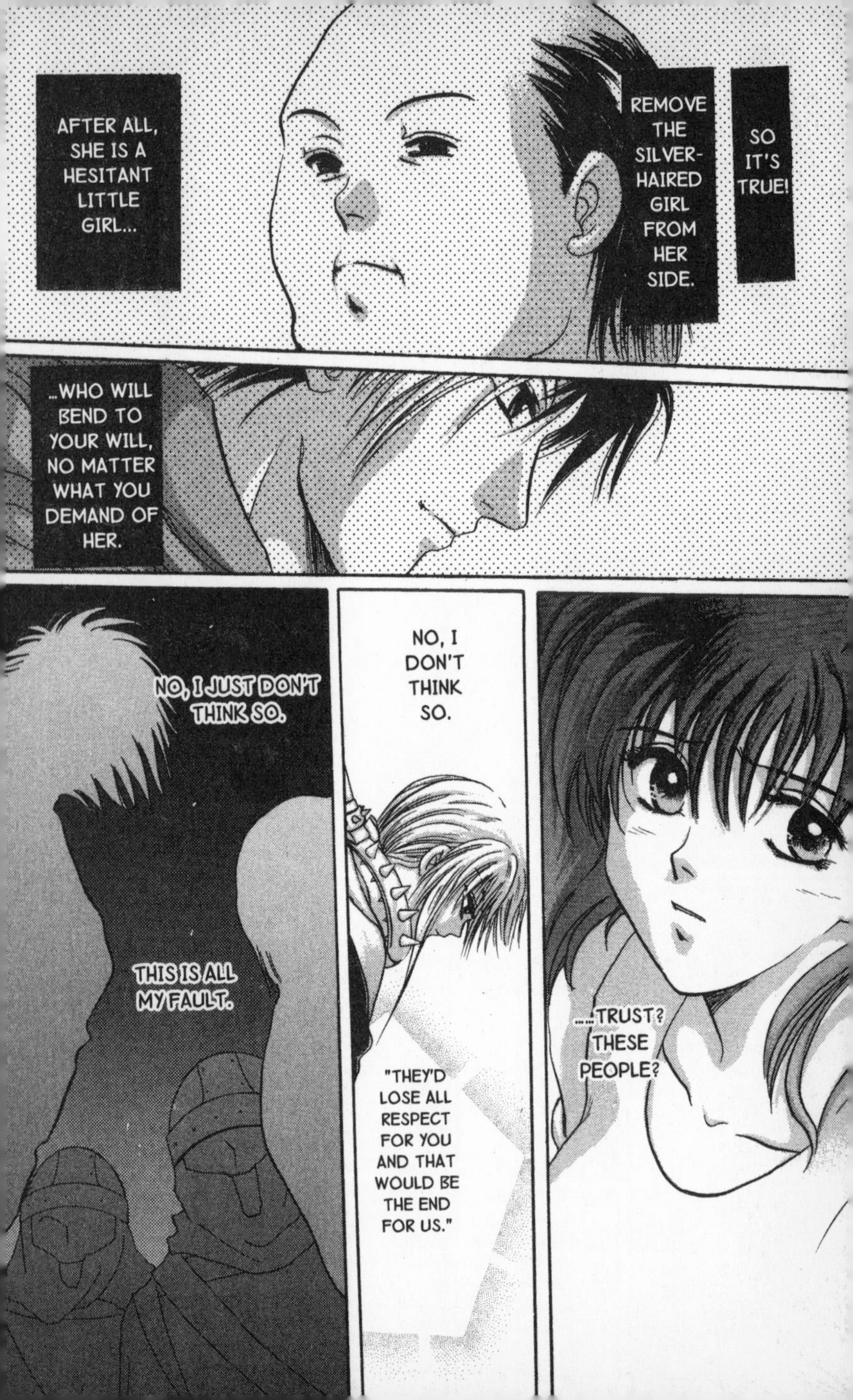
SO IT'S TRUE!
REMOVE THE SILVER-HAIRED GIRL FROM HER SIDE.
AFTER ALL, SHE IS A HESITANT LITTLE GIRL...
...WHO WILL BEND TO YOUR WILL, NO MATTER WHAT YOU DEMAND OF HER.
.....TRUST? THESE PEOPLE?
NO, I DON'T THINK SO.
"THEY'D LOSE ALL RESPECT FOR YOU AND THAT WOULD BE THE END FOR US."
NO, I JUST DON'T THINK SO.
THIS IS ALL MY FAULT.

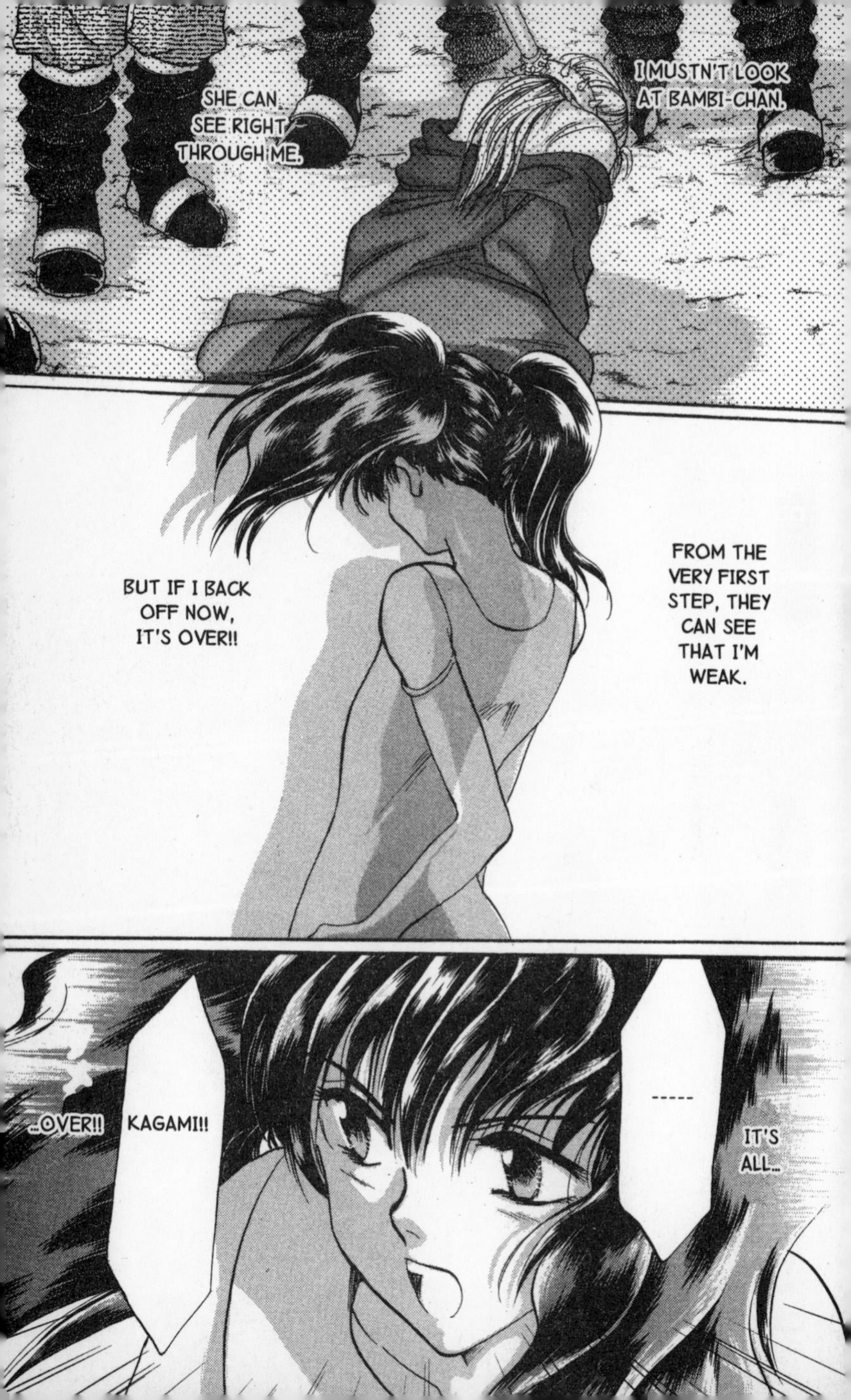

I MUSTN'T LOOK AT BAMBI-CHAN.
SHE CAN SEE RIGHT THROUGH ME.
FROM THE VERY FIRST STEP, THEY CAN SEE THAT I'M WEAK.
BUT IF I BACK OFF NOW, IT'S OVER!!

IT'S ALL..
KAGAMI!!
..OVER!!

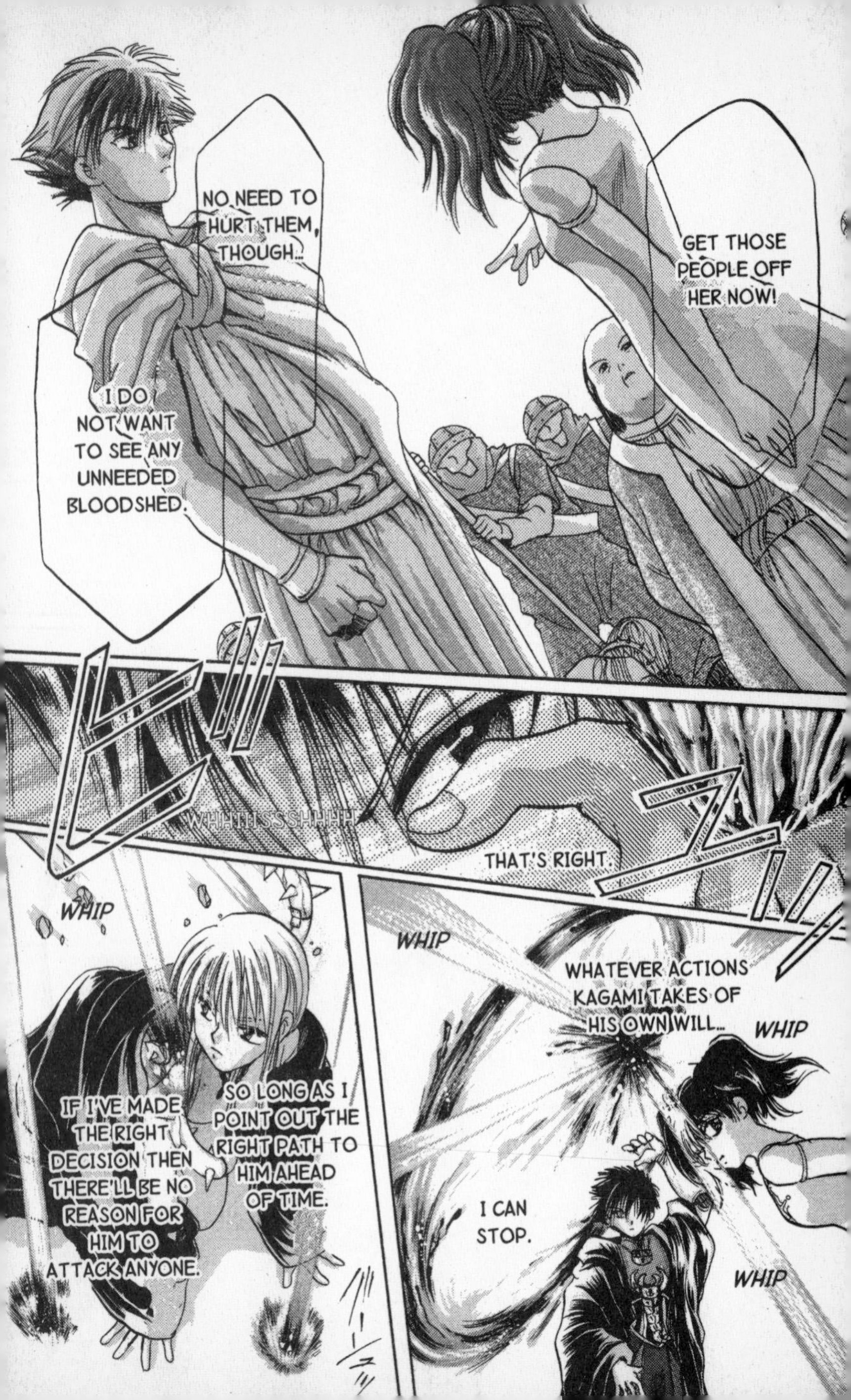
GET THOSE PEOPLE OFF HER NOW!
NO NEED TO HURT THEM, THOUGH...
I DO NOT WANT TO SEE ANY UNNEEDED BLOODSHED.
WHHHHSSSHHHH!!
THAT'S RIGHT.
WHIP
WHATEVER ACTIONS KAGAMI TAKES OF HIS OWN WILL...
WHIP
I CAN STOP.
WHIP
WHIP
SO LONG AS I POINT OUT THE RIGHT PATH TO HIM AHEAD OF TIME.
IF I'VE MADE THE RIGHT DECISION THEN THERE'LL BE NO REASON FOR HIM TO ATTACK ANYONE.

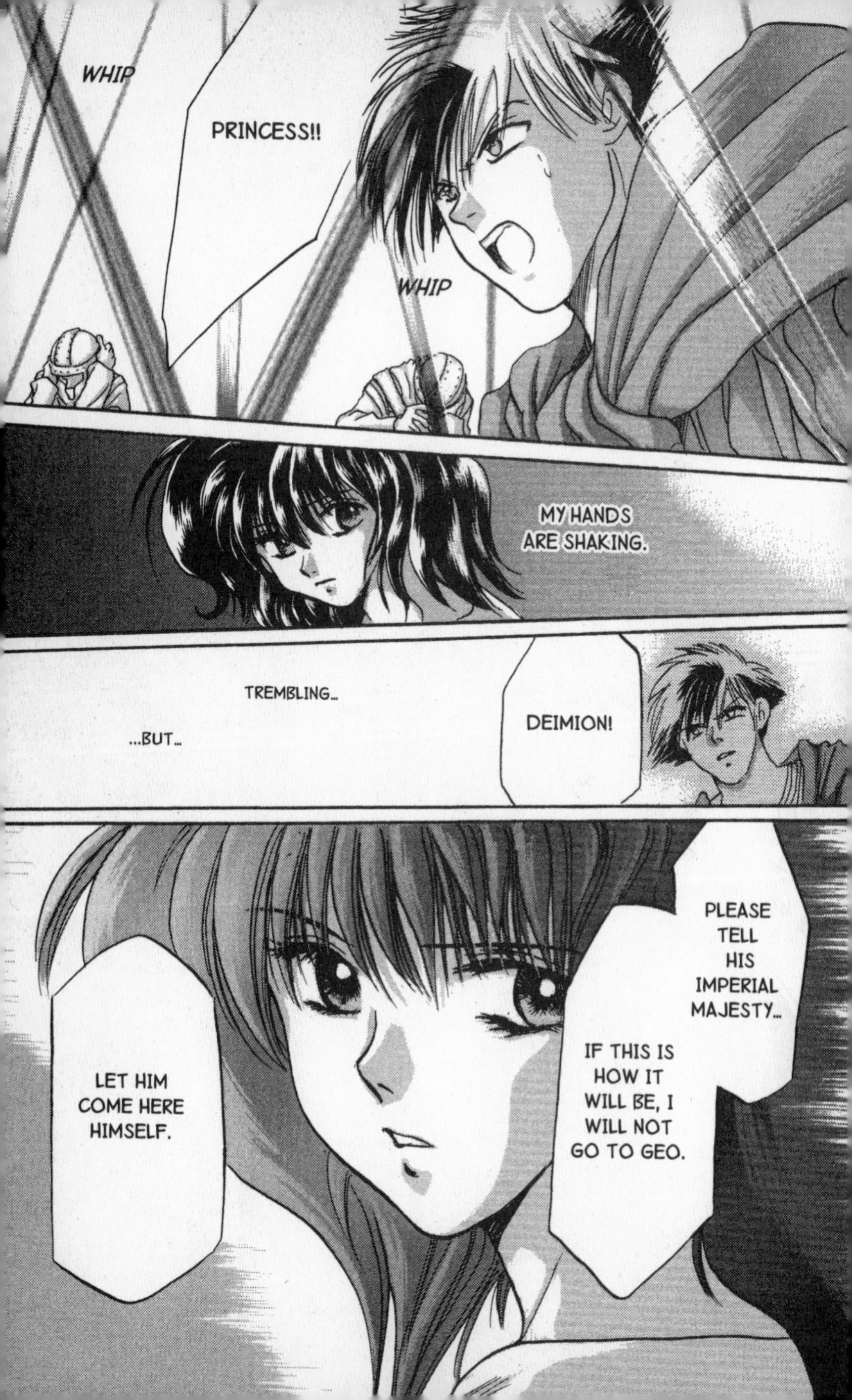

PRINCESS!!
WHIP
WHIP
MY HANDS ARE SHAKING.
DEIMION!
TREMBLING...
...BUT...
PLEASE TELL HIS IMPERIAL MAJESTY...
IF THIS IS HOW IT WILL BE, I WILL NOT GO TO GEO.
LET HIM COME HERE HIMSELF.

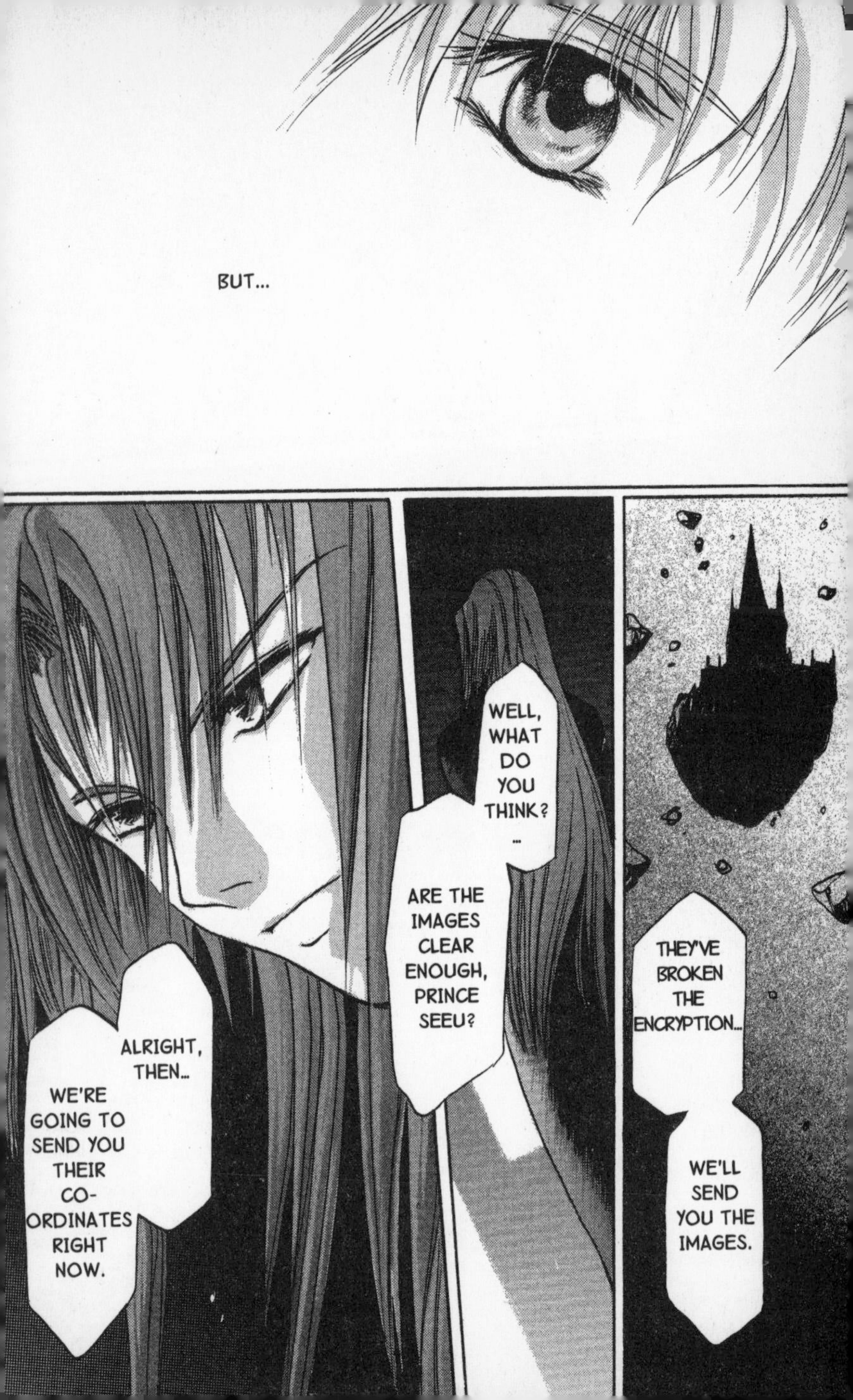
BUT...
THEY'VE BROKEN THE ENCRYPTION...
WE'LL SEND YOU THE IMAGES.
WELL, WHAT DO YOU THINK? ...
ARE THE IMAGES CLEAR ENOUGH, PRINCE SEEU?
ALRIGHT, THEN...
WE'RE GOING TO SEND YOU THEIR CO-ORDINATES RIGHT NOW.

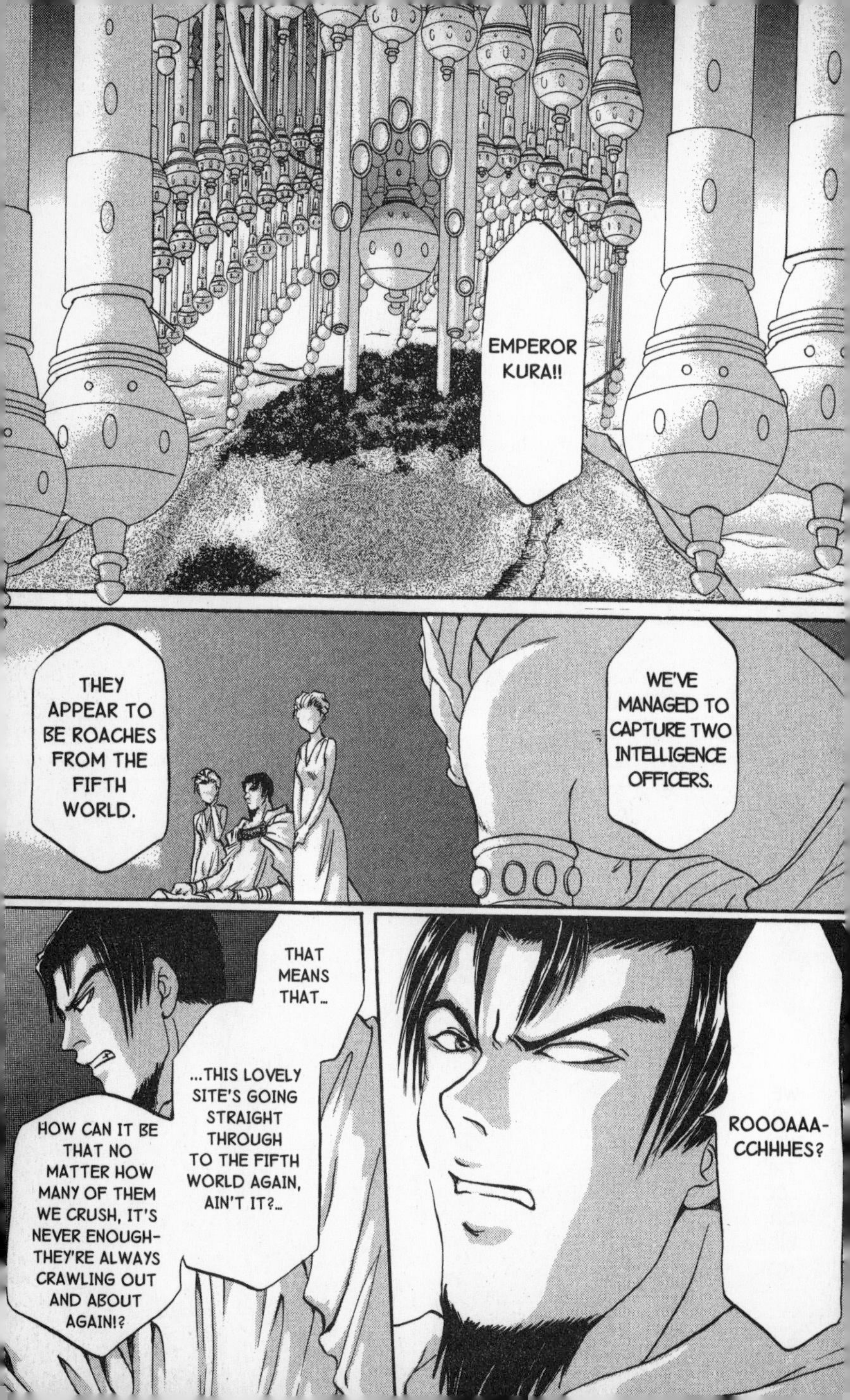
EMPEROR KURA!!
WE'VE MANAGED TO CAPTURE TWO INTELLIGENCE OFFICERS.
THEY APPEAR TO BE ROACHES FROM THE FIFTH WORLD.
ROOOAAA-CCHHHES?
THAT MEANS THAT...
...THIS LOVELY SITE'S GOING STRAIGHT THROUGH TO THE FIFTH WORLD AGAIN, AIN'T IT?...
HOW CAN IT BE THAT NO MATTER HOW MANY OF THEM WE CRUSH, IT'S NEVER ENOUGH- THEY'RE ALWAYS CRAWLING OUT AND ABOUT AGAIN!?

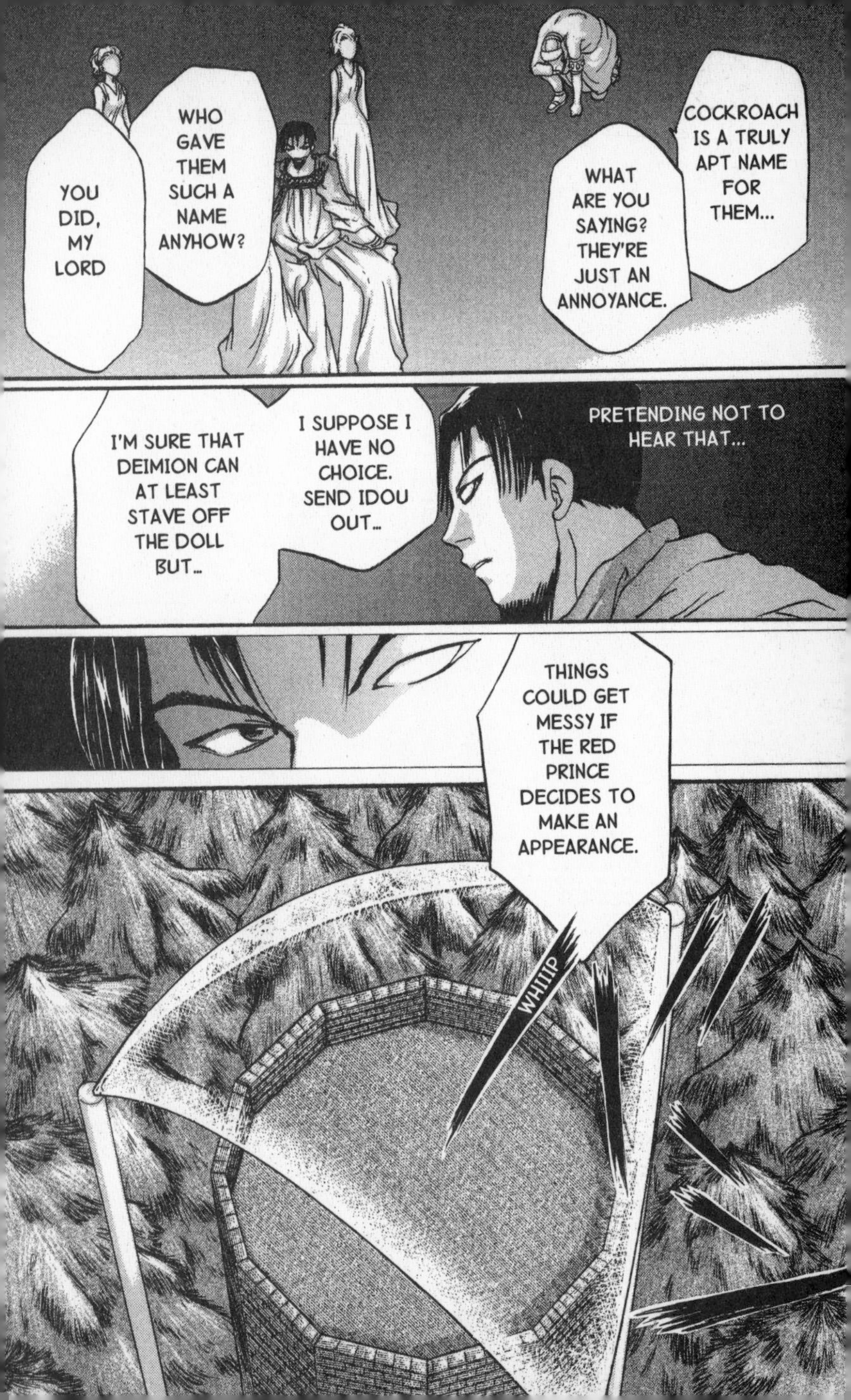
COCKROACH IS A TRULY APT NAME FOR THEM...
WHAT ARE YOU SAYING? THEY'RE JUST AN ANNOYANCE.
WHO GAVE THEM SUCH A NAME ANYHOW?
YOU DID, MY LORD
PRETENDING NOT TO HEAR THAT...
I SUPPOSE I HAVE NO CHOICE. SEND IDOU OUT...
I'M SURE THAT DEIMION CAN AT LEAST STAVE OFF THE DOLL BUT...
THINGS COULD GET MESSY IF THE RED PRINCE DECIDES TO MAKE AN APPEARANCE.
WHIIIP

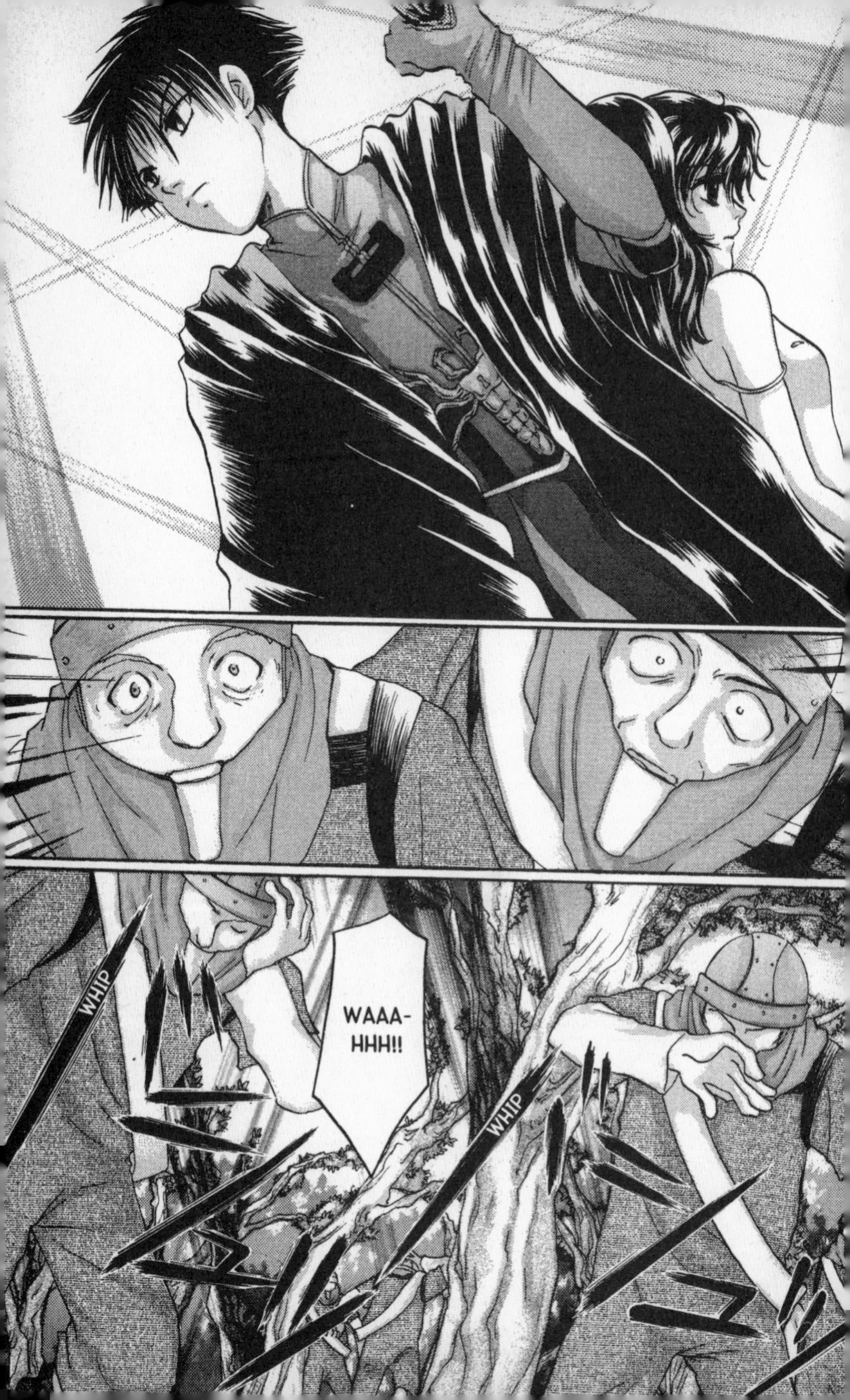
WHIP
WAAA-HHH!!
WHIP

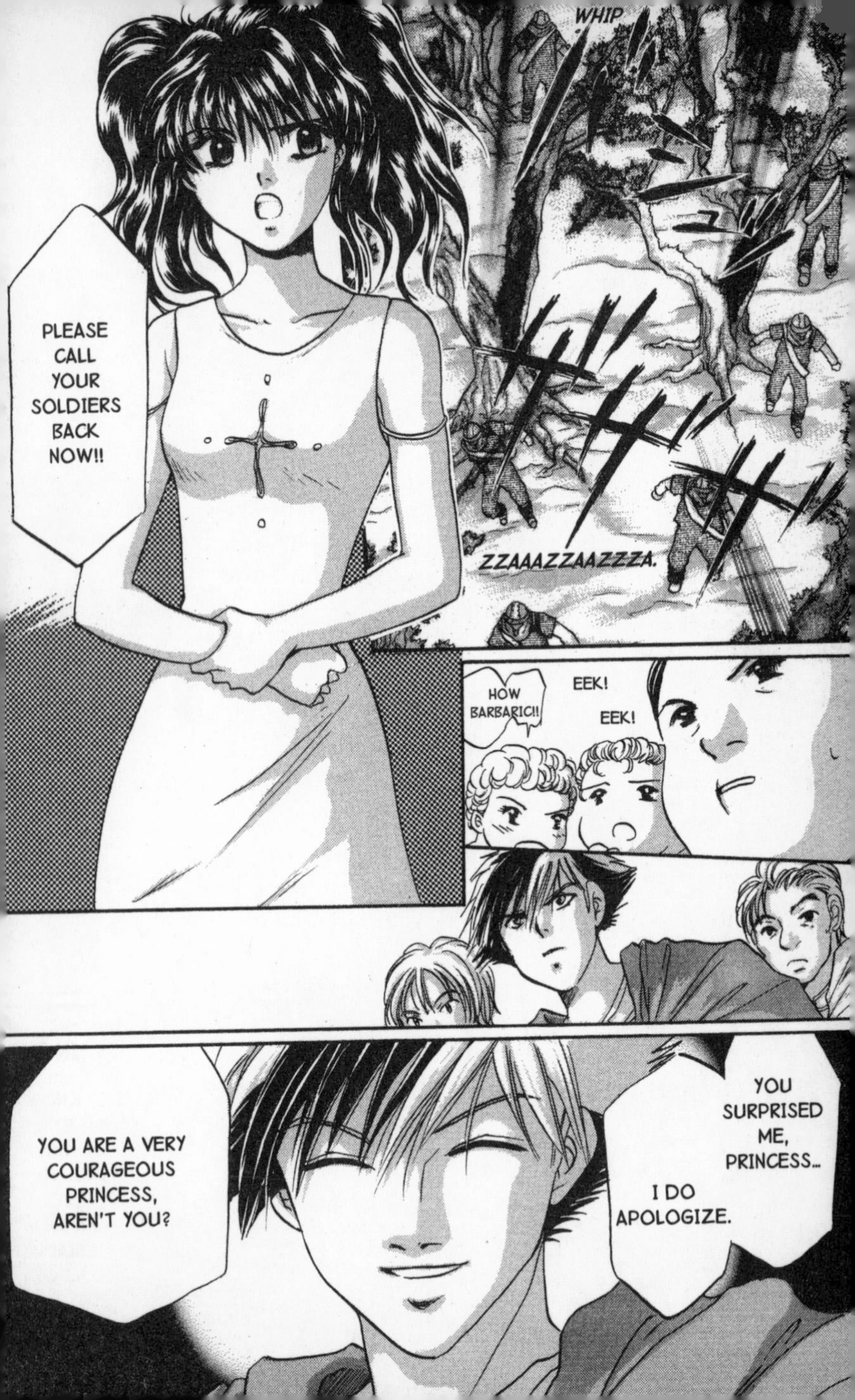
WHIP
ZZAAAZZAAZZZA.
EEK!
EEK!
HOW BARBARIC!!
PLEASE CALL YOUR SOLDIERS BACK NOW!!
YOU SURPRISED ME, PRINCESS...
I DO APOLOGIZE.
YOU ARE A VERY COURAGEOUS PRINCESS, AREN'T YOU?

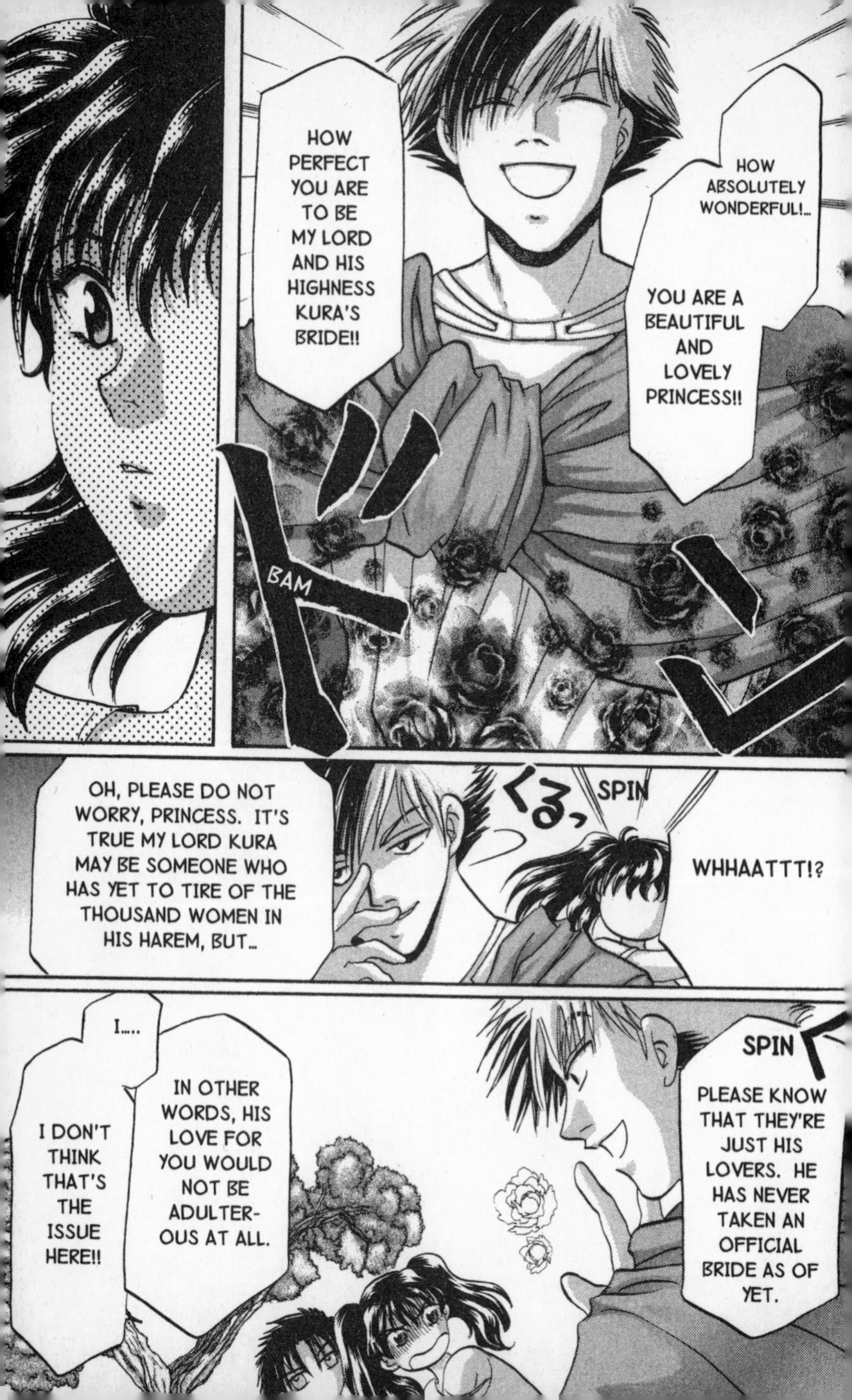
HOW ABSOLUTELY WONDERFUL!...
YOU ARE A BEAUTIFUL AND LOVELY PRINCESS!!
HOW PERFECT YOU ARE TO BE MY LORD AND HIS HIGHNESS KURA'S BRIDE!!
BAM
WHHAATTT!?
SPIN
くるっ
OH, PLEASE DO NOT WORRY, PRINCESS. IT'S TRUE MY LORD KURA MAY BE SOMEONE WHO HAS YET TO TIRE OF THE THOUSAND WOMEN IN HIS HAREM, BUT...
SPIN
PLEASE KNOW THAT THEY'RE JUST HIS LOVERS. HE HAS NEVER TAKEN AN OFFICIAL BRIDE AS OF YET.
IN OTHER WORDS, HIS LOVE FOR YOU WOULD NOT BE ADULTEROUS AT ALL.
I..... I DON'T THINK THAT'S THE ISSUE HERE!!

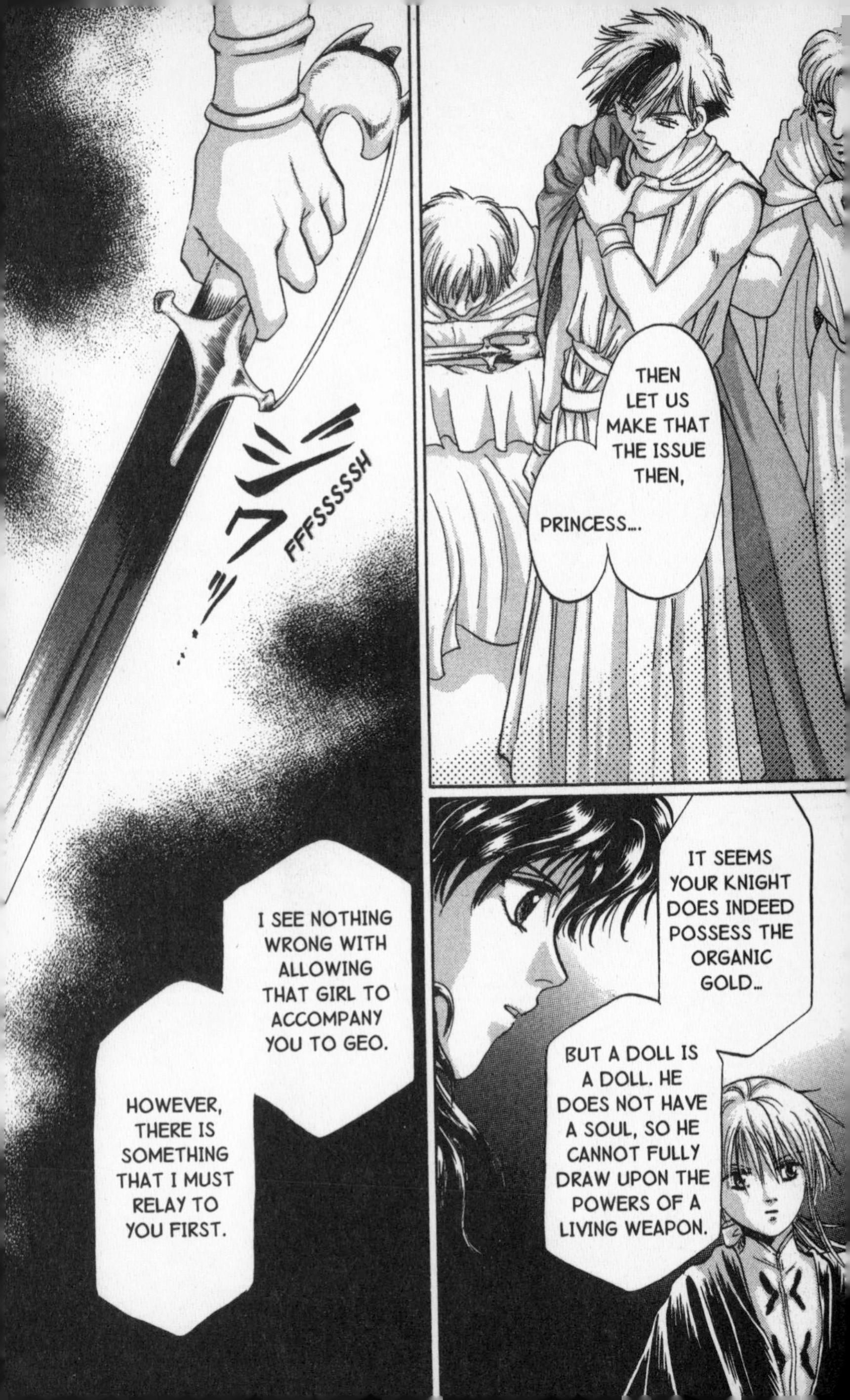
THEN LET US MAKE THAT THE ISSUE THEN,
PRINCESS....
IT SEEMS YOUR KNIGHT DOES INDEED POSSESS THE ORGANIC GOLD...
BUT A DOLL IS A DOLL. HE DOES NOT HAVE A SOUL, SO HE CANNOT FULLY DRAW UPON THE POWERS OF A LIVING WEAPON.
FFFSSSSSH
I SEE NOTHING WRONG WITH ALLOWING THAT GIRL TO ACCOMPANY YOU TO GEO.
HOWEVER, THERE IS SOMETHING THAT I MUST RELAY TO YOU FIRST.

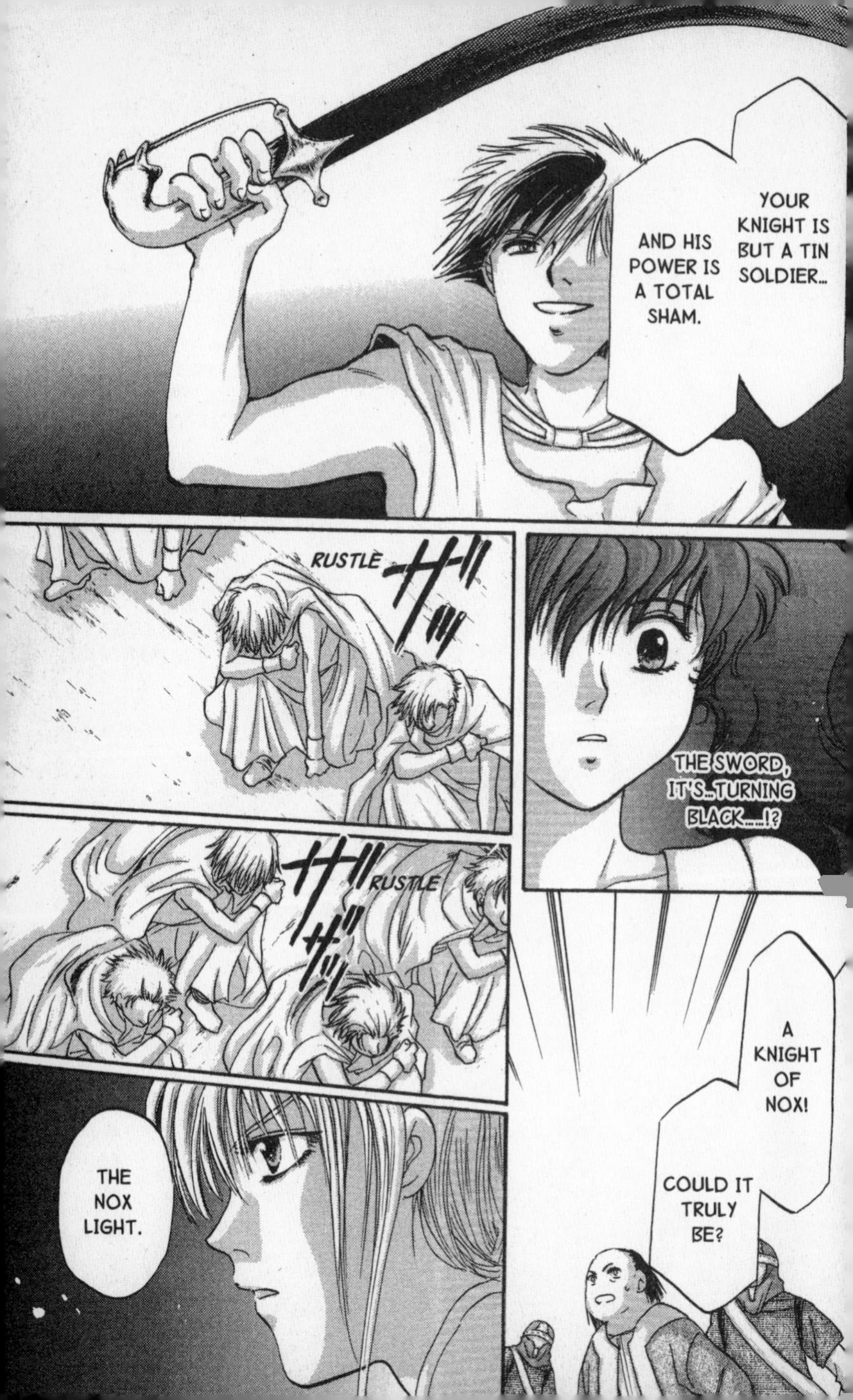
YOUR KNIGHT IS BUT A TIN SOLDIER...
AND HIS POWER IS A TOTAL SHAM.
THE SWORD, IT'S...TURNING BLACK......!?
RUSTLE
RUSTLE
A KNIGHT OF NOX!
COULD IT TRULY BE?
THE NOX LIGHT.

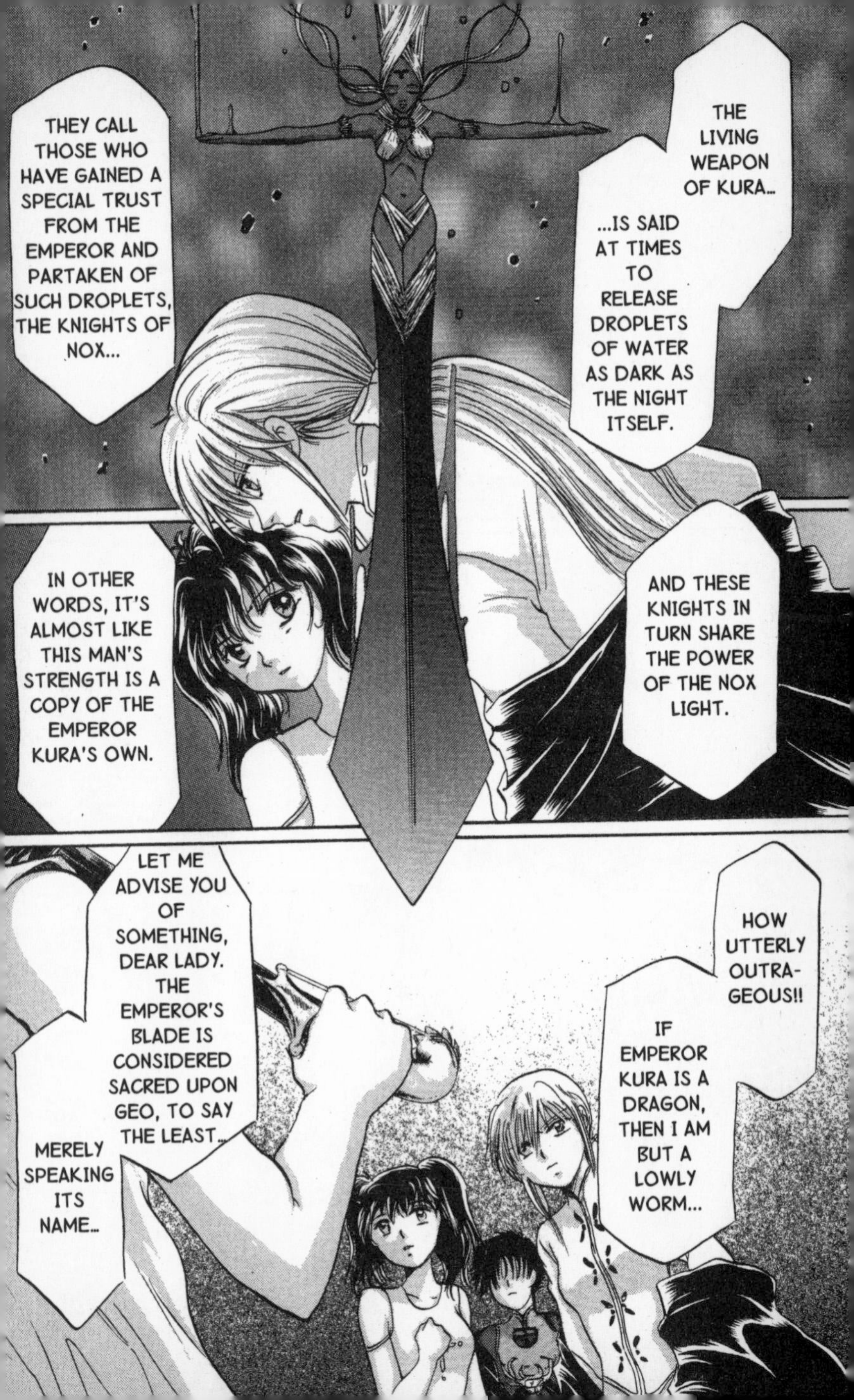
THE LIVING WEAPON OF KURA...
...IS SAID AT TIMES TO RELEASE DROPLETS OF WATER AS DARK AS THE NIGHT ITSELF.
THEY CALL THOSE WHO HAVE GAINED A SPECIAL TRUST FROM THE EMPEROR AND PARTAKEN OF SUCH DROPLETS, THE KNIGHTS OF NOX...
AND THESE KNIGHTS IN TURN SHARE THE POWER OF THE NOX LIGHT.
IN OTHER WORDS, IT'S ALMOST LIKE THIS MAN'S STRENGTH IS A COPY OF THE EMPEROR KURA'S OWN.
HOW UTTERLY OUTRA-GEOUS!!
IF EMPEROR KURA IS A DRAGON, THEN I AM BUT A LOWLY WORM...
LET ME ADVISE YOU OF SOMETHING, DEAR LADY. THE EMPEROR'S BLADE IS CONSIDERED SACRED UPON GEO, TO SAY THE LEAST...
MERELY SPEAKING ITS NAME...

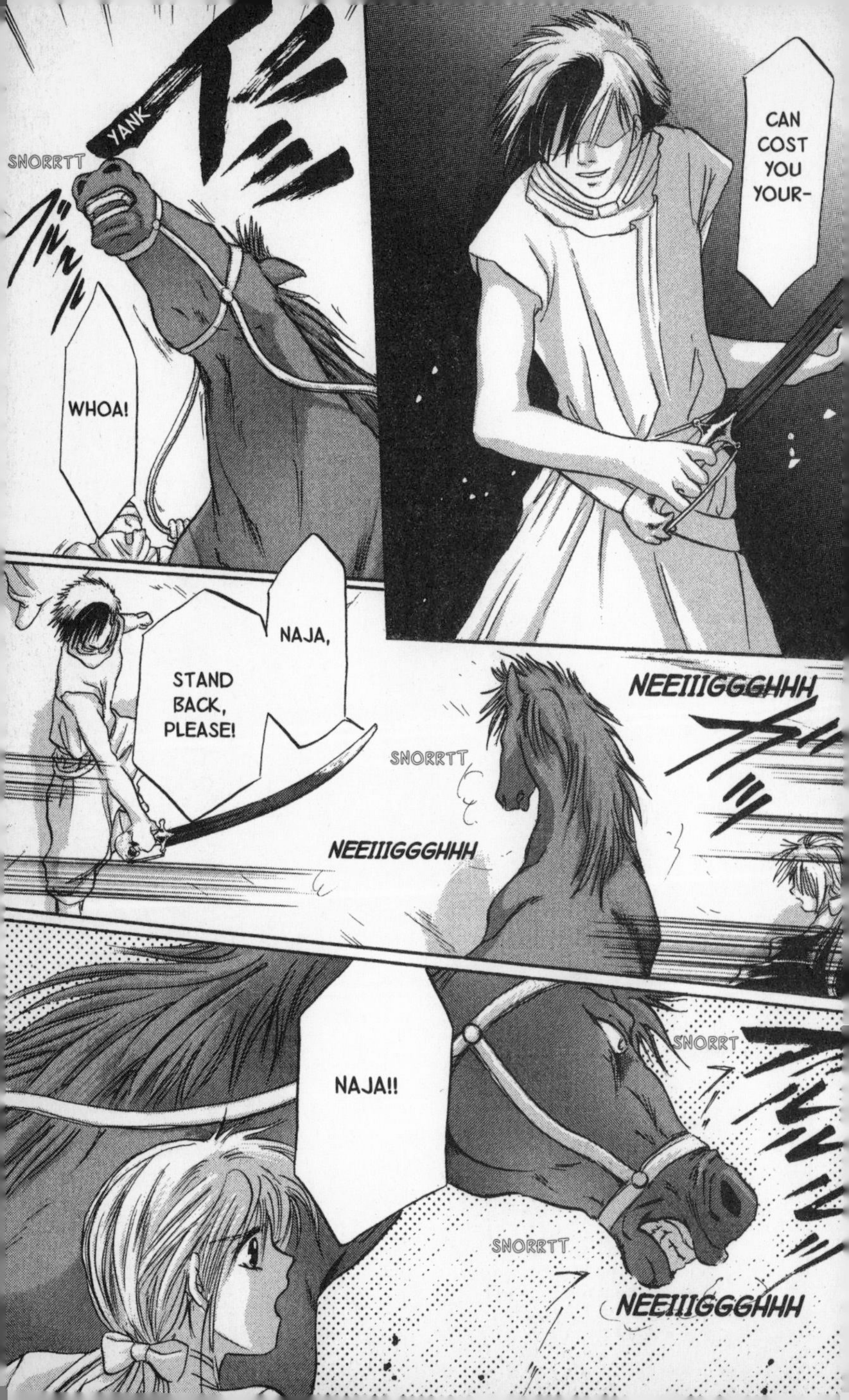

CAN COST YOU YOUR-
YANK
SNORRTT
WHOA!
NEEIIIGGGHHH
SNORRTT
NEEIIIGGGHHH
NAJA, STAND BACK, PLEASE!
SNORRT
SNORRTT
NEEIIIGGGHHH
NAJA!!

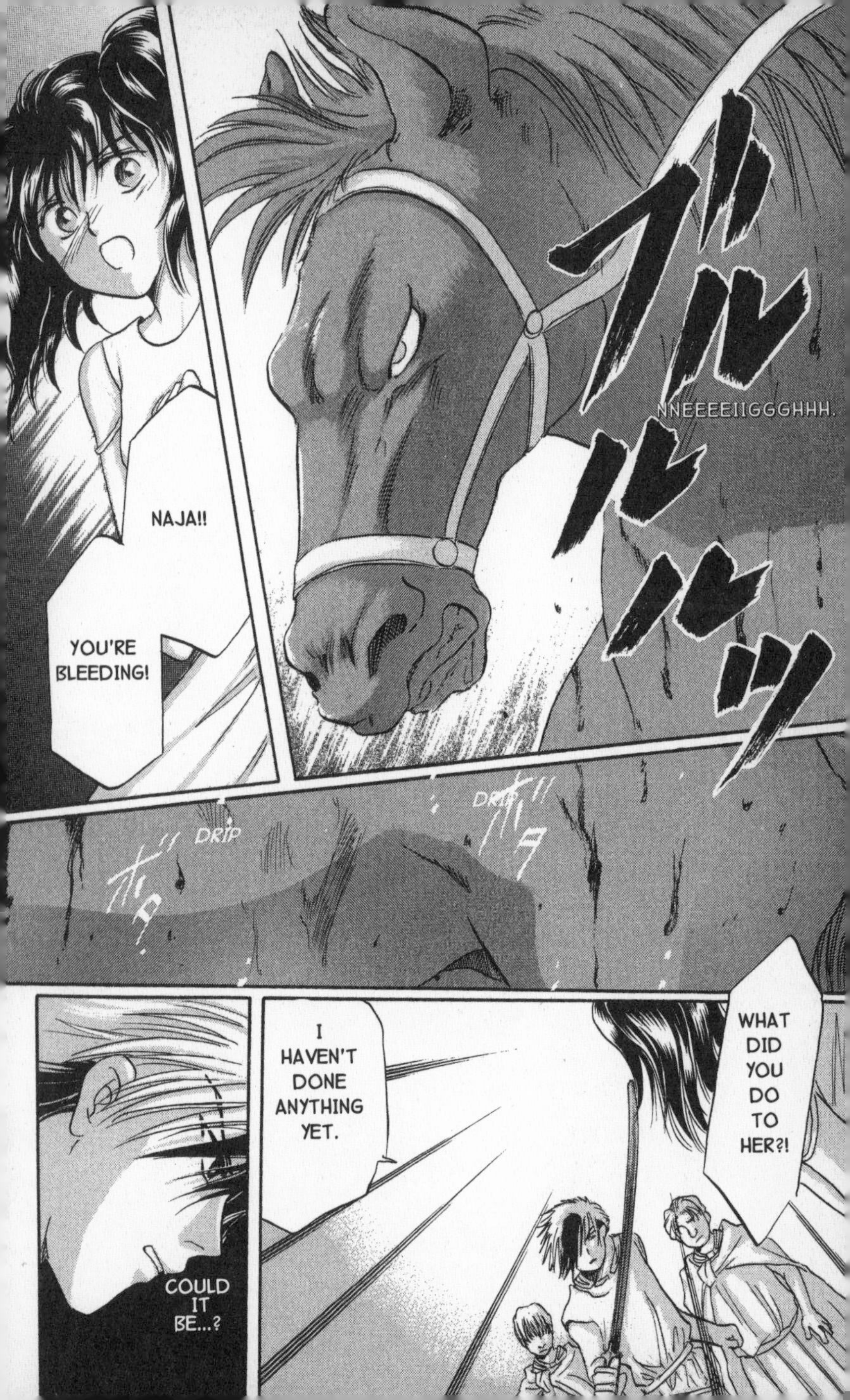
NNEEEEIIGGGHHH.
NAJA!!
YOU'RE BLEEDING!
DRIP
DRIP
WHAT DID YOU DO TO HER?!
I HAVEN'T DONE ANYTHING YET.
COULD IT BE...?

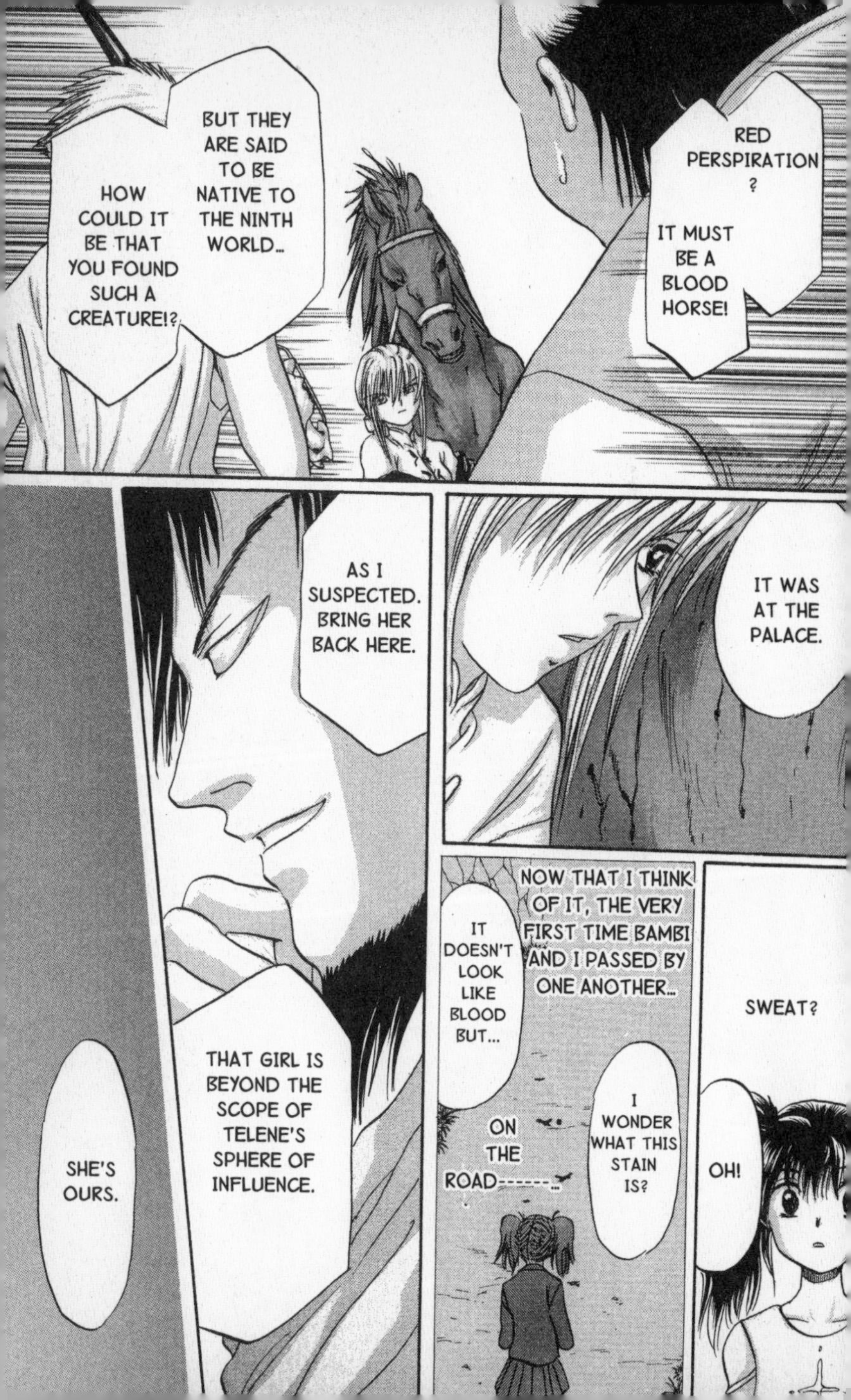
RED PERSPIRATION ?
IT MUST BE A BLOOD HORSE!
BUT THEY ARE SAID TO BE NATIVE TO THE NINTH WORLD...
HOW COULD IT BE THAT YOU FOUND SUCH A CREATURE!?
IT WAS AT THE PALACE.
SWEAT?
OH!
I WONDER WHAT THIS STAIN IS?
IT DOESN'T LOOK LIKE BLOOD BUT...
NOW THAT I THINK OF IT, THE VERY FIRST TIME BAMBI AND I PASSED BY ONE ANOTHER...
ON THE ROAD------...
AS I SUSPECTED. BRING HER BACK HERE.
THAT GIRL IS BEYOND THE SCOPE OF TELENE'S SPHERE OF INFLUENCE.
SHE'S OURS.

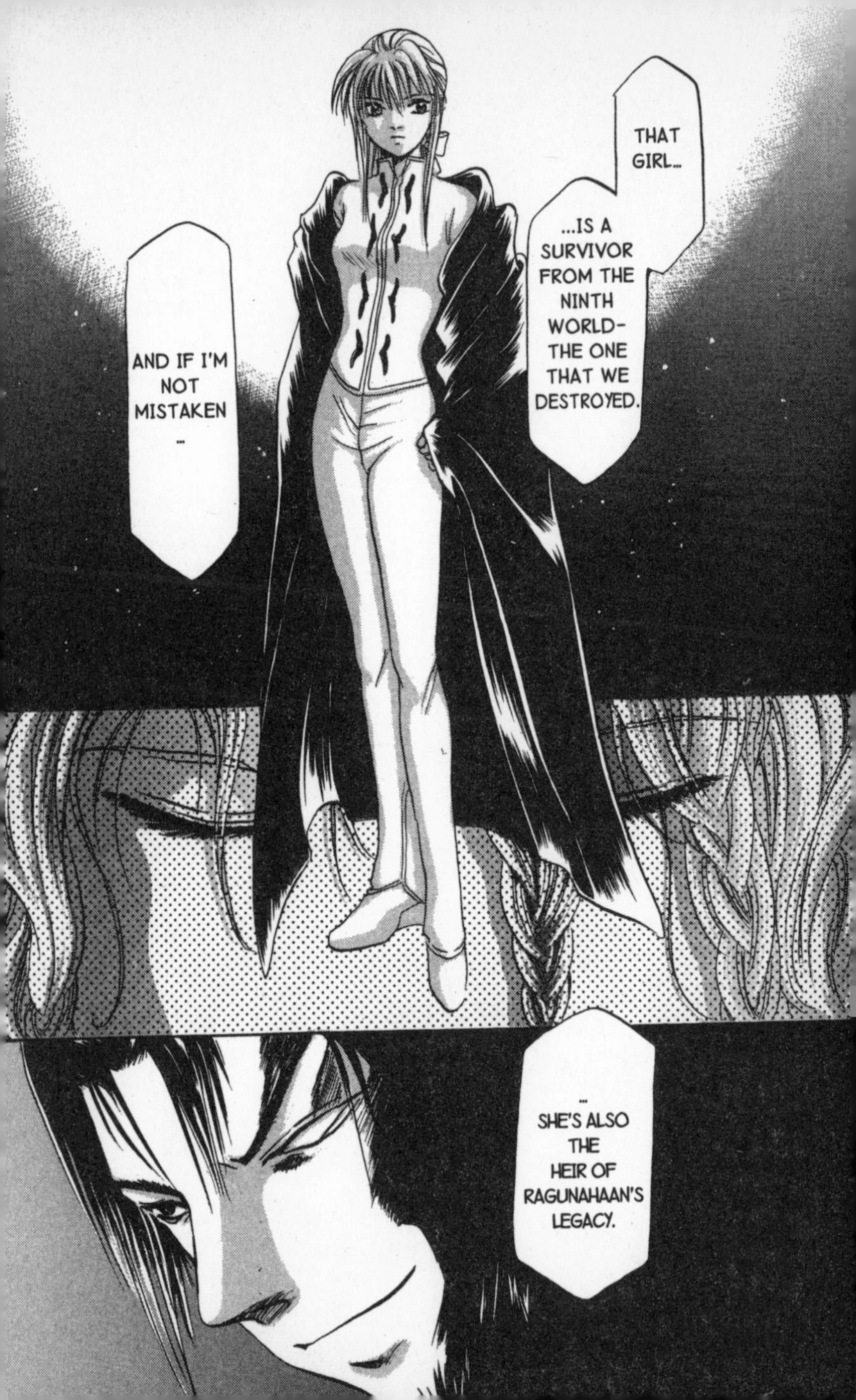
THAT GIRL...
...IS A SURVIVOR FROM THE NINTH WORLD- THE ONE THAT WE DESTROYED.
AND IF I'M NOT MISTAKEN ...
... SHE'S ALSO THE HEIR OF RAGUNAHAAN'S LEGACY.

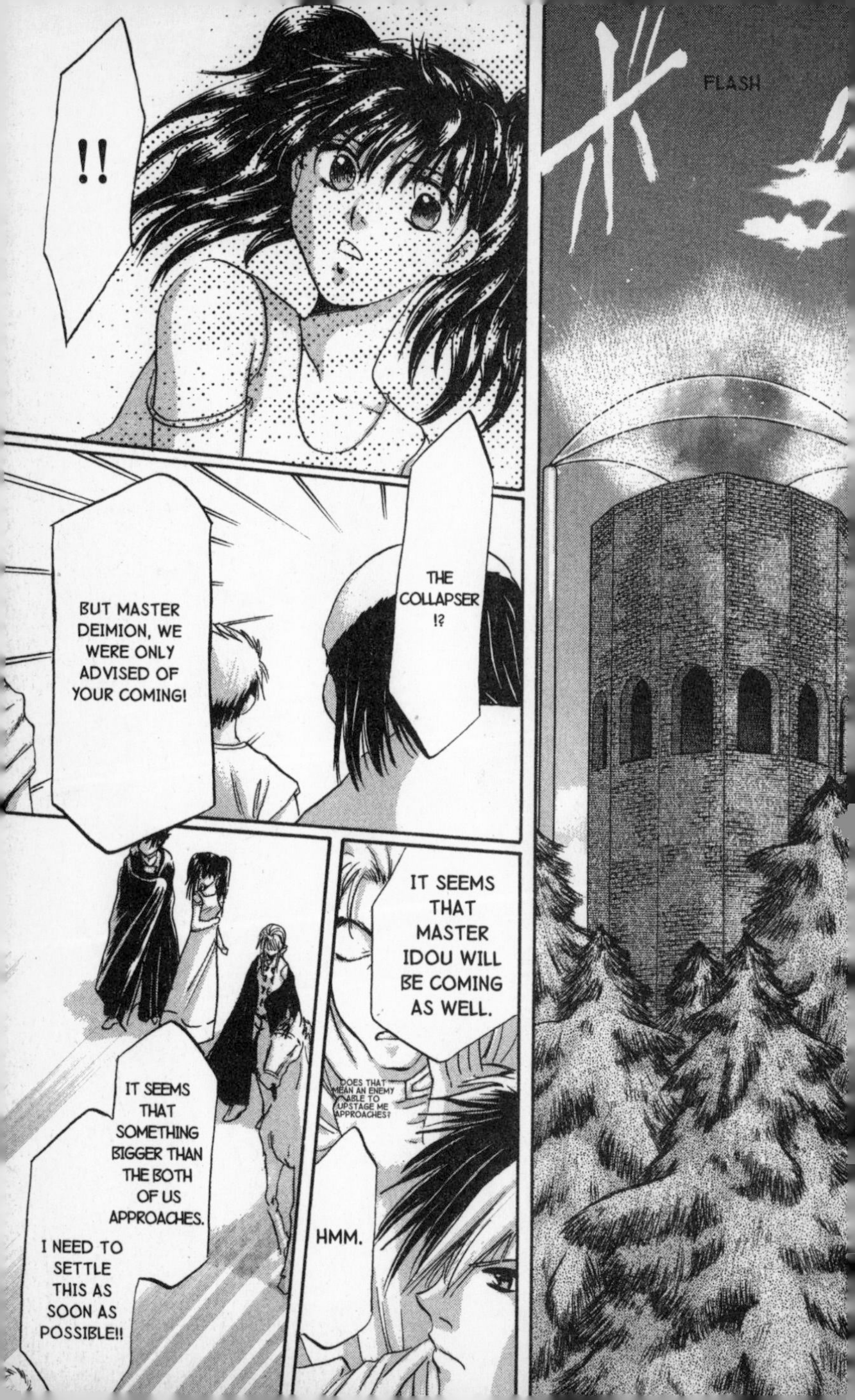
FLASH
!!
THE COLLAPSER !?
BUT MASTER DEIMION, WE WERE ONLY ADVISED OF YOUR COMING!
IT SEEMS THAT MASTER IDOU WILL BE COMING AS WELL.
DOES THAT MEAN AN ENEMY ABLE TO UPSTAGE ME APPROACHES?
HMM.
IT SEEMS THAT SOMETHING BIGGER THAN THE BOTH OF US APPROACHES.
I NEED TO SETTLE THIS AS SOON AS POSSIBLE!!

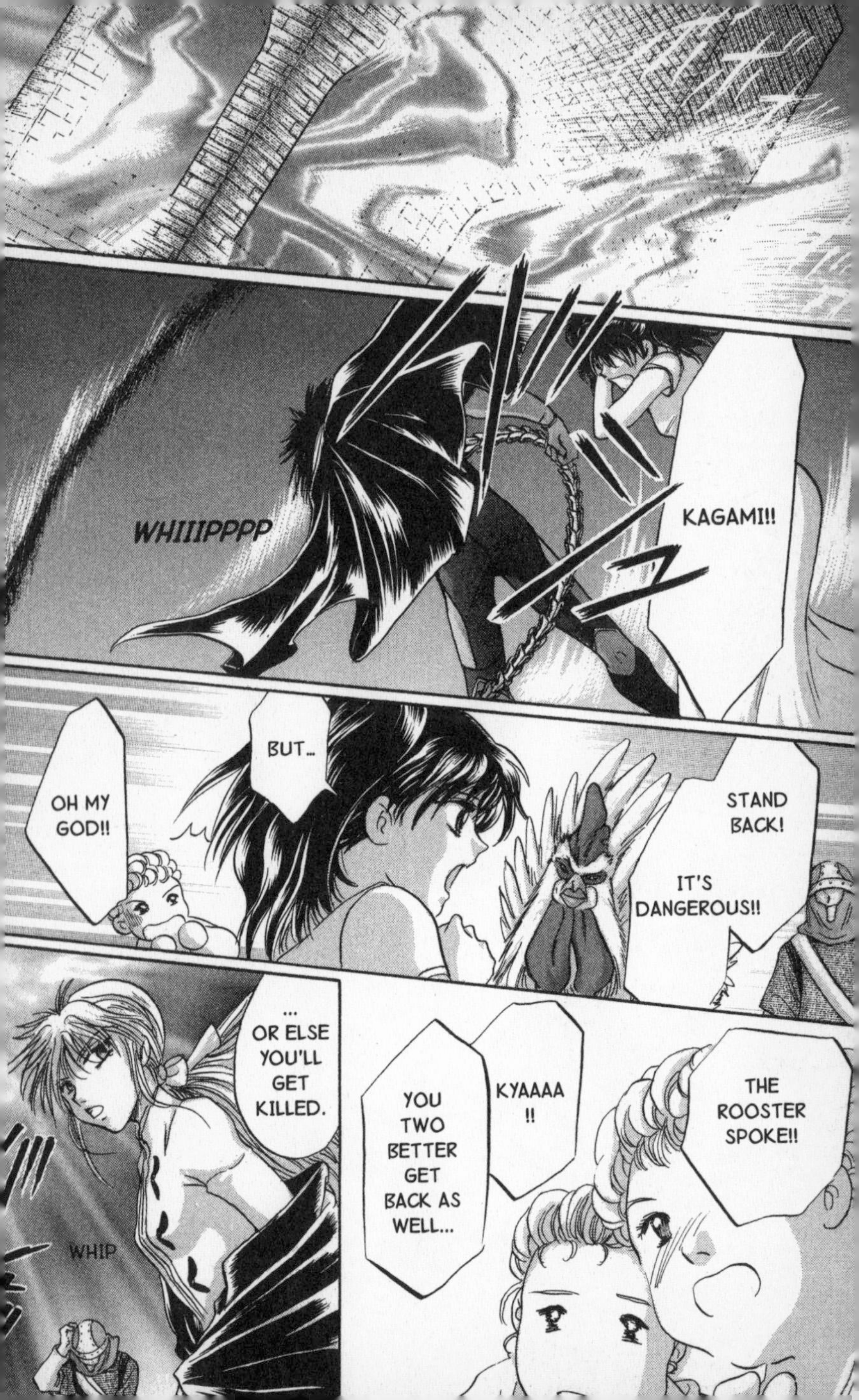
KAGAMI!!
WHIIIPPPP
STAND BACK!
IT'S DANGEROUS!!
BUT...
OH MY GOD!!
THE ROOSTER SPOKE!!
KYAAAA!!
YOU TWO BETTER GET BACK AS WELL...
... OR ELSE YOU'LL GET KILLED.
WHIP

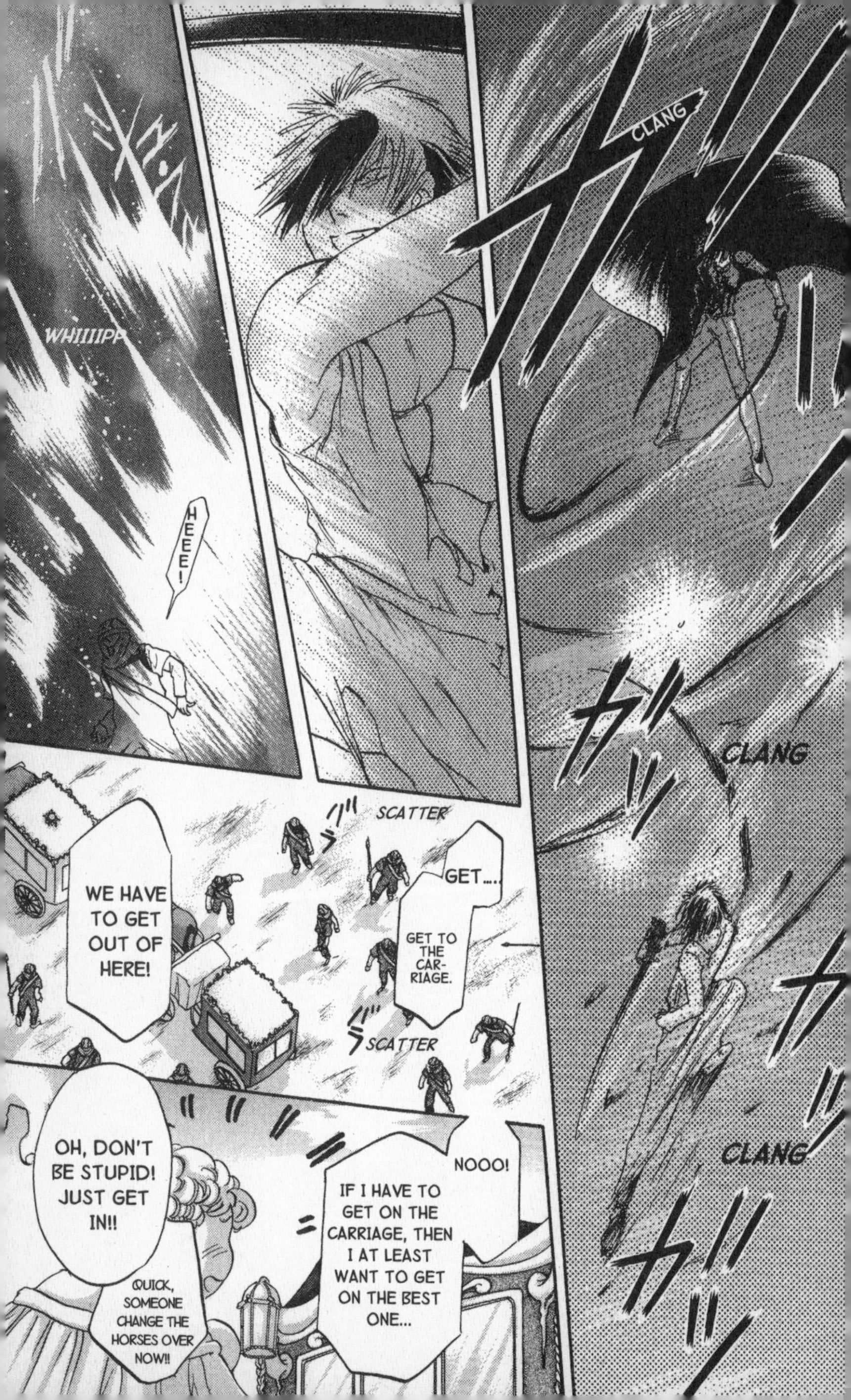
CLANG
CLANG
CLANG
WHIIIIPP
HEEEE!
SCATTER
GET....
GET TO THE CARRIAGE.
SCATTER
WE HAVE TO GET OUT OF HERE!
NOOO!
IF I HAVE TO GET ON THE CARRIAGE, THEN I AT LEAST WANT TO GET ON THE BEST ONE...
OH, DON'T BE STUPID! JUST GET IN!!
QUICK, SOMEONE CHANGE THE HORSES OVER NOW!!

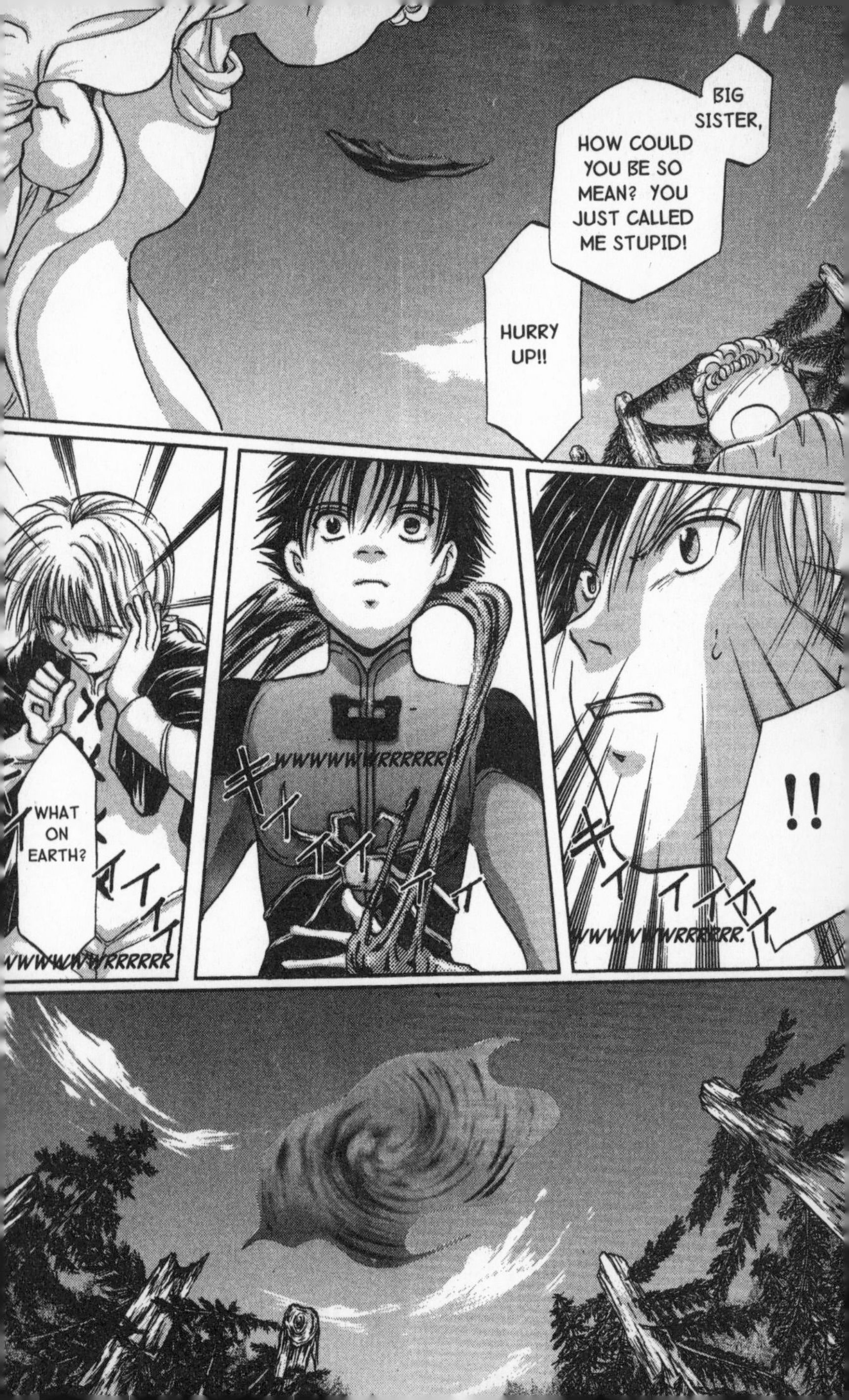
BIG SISTER, HOW COULD YOU BE SO MEAN? YOU JUST CALLED ME STUPID!
HURRY UP!!
!!
WWWWWWRRRRRR.
WWWWWWRRRRRR
WHAT ON EARTH?
WWWWWWRRRRRR

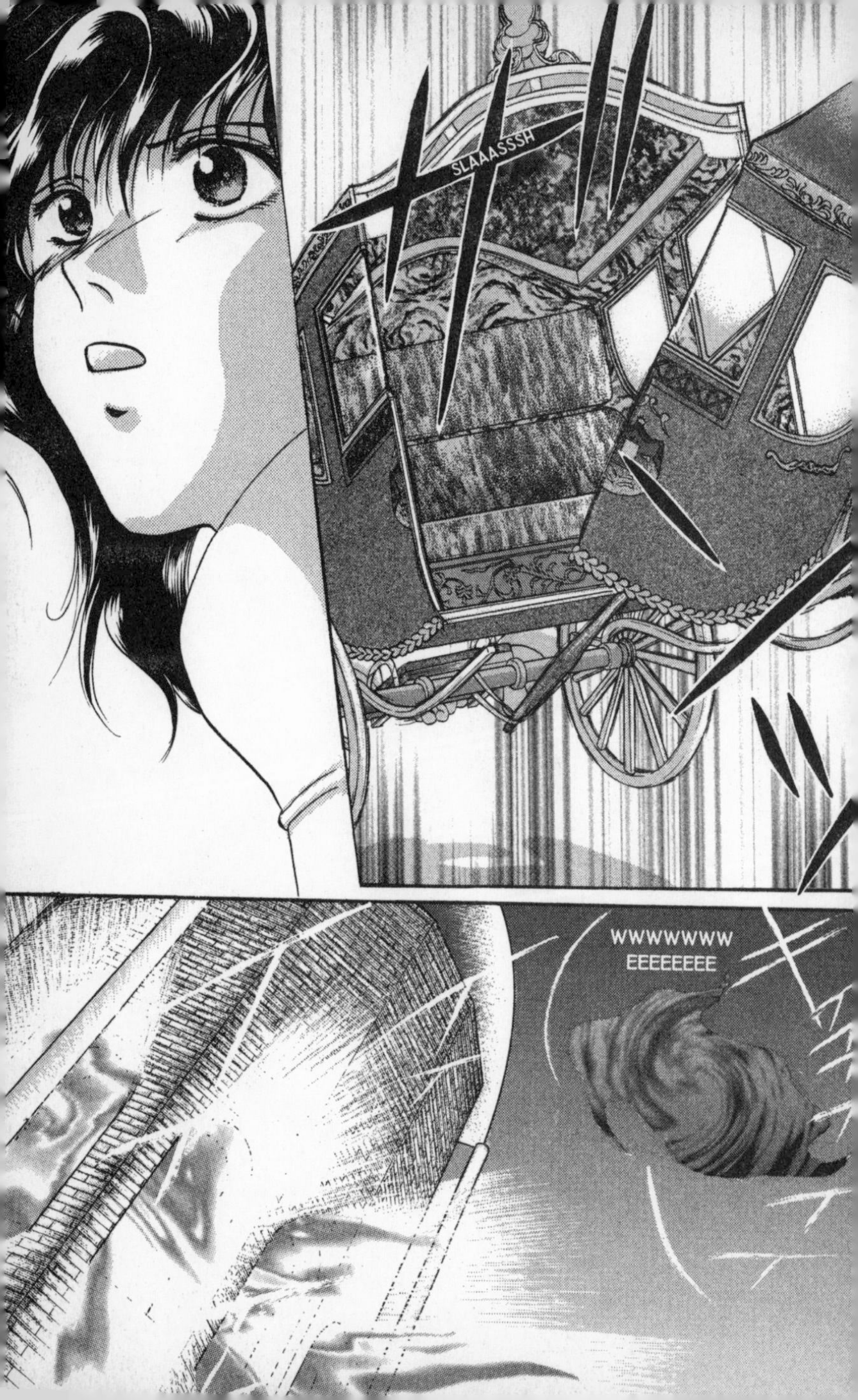
SLAAASSSH
WWWWWWW
EEEEEEE

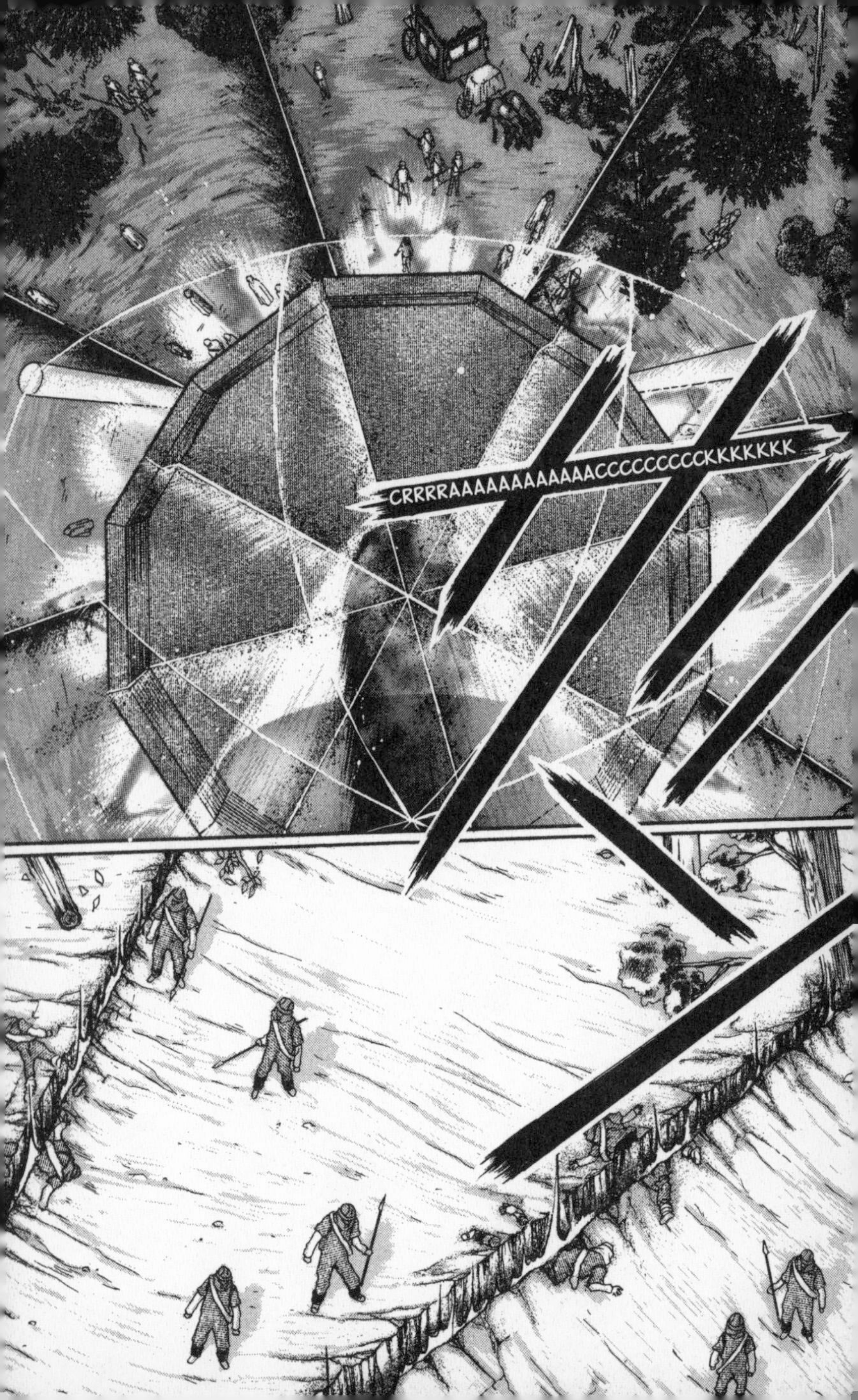
CRRRRAAAAAAAAAAAACCCCCCCCCKKKKKK

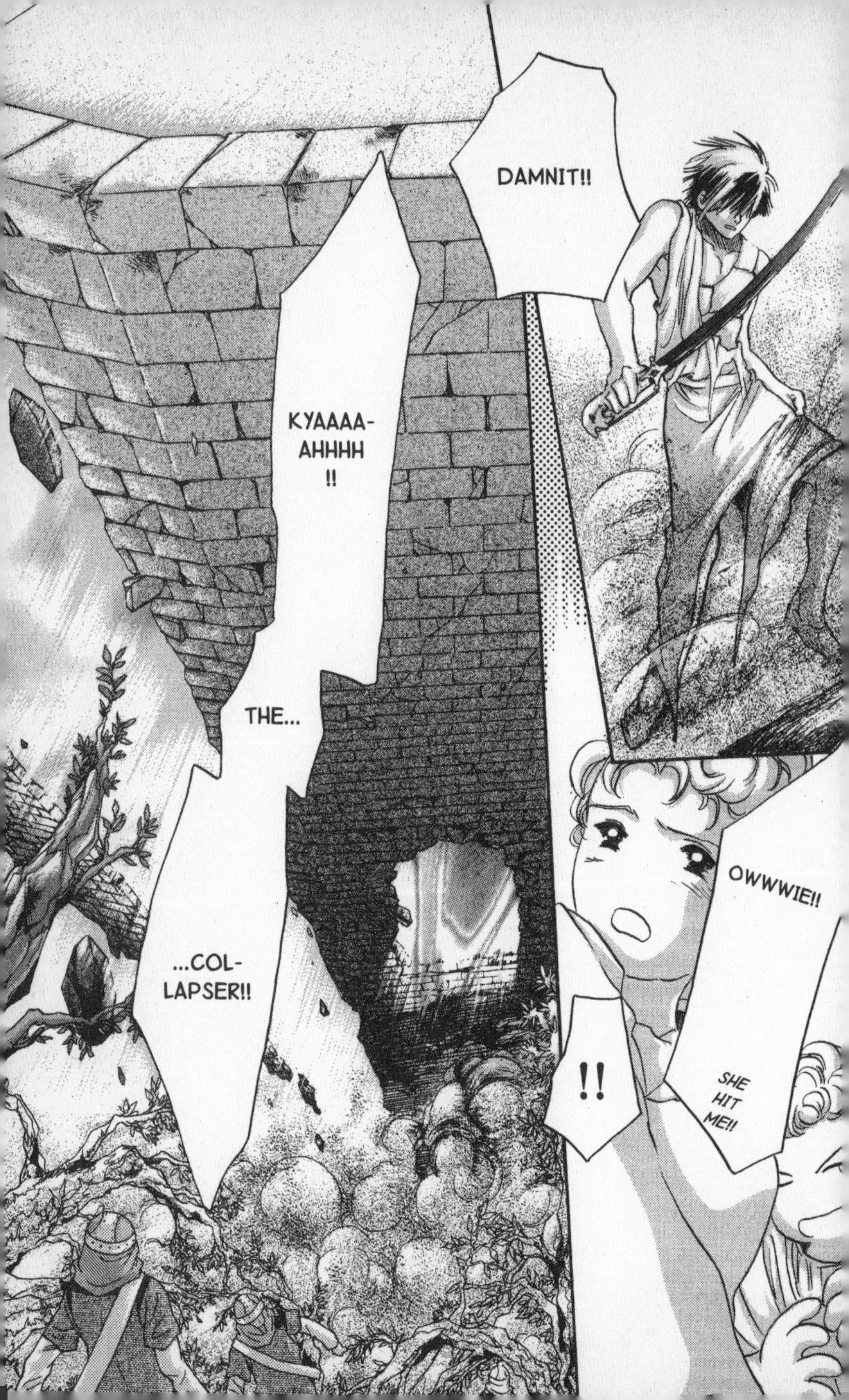
DAMNIT!!
OWWWIE!!
SHE HIT ME!!
!!
KYAAAA-AHHHH!!
THE...
...COL-LAPSER!!

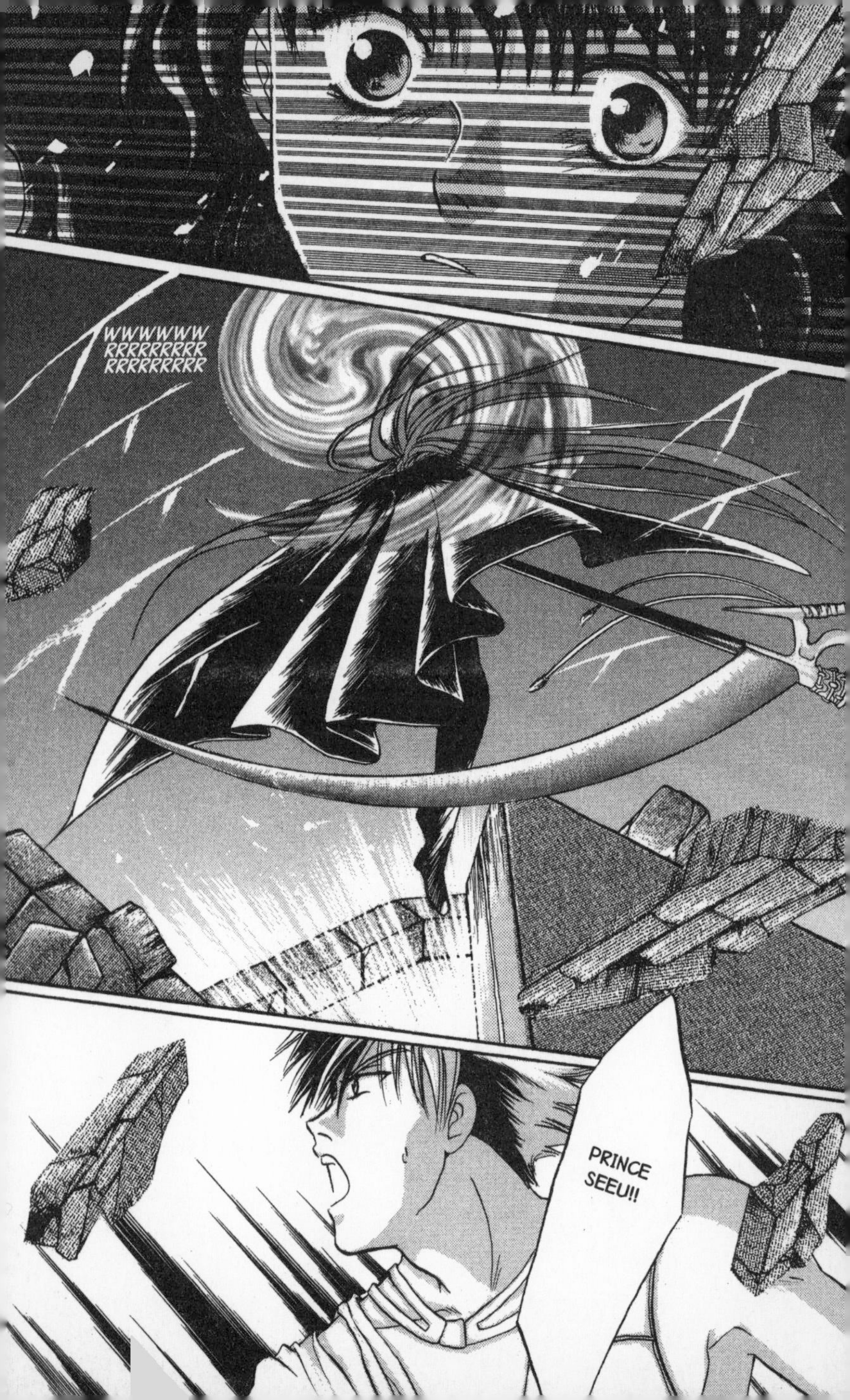
WWWWWW RRRRRRRRR RRRRRRRRR
PRINCE SEEU!!

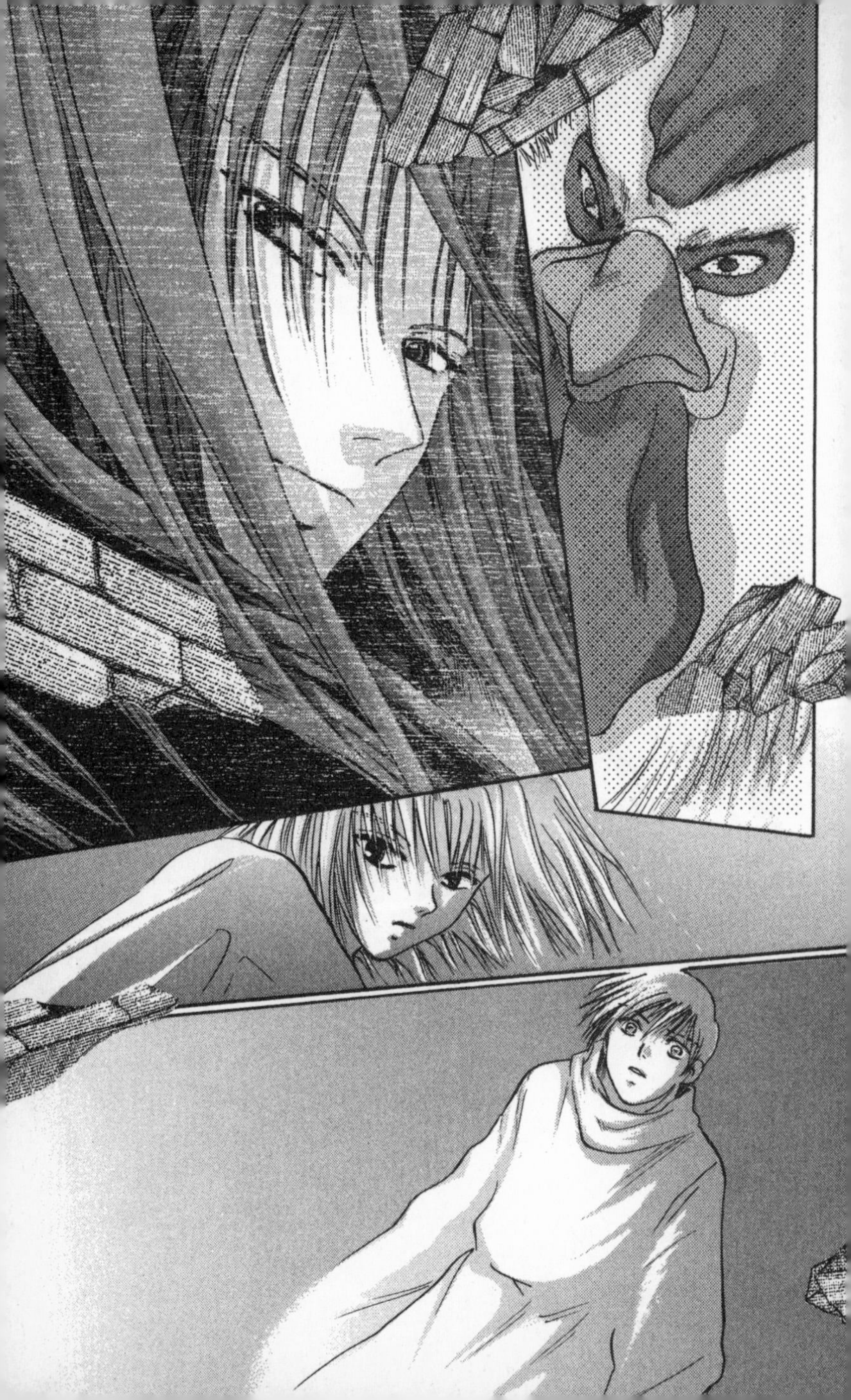

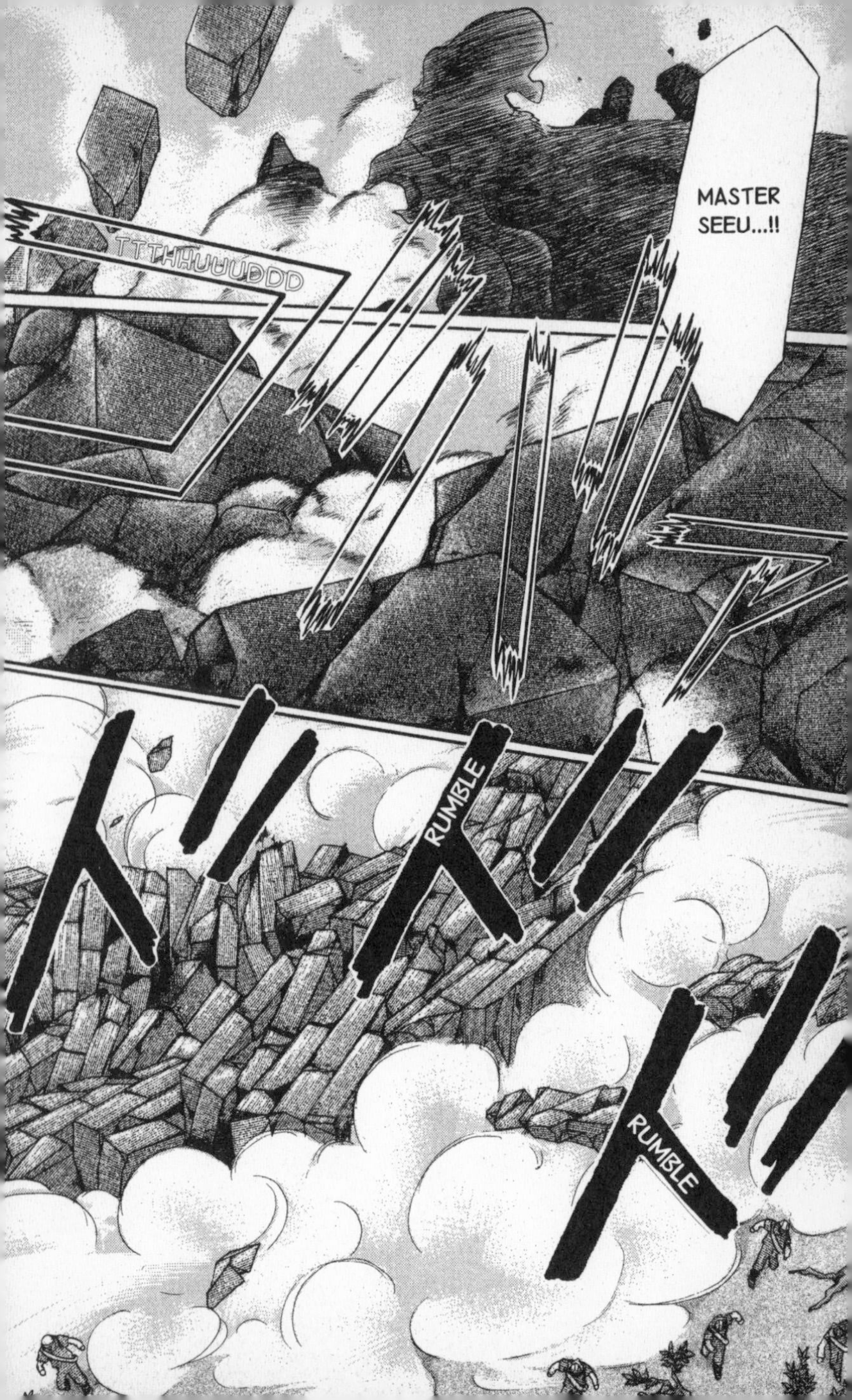
MASTER SEEU...!!
TTTHHUUUDDD
RUMBLE
RUMBLE

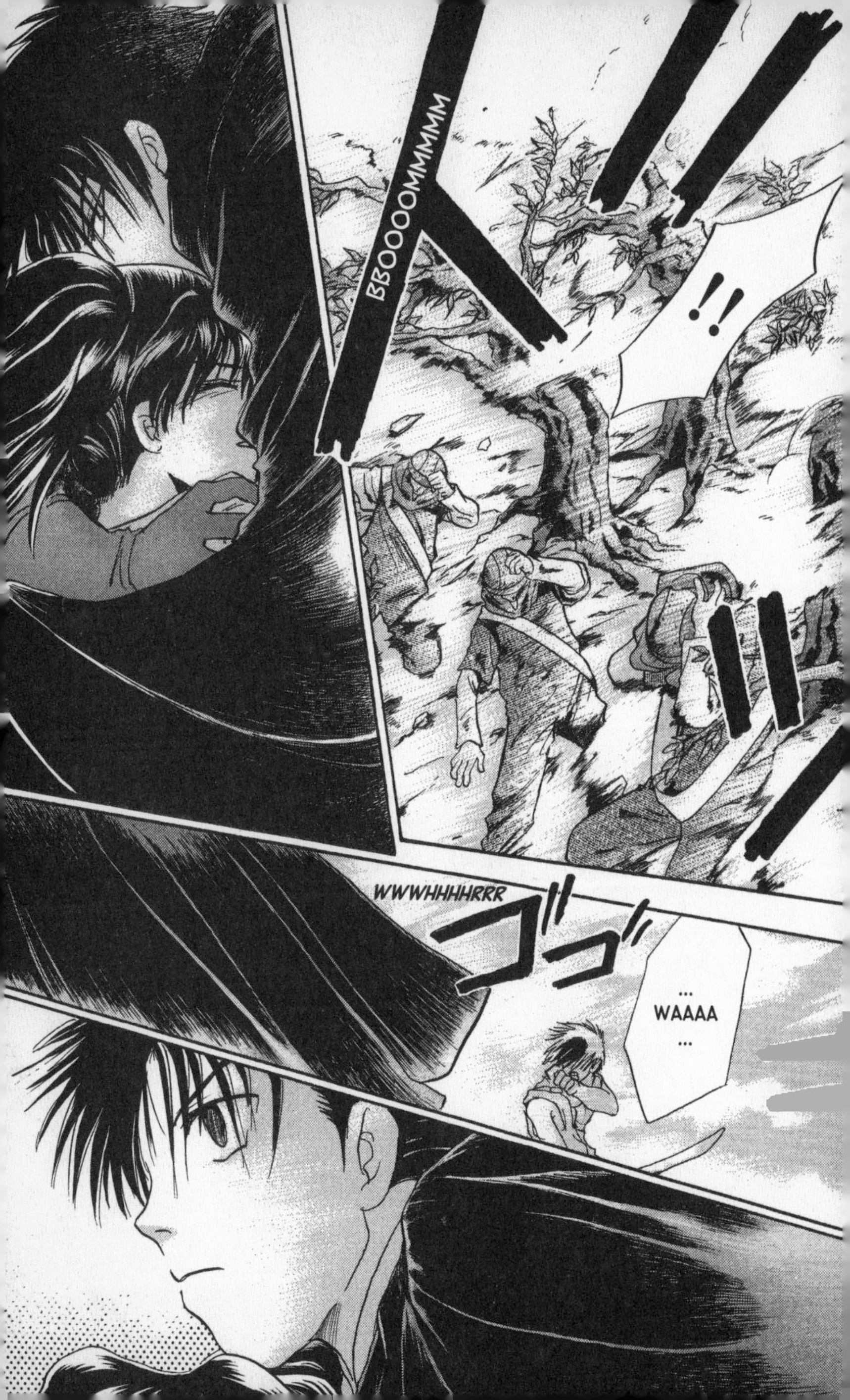
!!
BBOOOOMMMMM
WWWHHHHRRR
ゴゴ
... WAAAA ...

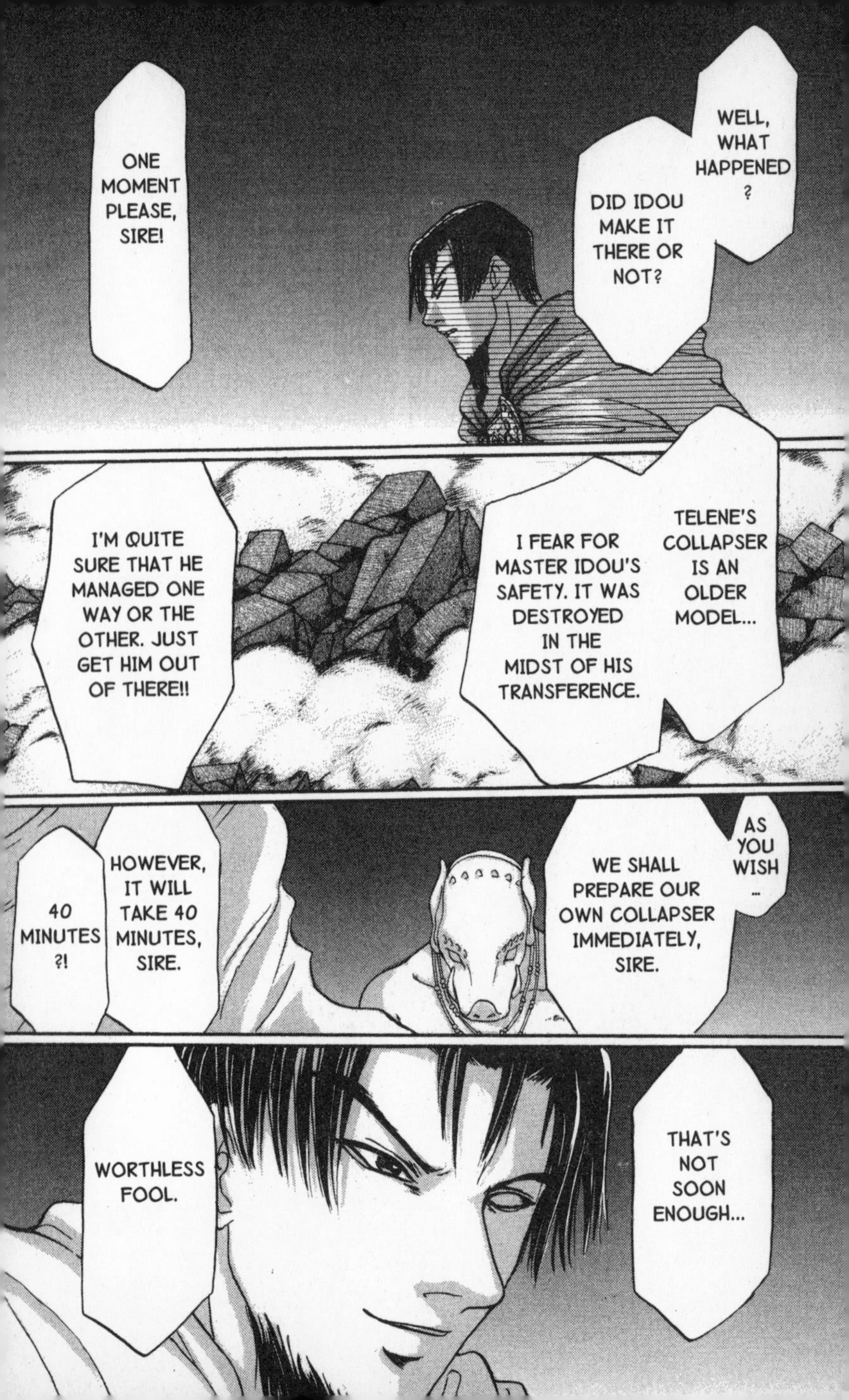
WELL, WHAT HAPPENED ?
DID IDOU MAKE IT THERE OR NOT?
ONE MOMENT PLEASE, SIRE!
TELENE'S COLLAPSER IS AN OLDER MODEL...
I FEAR FOR MASTER IDOU'S SAFETY. IT WAS DESTROYED IN THE MIDST OF HIS TRANSFERENCE.
I'M QUITE SURE THAT HE MANAGED ONE WAY OR THE OTHER. JUST GET HIM OUT OF THERE!!
AS YOU WISH ...
WE SHALL PREPARE OUR OWN COLLAPSER IMMEDIATELY, SIRE.
HOWEVER, IT WILL TAKE 40 MINUTES, SIRE.
40 MINUTES ?!
THAT'S NOT SOON ENOUGH...
WORTHLESS FOOL.

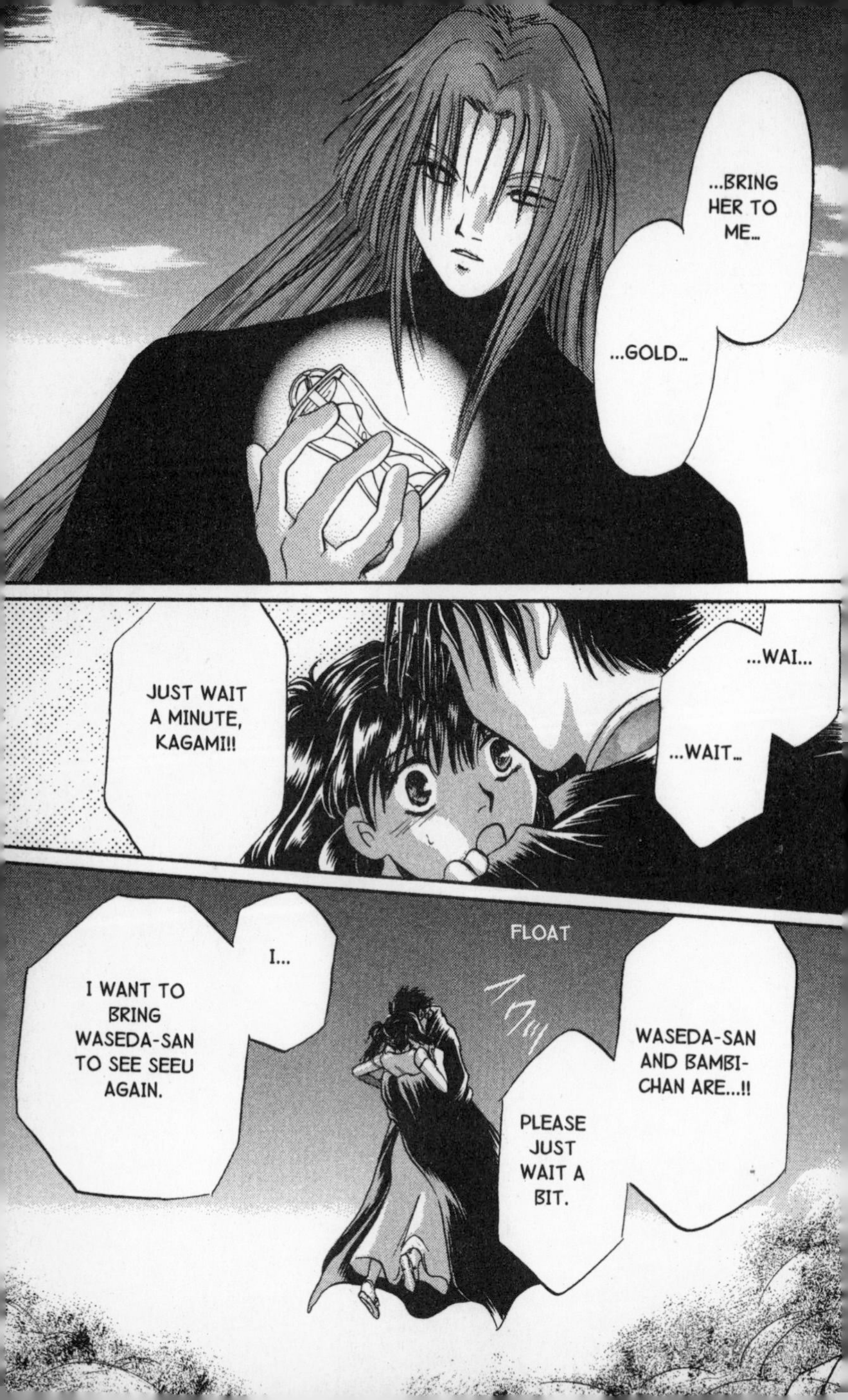
...BRING HER TO ME...
...GOLD...
...WAI...
...WAIT...
JUST WAIT A MINUTE, KAGAMI!!
FLOAT
WASEDA-SAN AND BAMBI-CHAN ARE...!!
PLEASE JUST WAIT A BIT.
I...
I WANT TO BRING WASEDA-SAN TO SEE SEEU AGAIN.

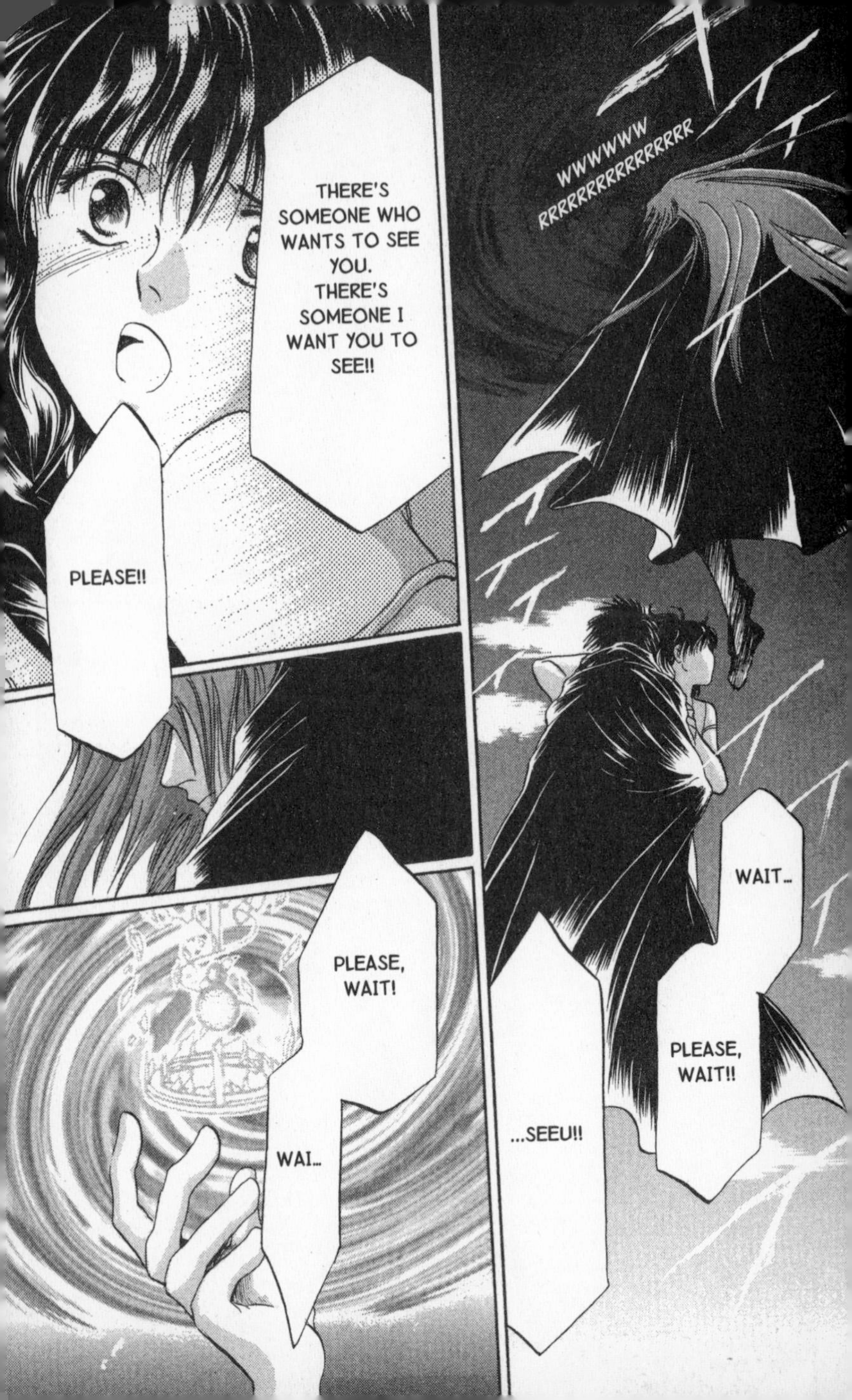
WWWWWW RRRRRRRRRRRR
WAIT...
PLEASE, WAIT!!
...SEEU!!
THERE'S SOMEONE WHO WANTS TO SEE YOU. THERE'S SOMEONE I WANT YOU TO SEE!!
PLEASE!!
PLEASE, WAIT!
WAI...

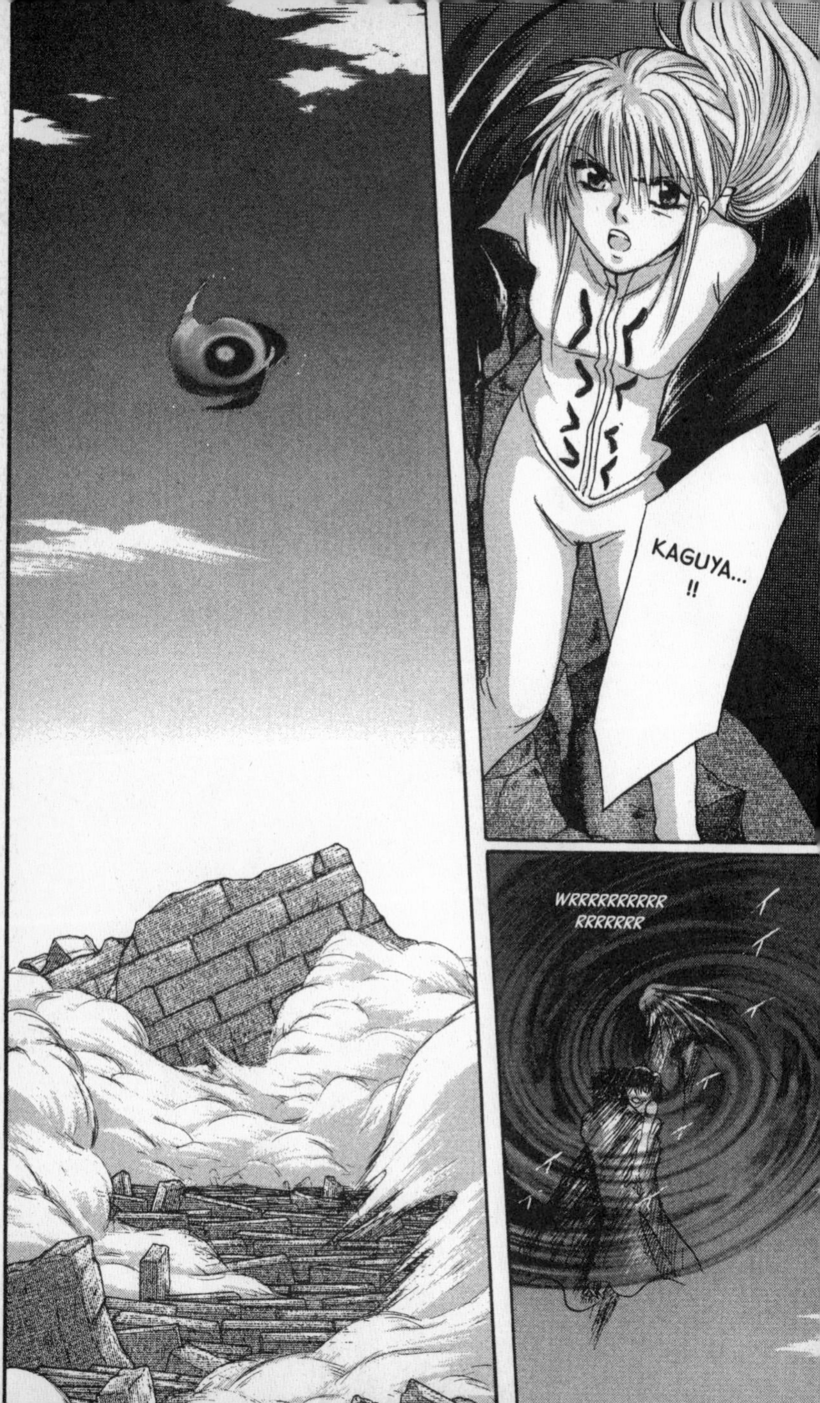
KAGUYA... !!
WRRRRRRRRRR RRRRRRR

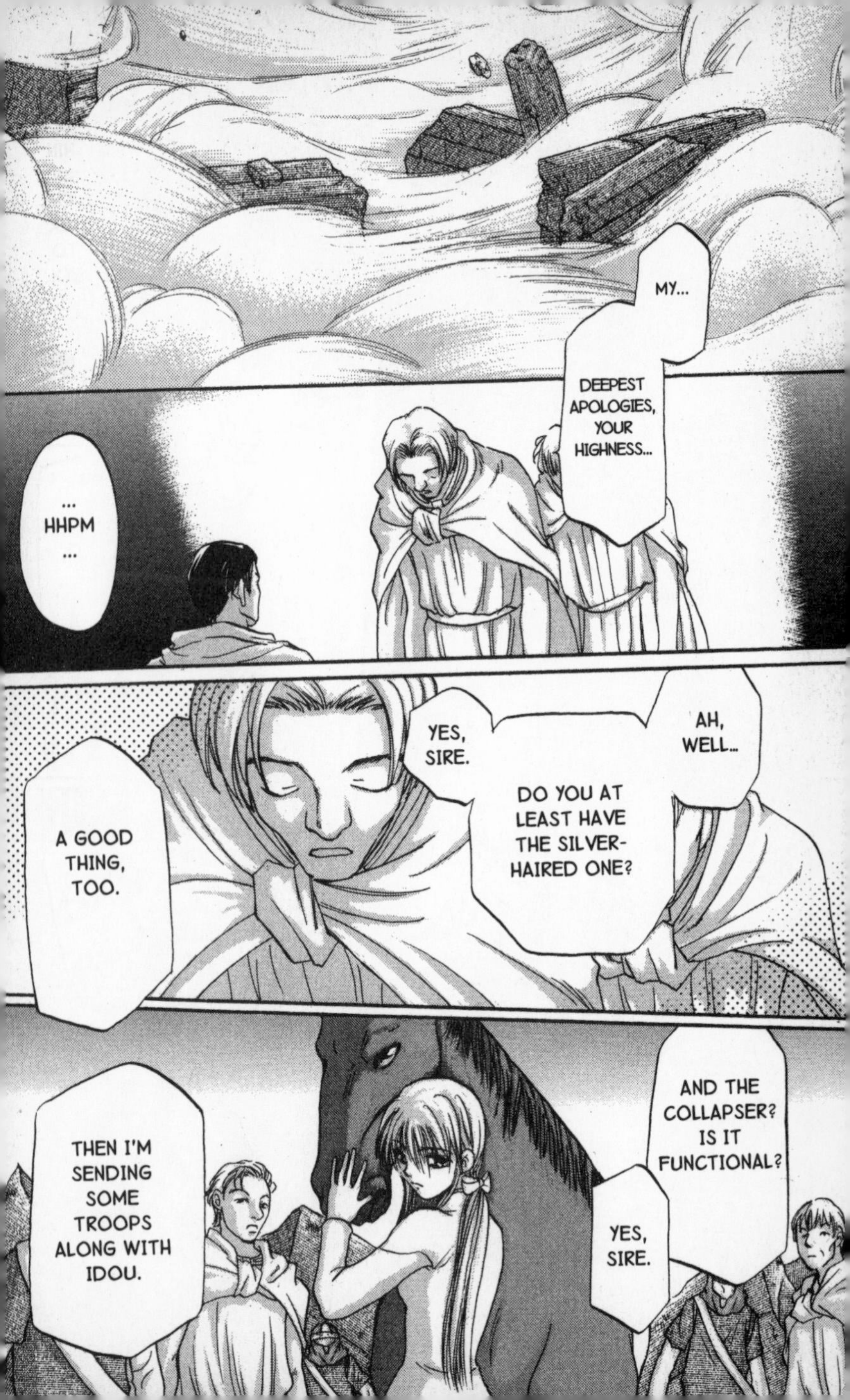
MY...
DEEPEST APOLOGIES, YOUR HIGHNESS...
... HHPM ...
AH, WELL...
DO YOU AT LEAST HAVE THE SILVER-HAIRED ONE?
YES, SIRE.
A GOOD THING, TOO.
AND THE COLLAPSER? IS IT FUNCTIONAL?
YES, SIRE.
THEN I'M SENDING SOME TROOPS ALONG WITH IDOU.

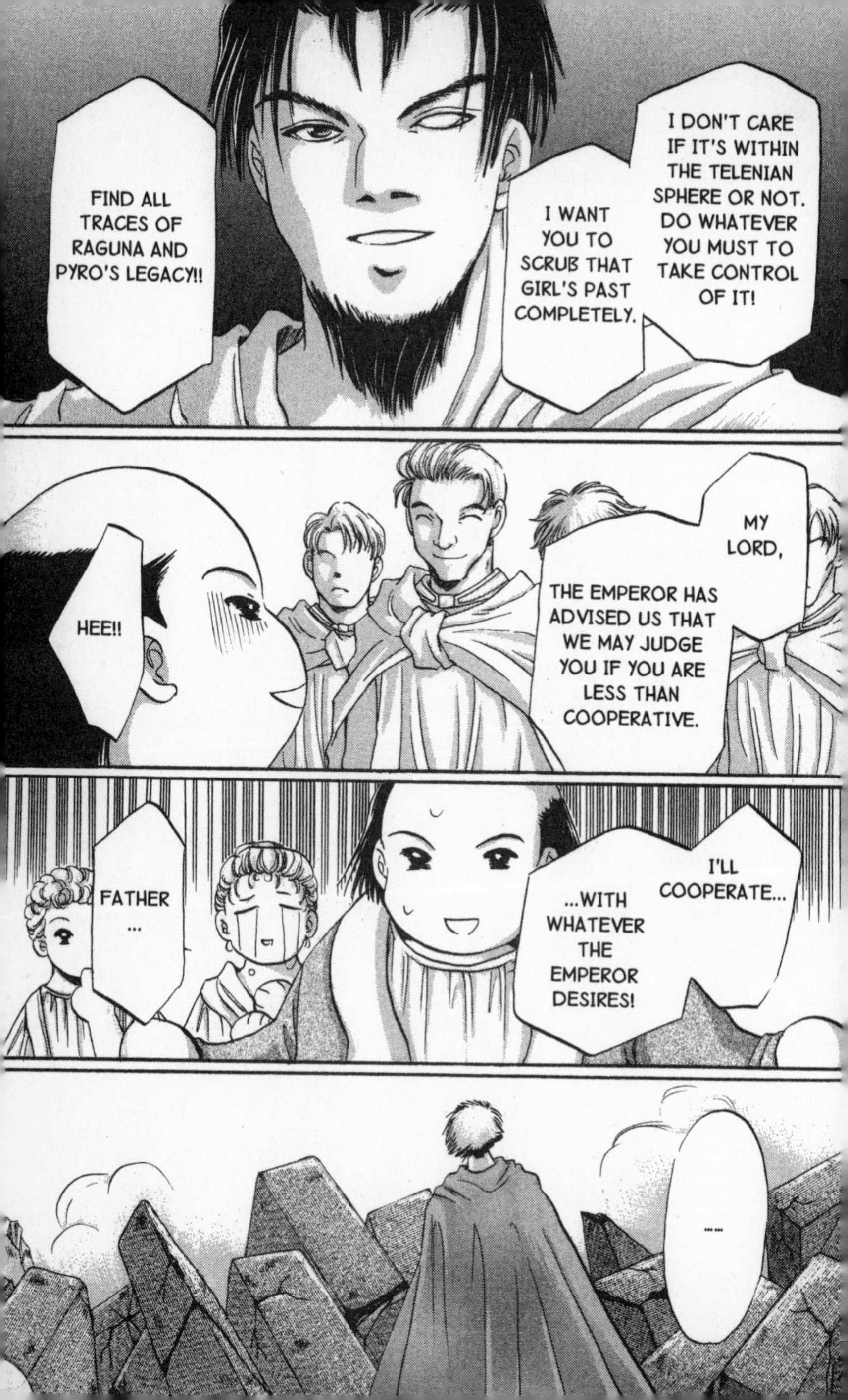
I DON'T CARE IF IT'S WITHIN THE TELENIAN SPHERE OR NOT. DO WHATEVER YOU MUST TO TAKE CONTROL OF IT!
I WANT YOU TO SCRUB THAT GIRL'S PAST COMPLETELY.
FIND ALL TRACES OF RAGUNA AND PYRO'S LEGACY!!
MY LORD,
THE EMPEROR HAS ADVISED US THAT WE MAY JUDGE YOU IF YOU ARE LESS THAN COOPERATIVE.
HEE!!
I'LL COOPERATE...
...WITH WHATEVER THE EMPEROR DESIRES!
FATHER ...
……

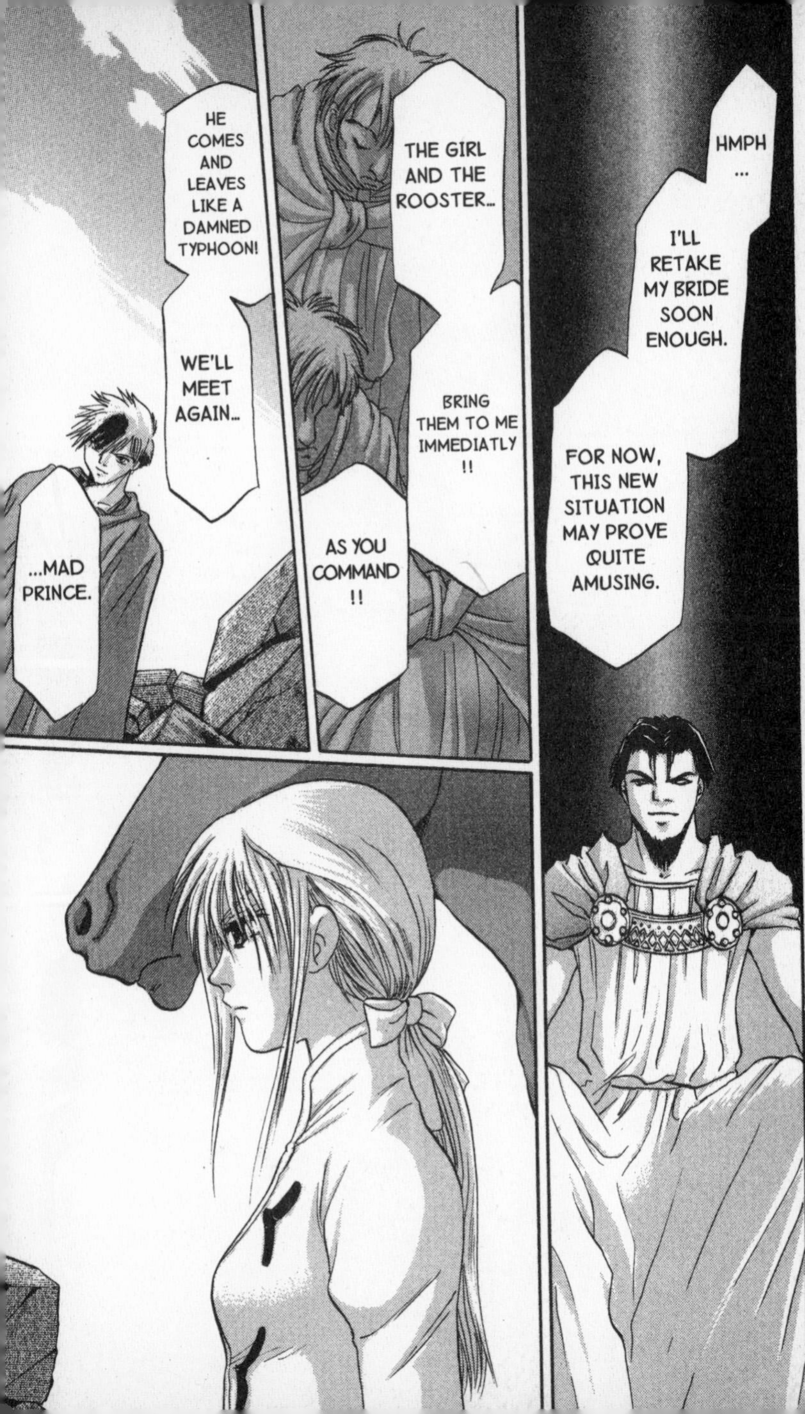
HMPH...
I'LL RETAKE MY BRIDE SOON ENOUGH.
FOR NOW, THIS NEW SITUATION MAY PROVE QUITE AMUSING.
THE GIRL AND THE ROOSTER...
BRING THEM TO ME IMMEDIATLY !!
AS YOU COMMAND !!
HE COMES AND LEAVES LIKE A DAMNED TYPHOON!
WE'LL MEET AGAIN...
...MAD PRINCE.

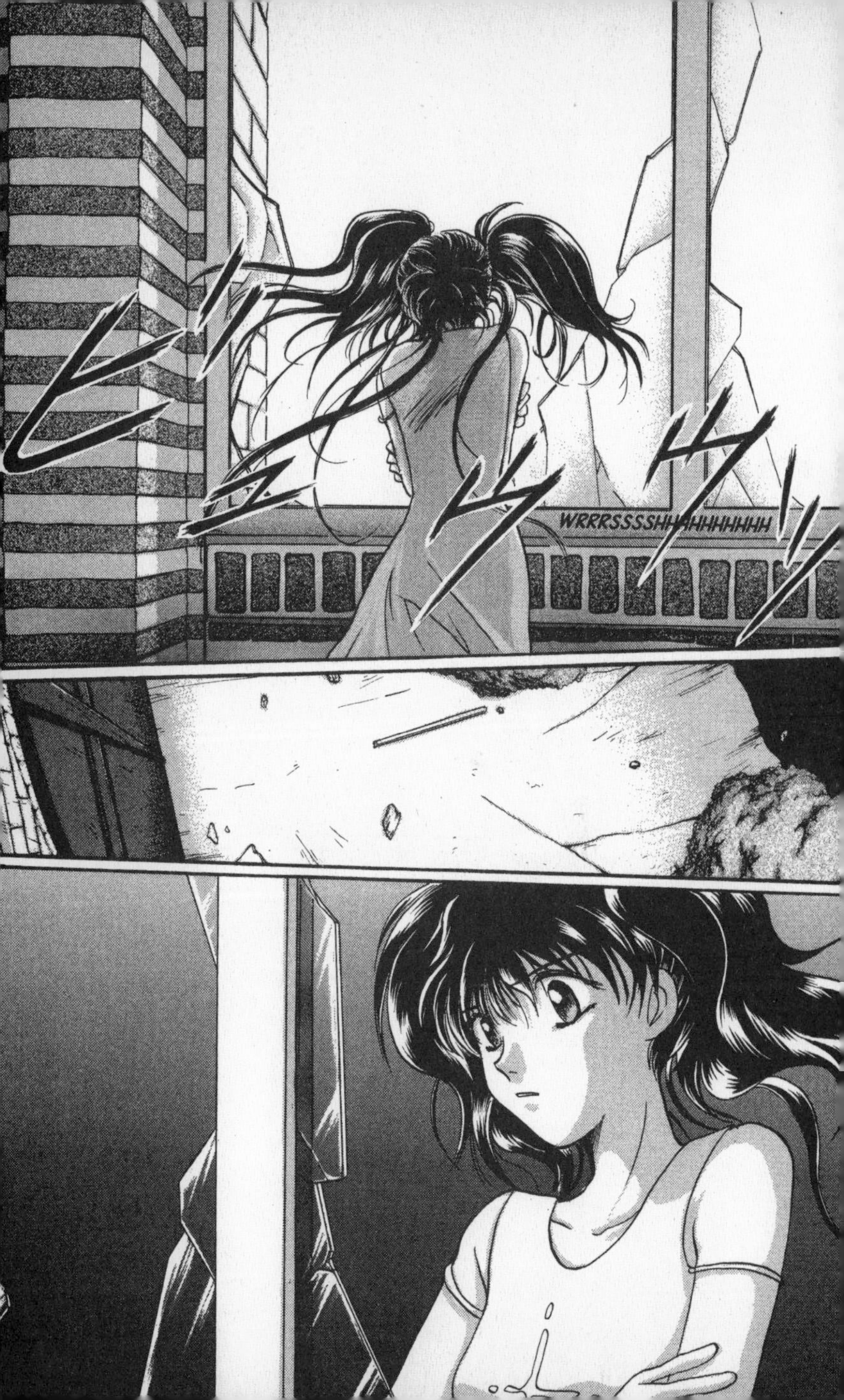
WRRRSSSSHHHHHHHHH

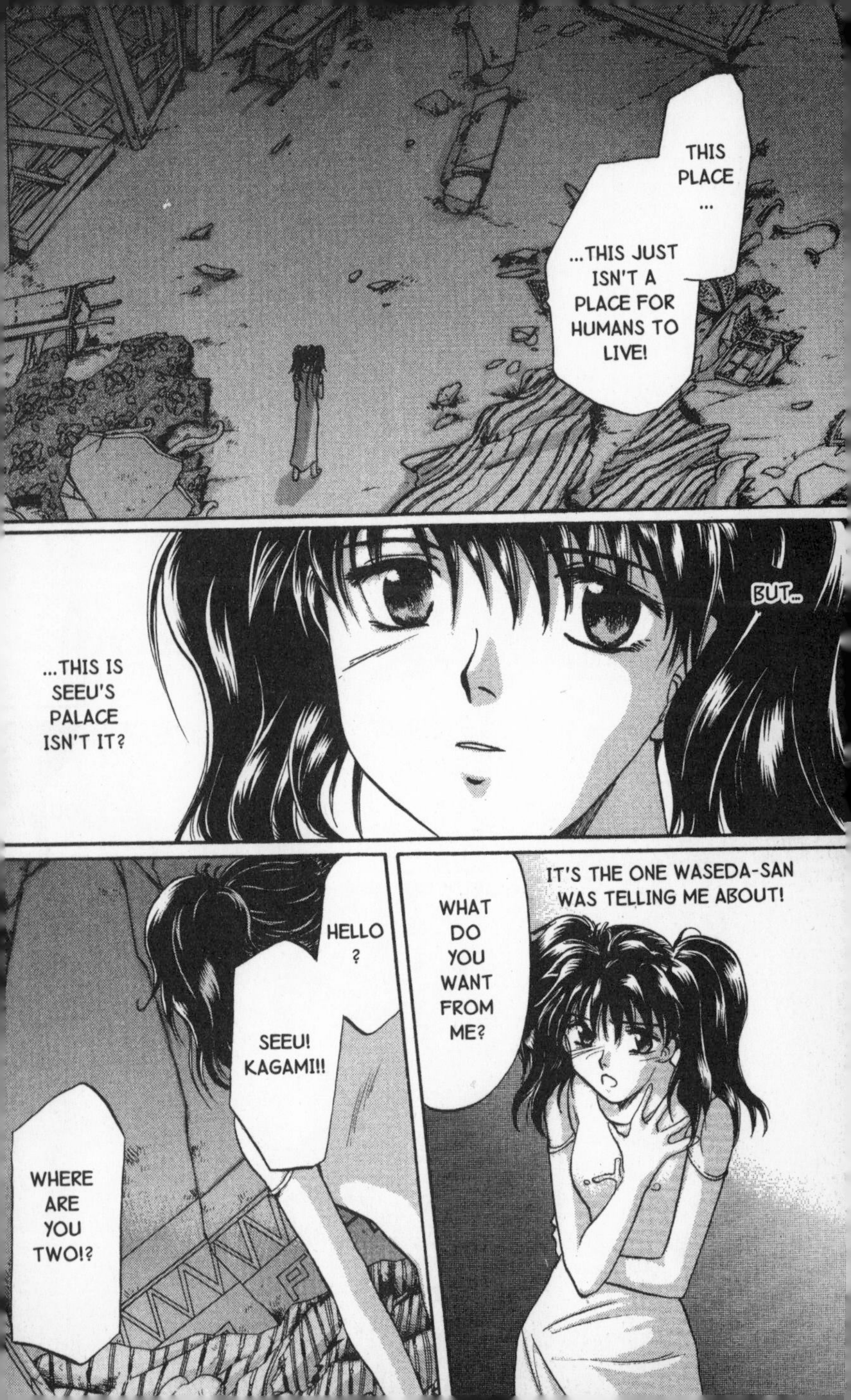
THIS PLACE ...
...THIS JUST ISN'T A PLACE FOR HUMANS TO LIVE!
BUT...
...THIS IS SEEU'S PALACE ISN'T IT?
IT'S THE ONE WASEDA-SAN WAS TELLING ME ABOUT!
WHAT DO YOU WANT FROM ME?
HELLO?
SEEU! KAGAMI!!
WHERE ARE YOU TWO!?

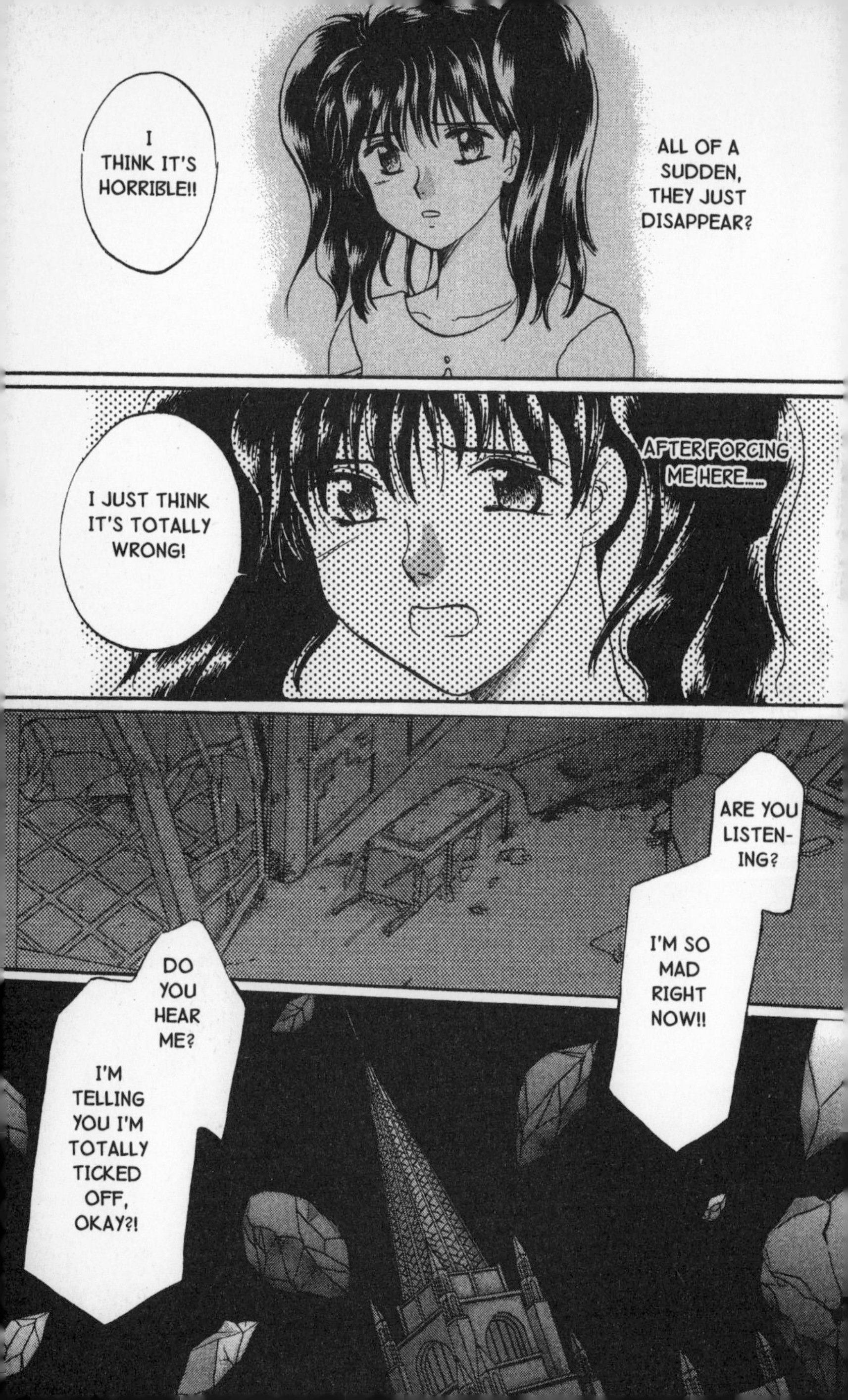
ALL OF A SUDDEN, THEY JUST DISAPPEAR?
I THINK IT'S HORRIBLE!!
AFTER FORCING ME HERE.....
I JUST THINK IT'S TOTALLY WRONG!
ARE YOU LISTEN-ING?
I'M SO MAD RIGHT NOW!!
DO YOU HEAR ME?
I'M TELLING YOU I'M TOTALLY TICKED OFF, OKAY?!

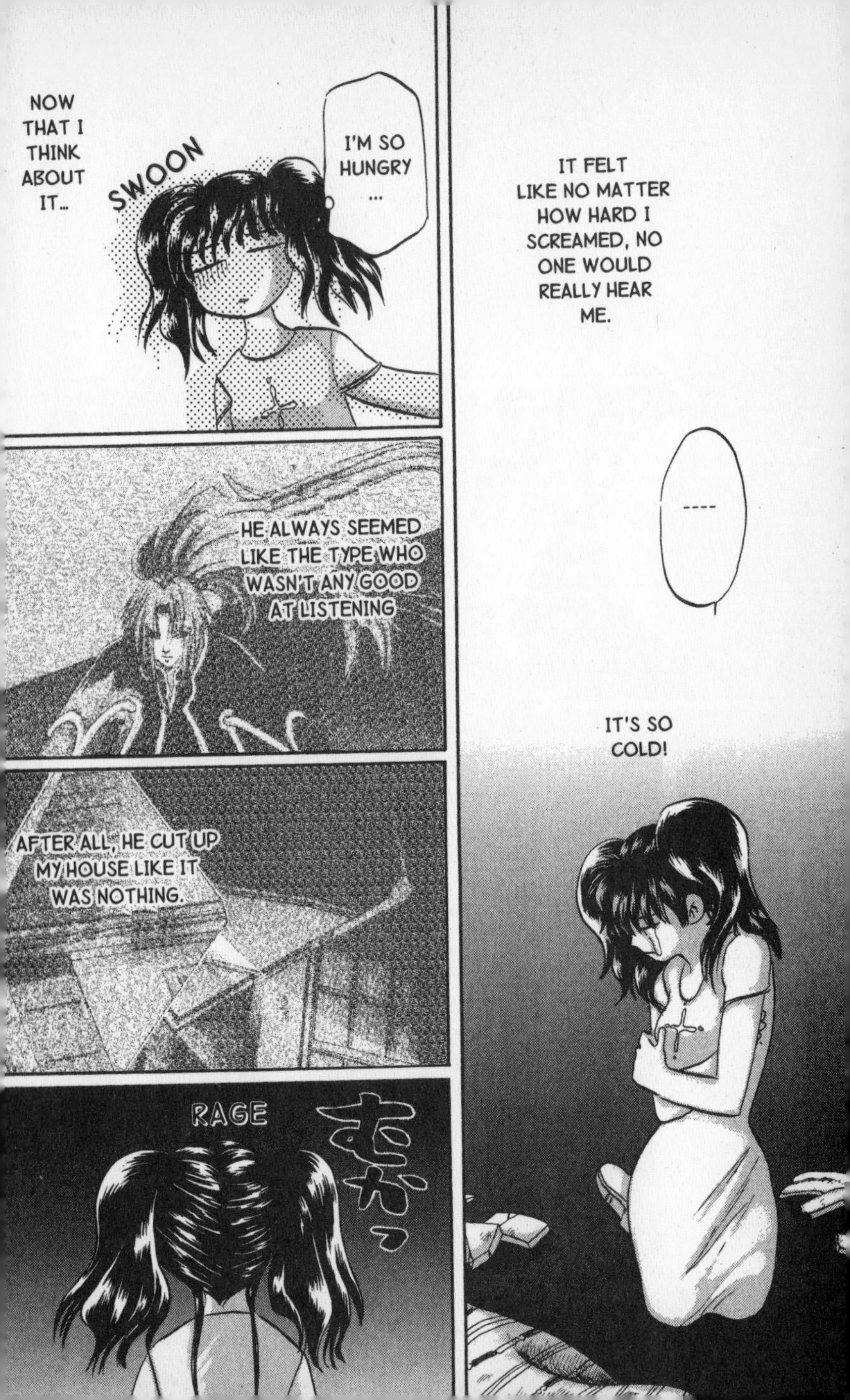
IT FELT LIKE NO MATTER HOW HARD I SCREAMED, NO ONE WOULD REALLY HEAR ME.

IT'S SO COLD!
I'M SO HUNGRY ...
SWOON
NOW THAT I THINK ABOUT IT...
HE ALWAYS SEEMED LIKE THE TYPE WHO WASN'T ANY GOOD AT LISTENING
AFTER ALL, HE CUT UP MY HOUSE LIKE IT WAS NOTHING.
むかっ
RAGE

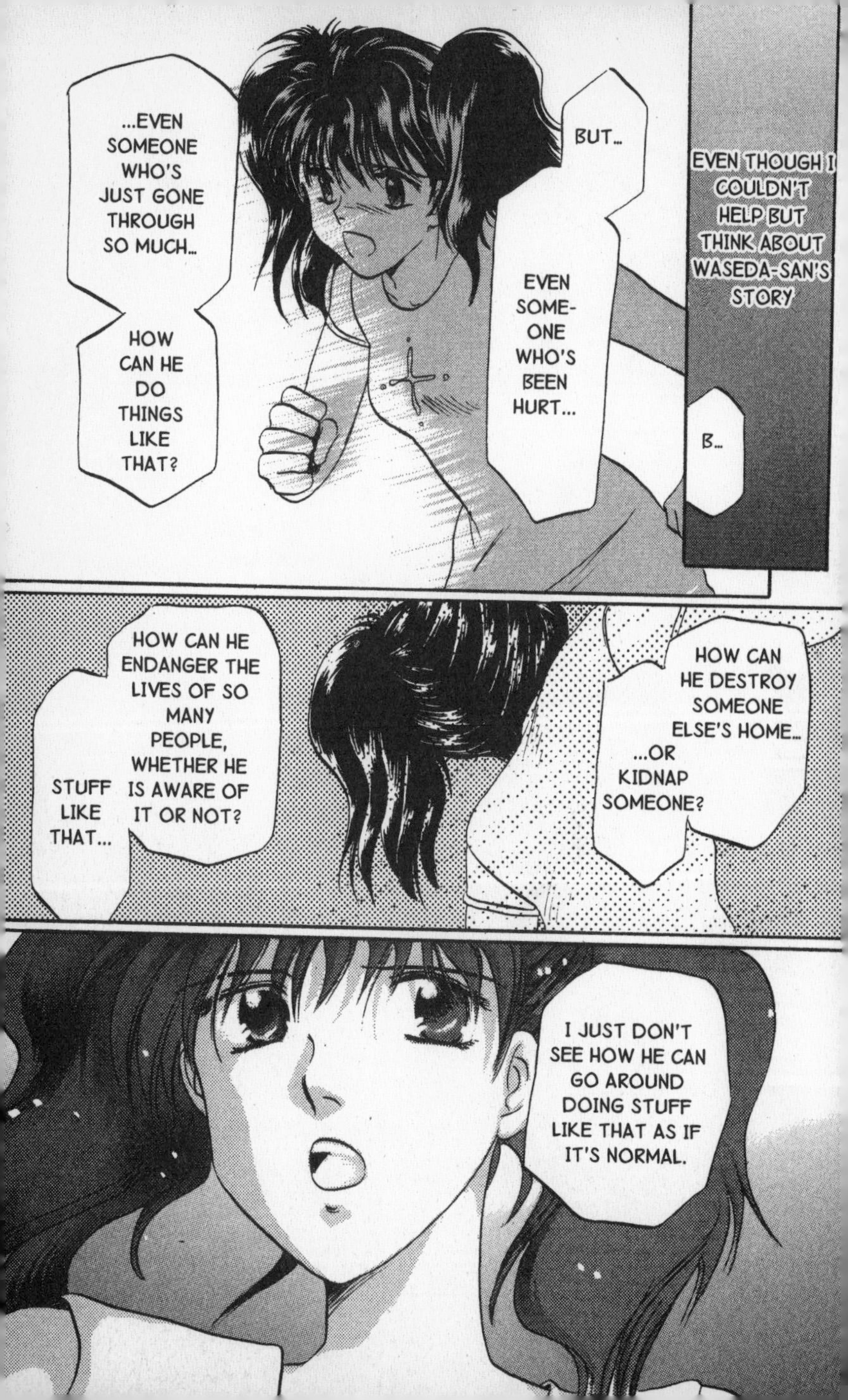
EVEN THOUGH I COULDN'T HELP BUT THINK ABOUT WASEDA-SAN'S STORY
B...
BUT...
EVEN SOME-ONE WHO'S BEEN HURT...
...EVEN SOMEONE WHO'S JUST GONE THROUGH SO MUCH...
HOW CAN HE DO THINGS LIKE THAT?
HOW CAN HE DESTROY SOMEONE ELSE'S HOME...
...OR KIDNAP SOMEONE?
HOW CAN HE ENDANGER THE LIVES OF SO MANY PEOPLE, WHETHER HE IS AWARE OF IT OR NOT?
STUFF LIKE THAT...
I JUST DON'T SEE HOW HE CAN GO AROUND DOING STUFF LIKE THAT AS IF IT'S NORMAL.

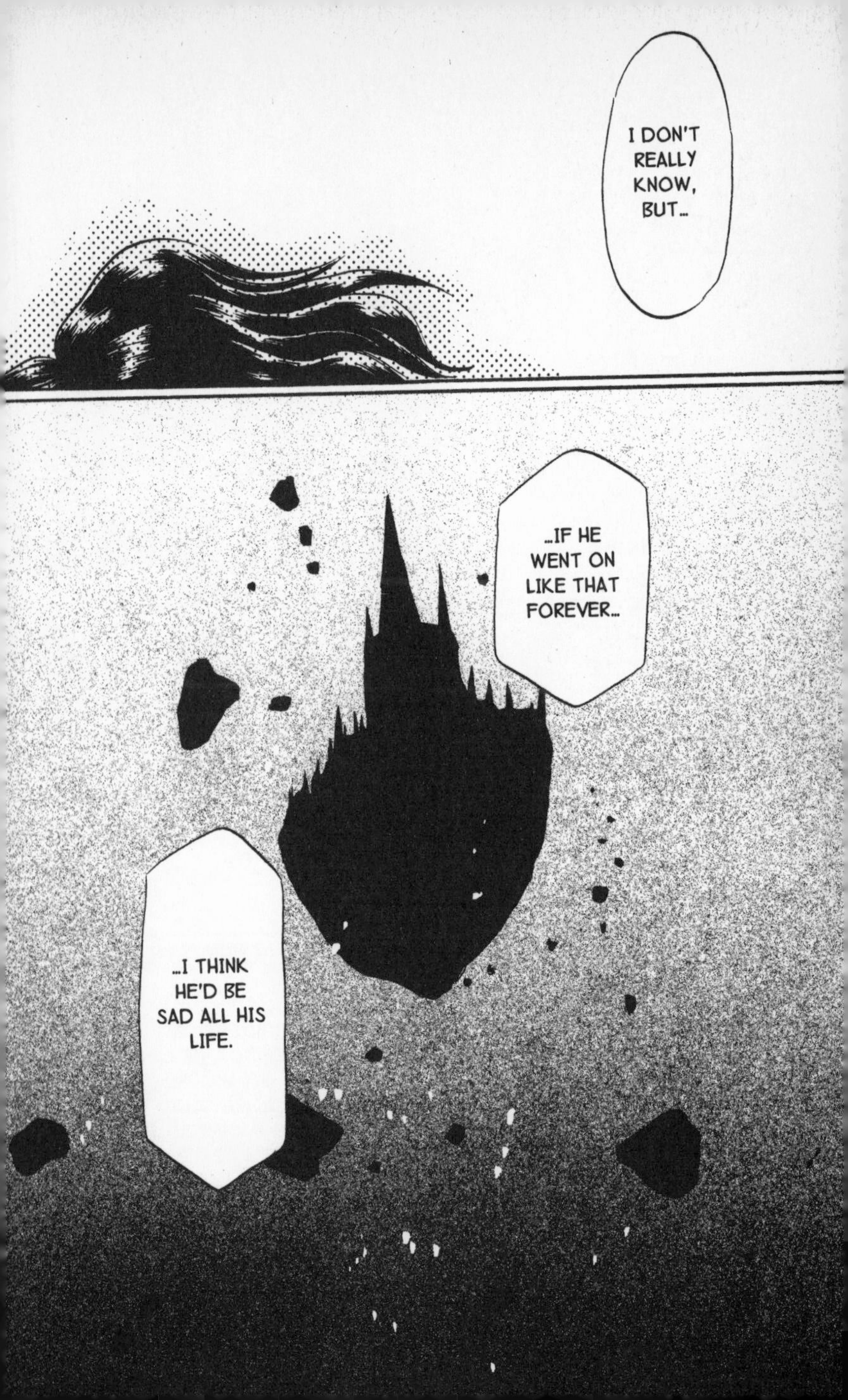
I DON'T REALLY KNOW, BUT...
...IF HE WENT ON LIKE THAT FOREVER...
...I THINK HE'D BE SAD ALL HIS LIFE.

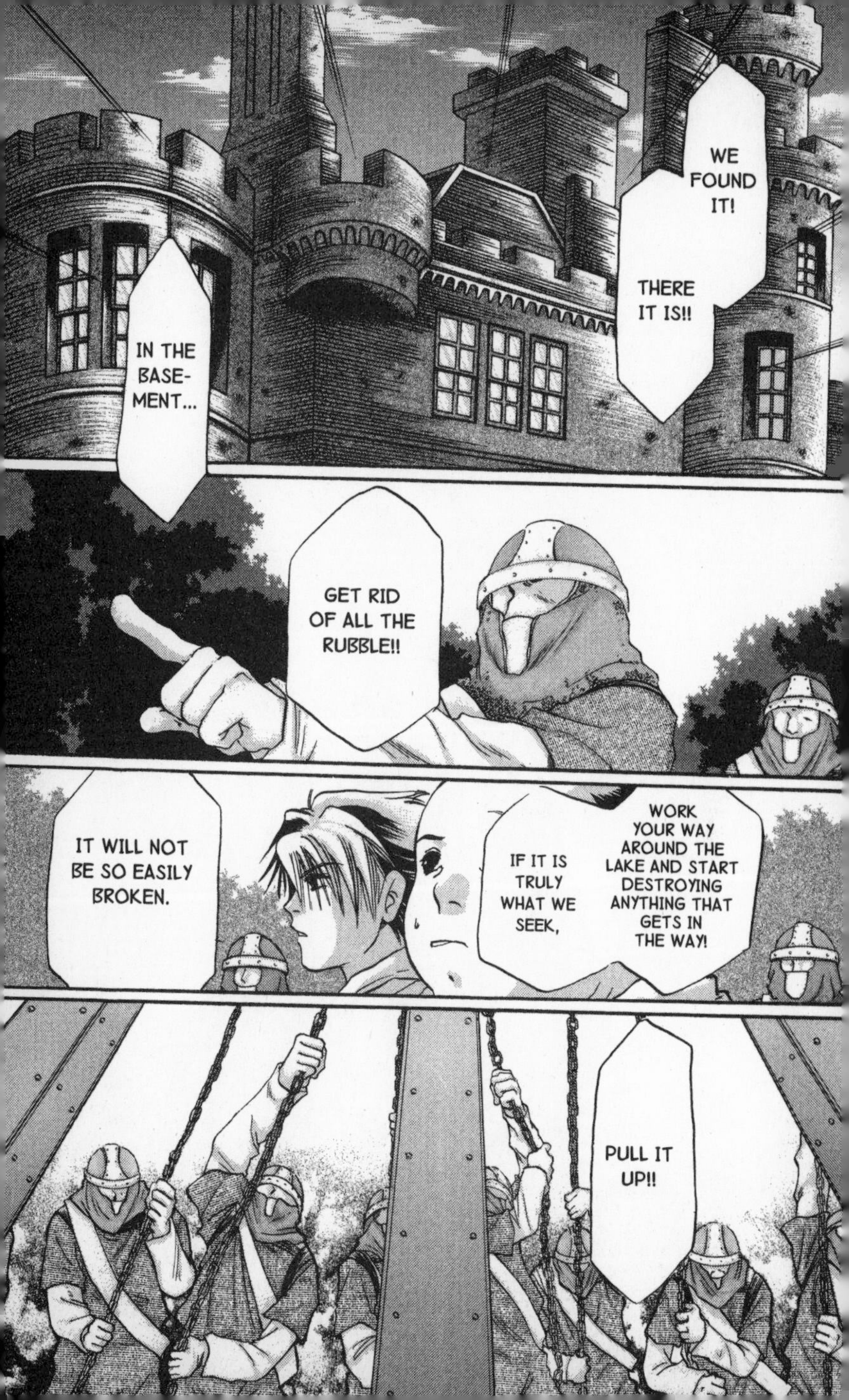
WE FOUND IT!
THERE IT IS!!
IN THE BASE-MENT...
GET RID OF ALL THE RUBBLE!!
WORK YOUR WAY AROUND THE LAKE AND START DESTROYING ANYTHING THAT GETS IN THE WAY!
IF IT IS TRULY WHAT WE SEEK,
IT WILL NOT BE SO EASILY BROKEN.
PULL IT UP!!

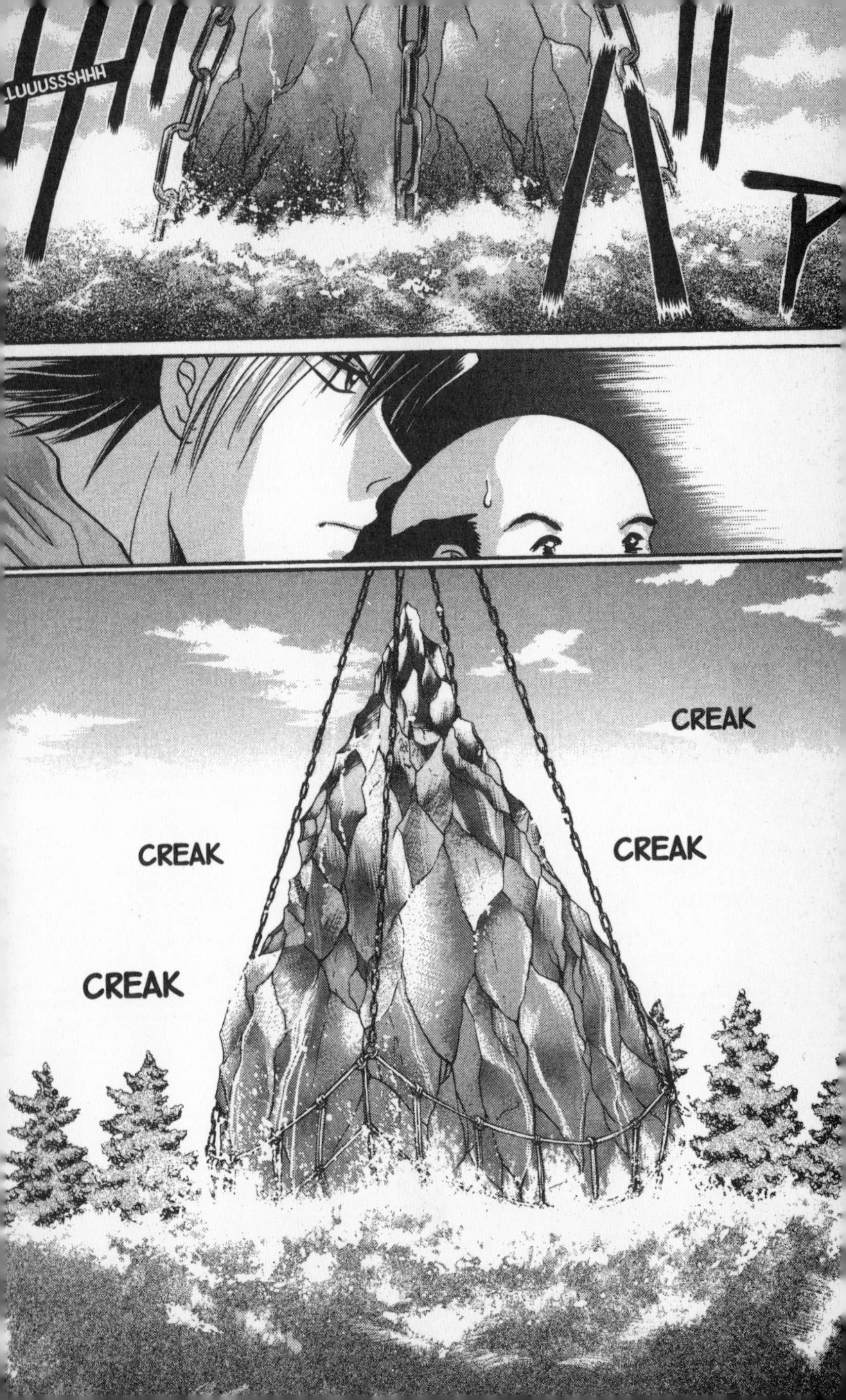
LUUUSSSHHH
CREAK
CREAK
CREAK

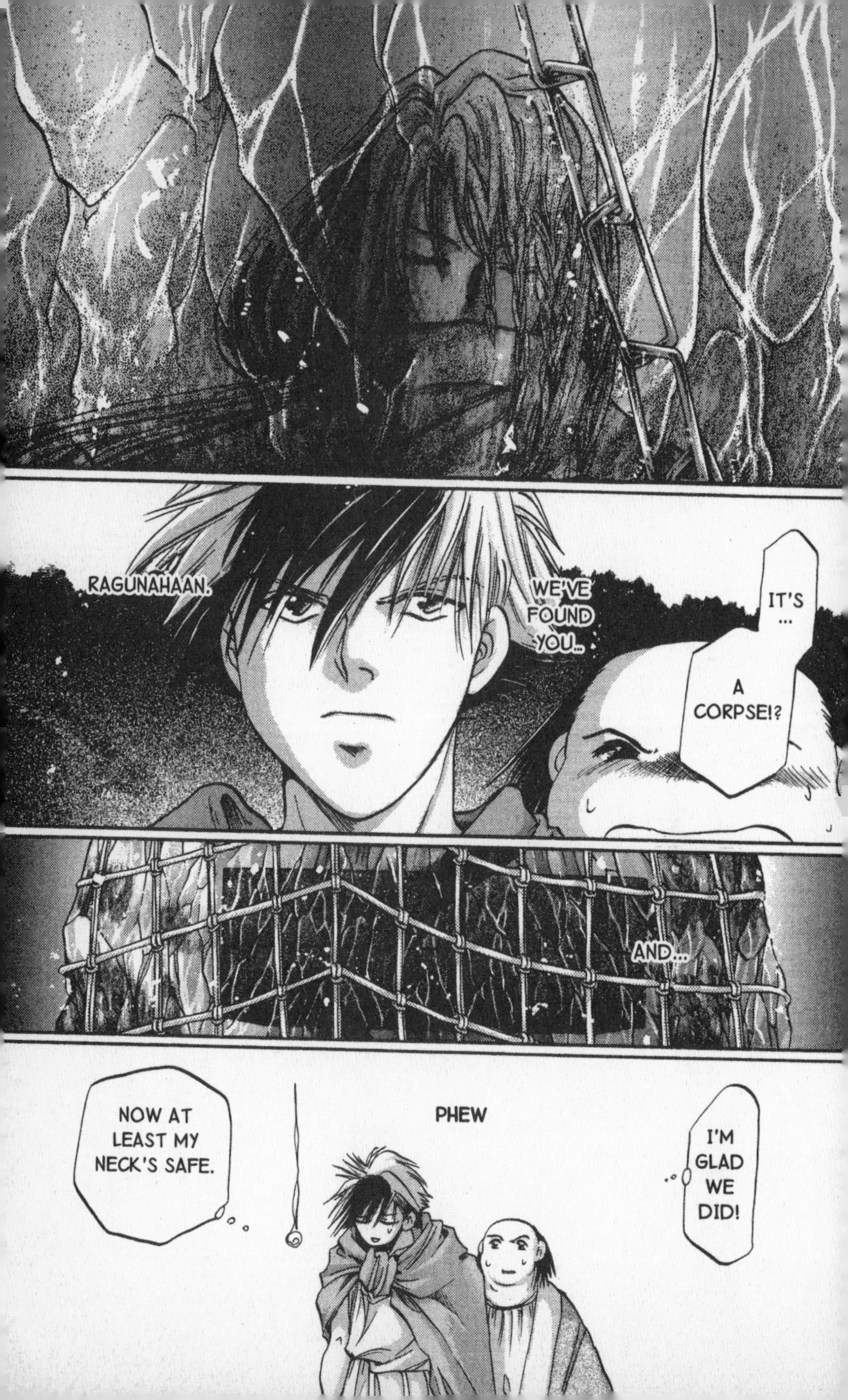
IT'S... A CORPSE!?
WE'VE FOUND YOU..
RAGUNAHAAN.
AND...
I'M GLAD WE DID!
PHEW
NOW AT LEAST MY NECK'S SAFE.

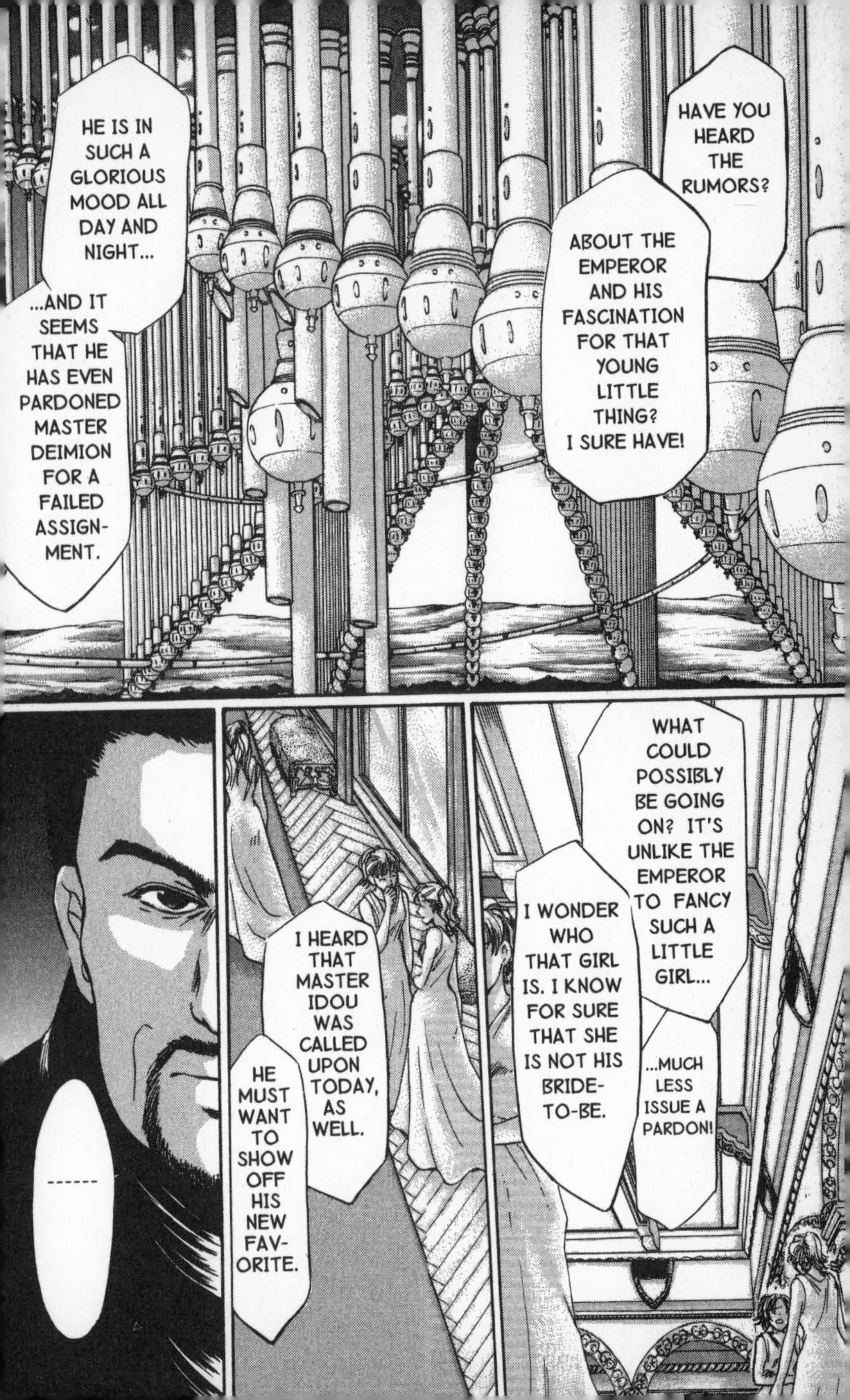
HAVE YOU HEARD THE RUMORS?
ABOUT THE EMPEROR AND HIS FASCINATION FOR THAT YOUNG LITTLE THING? I SURE HAVE!
HE IS IN SUCH A GLORIOUS MOOD ALL DAY AND NIGHT...
...AND IT SEEMS THAT HE HAS EVEN PARDONED MASTER DEIMION FOR A FAILED ASSIGN-MENT.
WHAT COULD POSSIBLY BE GOING ON? IT'S UNLIKE THE EMPEROR TO FANCY SUCH A LITTLE GIRL...
...MUCH LESS ISSUE A PARDON!
I WONDER WHO THAT GIRL IS. I KNOW FOR SURE THAT SHE IS NOT HIS BRIDE-TO-BE.
I HEARD THAT MASTER IDOU WAS CALLED UPON TODAY, AS WELL.
HE MUST WANT TO SHOW OFF HIS NEW FAV-ORITE.

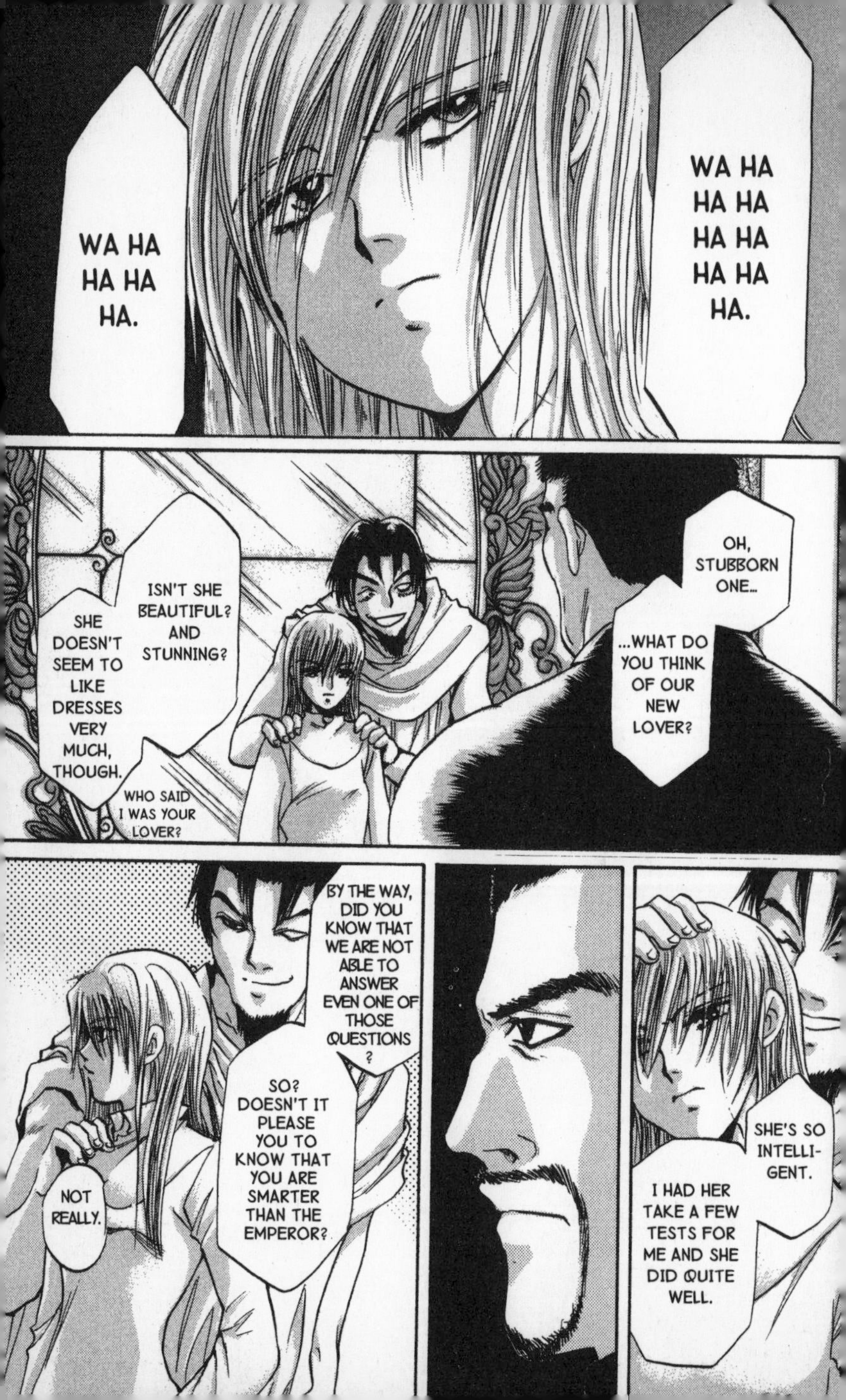
WA HA HA HA HA HA HA HA HA.
WA HA HA HA HA.
OH, STUBBORN ONE...
...WHAT DO YOU THINK OF OUR NEW LOVER?
ISN'T SHE BEAUTIFUL? AND STUNNING?
SHE DOESN'T SEEM TO LIKE DRESSES VERY MUCH, THOUGH.
WHO SAID I WAS YOUR LOVER?
SHE'S SO INTELLI-GENT.
I HAD HER TAKE A FEW TESTS FOR ME AND SHE DID QUITE WELL.
BY THE WAY, DID YOU KNOW THAT WE ARE NOT ABLE TO ANSWER EVEN ONE OF THOSE QUESTIONS?
SO? DOESN'T IT PLEASE YOU TO KNOW THAT YOU ARE SMARTER THAN THE EMPEROR?
NOT REALLY.

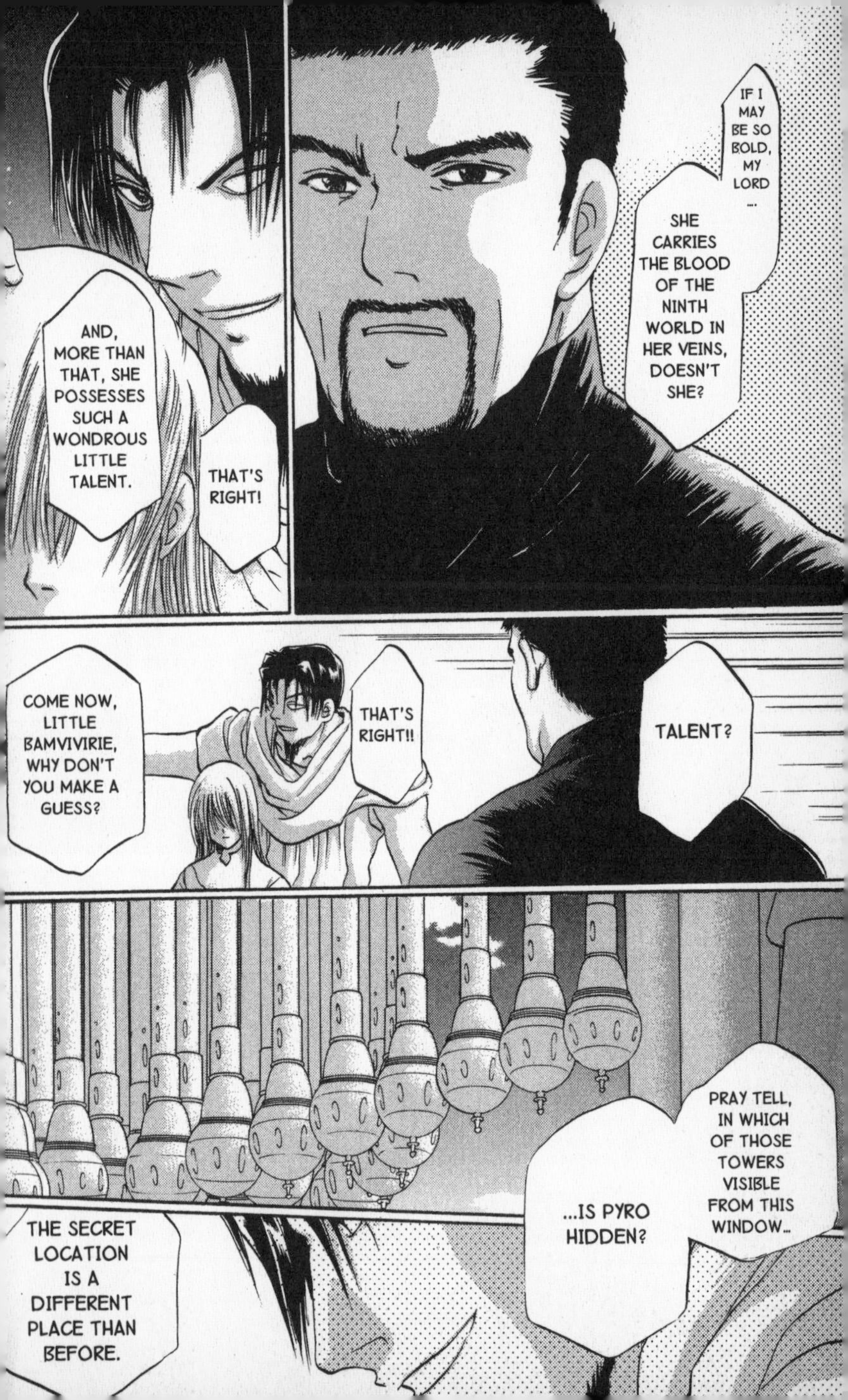
IF I MAY BE SO BOLD, MY LORD ...
SHE CARRIES THE BLOOD OF THE NINTH WORLD IN HER VEINS, DOESN'T SHE?
THAT'S RIGHT!
AND, MORE THAN THAT, SHE POSSESSES SUCH A WONDROUS LITTLE TALENT.
TALENT?
THAT'S RIGHT!!
COME NOW, LITTLE BAMVIVIRIE, WHY DON'T YOU MAKE A GUESS?
PRAY TELL, IN WHICH OF THOSE TOWERS VISIBLE FROM THIS WINDOW...
...IS PYRO HIDDEN?
THE SECRET LOCATION IS A DIFFERENT PLACE THAN BEFORE.

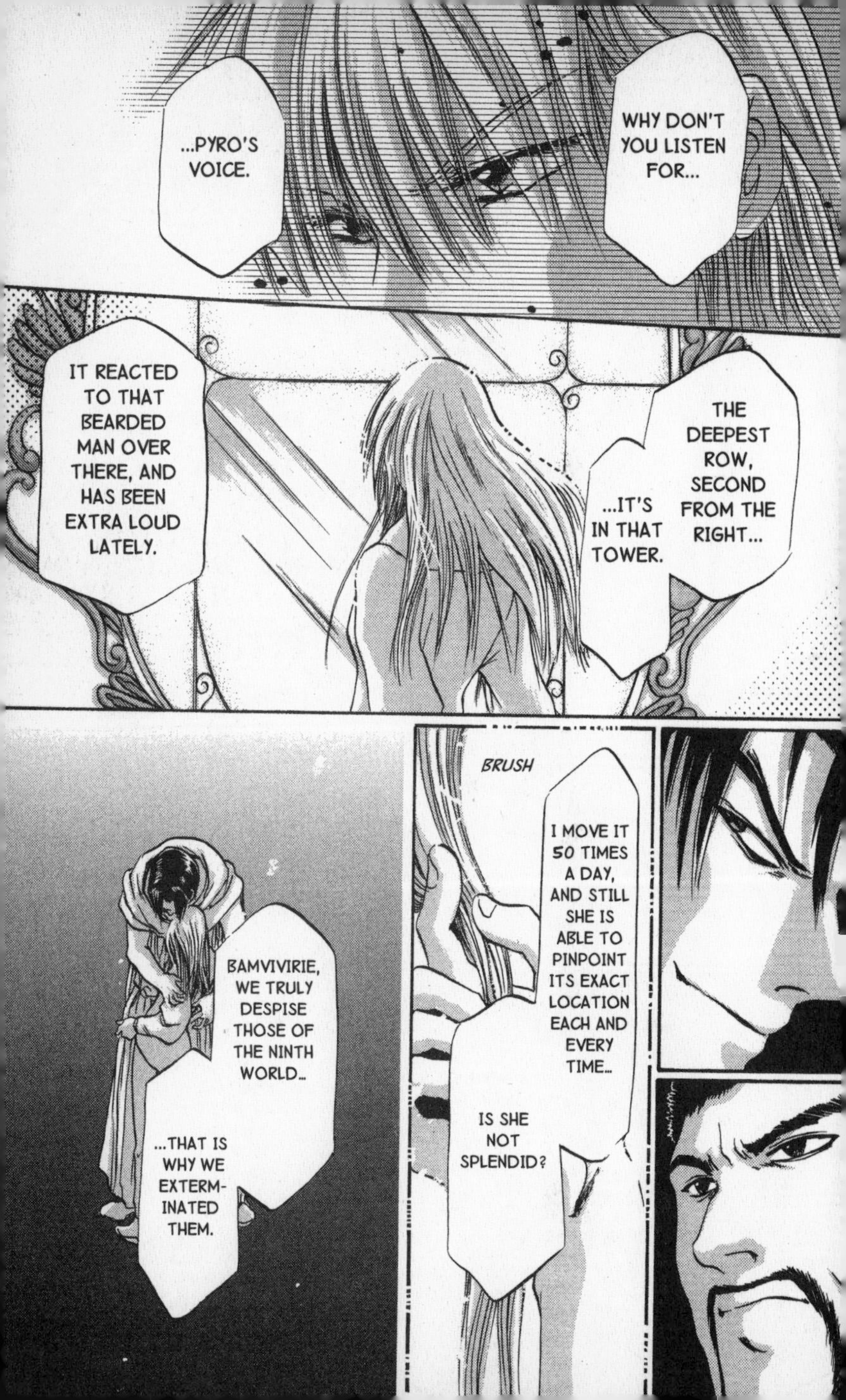
WHY DON'T YOU LISTEN FOR...
...PYRO'S VOICE.
THE DEEPEST ROW, SECOND FROM THE RIGHT...
...IT'S IN THAT TOWER.
IT REACTED TO THAT BEARDED MAN OVER THERE, AND HAS BEEN EXTRA LOUD LATELY.
BRUSH
I MOVE IT 50 TIMES A DAY, AND STILL SHE IS ABLE TO PINPOINT ITS EXACT LOCATION EACH AND EVERY TIME...
IS SHE NOT SPLENDID?
BAMVIVIRIE, WE TRULY DESPISE THOSE OF THE NINTH WORLD...
...THAT IS WHY WE EXTERM-INATED THEM.

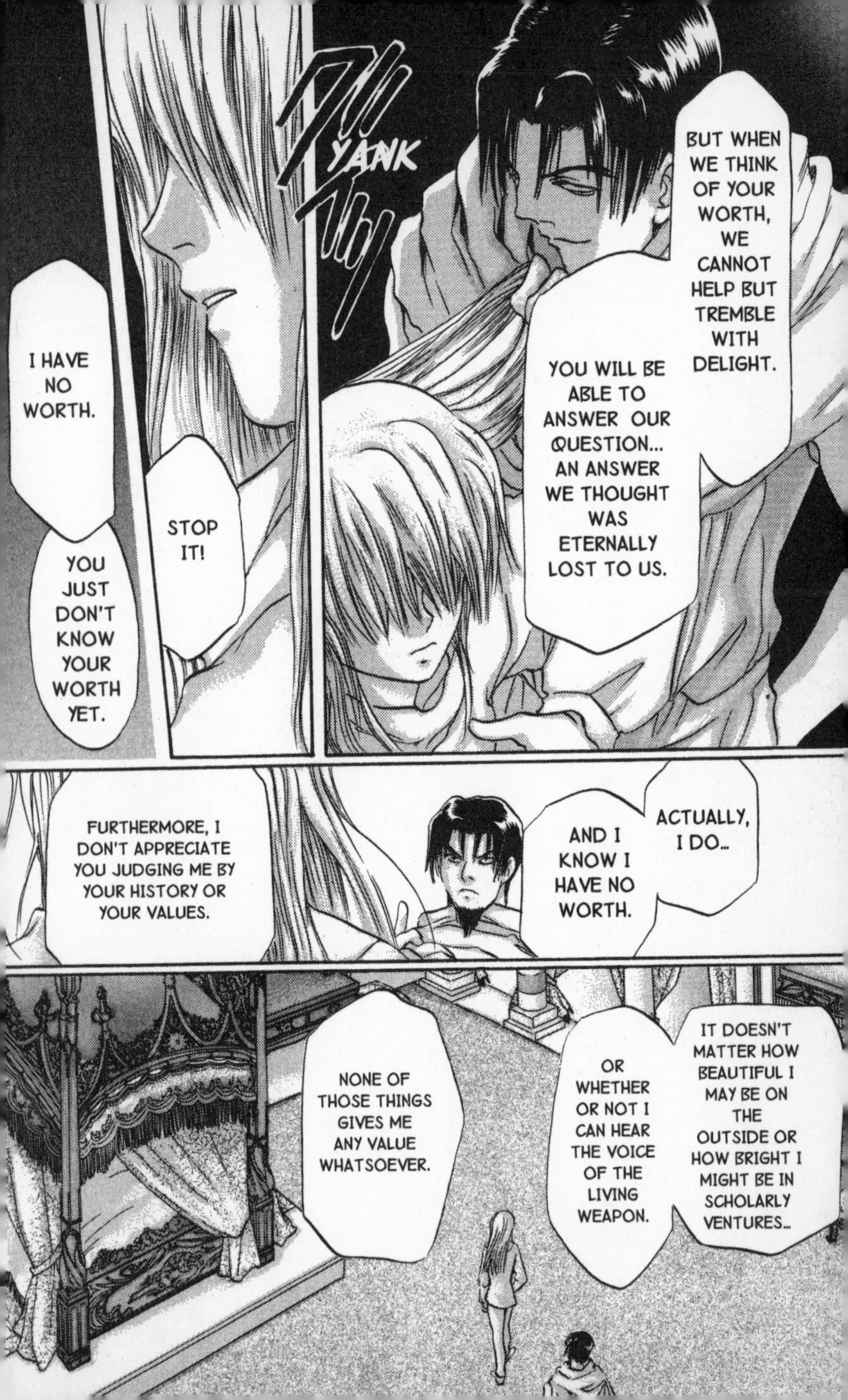
BUT WHEN WE THINK OF YOUR WORTH, WE CANNOT HELP BUT TREMBLE WITH DELIGHT.
YANK
YOU WILL BE ABLE TO ANSWER OUR QUESTION... AN ANSWER WE THOUGHT WAS ETERNALLY LOST TO US.
STOP IT!
I HAVE NO WORTH.
YOU JUST DON'T KNOW YOUR WORTH YET.
ACTUALLY, I DO...
AND I KNOW I HAVE NO WORTH.
FURTHERMORE, I DON'T APPRECIATE YOU JUDGING ME BY YOUR HISTORY OR YOUR VALUES.
IT DOESN'T MATTER HOW BEAUTIFUL I MAY BE ON THE OUTSIDE OR HOW BRIGHT I MIGHT BE IN SCHOLARLY VENTURES...
OR WHETHER OR NOT I CAN HEAR THE VOICE OF THE LIVING WEAPON.
NONE OF THOSE THINGS GIVES ME ANY VALUE WHATSOEVER.

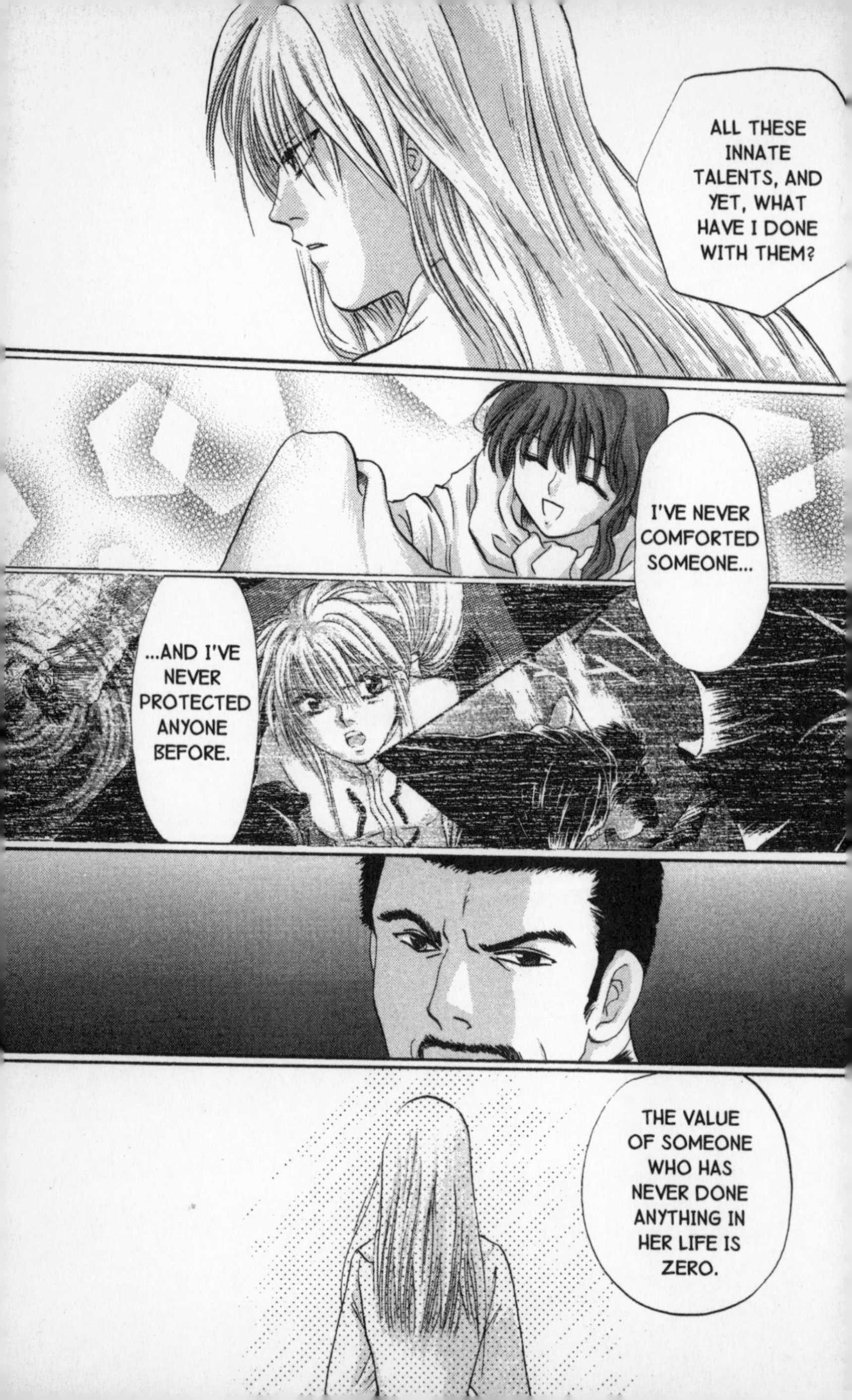
ALL THESE INNATE TALENTS, AND YET, WHAT HAVE I DONE WITH THEM?
I'VE NEVER COMFORTED SOMEONE...
...AND I'VE NEVER PROTECTED ANYONE BEFORE.
THE VALUE OF SOMEONE WHO HAS NEVER DONE ANYTHING IN HER LIFE IS ZERO.

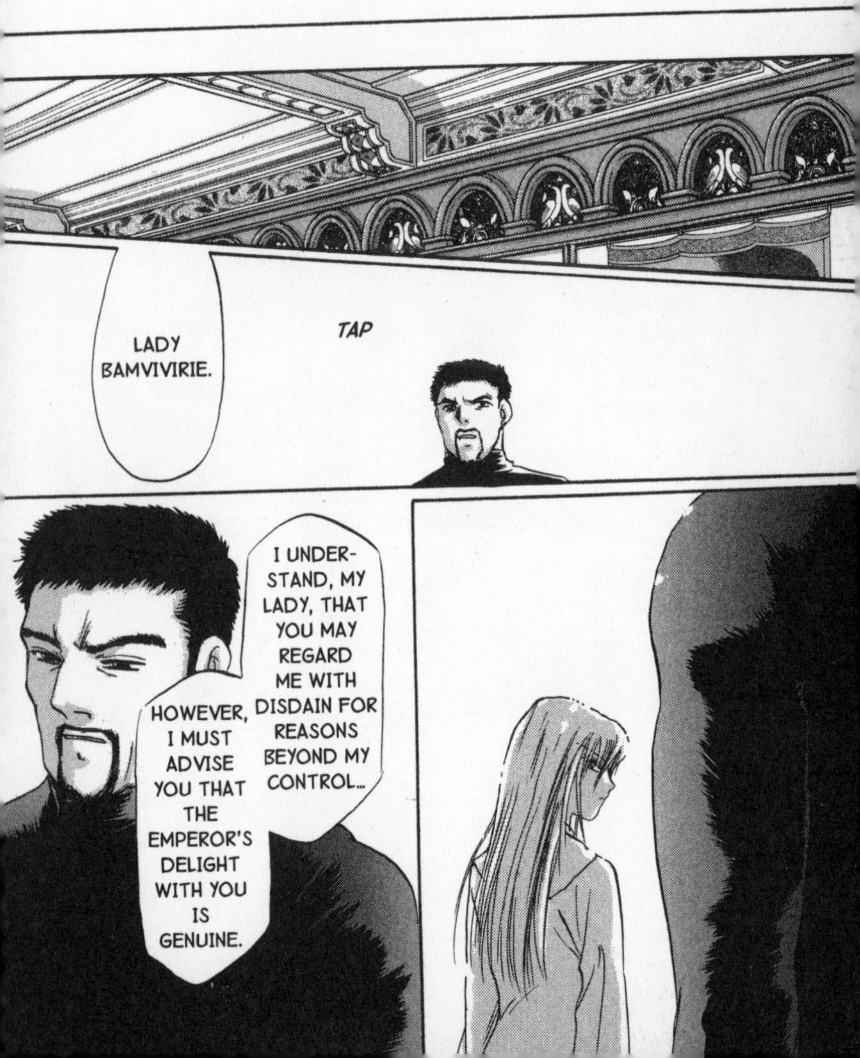
TAP
LADY BAMVIVIRIE.
I UNDER-STAND, MY LADY, THAT YOU MAY REGARD ME WITH DISDAIN FOR REASONS BEYOND MY CONTROL...
HOWEVER, I MUST ADVISE YOU THAT THE EMPEROR'S DELIGHT WITH YOU IS GENUINE.

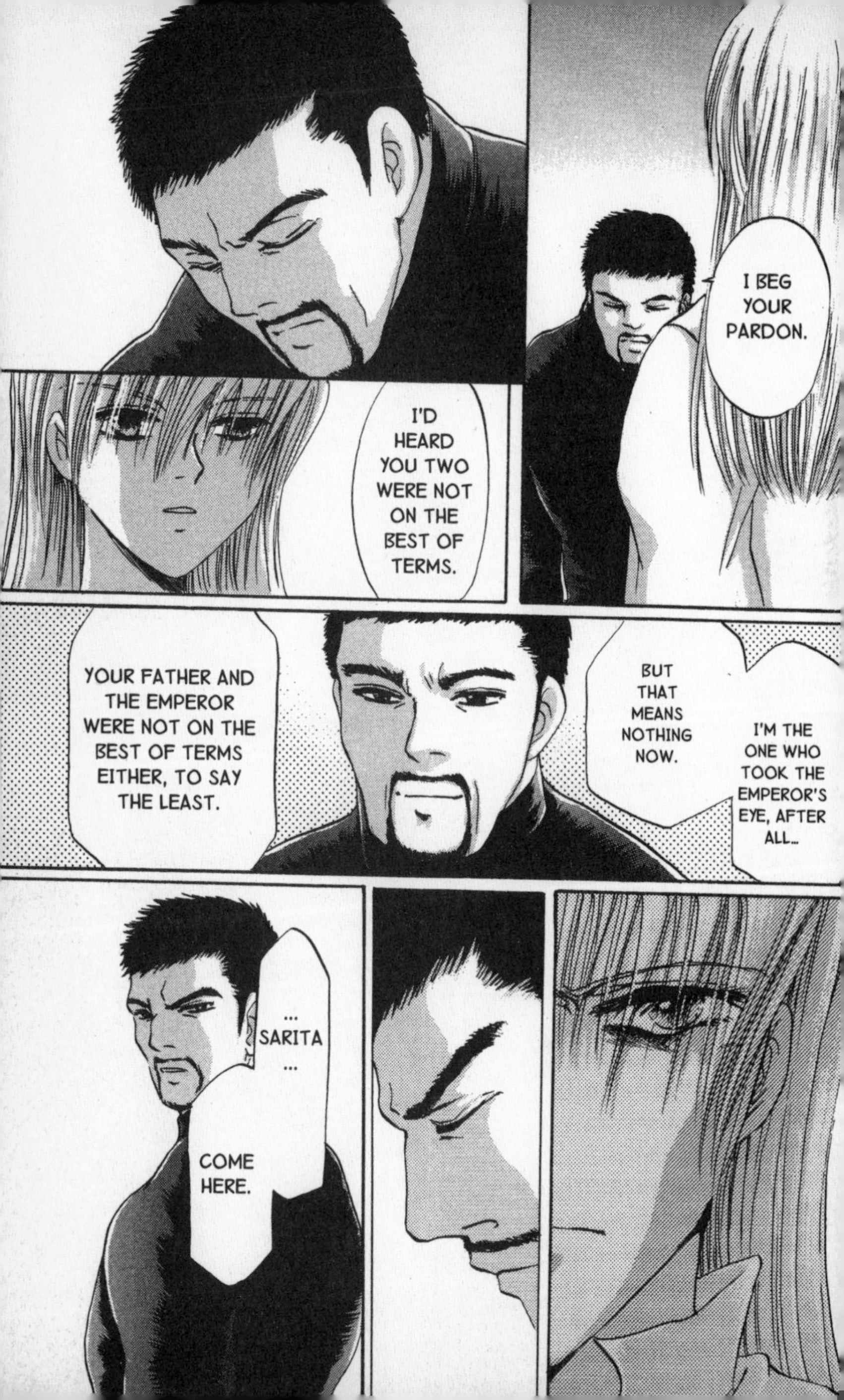
I BEG YOUR PARDON.
I'D HEARD YOU TWO WERE NOT ON THE BEST OF TERMS.
I'M THE ONE WHO TOOK THE EMPEROR'S EYE, AFTER ALL...
BUT THAT MEANS NOTHING NOW.
YOUR FATHER AND THE EMPEROR WERE NOT ON THE BEST OF TERMS EITHER, TO SAY THE LEAST.
...SARITA...
COME HERE.

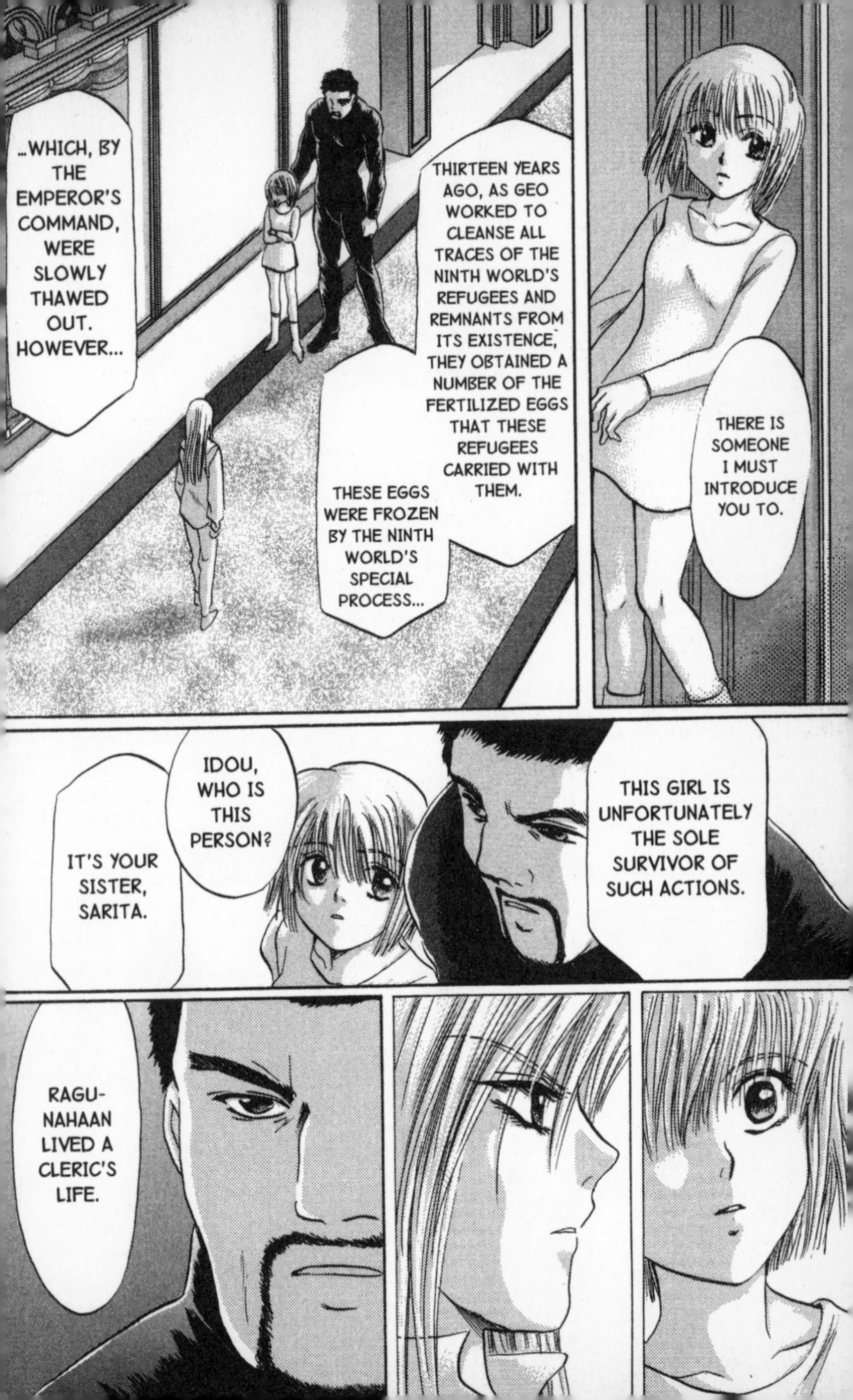
THERE IS SOMEONE I MUST INTRODUCE YOU TO.
THIRTEEN YEARS AGO, AS GEO WORKED TO CLEANSE ALL TRACES OF THE NINTH WORLD'S REFUGEES AND REMNANTS FROM ITS EXISTENCE, THEY OBTAINED A NUMBER OF THE FERTILIZED EGGS THAT THESE REFUGEES CARRIED WITH THEM.
THESE EGGS WERE FROZEN BY THE NINTH WORLD'S SPECIAL PROCESS...
...WHICH, BY THE EMPEROR'S COMMAND, WERE SLOWLY THAWED OUT. HOWEVER...
THIS GIRL IS UNFORTUNATELY THE SOLE SURVIVOR OF SUCH ACTIONS.
IDOU, WHO IS THIS PERSON?
IT'S YOUR SISTER, SARITA.
RAGU-NAHAAN LIVED A CLERIC'S LIFE.

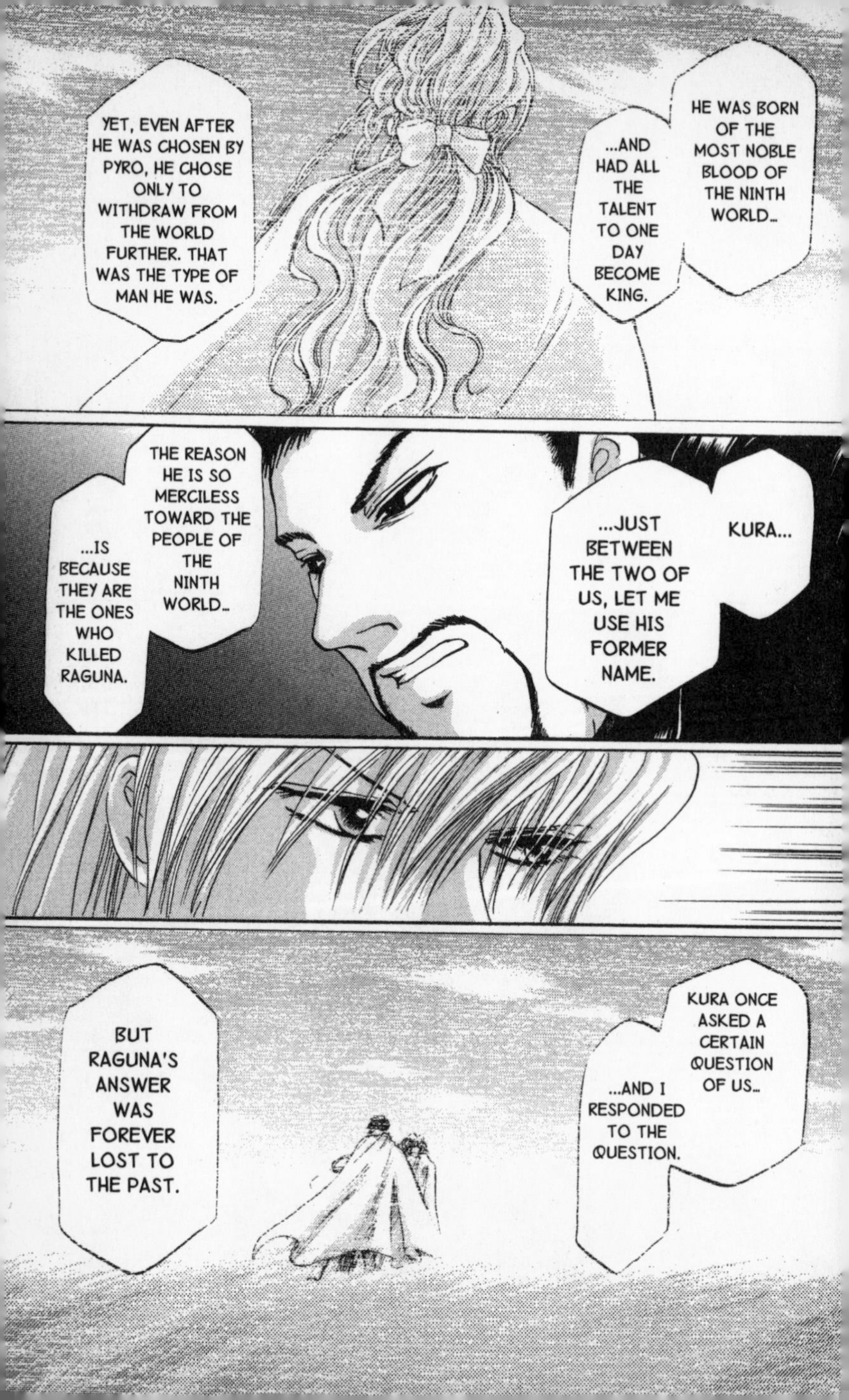
HE WAS BORN OF THE MOST NOBLE BLOOD OF THE NINTH WORLD...
...AND HAD ALL THE TALENT TO ONE DAY BECOME KING.
YET, EVEN AFTER HE WAS CHOSEN BY PYRO, HE CHOSE ONLY TO WITHDRAW FROM THE WORLD FURTHER. THAT WAS THE TYPE OF MAN HE WAS.
KURA...
...JUST BETWEEN THE TWO OF US, LET ME USE HIS FORMER NAME.
THE REASON HE IS SO MERCILESS TOWARD THE PEOPLE OF THE NINTH WORLD...
...IS BECAUSE THEY ARE THE ONES WHO KILLED RAGUNA.
KURA ONCE ASKED A CERTAIN QUESTION OF US...
...AND I RESPONDED TO THE QUESTION.
BUT RAGUNA'S ANSWER WAS FOREVER LOST TO THE PAST.

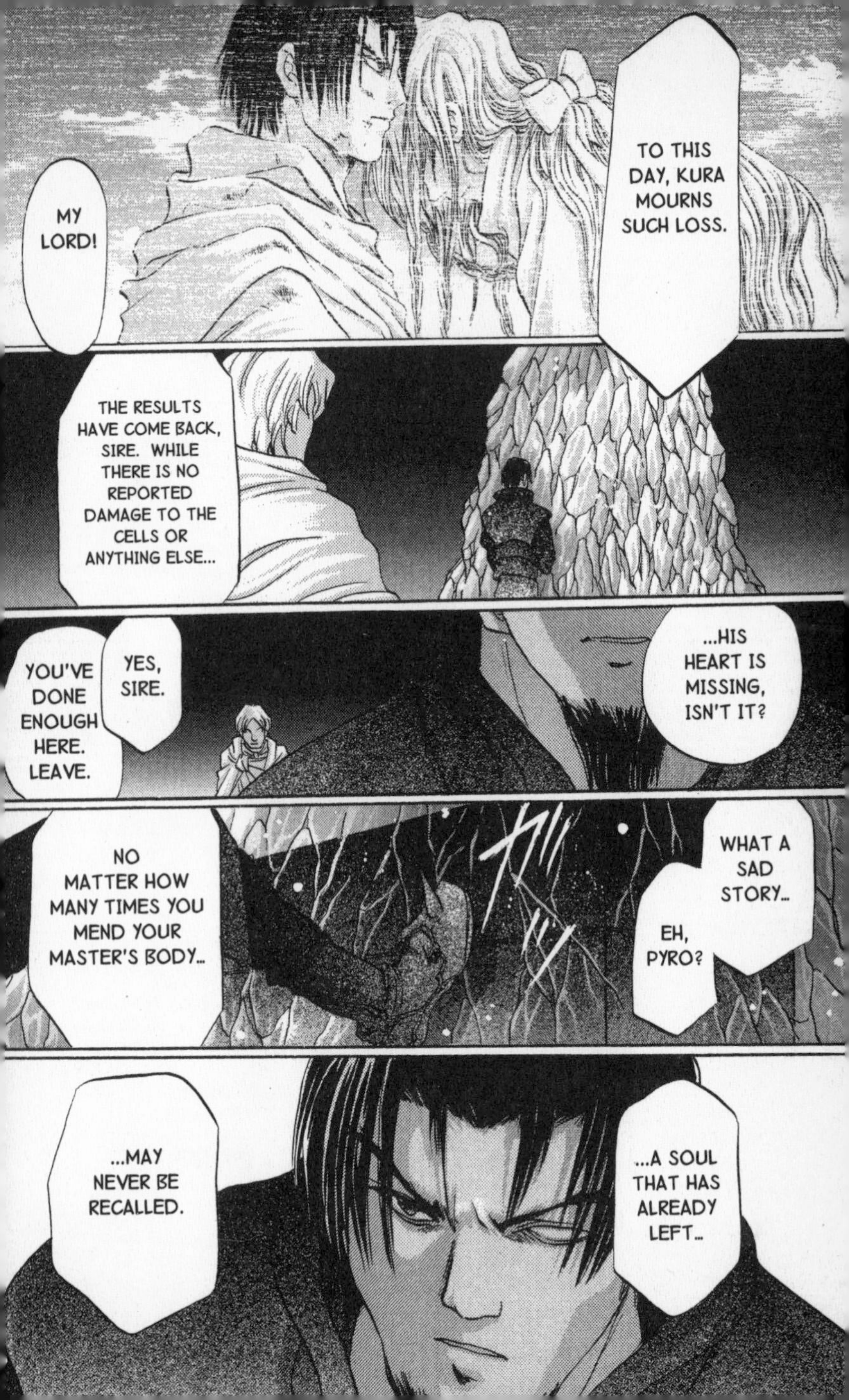
TO THIS DAY, KURA MOURNS SUCH LOSS.
MY LORD!
THE RESULTS HAVE COME BACK, SIRE. WHILE THERE IS NO REPORTED DAMAGE TO THE CELLS OR ANYTHING ELSE...
...HIS HEART IS MISSING, ISN'T IT?
YES, SIRE.
YOU'VE DONE ENOUGH HERE. LEAVE.
WHAT A SAD STORY...
EH, PYRO?
NO MATTER HOW MANY TIMES YOU MEND YOUR MASTER'S BODY...
...A SOUL THAT HAS ALREADY LEFT...
...MAY NEVER BE RECALLED.

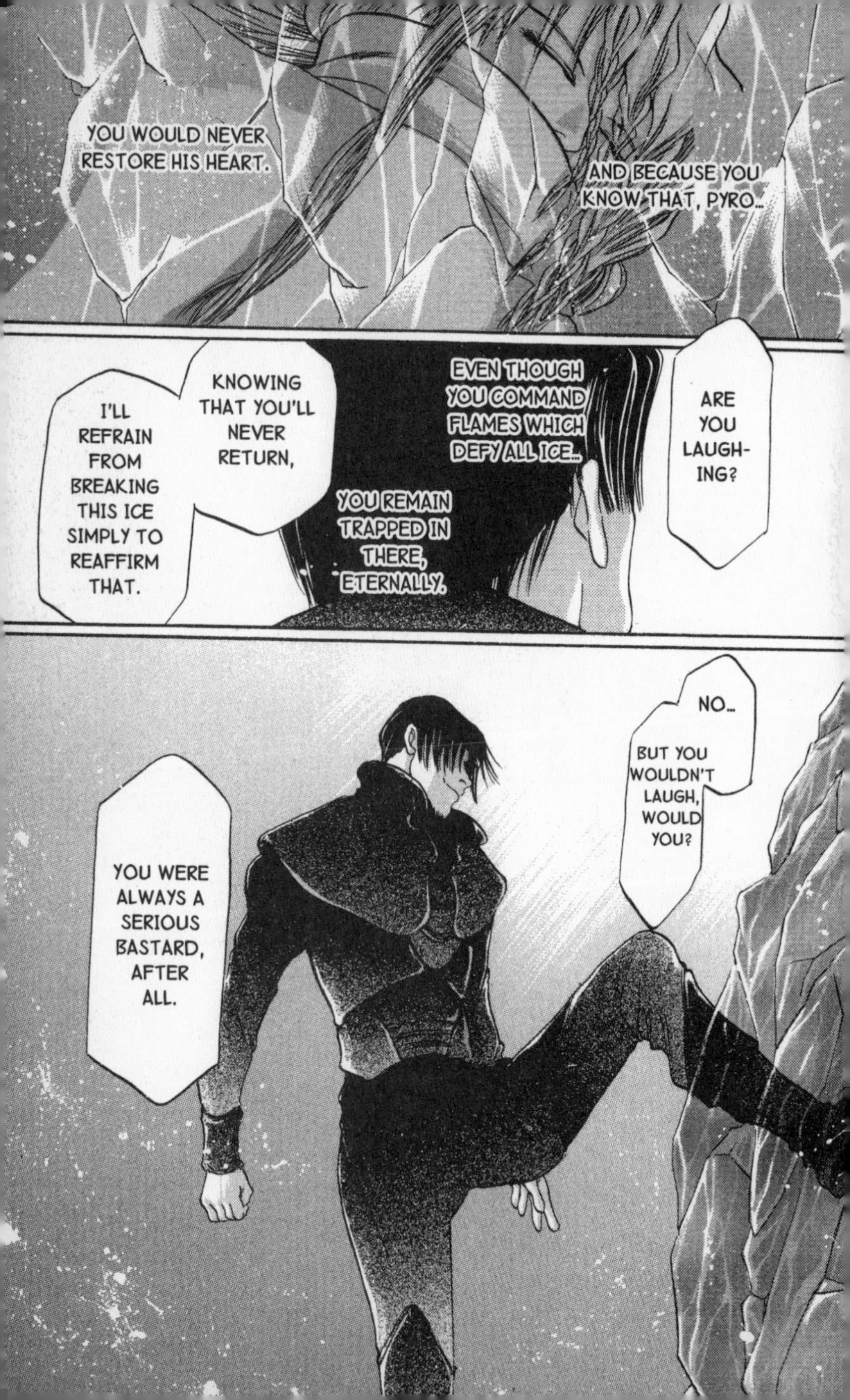

AND BECAUSE YOU KNOW THAT, PYRO...
YOU WOULD NEVER RESTORE HIS HEART.
ARE YOU LAUGHING?
EVEN THOUGH YOU COMMAND FLAMES WHICH DEFY ALL ICE...
YOU REMAIN TRAPPED IN THERE, ETERNALLY.
KNOWING THAT YOU'LL NEVER RETURN,
I'LL REFRAIN FROM BREAKING THIS ICE SIMPLY TO REAFFIRM THAT.
NO...
BUT YOU WOULDN'T LAUGH, WOULD YOU?
YOU WERE ALWAYS A SERIOUS BASTARD, AFTER ALL.

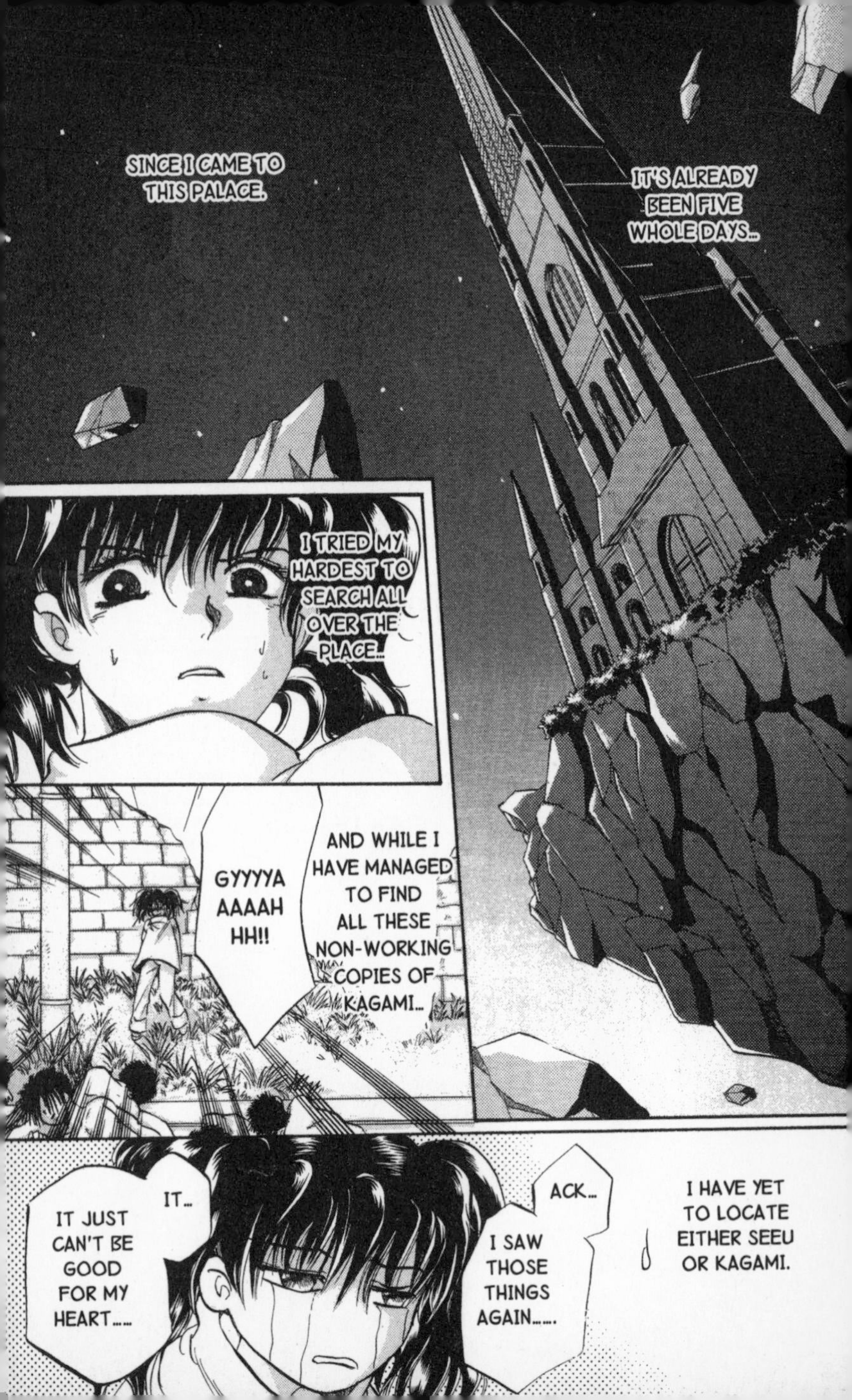
IT'S ALREADY BEEN FIVE WHOLE DAYS...
SINCE I CAME TO THIS PALACE.
I TRIED MY HARDEST TO SEARCH ALL OVER THE PLACE...
AND WHILE I HAVE MANAGED TO FIND ALL THESE NON-WORKING COPIES OF KAGAMI...
GYYYYA AAAAH HH!!
I HAVE YET TO LOCATE EITHER SEEU OR KAGAMI.
ACK...
I SAW THOSE THINGS AGAIN......
IT...
IT JUST CAN'T BE GOOD FOR MY HEART.....

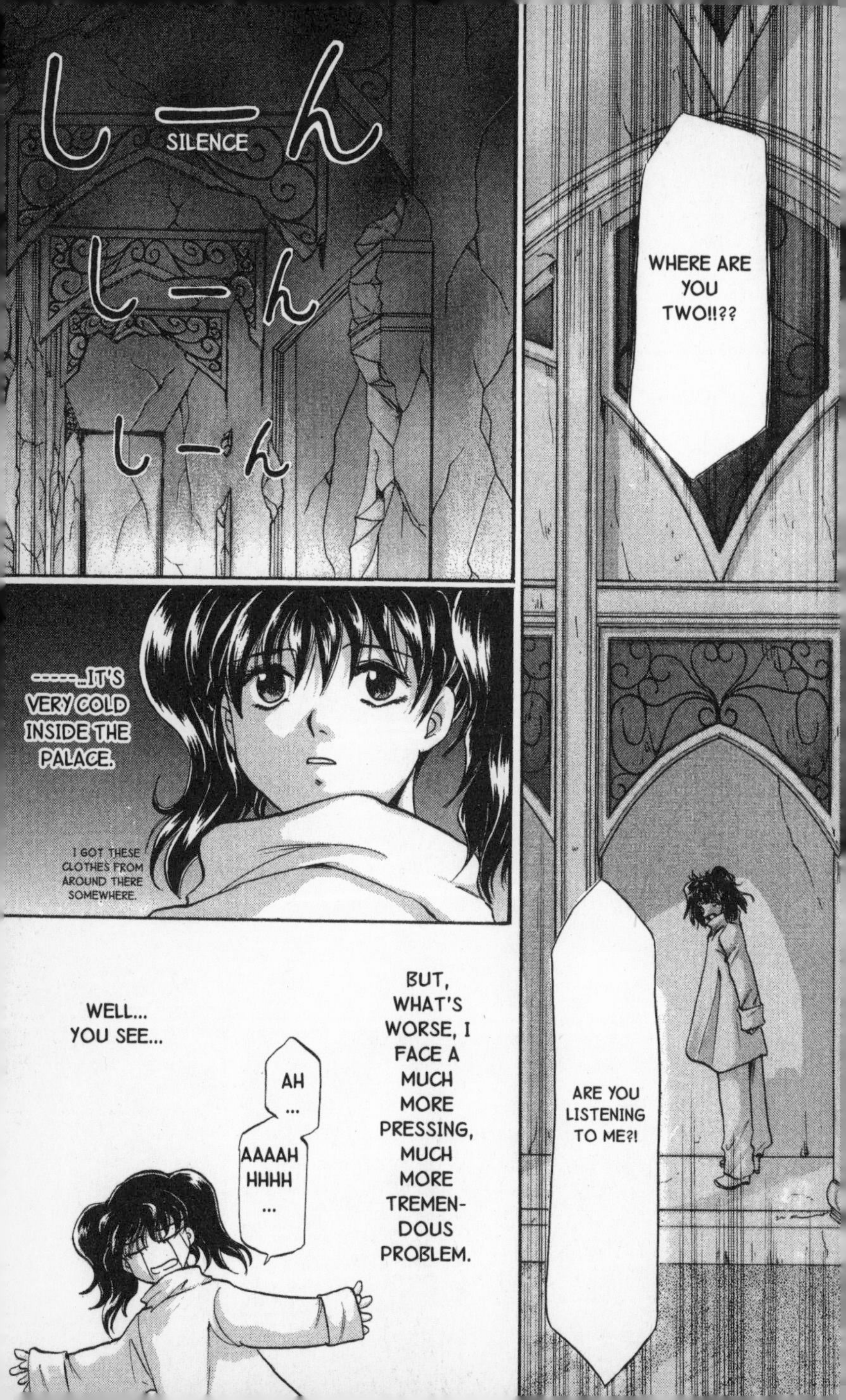
WHERE ARE YOU TWO!!??
しーん
SILENCE
しーん
しーん
ARE YOU LISTENING TO ME?!
------...IT'S VERY COLD INSIDE THE PALACE.
I GOT THESE CLOTHES FROM AROUND THERE SOMEWHERE.
BUT, WHAT'S WORSE, I FACE A MUCH MORE PRESSING, MUCH MORE TREMEN-DOUS PROBLEM.
AH ...
AAAAHHHHH ...
WELL... YOU SEE...

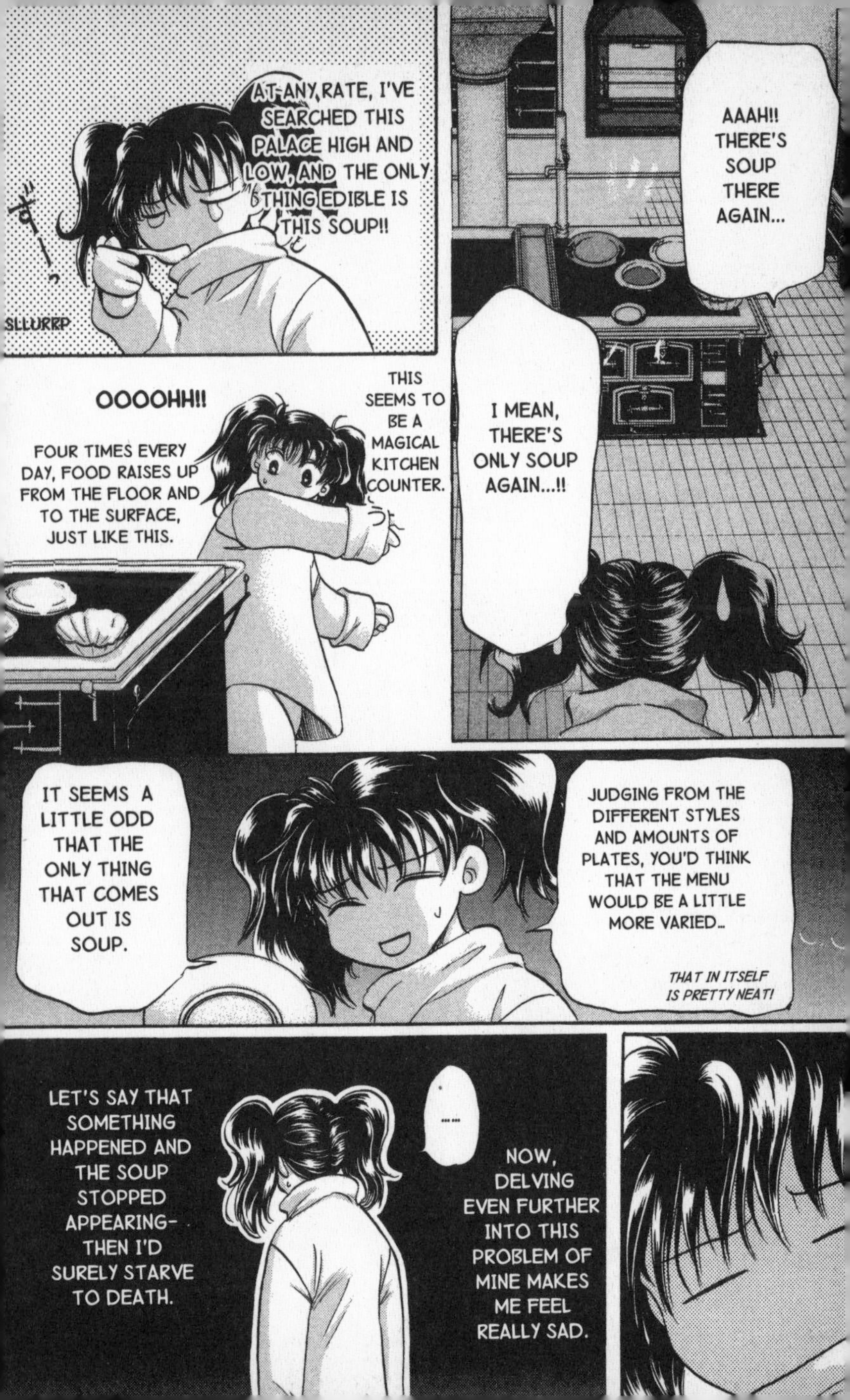
AAAH!! THERE'S SOUP THERE AGAIN...
I MEAN, THERE'S ONLY SOUP AGAIN...!!
AT ANY RATE, I'VE SEARCHED THIS PALACE HIGH AND LOW, AND THE ONLY THING EDIBLE IS THIS SOUP!!
SLLURRP
THIS SEEMS TO BE A MAGICAL KITCHEN COUNTER.
OOOOHH!!
FOUR TIMES EVERY DAY, FOOD RAISES UP FROM THE FLOOR AND TO THE SURFACE, JUST LIKE THIS.
JUDGING FROM THE DIFFERENT STYLES AND AMOUNTS OF PLATES, YOU'D THINK THAT THE MENU WOULD BE A LITTLE MORE VARIED...
THAT IN ITSELF IS PRETTY NEAT!
IT SEEMS A LITTLE ODD THAT THE ONLY THING THAT COMES OUT IS SOUP.
......
NOW, DELVING EVEN FURTHER INTO THIS PROBLEM OF MINE MAKES ME FEEL REALLY SAD.
LET'S SAY THAT SOMETHING HAPPENED AND THE SOUP STOPPED APPEARING- THEN I'D SURELY STARVE TO DEATH.

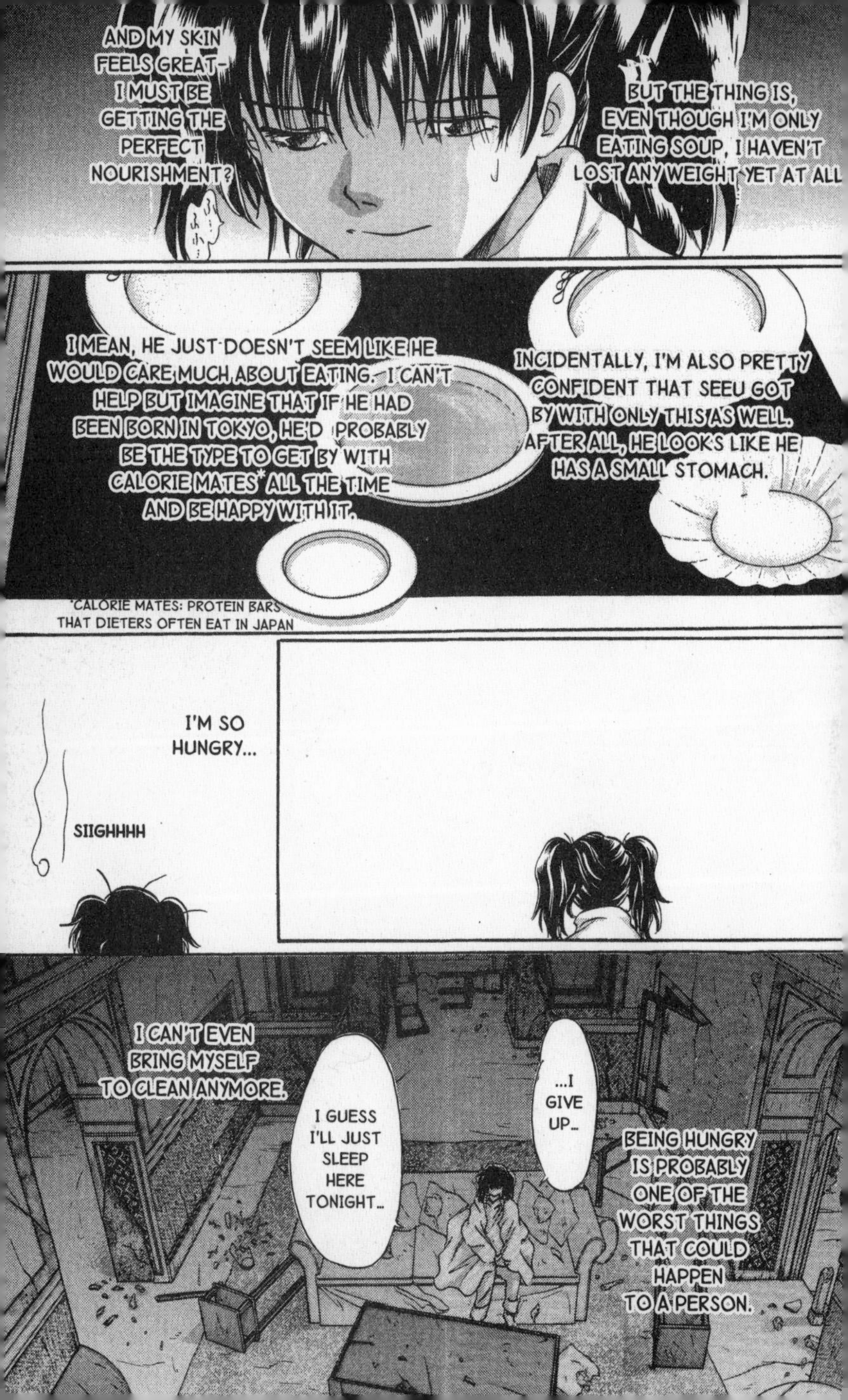
BUT THE THING IS, EVEN THOUGH I'M ONLY EATING SOUP, I HAVEN'T LOST ANY WEIGHT YET AT ALL
AND MY SKIN FEELS GREAT- I MUST BE GETTING THE PERFECT NOURISHMENT?
INCIDENTALLY, I'M ALSO PRETTY CONFIDENT THAT SEEU GOT BY WITH ONLY THIS AS WELL. AFTER ALL, HE LOOKS LIKE HE HAS A SMALL STOMACH.
I MEAN, HE JUST DOESN'T SEEM LIKE HE WOULD CARE MUCH ABOUT EATING. I CAN'T HELP BUT IMAGINE THAT IF HE HAD BEEN BORN IN TOKYO, HE'D PROBABLY BE THE TYPE TO GET BY WITH CALORIE MATES* ALL THE TIME AND BE HAPPY WITH IT.
I'M SO HUNGRY...
SIIGHHHH
BEING HUNGRY IS PROBABLY ONE OF THE WORST THINGS THAT COULD HAPPEN TO A PERSON.
...I GIVE UP...
I GUESS I'LL JUST SLEEP HERE TONIGHT...
I CAN'T EVEN BRING MYSELF TO CLEAN ANYMORE.

*CALORIE MATES: PROTEIN BARS THAT DIETERS OFTEN EAT IN JAPAN

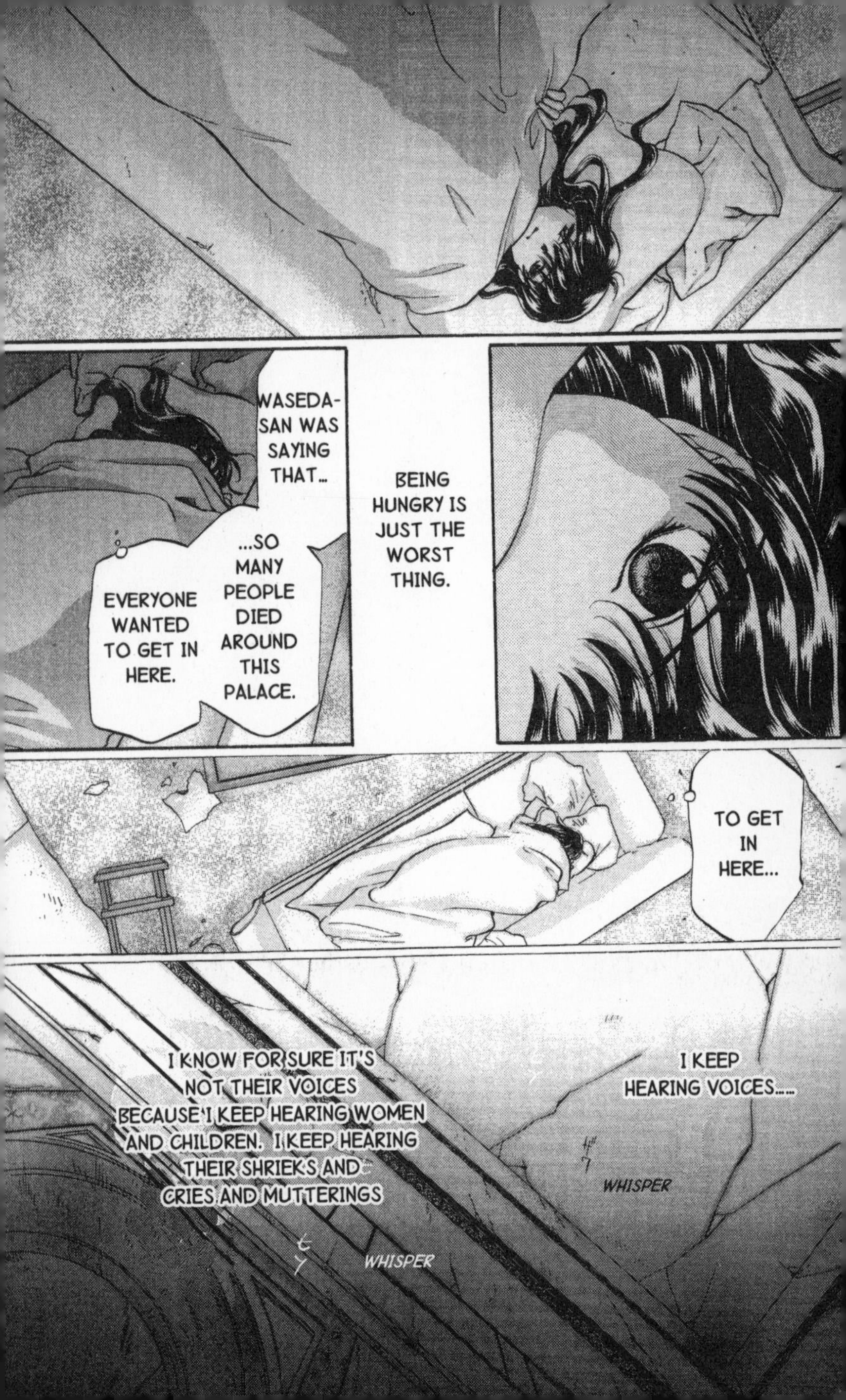
BEING HUNGRY IS JUST THE WORST THING.
WASEDA-SAN WAS SAYING THAT...
...SO MANY PEOPLE DIED AROUND THIS PALACE.
EVERYONE WANTED TO GET IN HERE.
TO GET IN HERE...
I KEEP HEARING VOICES.....
WHISPER
I KNOW FOR SURE IT'S NOT THEIR VOICES BECAUSE I KEEP HEARING WOMEN AND CHILDREN. I KEEP HEARING THEIR SHRIEKS AND CRIES AND MUTTERINGS
WHISPER

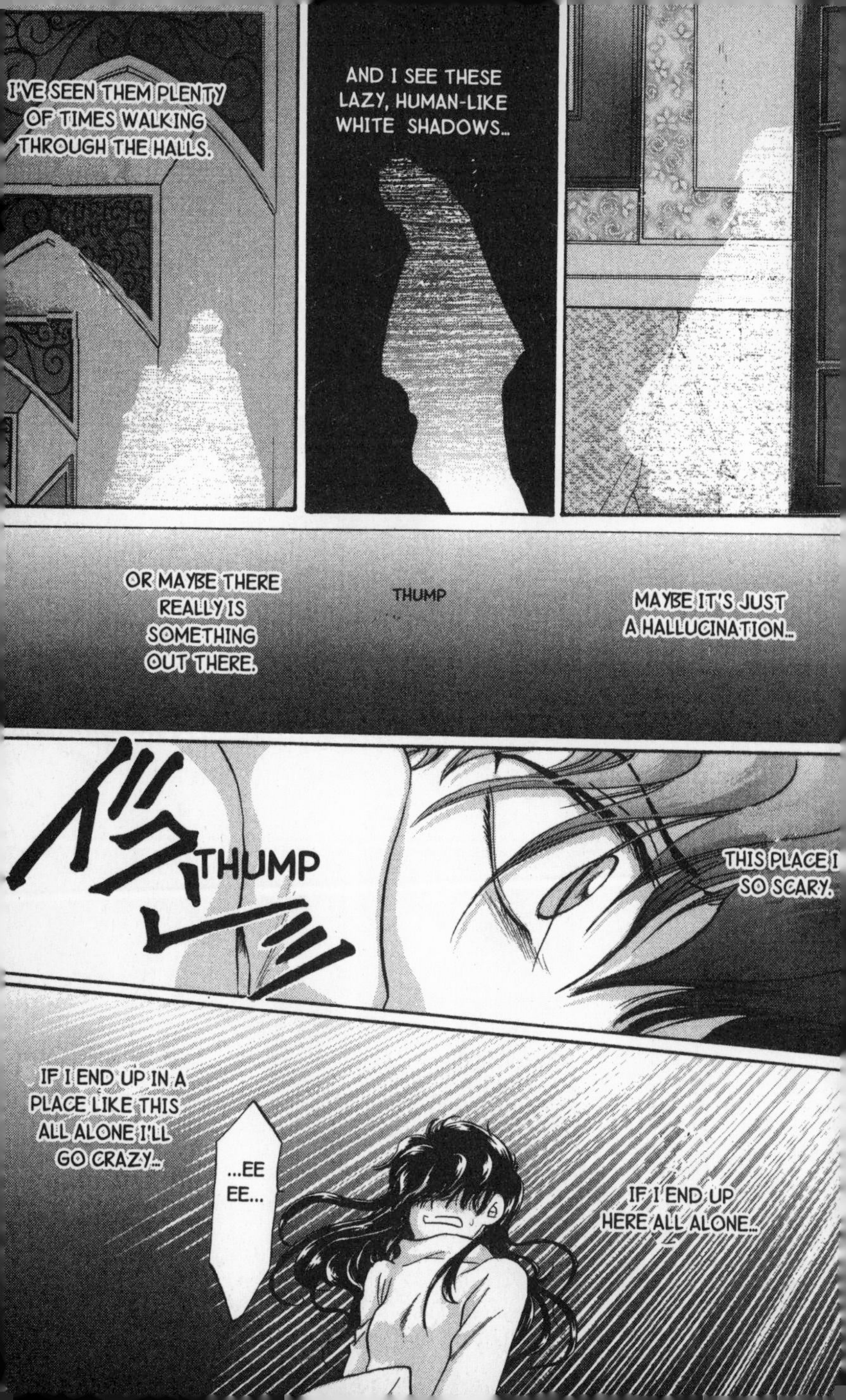
AND I SEE THESE LAZY, HUMAN-LIKE WHITE SHADOWS...
I'VE SEEN THEM PLENTY OF TIMES WALKING THROUGH THE HALLS.
MAYBE IT'S JUST A HALLUCINATION...
THUMP
OR MAYBE THERE REALLY IS SOMETHING OUT THERE.
THIS PLACE I SO SCARY.
THUMP
IF I END UP HERE ALL ALONE...
...EE EE...
IF I END UP IN A PLACE LIKE THIS ALL ALONE I'LL GO CRAZY...

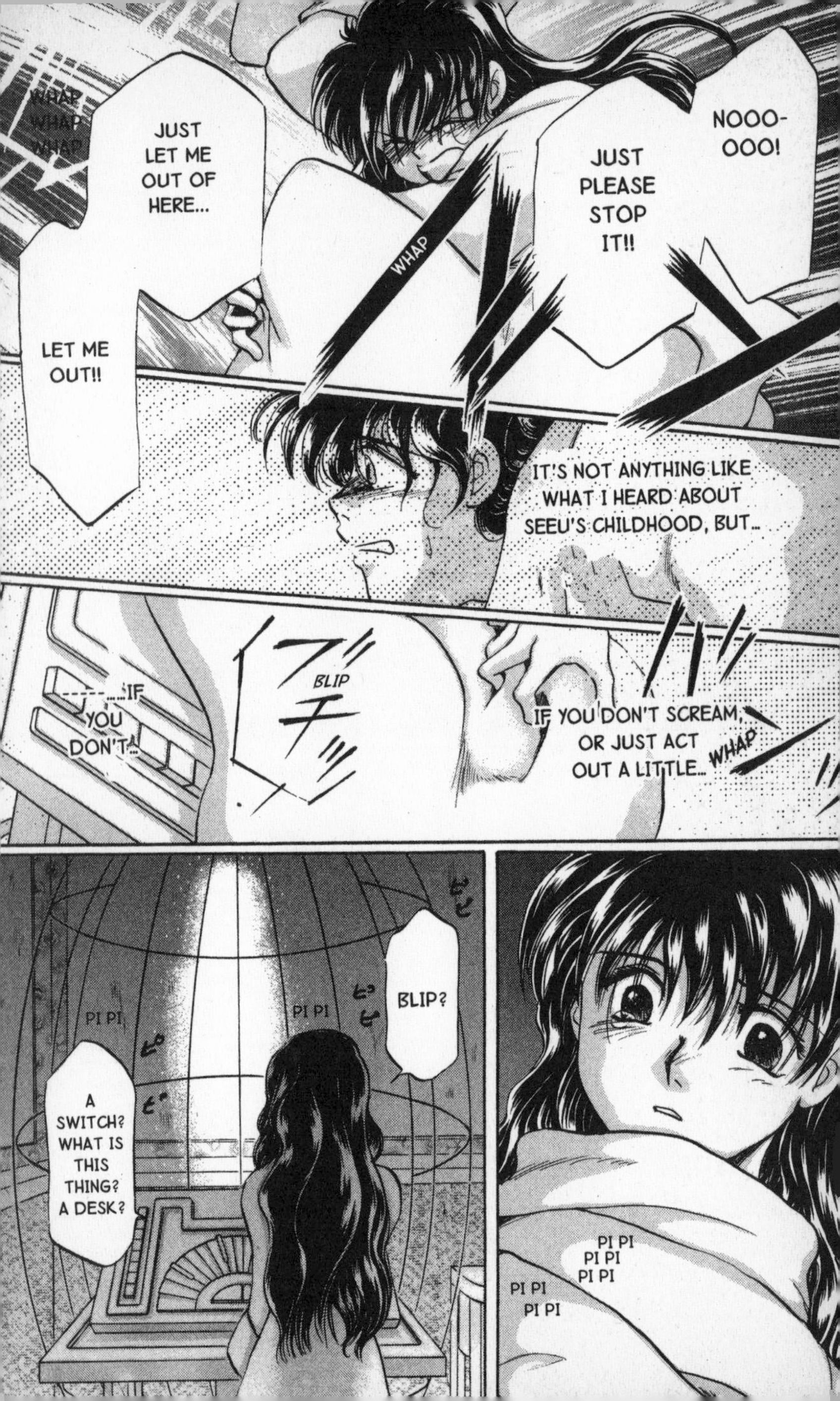
NOOO-OOO!
JUST PLEASE STOP IT!!
WHAP
WHAP WHAP WHAP
JUST LET ME OUT OF HERE...
LET ME OUT!!
IT'S NOT ANYTHING LIKE WHAT I HEARD ABOUT SEEU'S CHILDHOOD, BUT...
IF YOU DON'T SCREAM, OR JUST ACT OUT A LITTLE...
WHAP
BLIP
......IF YOU DON'T...
PI PI
PI PI
PI PI
PI PI
PI PI
BLIP?
PI PI
PI PI
A SWITCH? WHAT IS THIS THING? A DESK?

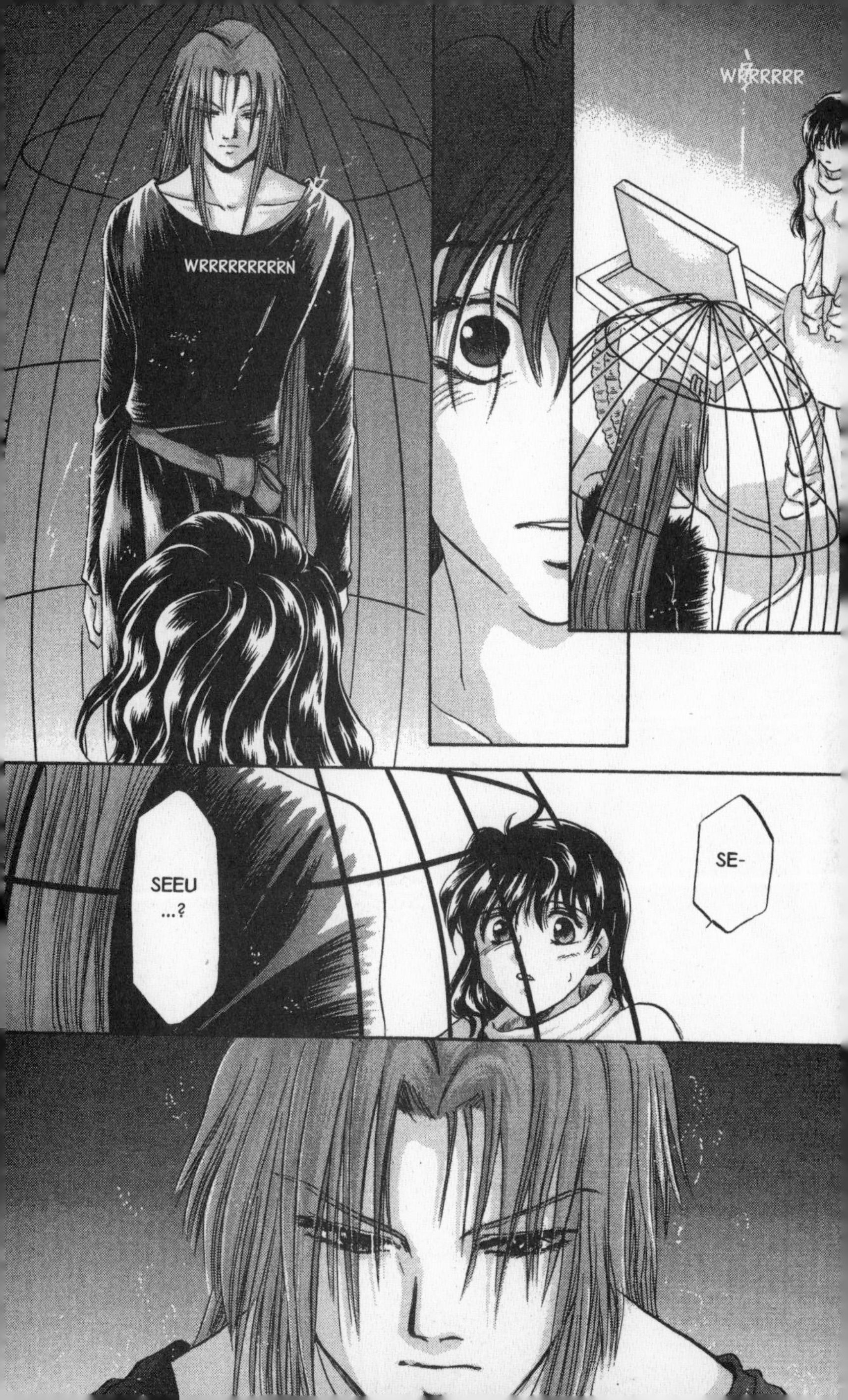
WRRRRRR
WRRRRRRRRRN
SE-
SEEU ...?

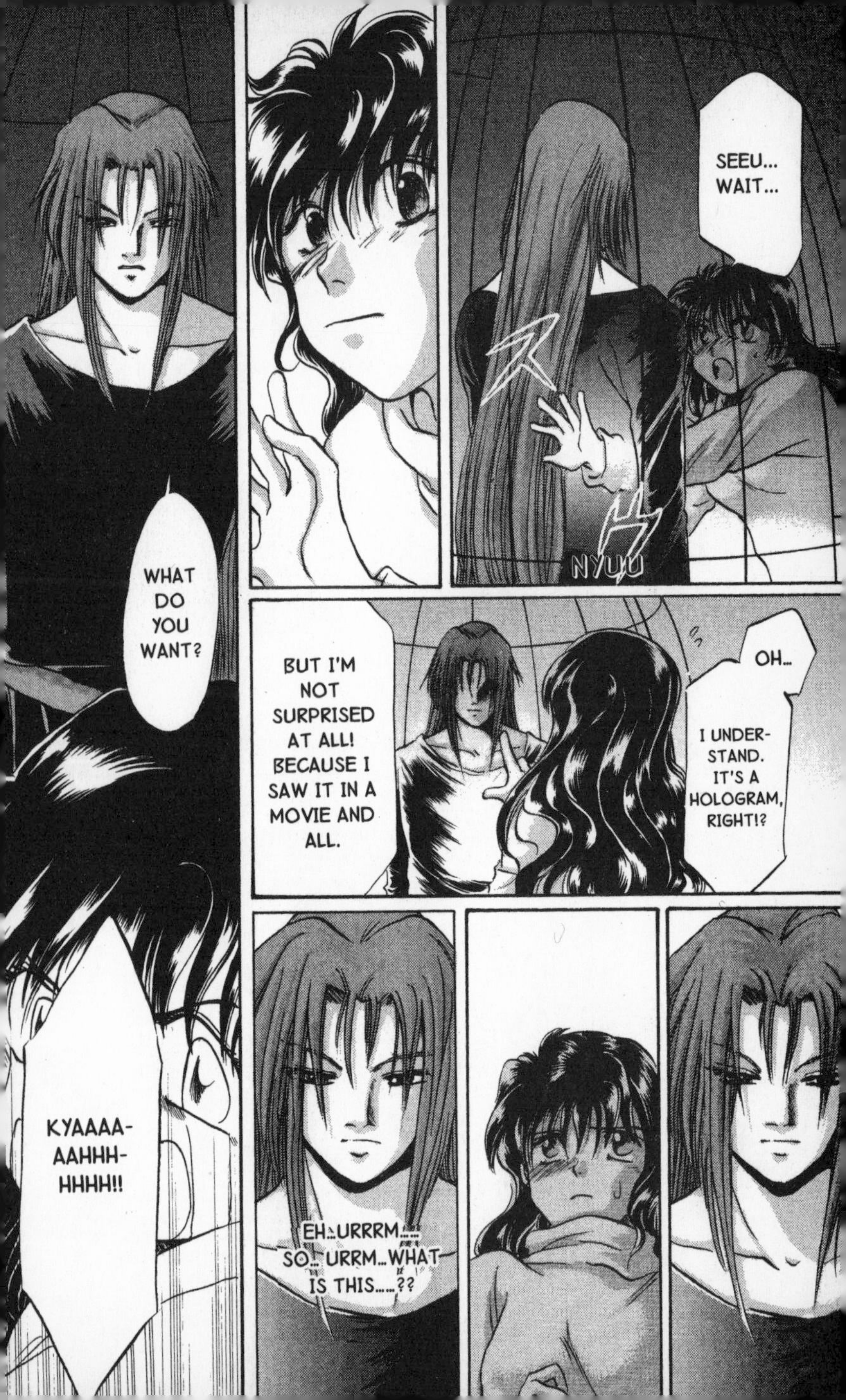
SEEU... WAIT...
NYUU
OH...
I UNDER-STAND. IT'S A HOLOGRAM, RIGHT!?
BUT I'M NOT SURPRISED AT ALL! BECAUSE I SAW IT IN A MOVIE AND ALL.
EH...URRRM..... SO... URRM...WHAT IS THIS.....??
WHAT DO YOU WANT?
KYAAAA-AAHHH-HHHH!!

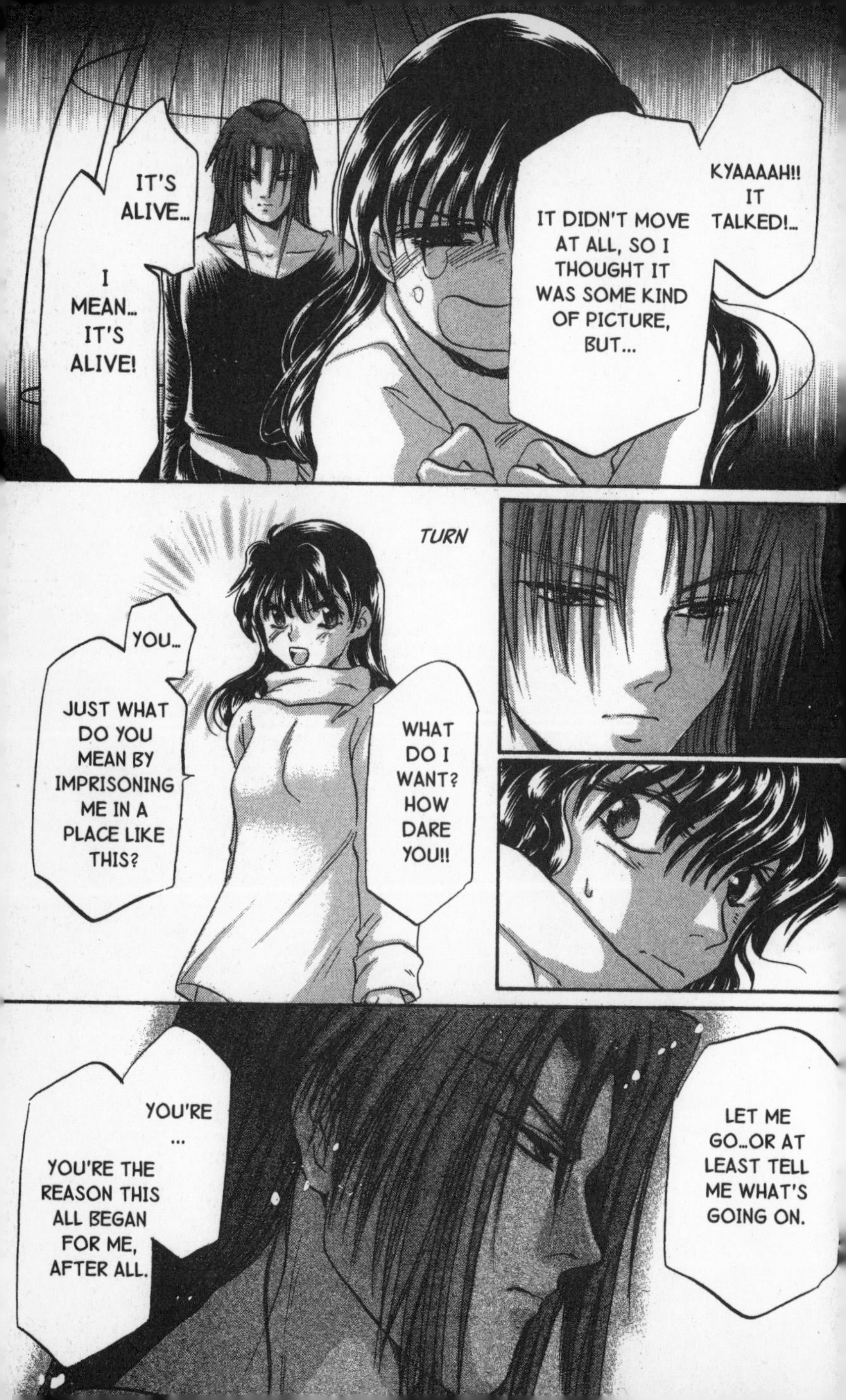
KYAAAAH!! IT TALKED!...
IT DIDN'T MOVE AT ALL, SO I THOUGHT IT WAS SOME KIND OF PICTURE, BUT...
IT'S ALIVE...
I MEAN... IT'S ALIVE!
TURN
WHAT DO I WANT? HOW DARE YOU!!
YOU...
JUST WHAT DO YOU MEAN BY IMPRISONING ME IN A PLACE LIKE THIS?
LET ME GO...OR AT LEAST TELL ME WHAT'S GOING ON.
YOU'RE ...
YOU'RE THE REASON THIS ALL BEGAN FOR ME, AFTER ALL.

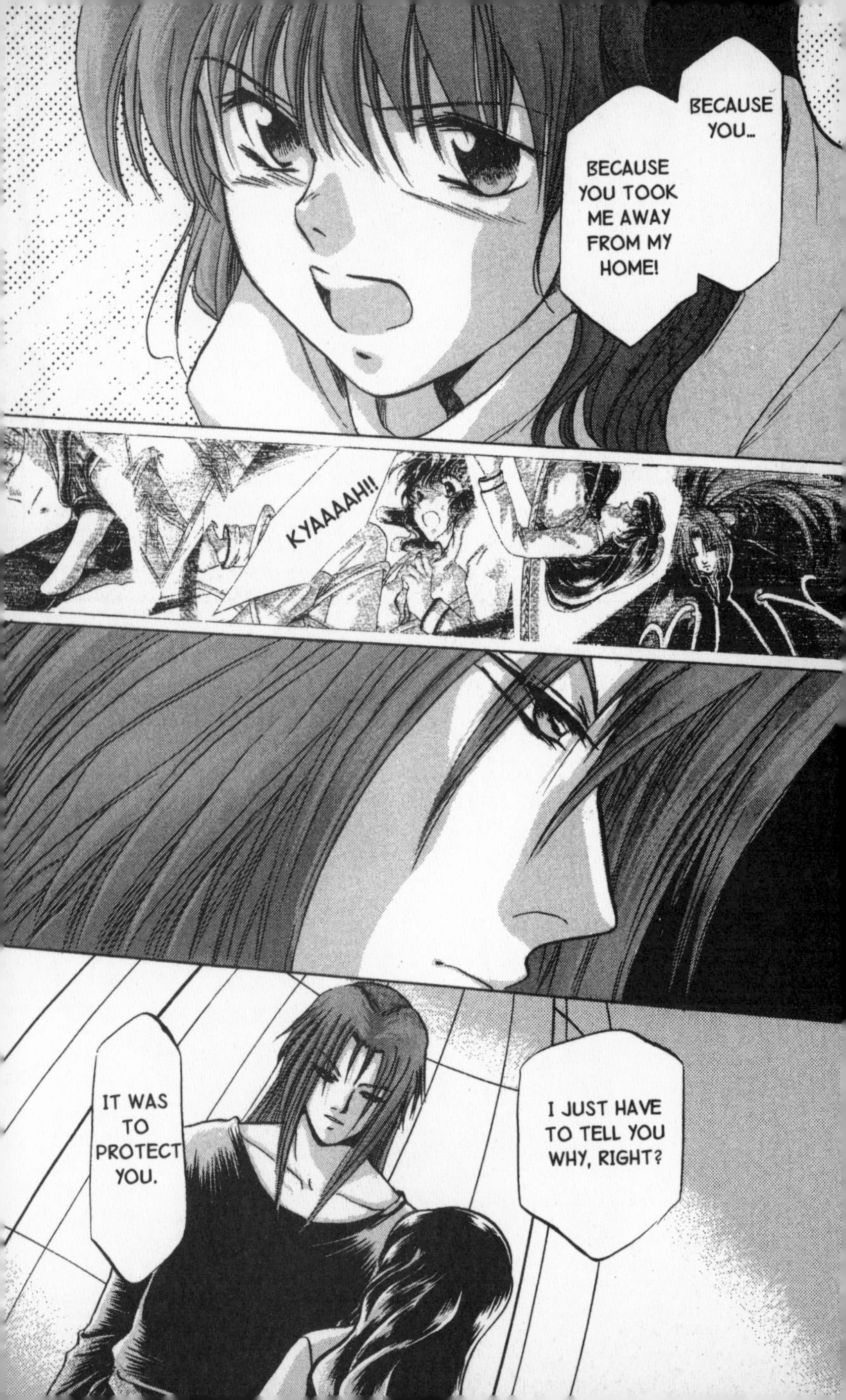
BECAUSE YOU...
BECAUSE YOU TOOK ME AWAY FROM MY HOME!
KYAAAAH!!
I JUST HAVE TO TELL YOU WHY, RIGHT?
IT WAS TO PROTECT YOU.

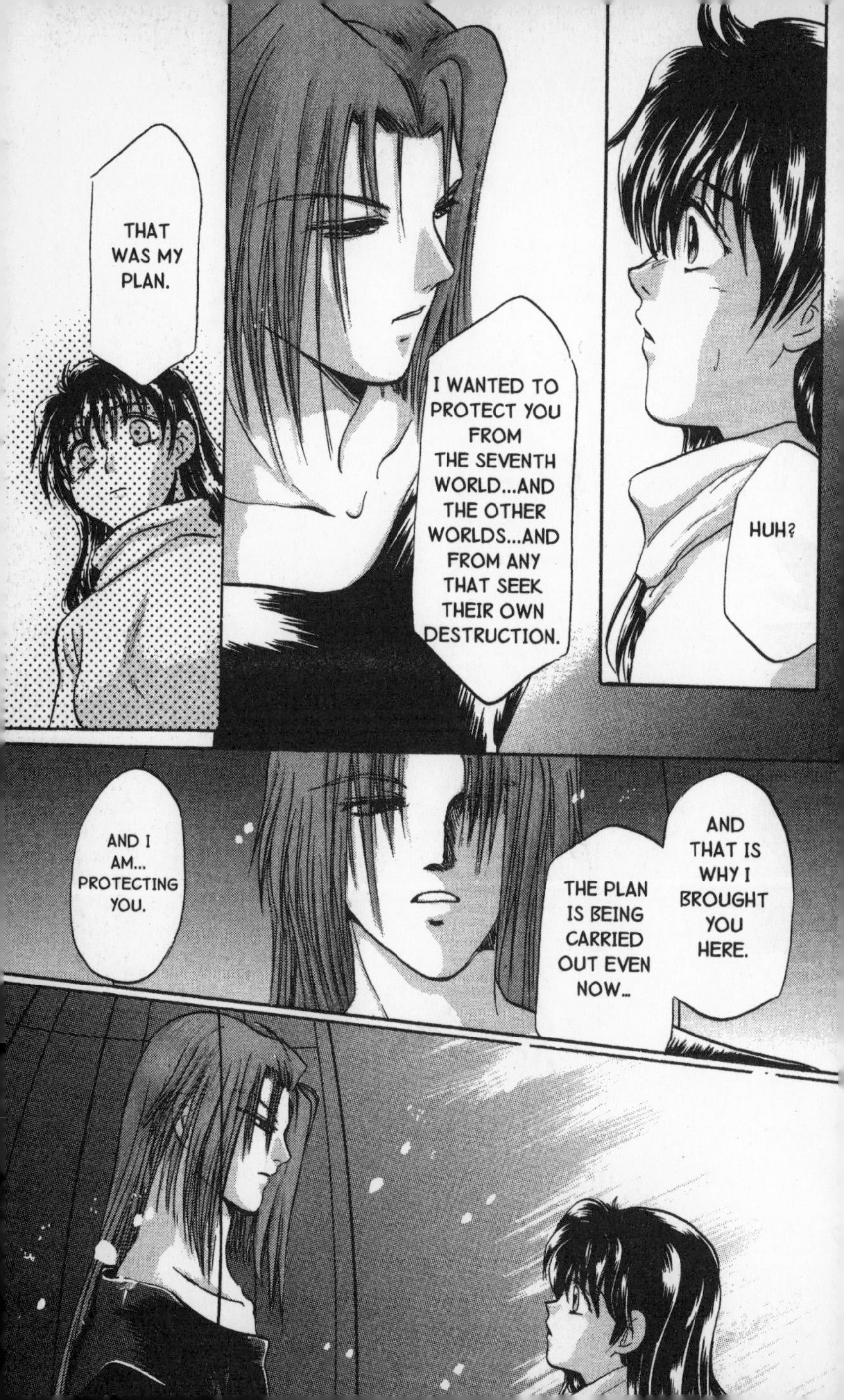
HUH?
I WANTED TO PROTECT YOU FROM THE SEVENTH WORLD...AND THE OTHER WORLDS...AND FROM ANY THAT SEEK THEIR OWN DESTRUCTION.
THAT WAS MY PLAN.
AND THAT IS WHY I BROUGHT YOU HERE.
THE PLAN IS BEING CARRIED OUT EVEN NOW...
AND I AM... PROTECTING YOU.

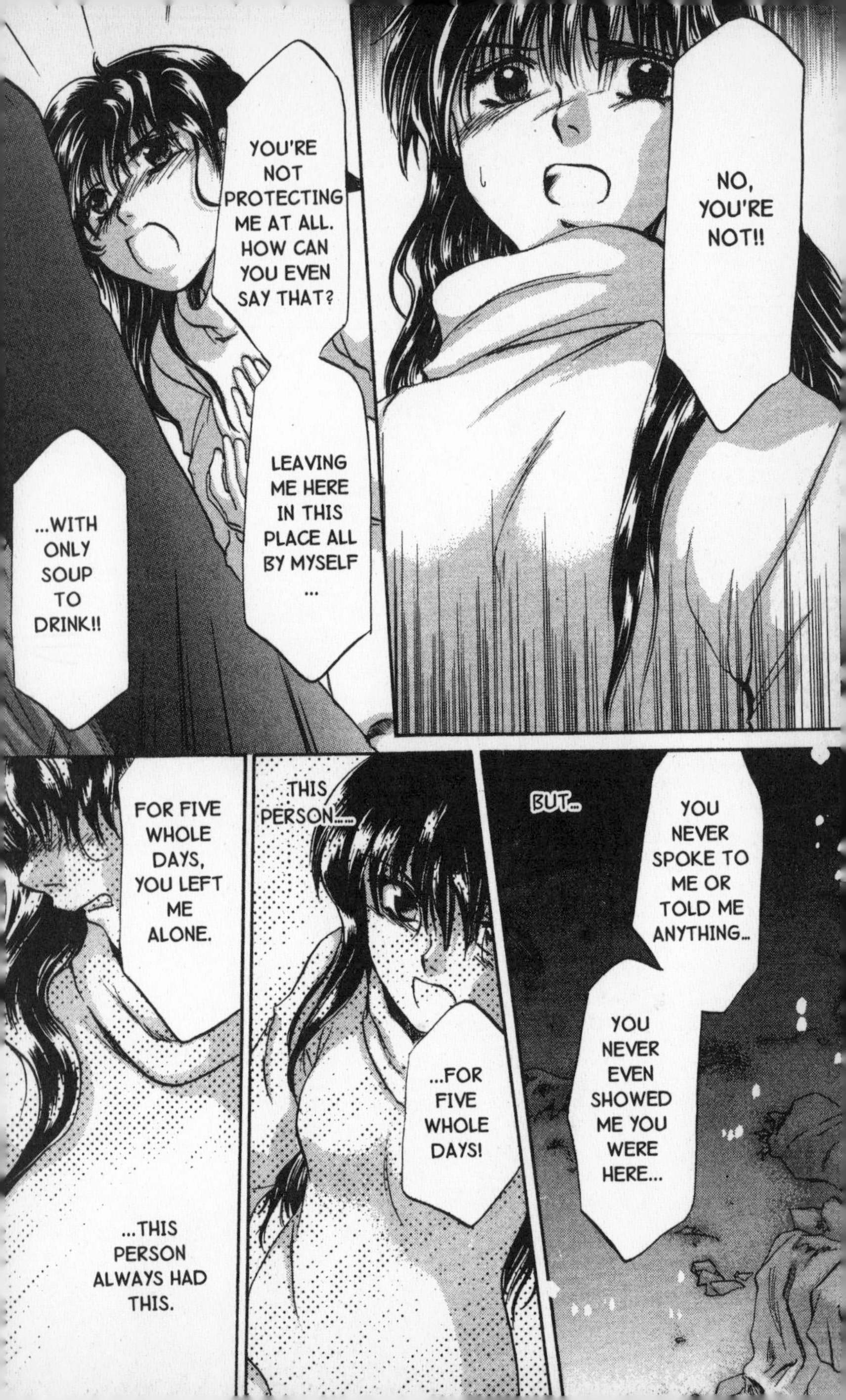
NO, YOU'RE NOT!!
YOU'RE NOT PROTECTING ME AT ALL. HOW CAN YOU EVEN SAY THAT?
LEAVING ME HERE IN THIS PLACE ALL BY MYSELF ...
...WITH ONLY SOUP TO DRINK!!
BUT...
YOU NEVER SPOKE TO ME OR TOLD ME ANYTHING...
YOU NEVER EVEN SHOWED ME YOU WERE HERE...
THIS PERSON.....
...FOR FIVE WHOLE DAYS!
FOR FIVE WHOLE DAYS, YOU LEFT ME ALONE.
...THIS PERSON ALWAYS HAD THIS.

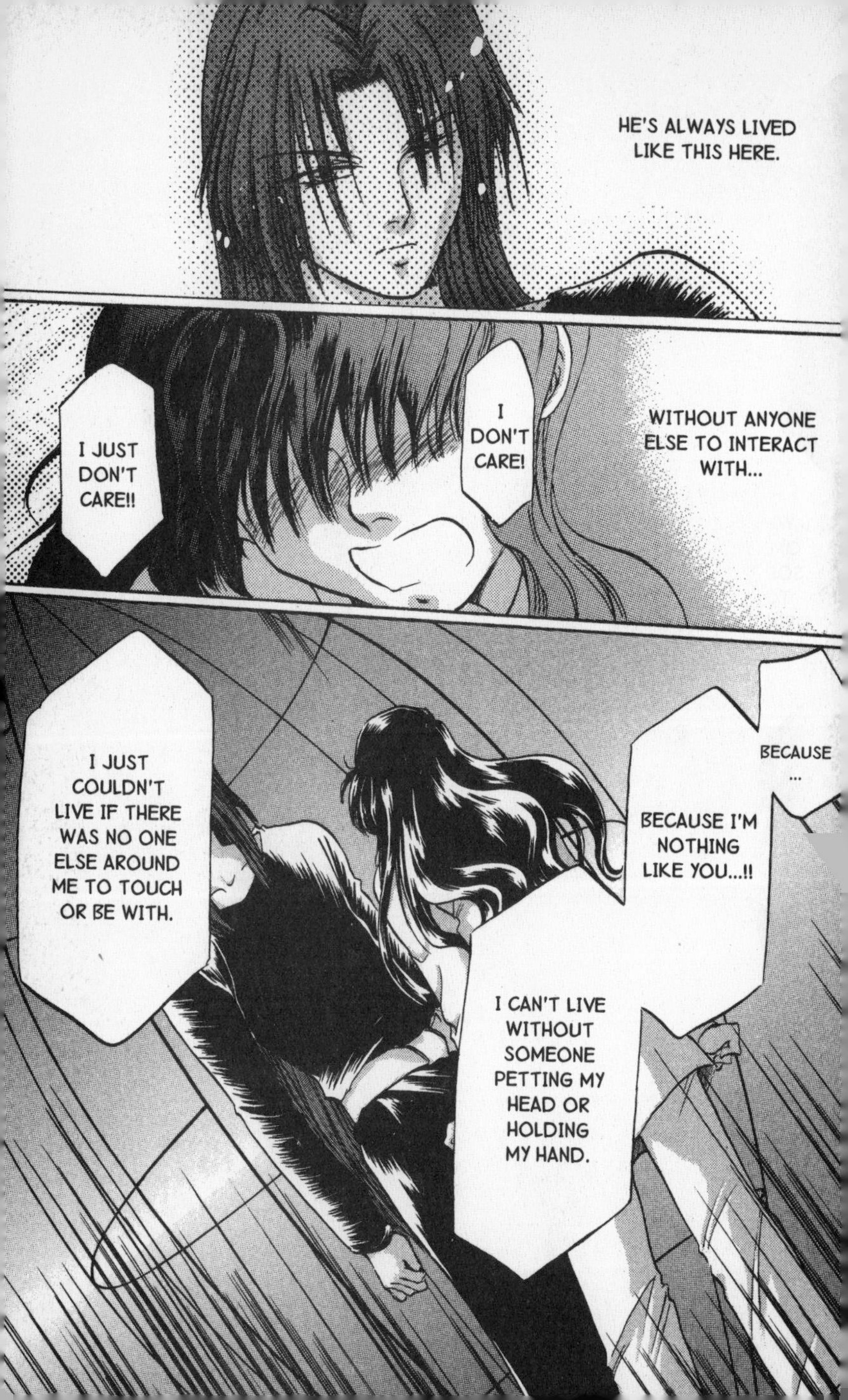
HE'S ALWAYS LIVED LIKE THIS HERE.
WITHOUT ANYONE ELSE TO INTERACT WITH...
I DON'T CARE!
I JUST DON'T CARE!!
BECAUSE ...
BECAUSE I'M NOTHING LIKE YOU...!!
I CAN'T LIVE WITHOUT SOMEONE PETTING MY HEAD OR HOLDING MY HAND.
I JUST COULDN'T LIVE IF THERE WAS NO ONE ELSE AROUND ME TO TOUCH OR BE WITH.

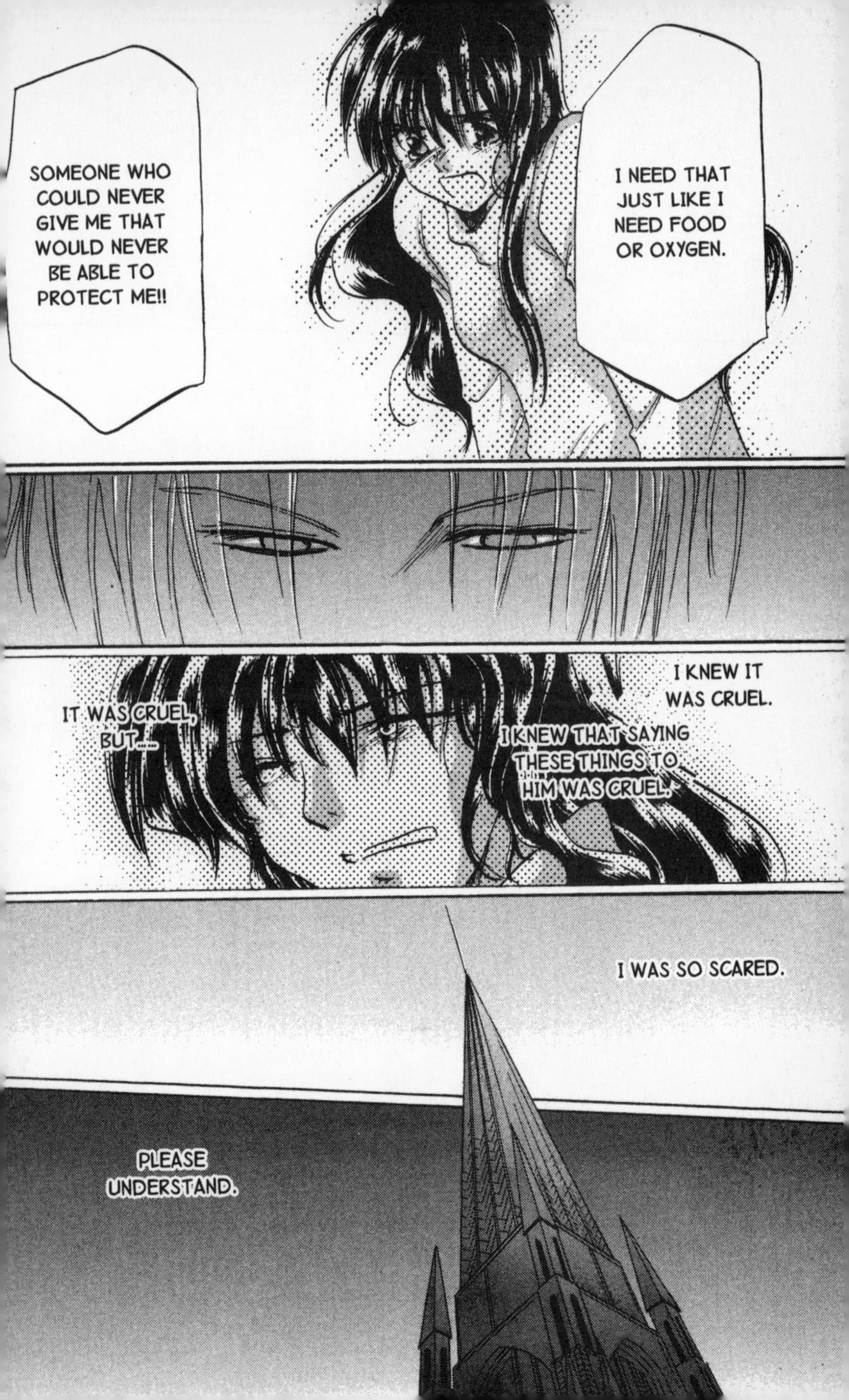
I NEED THAT JUST LIKE I NEED FOOD OR OXYGEN.
SOMEONE WHO COULD NEVER GIVE ME THAT WOULD NEVER BE ABLE TO PROTECT ME!!
I KNEW IT WAS CRUEL.
I KNEW THAT SAYING THESE THINGS TO HIM WAS CRUEL.
IT WAS CRUEL, BUT.....
I WAS SO SCARED.
PLEASE UNDERSTAND.

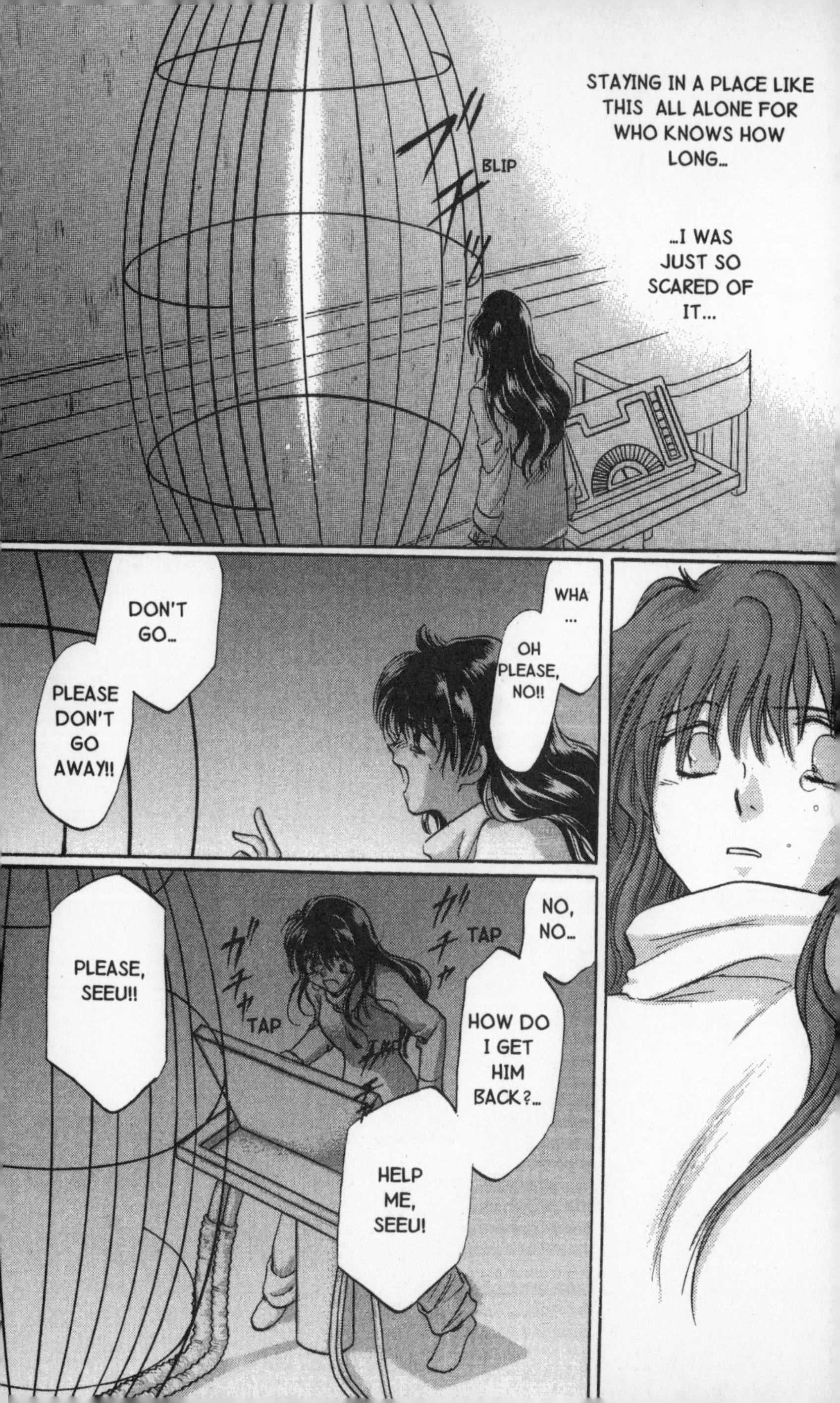
STAYING IN A PLACE LIKE THIS ALL ALONE FOR WHO KNOWS HOW LONG...
BLIP
...I WAS JUST SO SCARED OF IT...
WHA...
OH PLEASE, NO!!
DON'T GO...
PLEASE DON'T GO AWAY!!
NO, NO...
TAP
HOW DO I GET HIM BACK?...
TAP
PLEASE, SEEU!!
HELP ME, SEEU!

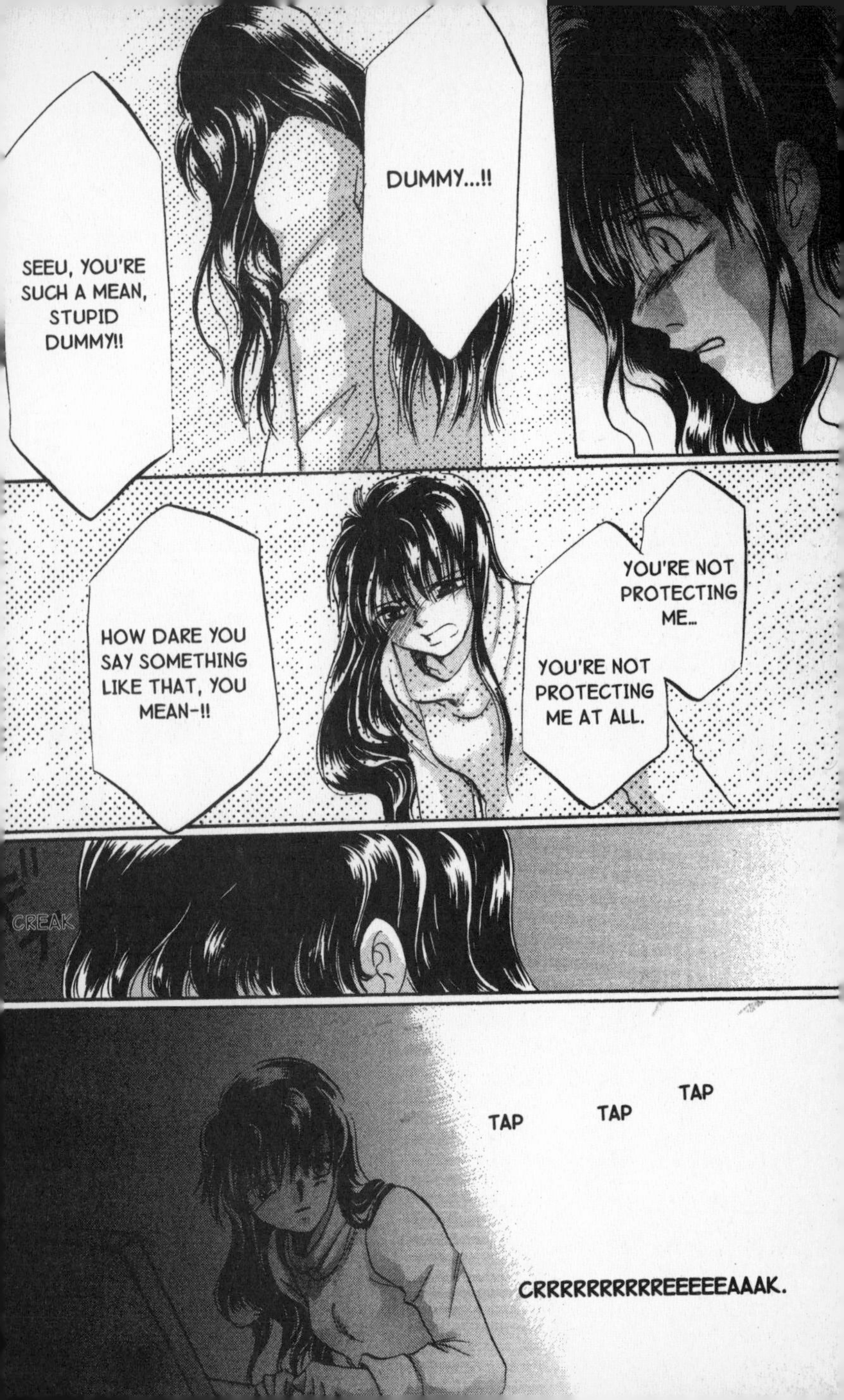
DUMMY...!!
SEEU, YOU'RE SUCH A MEAN, STUPID DUMMY!!
YOU'RE NOT PROTECTING ME..
YOU'RE NOT PROTECTING ME AT ALL.
HOW DARE YOU SAY SOMETHING LIKE THAT, YOU MEAN-!!
CREAK
TAP
TAP
TAP
CRRRRRRRRRREEEEEAAAK.

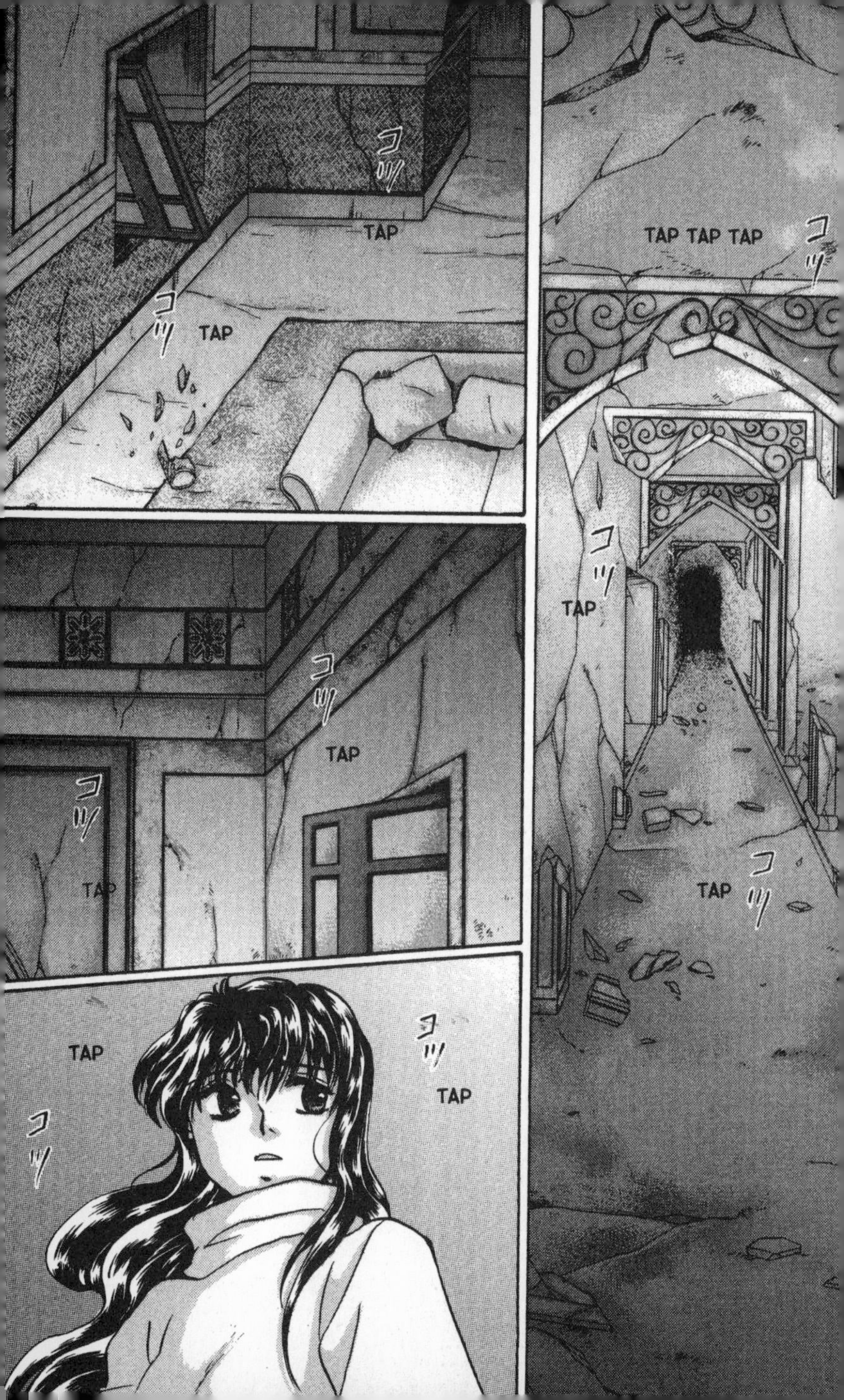
コッ
TAP TAP TAP
コッ
TAP
コッ
TAP
コッ
TAP
コッ
TAP
コッ
TAP
コッ
TAP
コッ
TAP
コッ
TAP

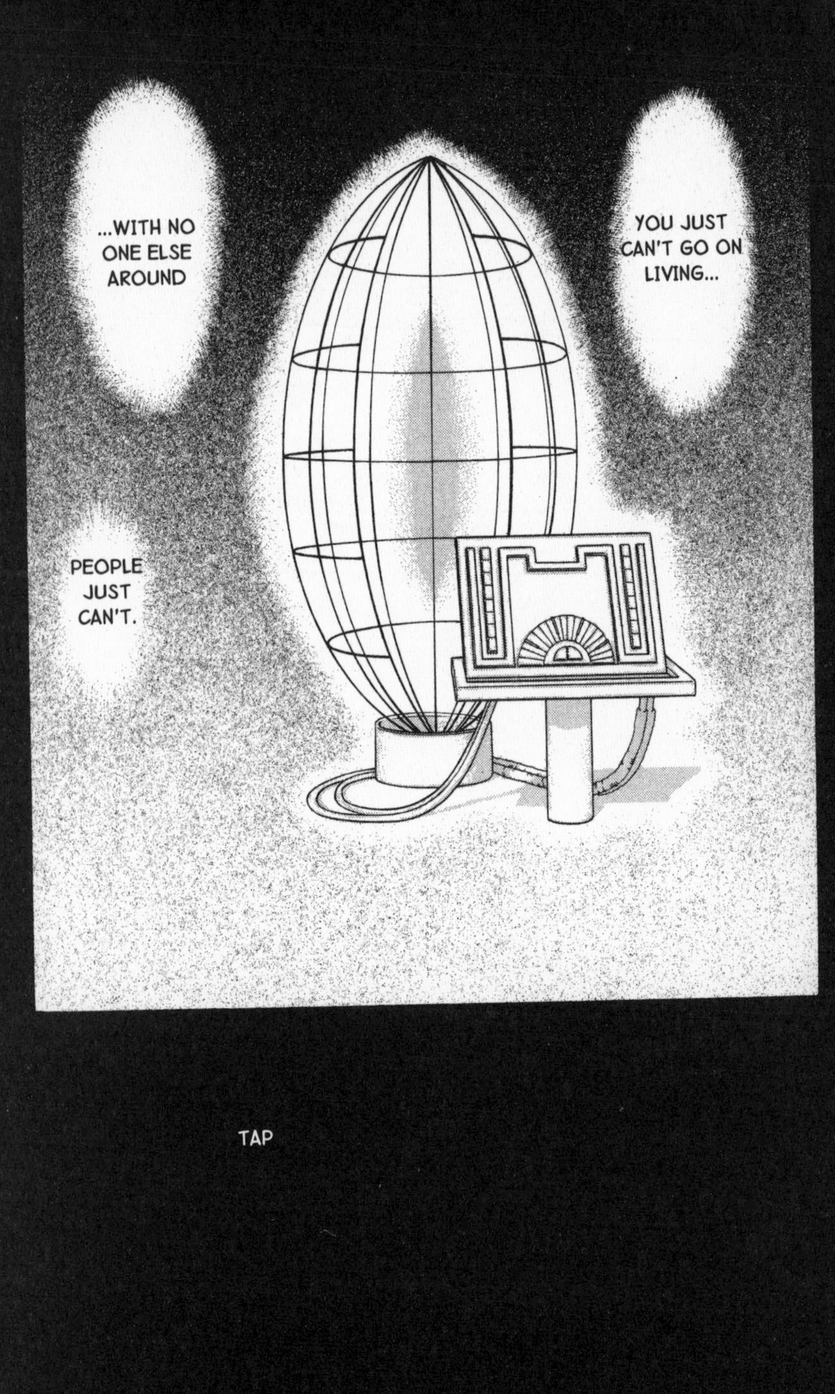
YOU JUST CAN'T GO ON LIVING...
...WITH NO ONE ELSE AROUND
PEOPLE JUST CAN'T.
TAP

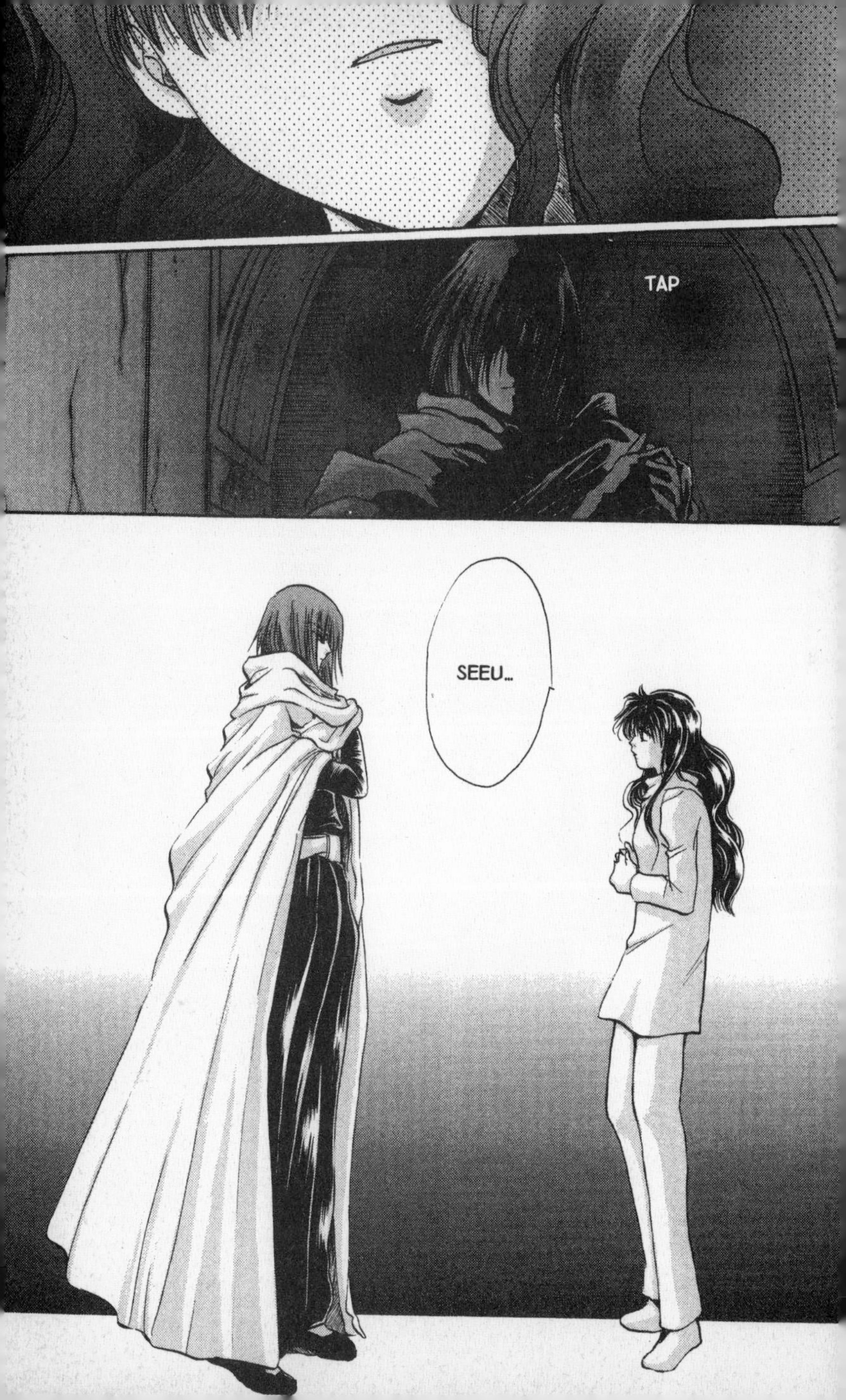
TAP
SEEU...

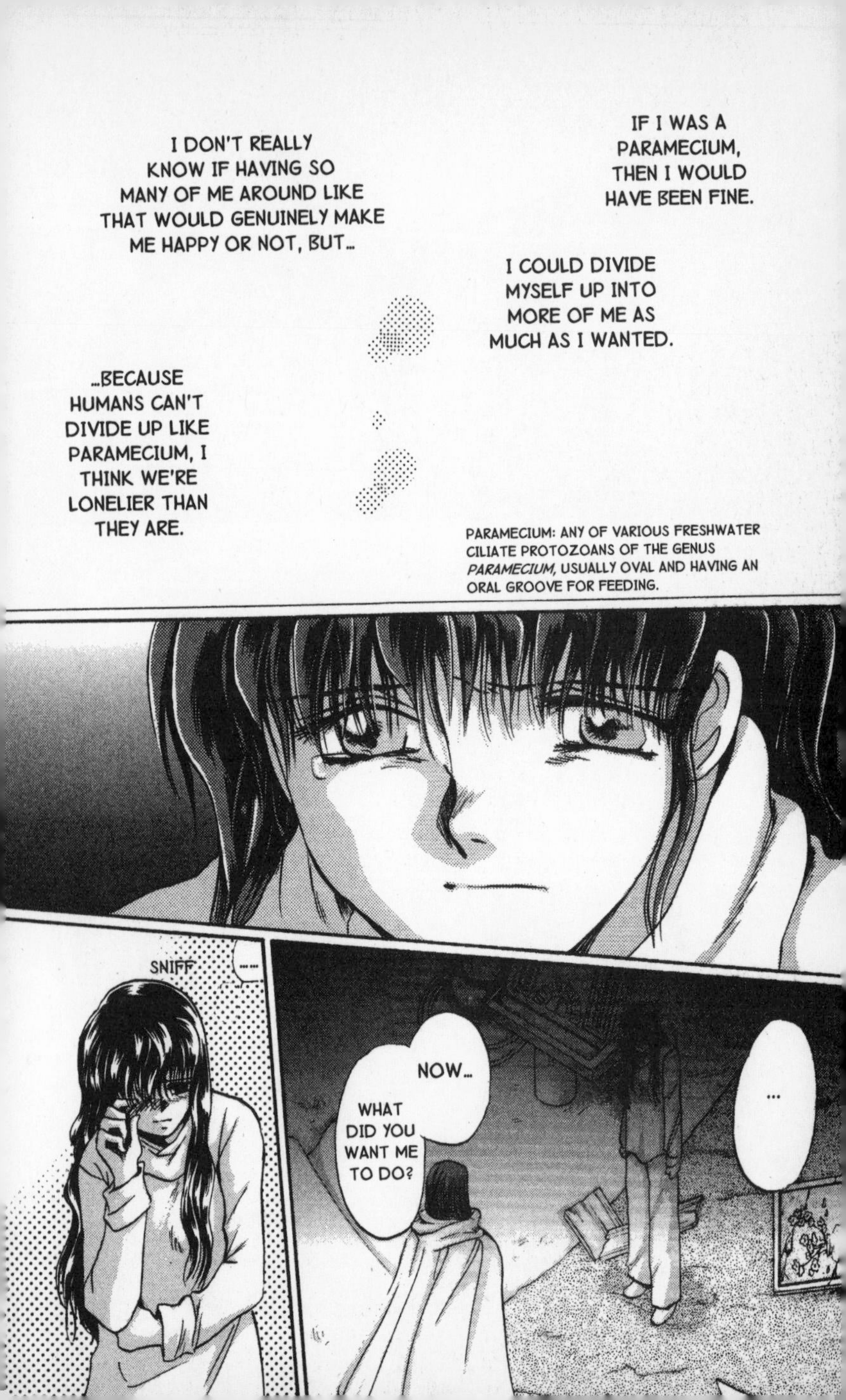
IF I WAS A PARAMECIUM, THEN I WOULD HAVE BEEN FINE.
I COULD DIVIDE MYSELF UP INTO MORE OF ME AS MUCH AS I WANTED.
I DON'T REALLY KNOW IF HAVING SO MANY OF ME AROUND LIKE THAT WOULD GENUINELY MAKE ME HAPPY OR NOT, BUT...
...BECAUSE HUMANS CAN'T DIVIDE UP LIKE PARAMECIUM, I THINK WE'RE LONELIER THAN THEY ARE.
...
NOW...
WHAT DID YOU WANT ME TO DO?
......
SNIFF

PARAMECIUM: ANY OF VARIOUS FRESHWATER CILIATE PROTOZOANS OF THE GENUS *PARAMECIUM,* USUALLY OVAL AND HAVING AN ORAL GROOVE FOR FEEDING.

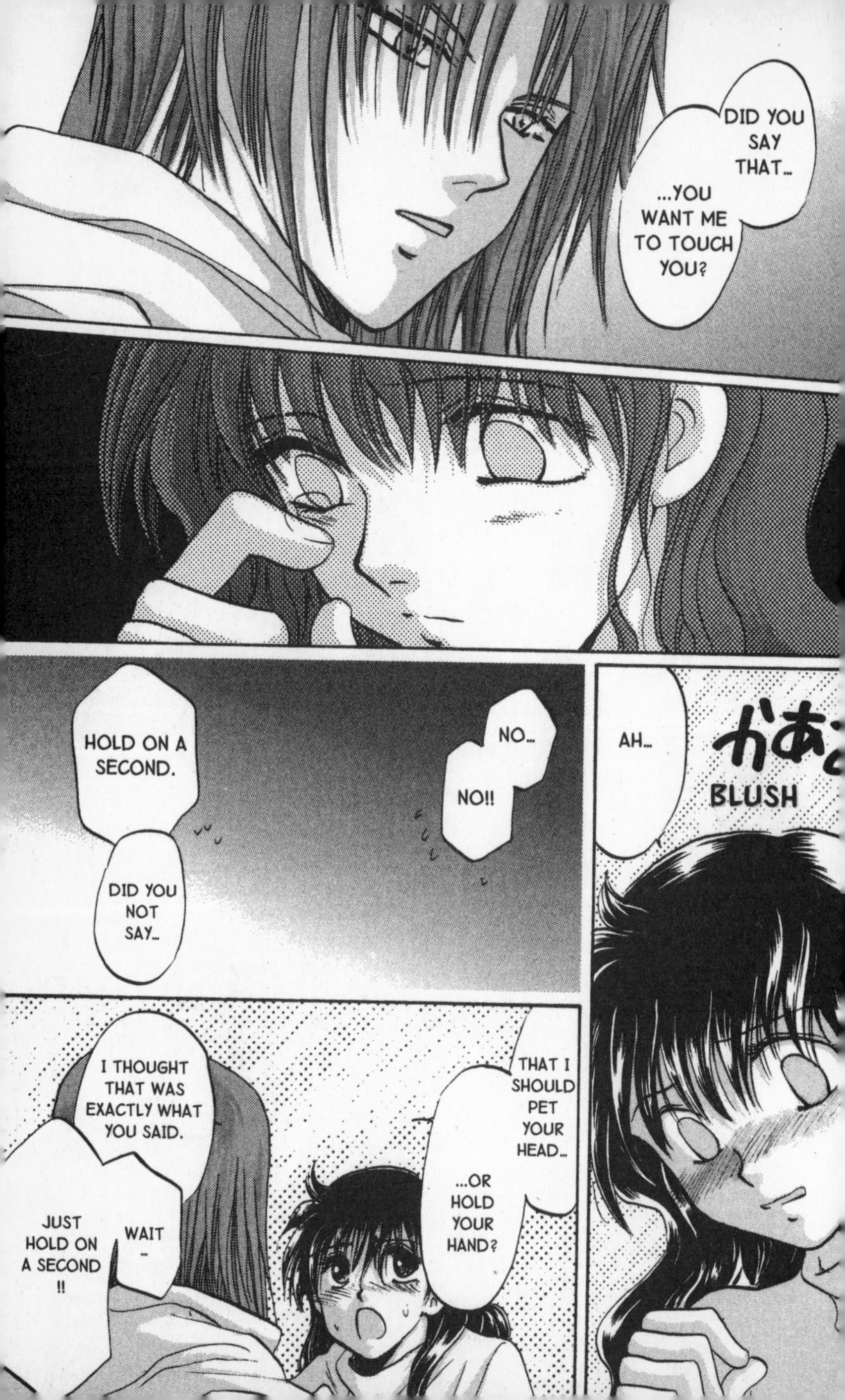
DID YOU SAY THAT...
...YOU WANT ME TO TOUCH YOU?
AH...
かあ
BLUSH
NO...
NO!!
HOLD ON A SECOND.
DID YOU NOT SAY...
THAT I SHOULD PET YOUR HEAD...
...OR HOLD YOUR HAND?
I THOUGHT THAT WAS EXACTLY WHAT YOU SAID.
WAIT...
JUST HOLD ON A SECOND!!

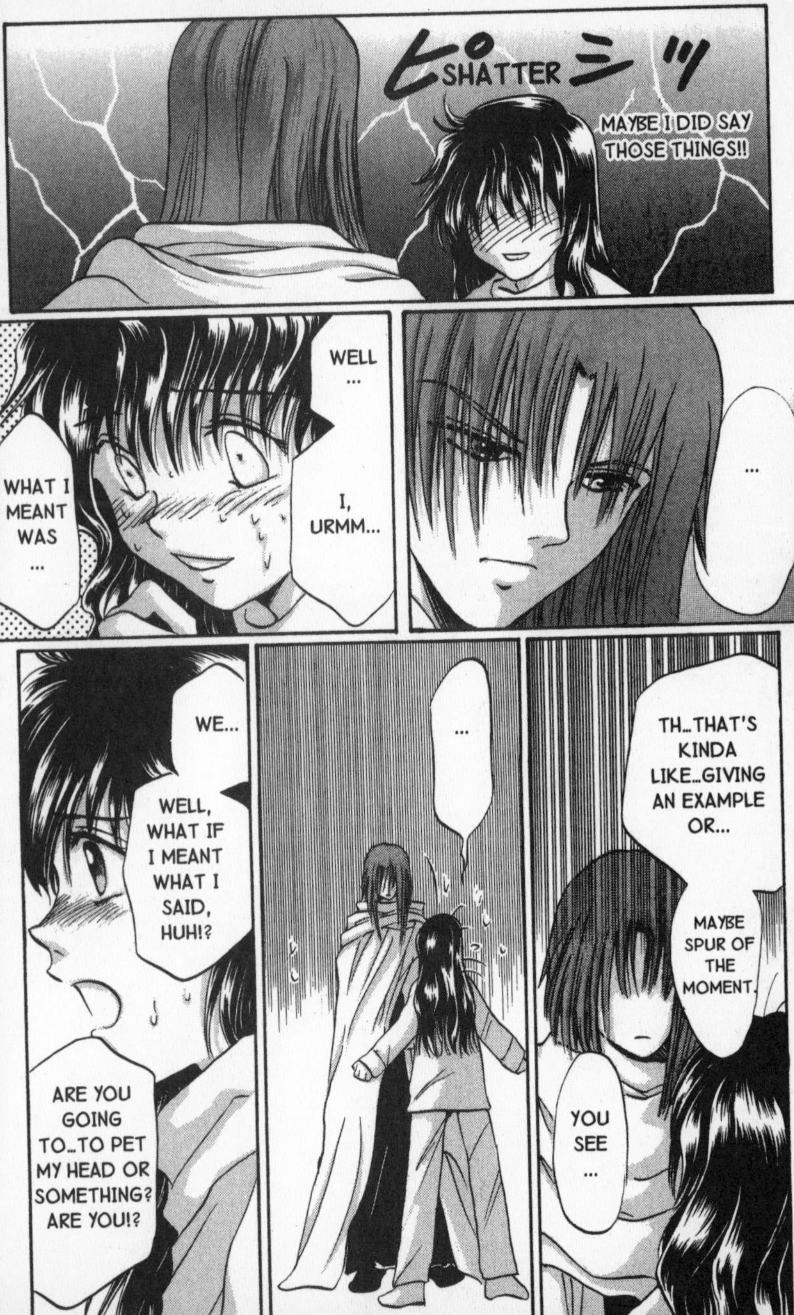
ピSHATTERシッ
MAYBE I DID SAY THOSE THINGS!!
...
WELL ...
I, URMM...
WHAT I MEANT WAS ...
TH...THAT'S KINDA LIKE...GIVING AN EXAMPLE OR...
MAYBE SPUR OF THE MOMENT.
YOU SEE ...
...
WE...
WELL, WHAT IF I MEANT WHAT I SAID, HUH!?
ARE YOU GOING TO...TO PET MY HEAD OR SOMETHING? ARE YOU!?

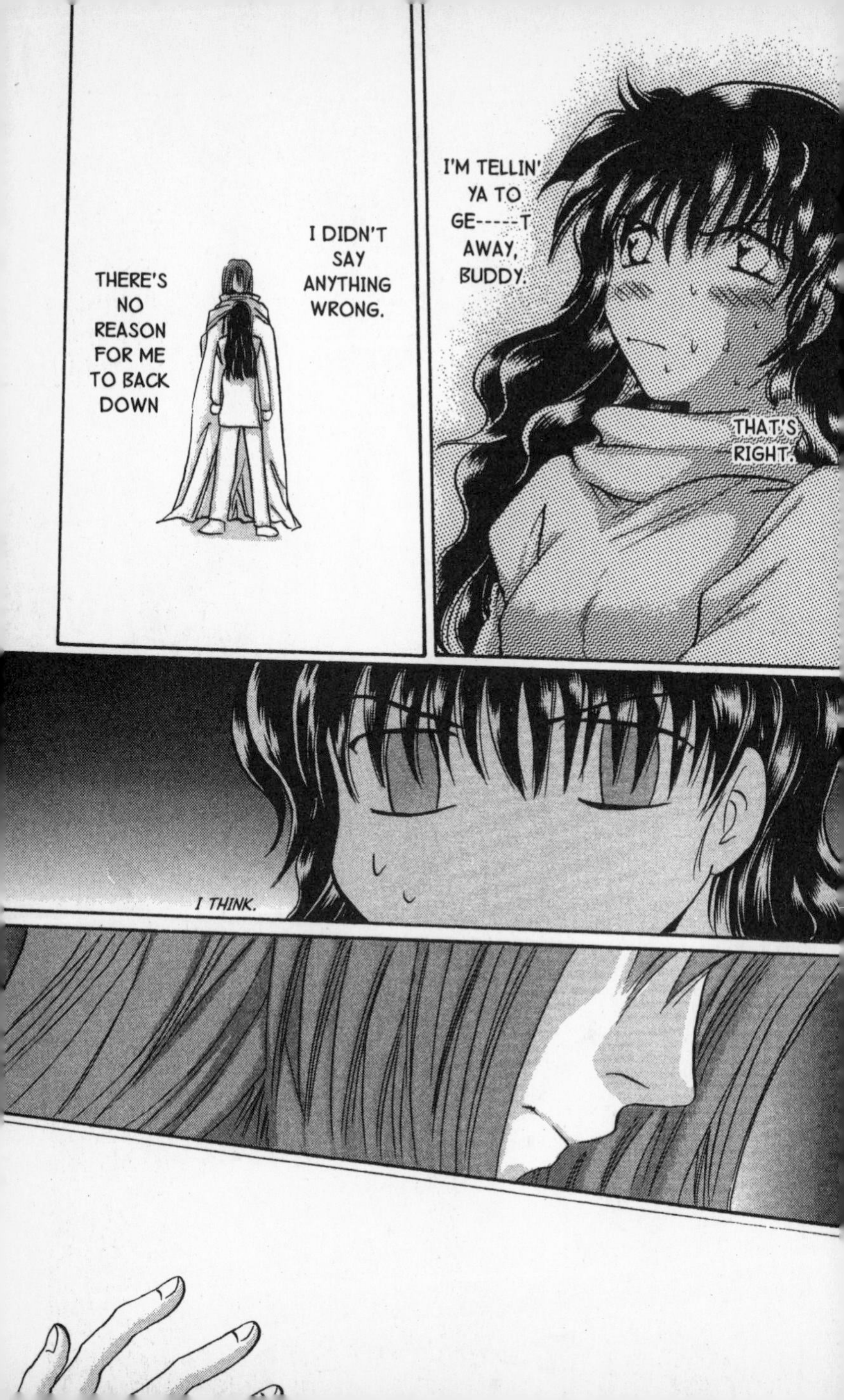
I'M TELLIN' YA TO GE-----T AWAY, BUDDY.
THAT'S RIGHT.
I DIDN'T SAY ANYTHING WRONG.
THERE'S NO REASON FOR ME TO BACK DOWN
I THINK.

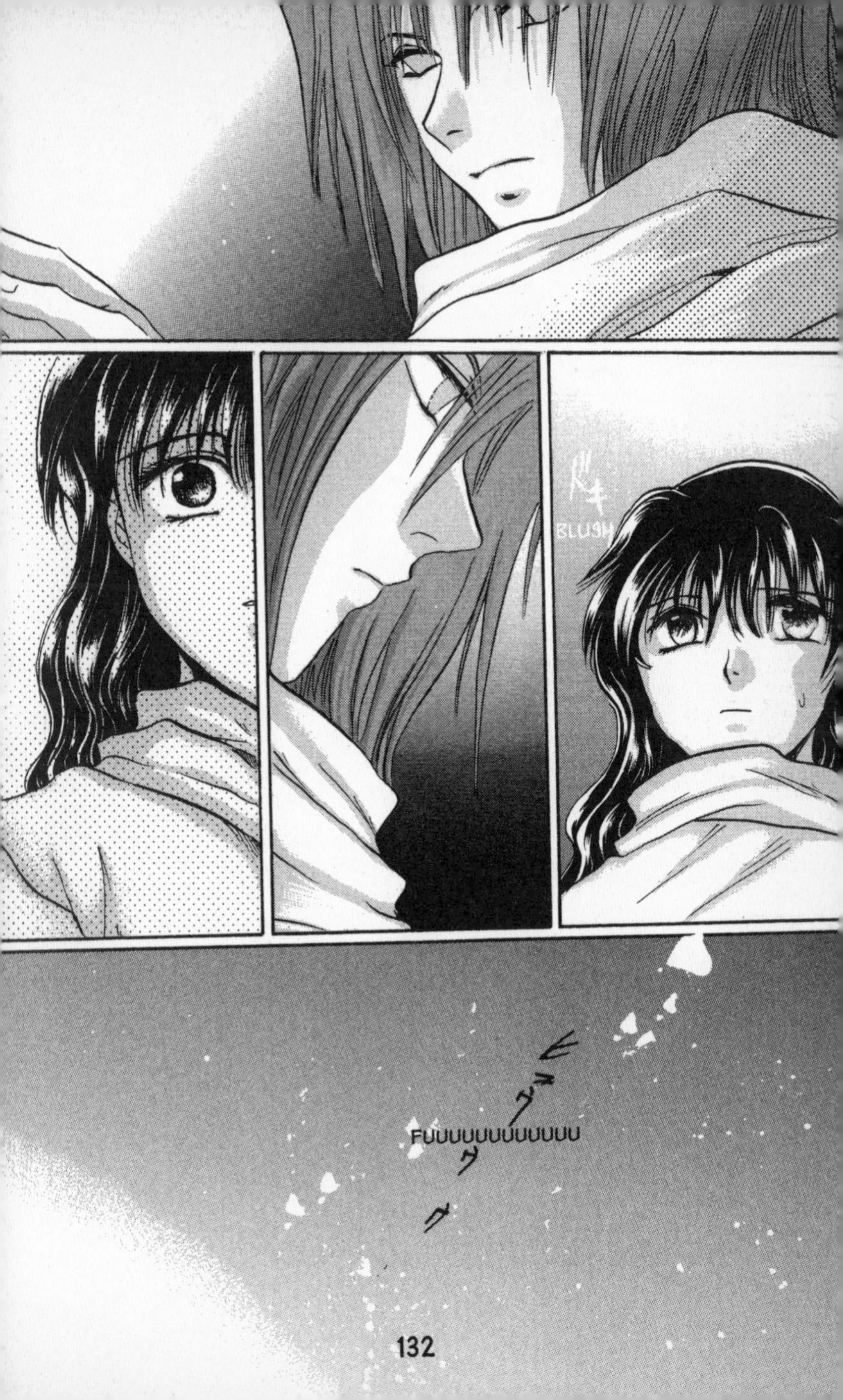
ドキ
BLUSH
ヒュウウウ
FUUUUUUUUUUUU

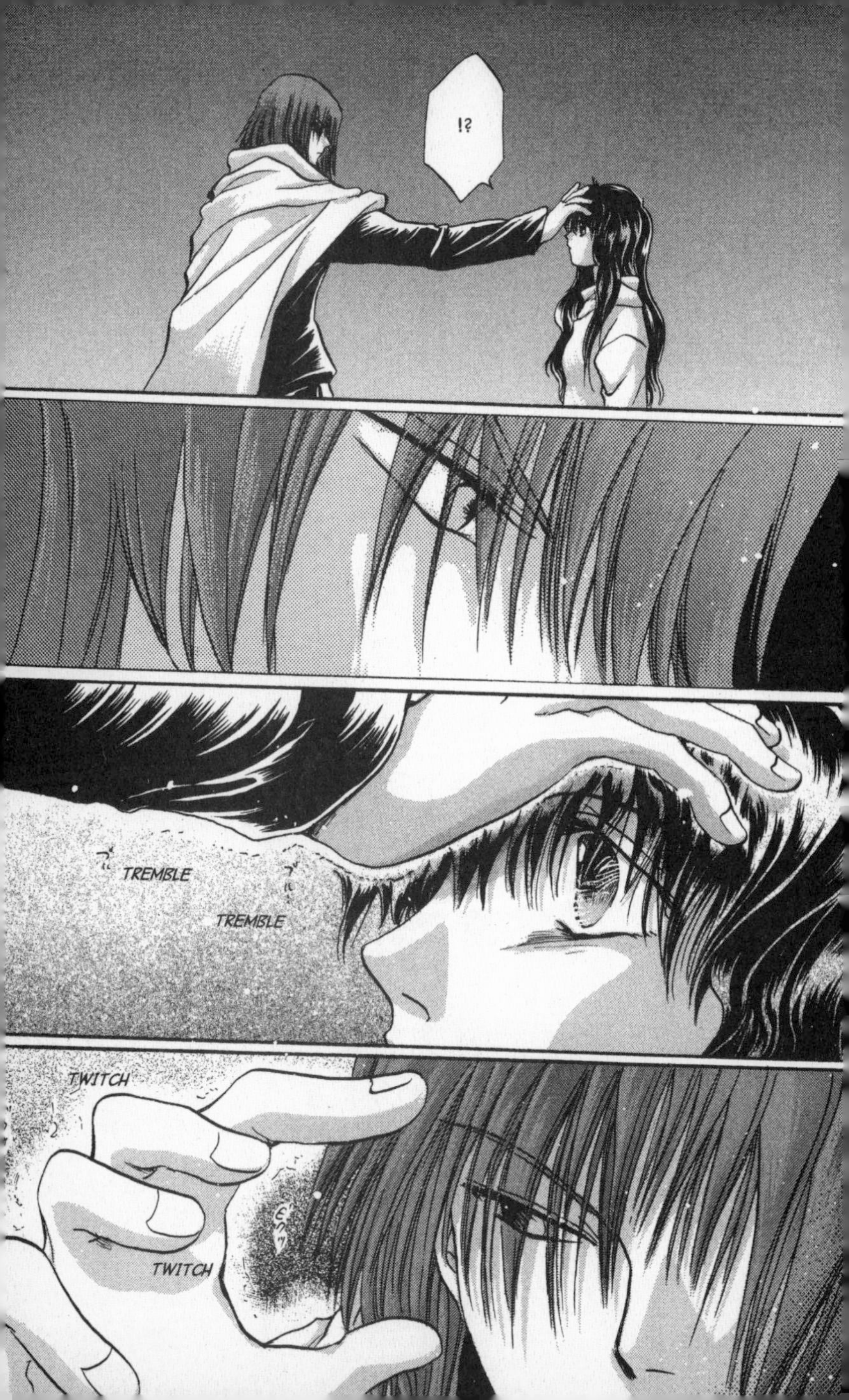
!?
TREMBLE
TREMBLE
TWITCH
TWITCH

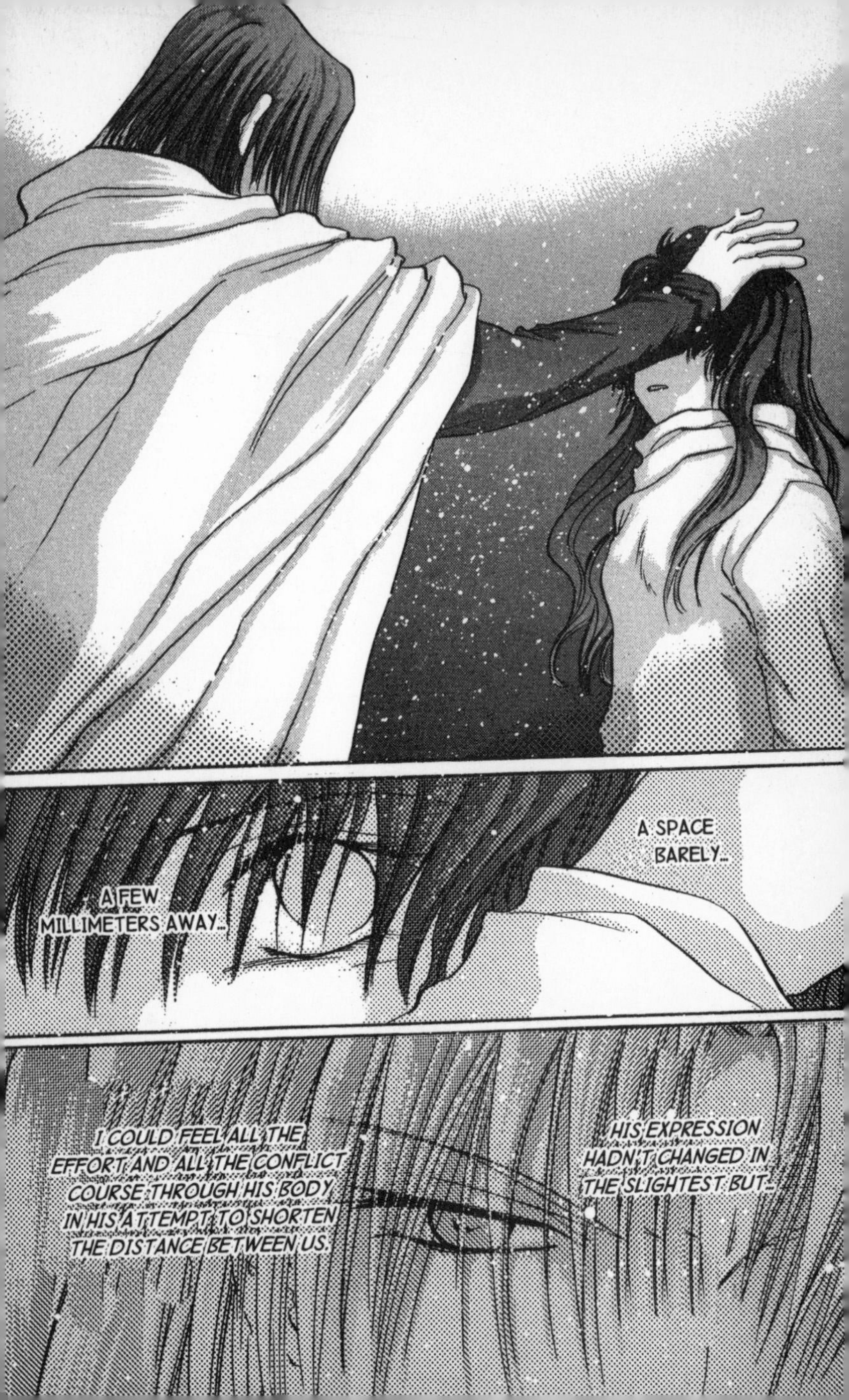
A SPACE BARELY...
A FEW MILLIMETERS AWAY...
HIS EXPRESSION HADN'T CHANGED IN THE SLIGHTEST BUT...
I COULD FEEL ALL THE EFFORT AND ALL THE CONFLICT COURSE THROUGH HIS BODY IN HIS ATTEMPT TO SHORTEN THE DISTANCE BETWEEN US.

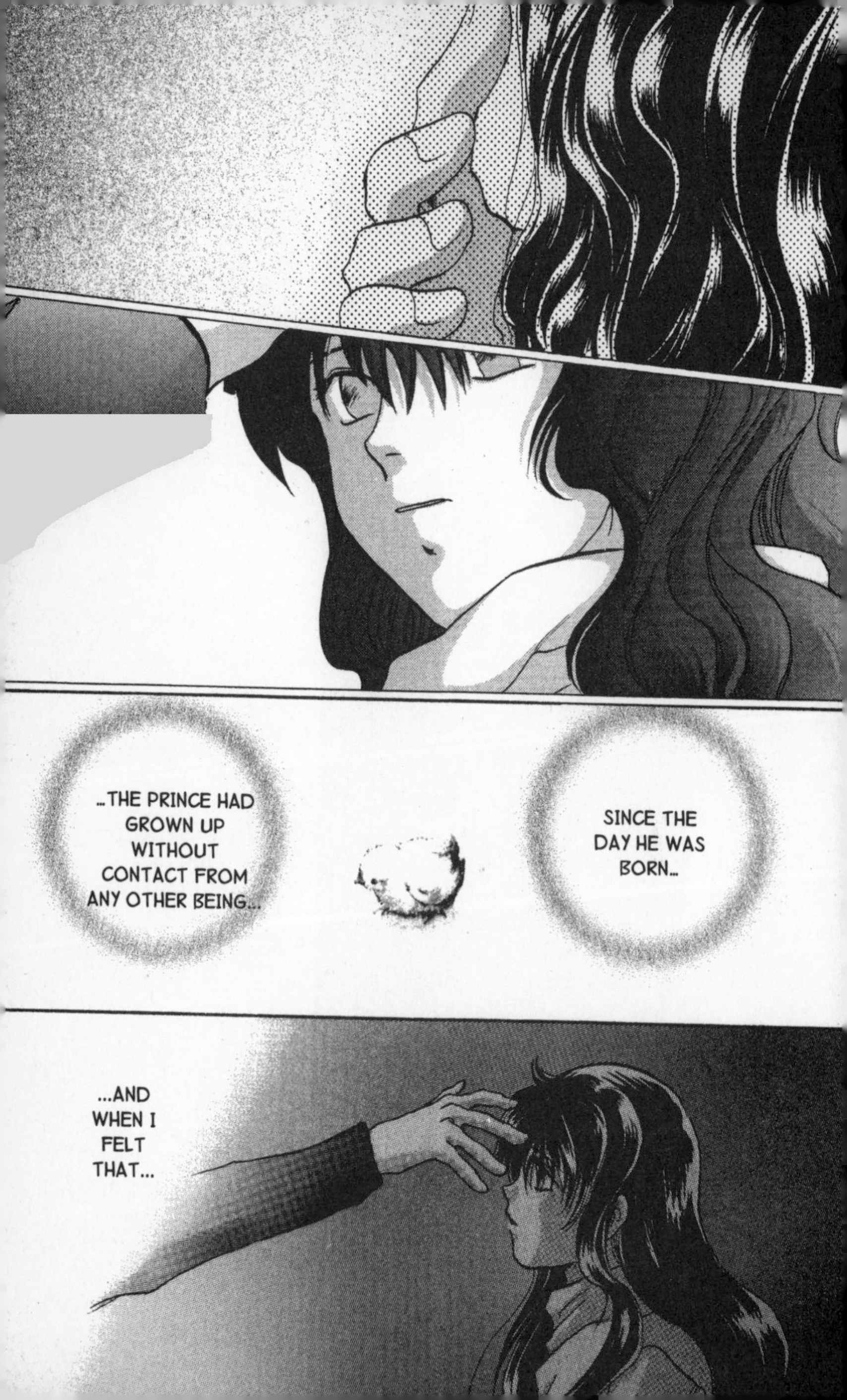
SINCE THE DAY HE WAS BORN...
...THE PRINCE HAD GROWN UP WITHOUT CONTACT FROM ANY OTHER BEING...
...AND WHEN I FELT THAT...

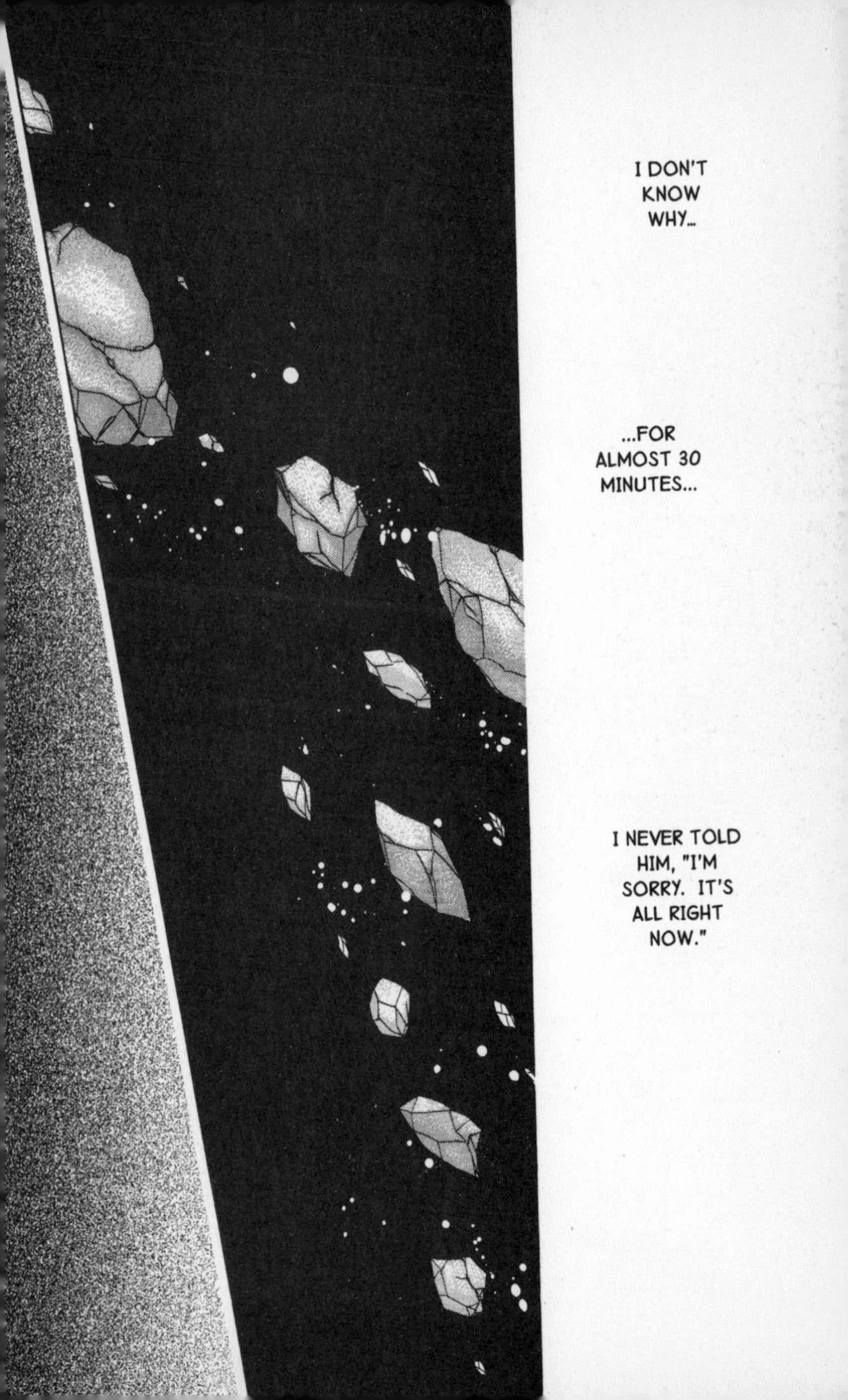
I DON'T KNOW WHY...
...FOR ALMOST 30 MINUTES...
I NEVER TOLD HIM, "I'M SORRY. IT'S ALL RIGHT NOW."

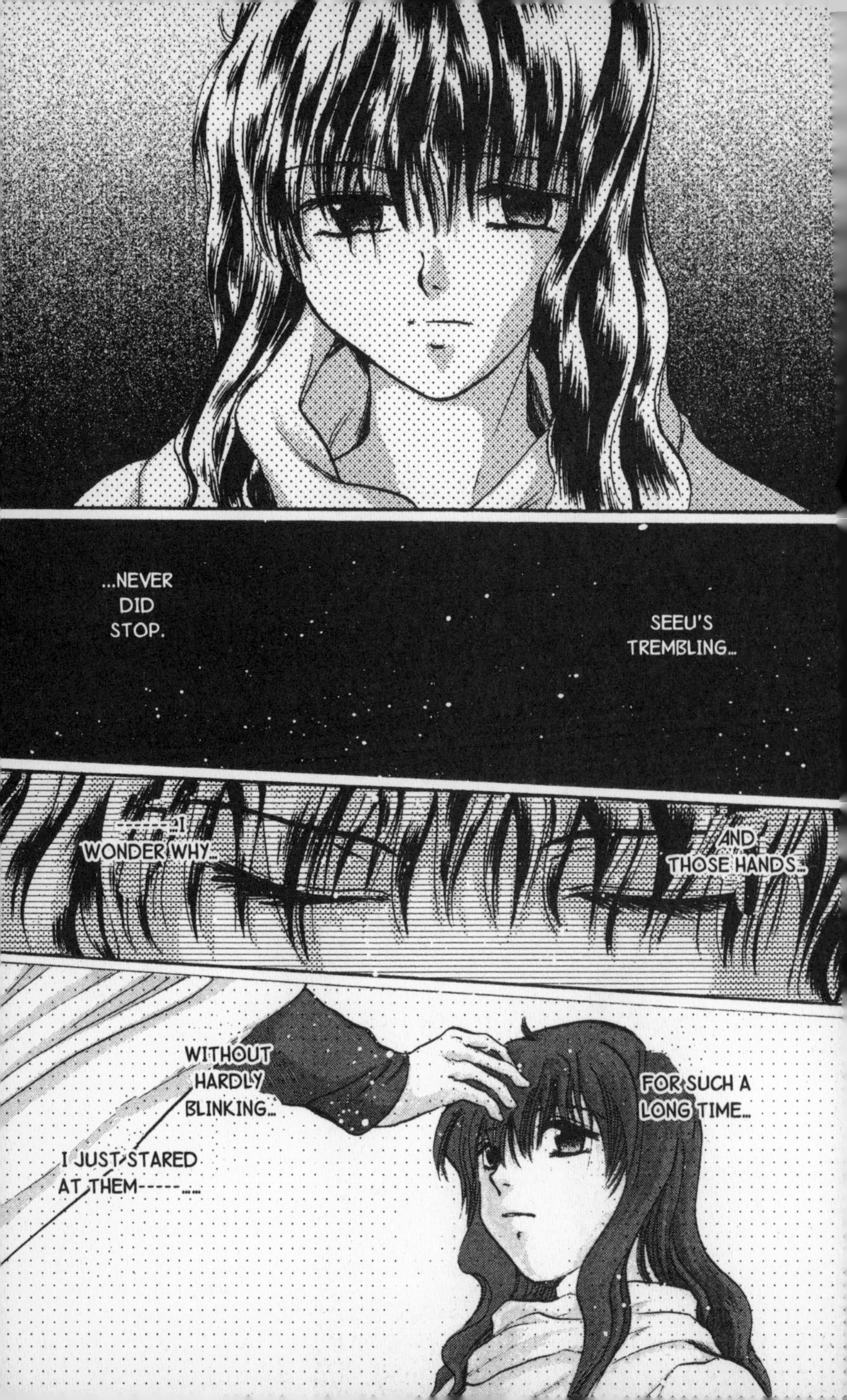
SEEU'S TREMBLING...
...NEVER DID STOP.
AND THOSE HANDS...
------...I WONDER WHY...
FOR SUCH A LONG TIME...
WITHOUT HARDLY BLINKING...
I JUST STARED AT THEM-----......

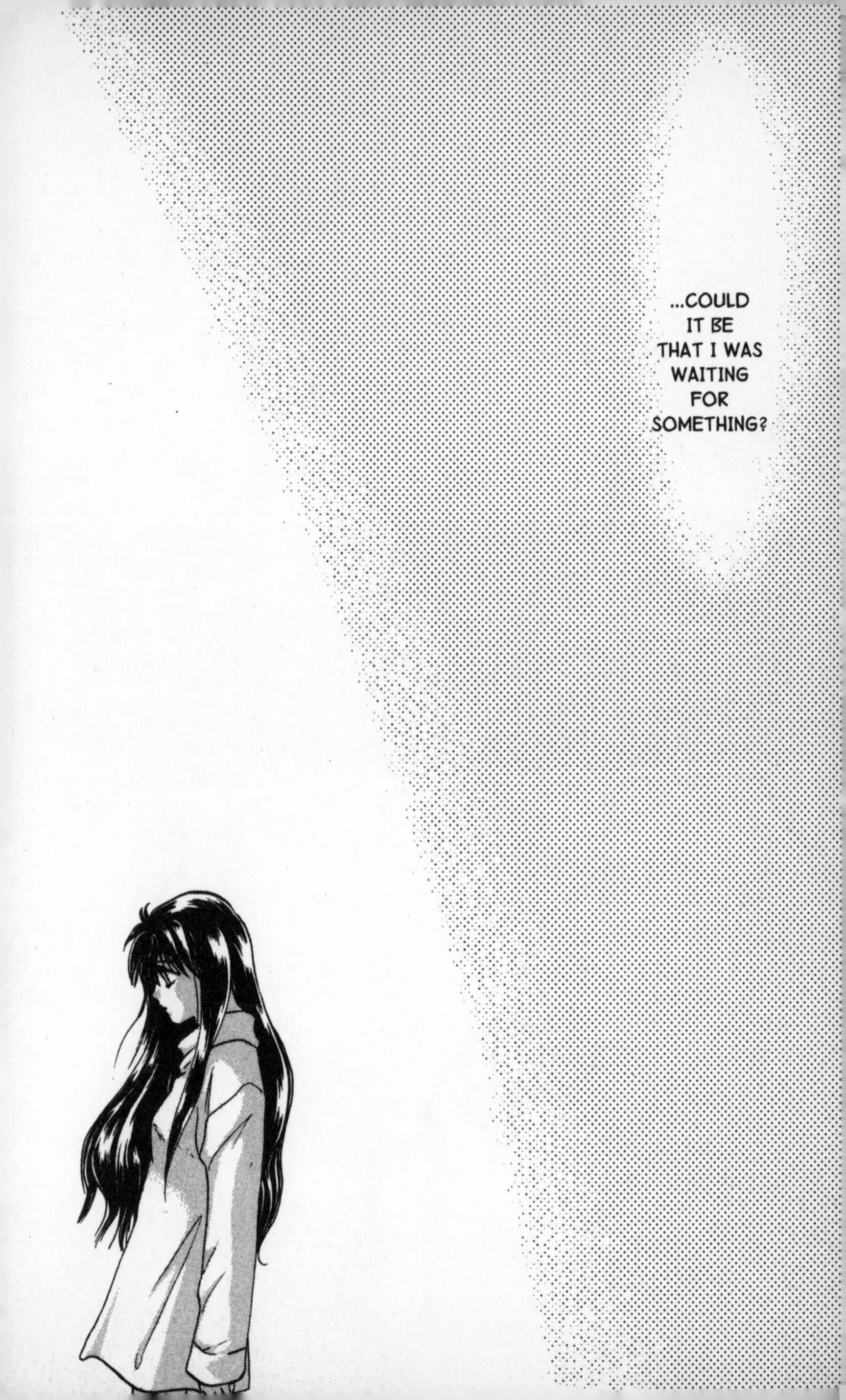
...COULD IT BE THAT I WAS WAITING FOR SOMETHING?

WHY?

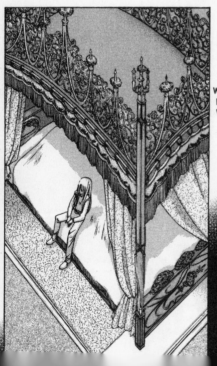

I
WON-
DER
WHY
?

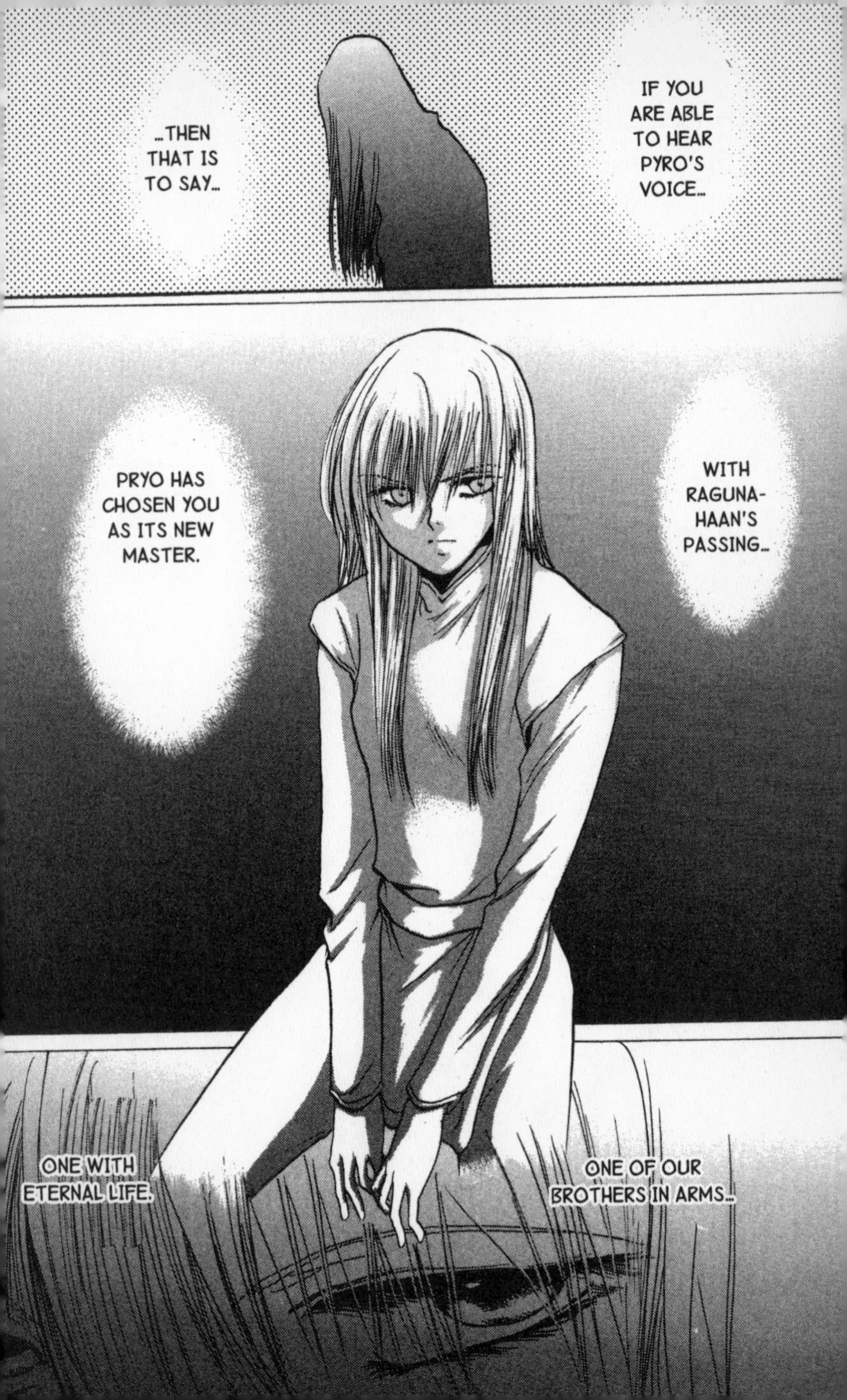
IF YOU ARE ABLE TO HEAR PYRO'S VOICE...
...THEN THAT IS TO SAY...
WITH RAGUNA-HAAN'S PASSING...
PRYO HAS CHOSEN YOU AS ITS NEW MASTER.
ONE OF OUR BROTHERS IN ARMS...
ONE WITH ETERNAL LIFE.

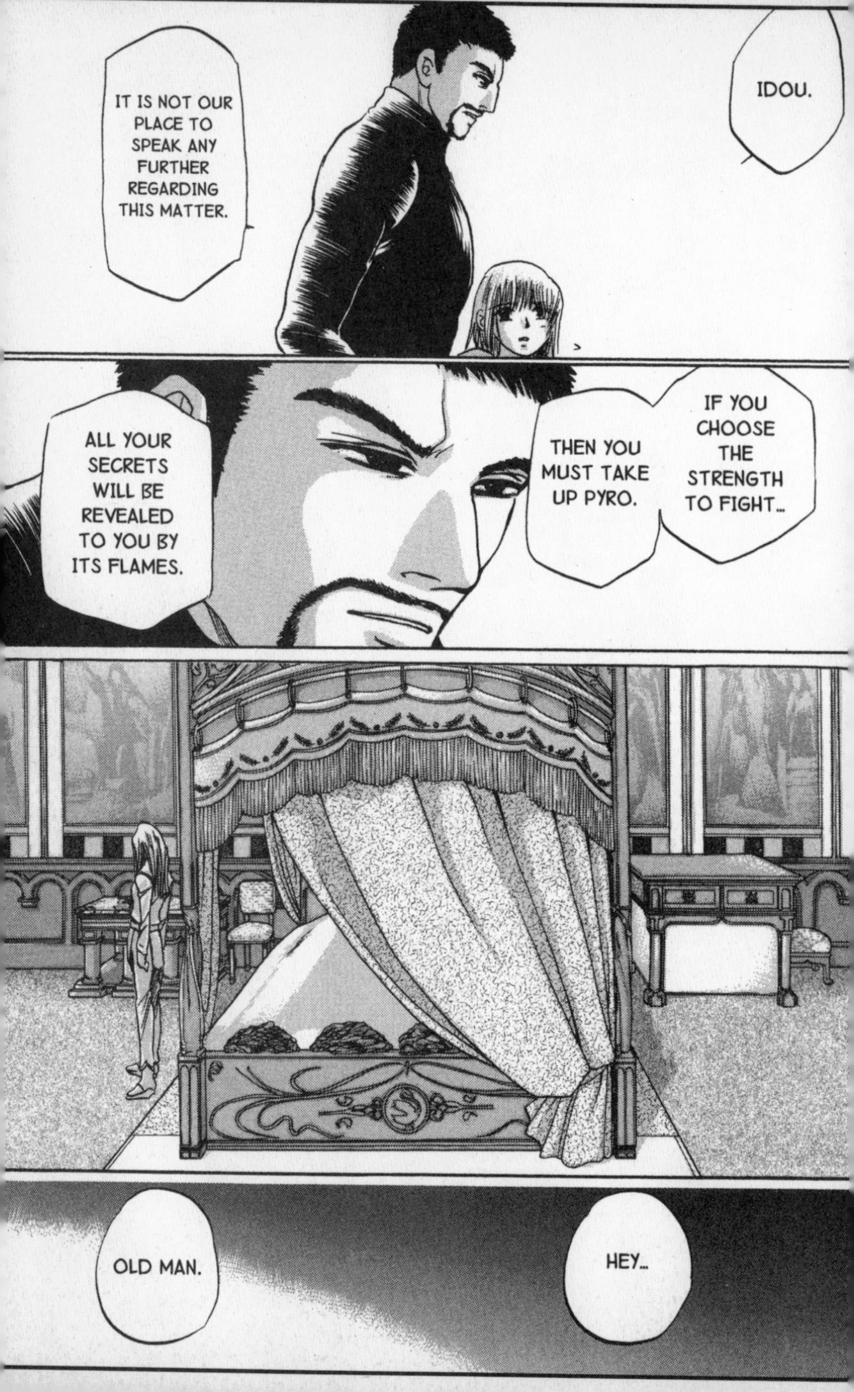
IDOU.
IT IS NOT OUR PLACE TO SPEAK ANY FURTHER REGARDING THIS MATTER.
IF YOU CHOOSE THE STRENGTH TO FIGHT...
THEN YOU MUST TAKE UP PYRO.
ALL YOUR SECRETS WILL BE REVEALED TO YOU BY ITS FLAMES.
HEY...
OLD MAN.

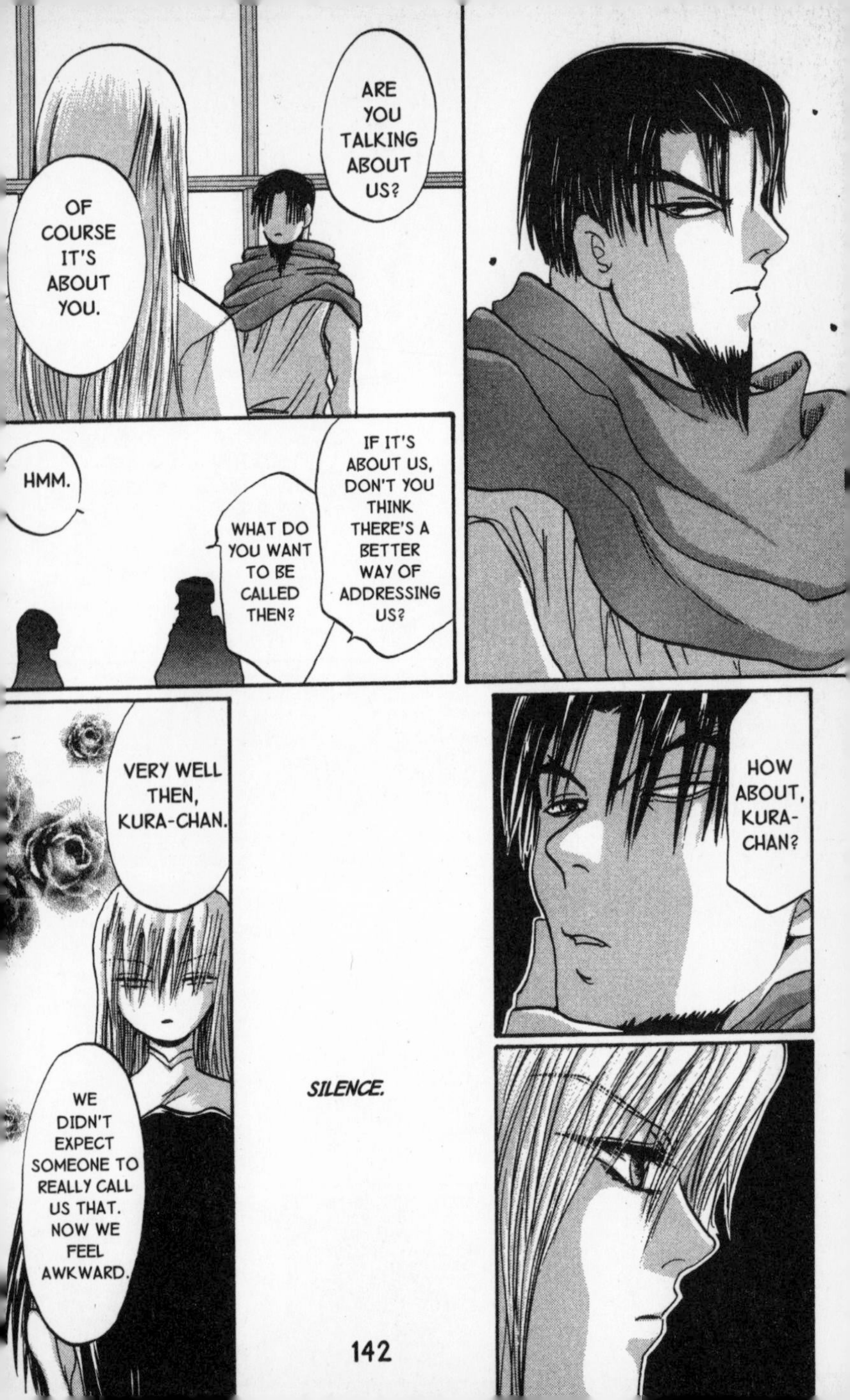
ARE YOU TALKING ABOUT US?
OF COURSE IT'S ABOUT YOU.
IF IT'S ABOUT US, DON'T YOU THINK THERE'S A BETTER WAY OF ADDRESSING US?
WHAT DO YOU WANT TO BE CALLED THEN?
HMM.
HOW ABOUT, KURA-CHAN?
SILENCE.
VERY WELL THEN, KURA-CHAN.
WE DIDN'T EXPECT SOMEONE TO REALLY CALL US THAT. NOW WE FEEL AWKWARD.

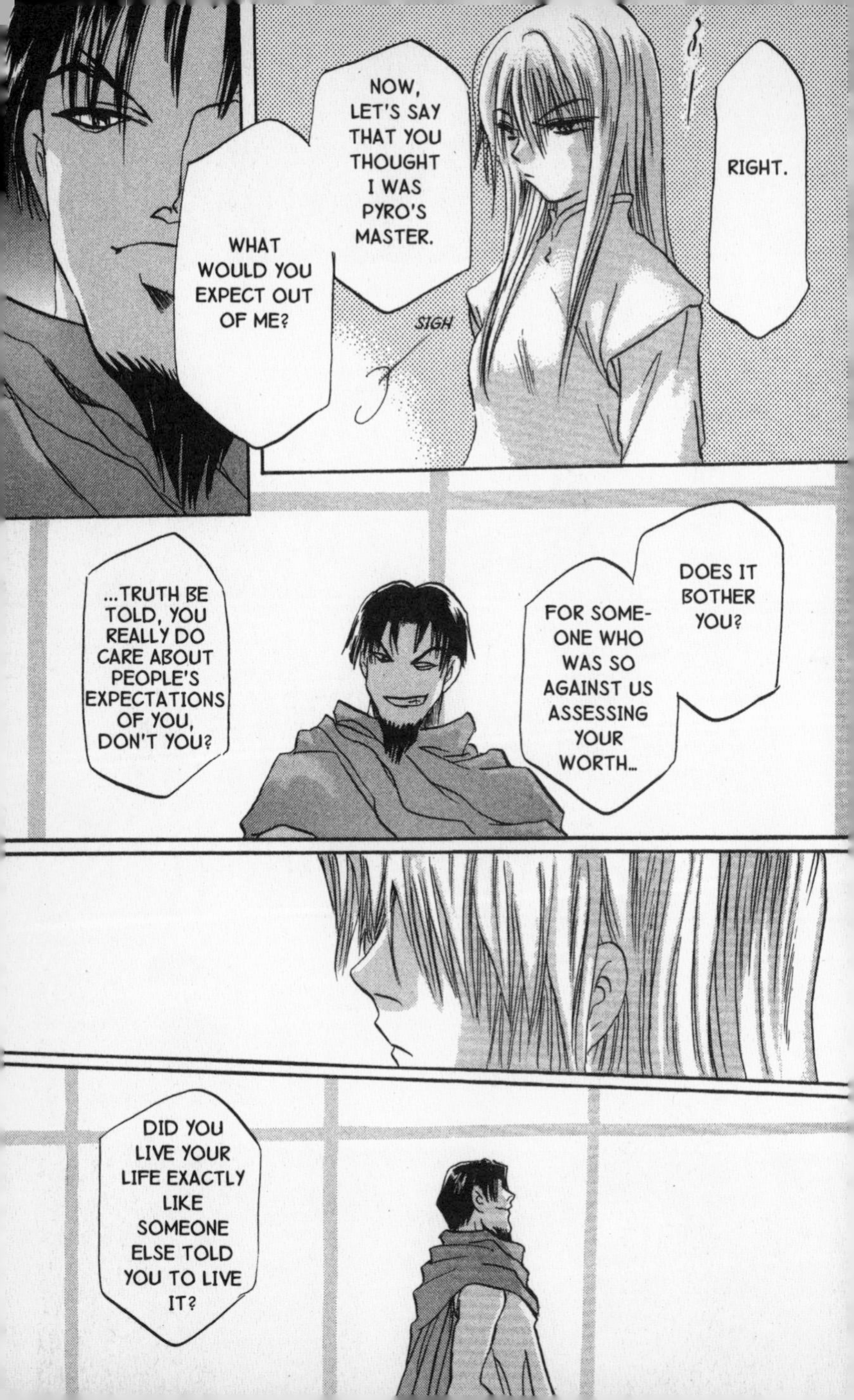
RIGHT.
SIGH
NOW, LET'S SAY THAT YOU THOUGHT I WAS PYRO'S MASTER.
WHAT WOULD YOU EXPECT OUT OF ME?
DOES IT BOTHER YOU?
FOR SOME-ONE WHO WAS SO AGAINST US ASSESSING YOUR WORTH...
...TRUTH BE TOLD, YOU REALLY DO CARE ABOUT PEOPLE'S EXPECTATIONS OF YOU, DON'T YOU?
DID YOU LIVE YOUR LIFE EXACTLY LIKE SOMEONE ELSE TOLD YOU TO LIVE IT?

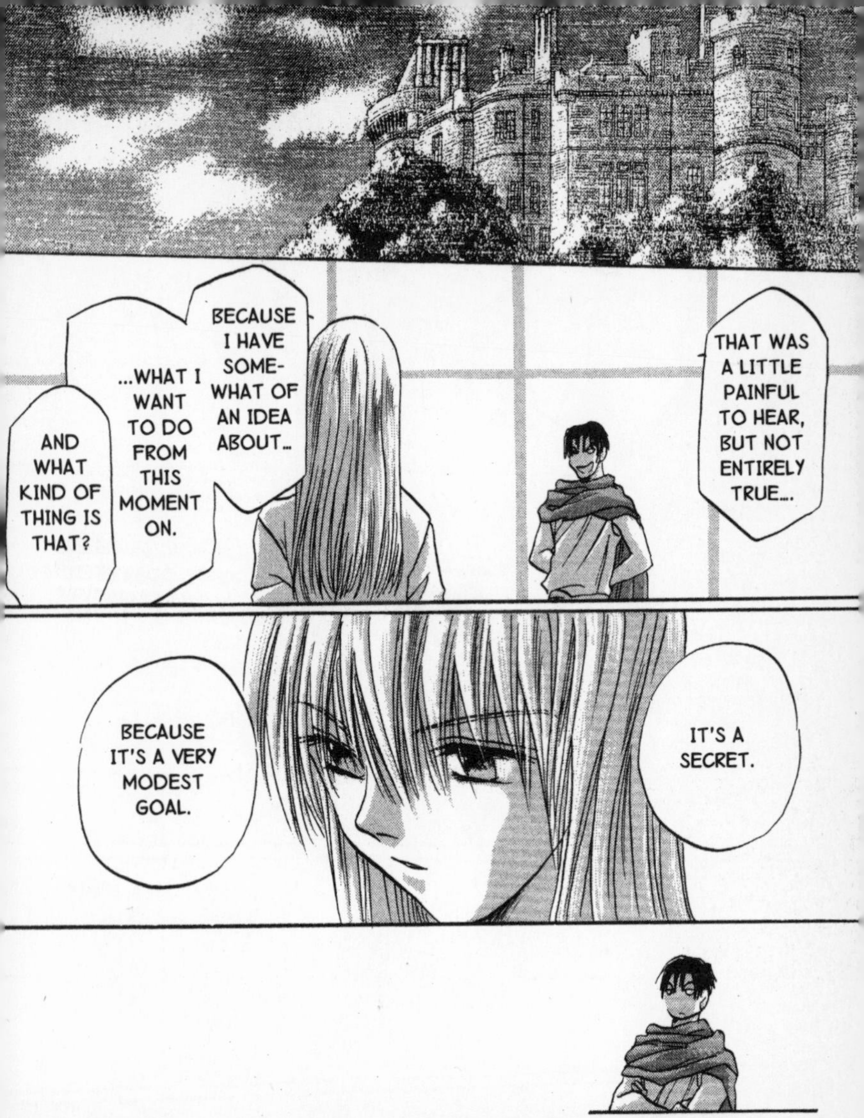
THAT WAS A LITTLE PAINFUL TO HEAR, BUT NOT ENTIRELY TRUE....
BECAUSE I HAVE SOME-WHAT OF AN IDEA ABOUT...
...WHAT I WANT TO DO FROM THIS MOMENT ON.
AND WHAT KIND OF THING IS THAT?
IT'S A SECRET.
BECAUSE IT'S A VERY MODEST GOAL.

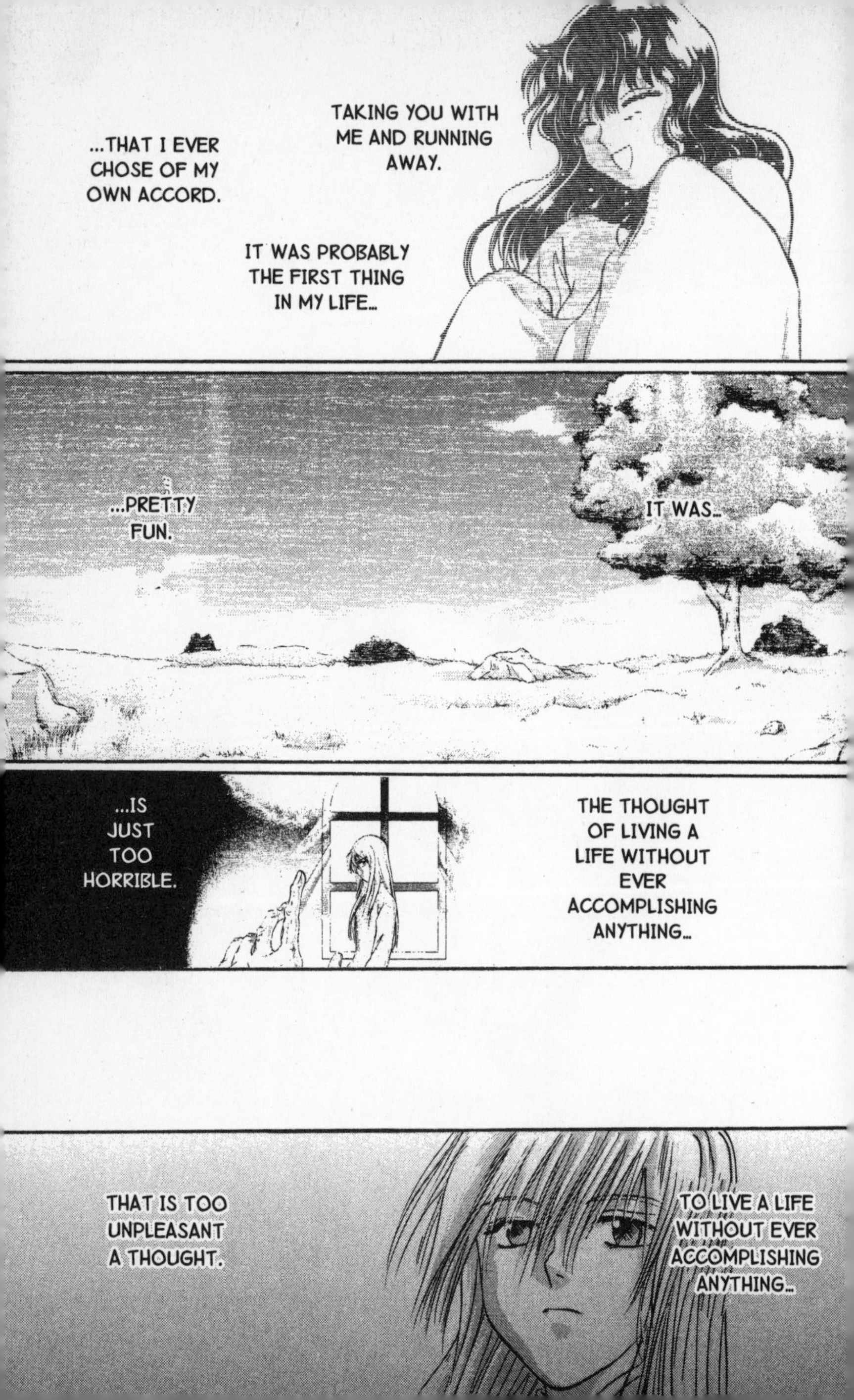
TAKING YOU WITH ME AND RUNNING AWAY.
IT WAS PROBABLY THE FIRST THING IN MY LIFE..
...THAT I EVER CHOSE OF MY OWN ACCORD.
IT WAS..
...PRETTY FUN.
THE THOUGHT OF LIVING A LIFE WITHOUT EVER ACCOMPLISHING ANYTHING...
...IS JUST TOO HORRIBLE.
TO LIVE A LIFE WITHOUT EVER ACCOMPLISHING ANYTHING..
THAT IS TOO UNPLEASANT A THOUGHT.

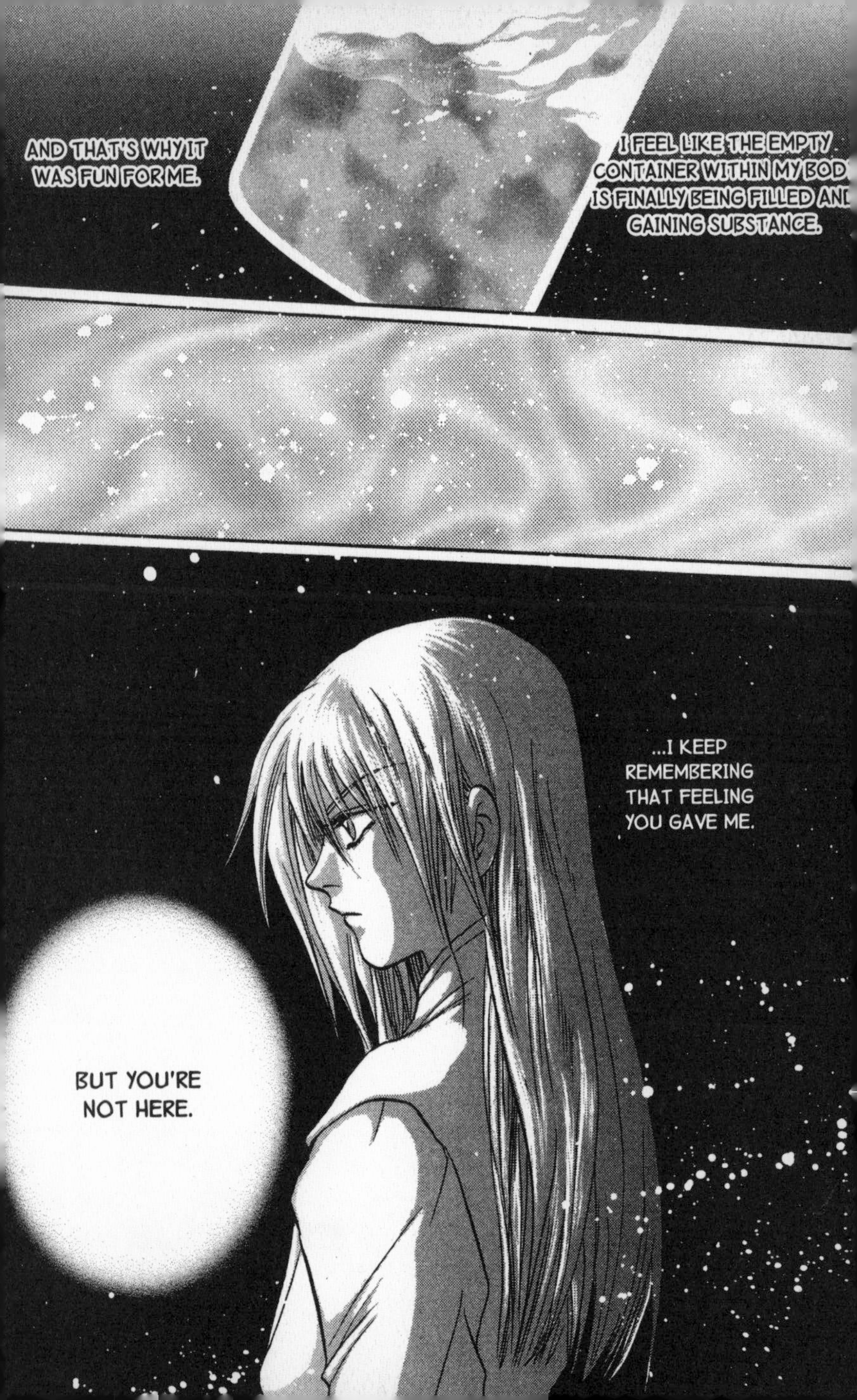
I FEEL LIKE THE EMPTY CONTAINER WITHIN MY BOD IS FINALLY BEING FILLED AN GAINING SUBSTANCE.
AND THAT'S WHY IT WAS FUN FOR ME.
...I KEEP REMEMBERING THAT FEELING YOU GAVE ME.
BUT YOU'RE NOT HERE.

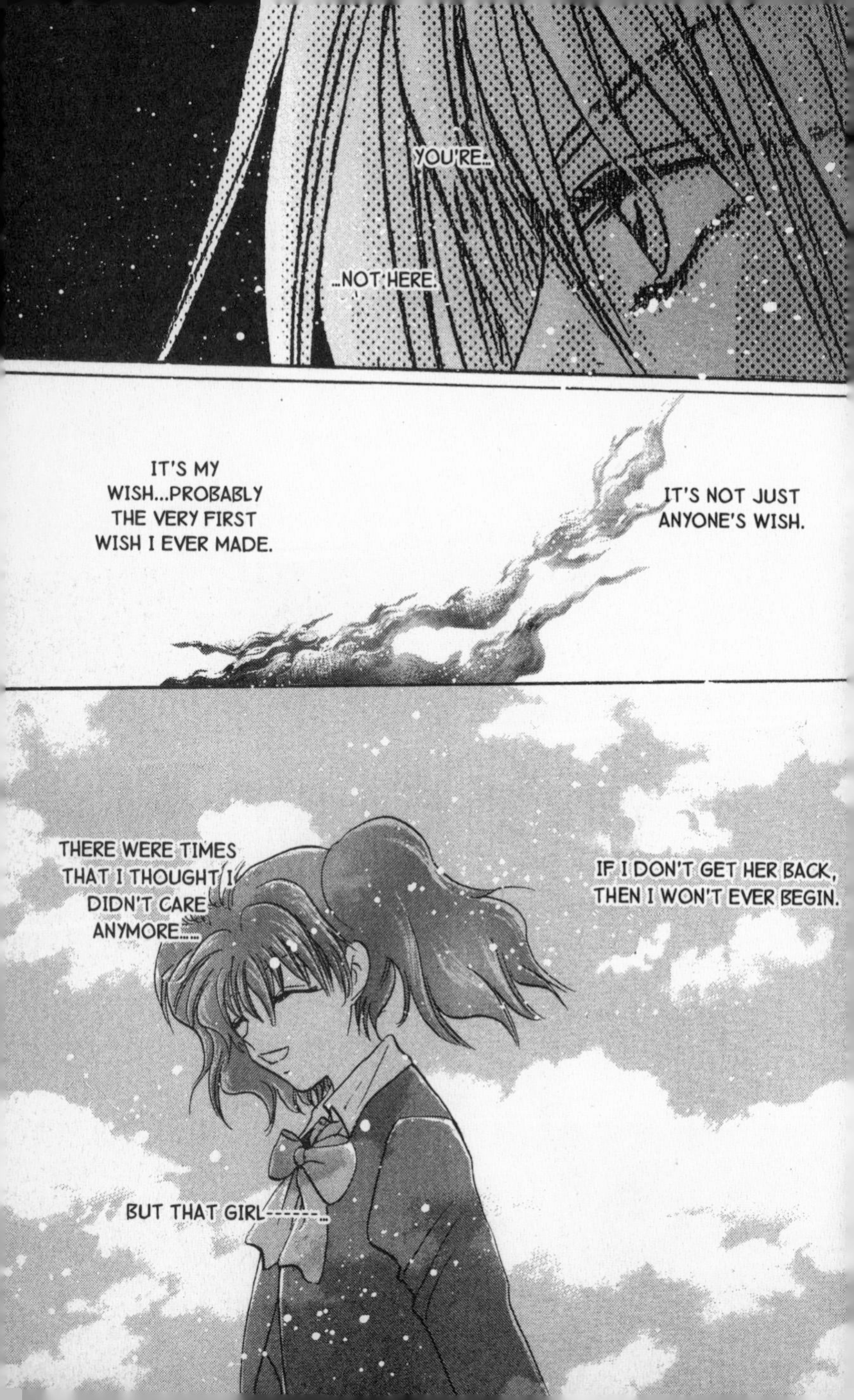
YOU'RE..
...NOT HERE.
IT'S NOT JUST ANYONE'S WISH.
IT'S MY WISH...PROBABLY THE VERY FIRST WISH I EVER MADE.
IF I DON'T GET HER BACK, THEN I WON'T EVER BEGIN.
THERE WERE TIMES THAT I THOUGHT I DIDN'T CARE ANYMORE......
BUT THAT GIRL------...

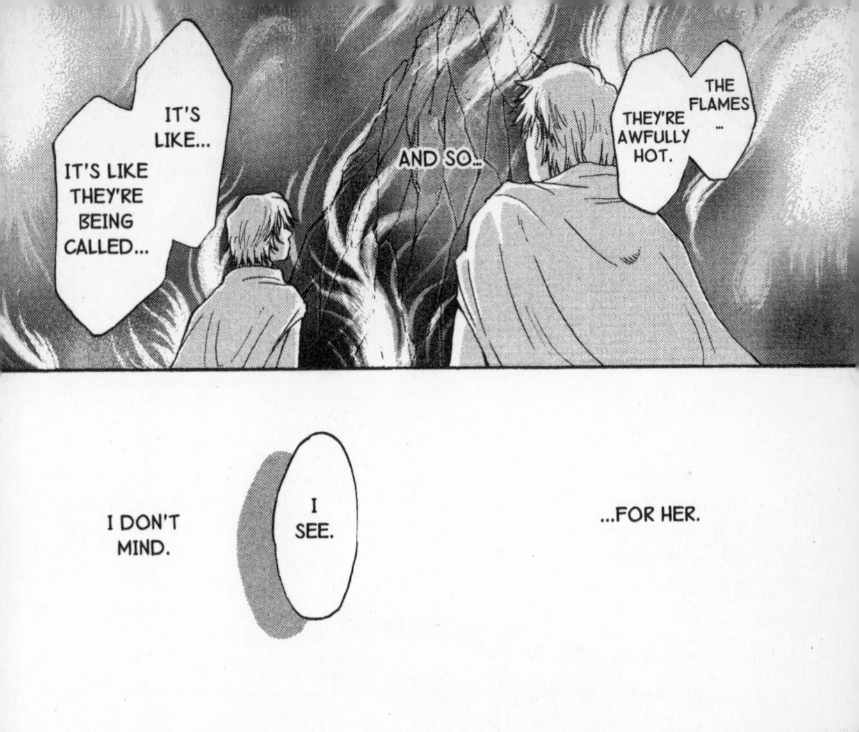
THE FLAMES ...
THEY'RE AWFULLY HOT.
AND SO...
IT'S LIKE...
IT'S LIKE THEY'RE BEING CALLED...
...FOR HER.
I SEE.
I DON'T MIND.
NO SECOND THOUGHTS?
AS KIND AS WE ARE...
...PROVIDING WEAPONS TO THOSE WHO DO NOT PLEDGE THEIR ALLEGIANCE TO US.

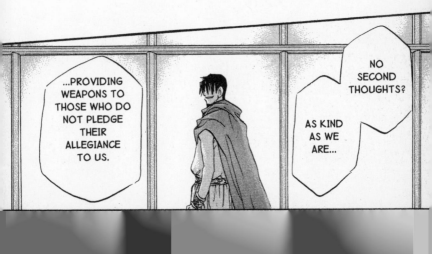

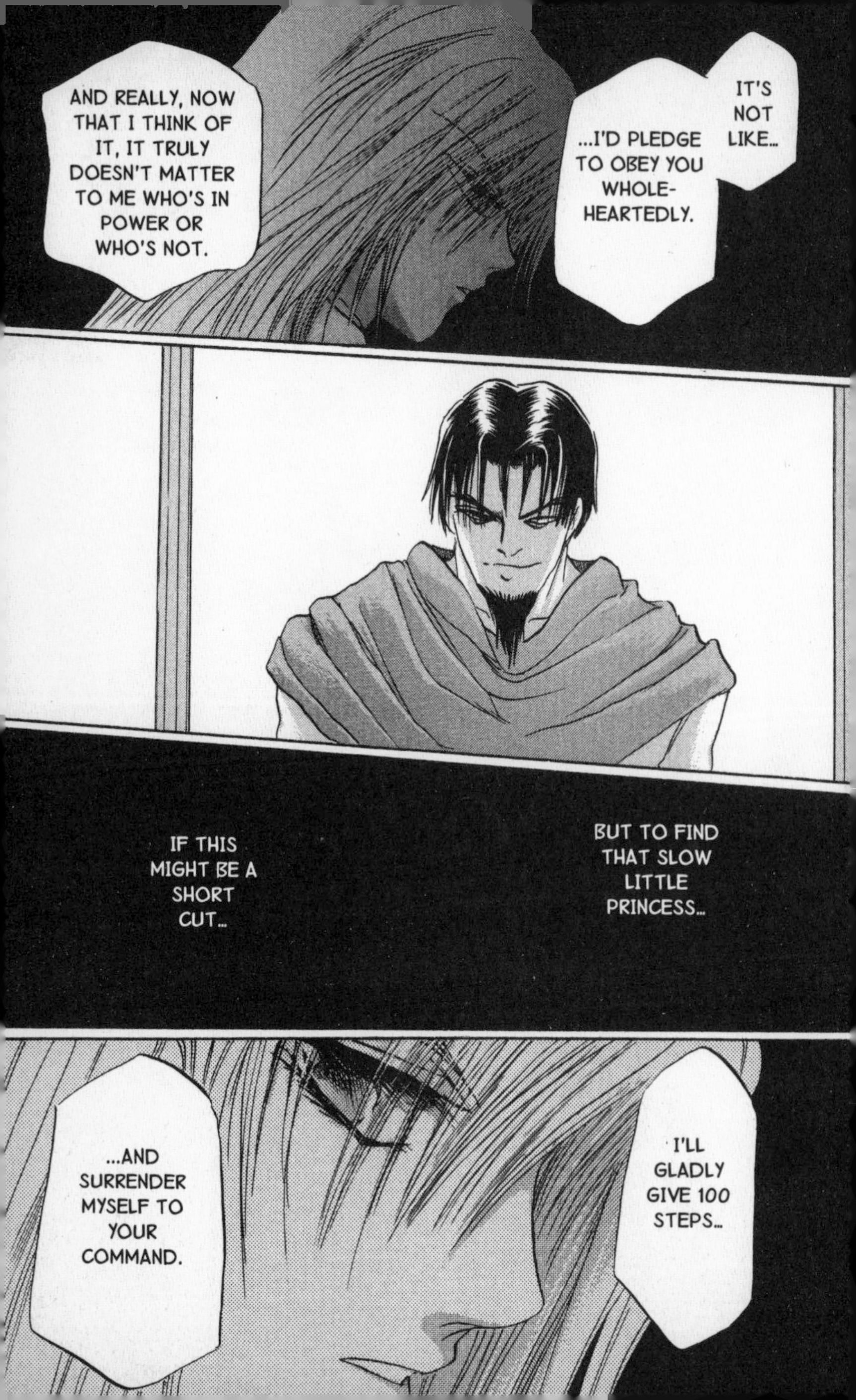
IT'S NOT LIKE...
...I'D PLEDGE TO OBEY YOU WHOLE-HEARTEDLY.
AND REALLY, NOW THAT I THINK OF IT, IT TRULY DOESN'T MATTER TO ME WHO'S IN POWER OR WHO'S NOT.
BUT TO FIND THAT SLOW LITTLE PRINCESS...
IF THIS MIGHT BE A SHORT CUT...
I'LL GLADLY GIVE 100 STEPS...
...AND SURRENDER MYSELF TO YOUR COMMAND.

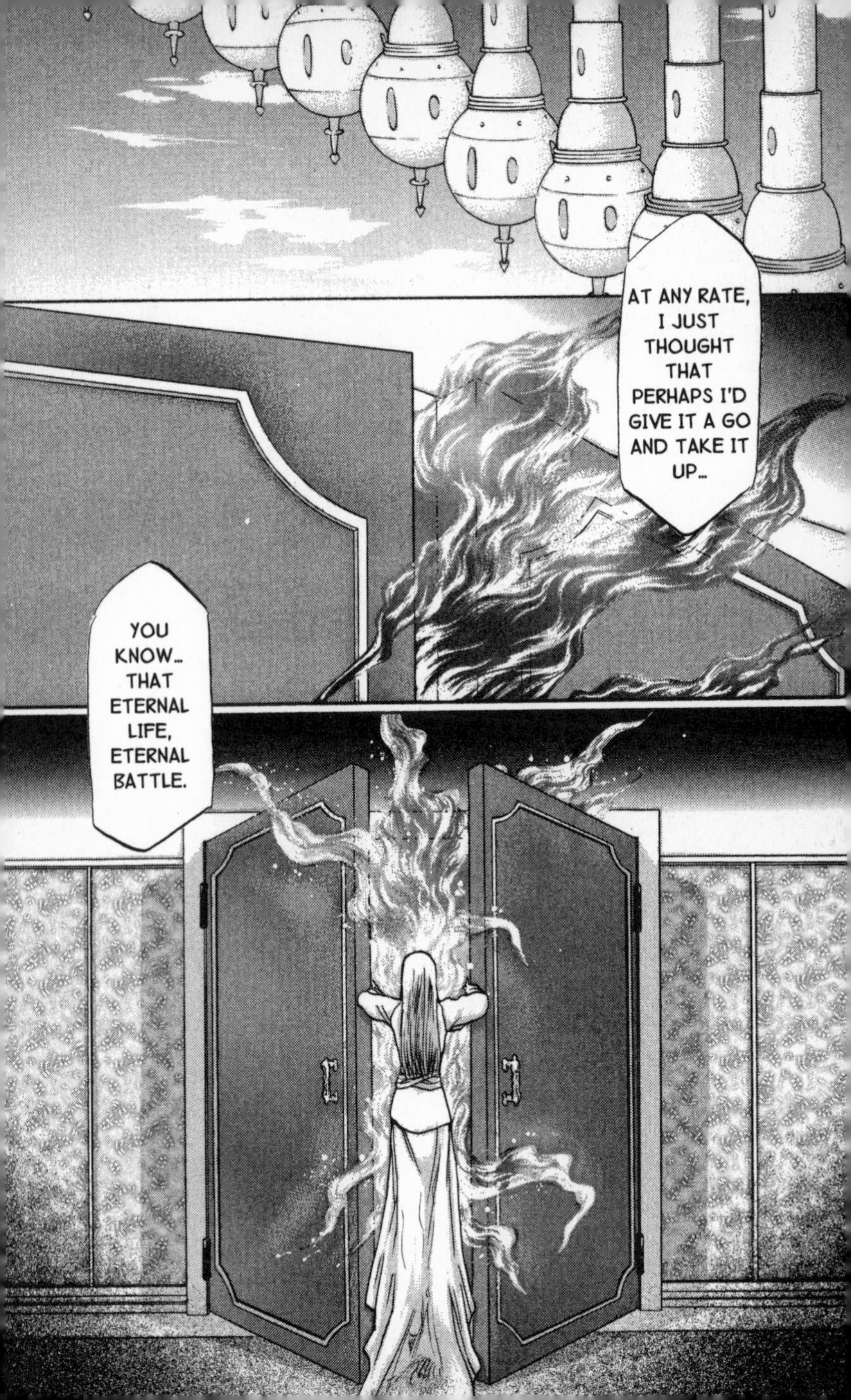
AT ANY RATE, I JUST THOUGHT THAT PERHAPS I'D GIVE IT A GO AND TAKE IT UP...
YOU KNOW... THAT ETERNAL LIFE, ETERNAL BATTLE.

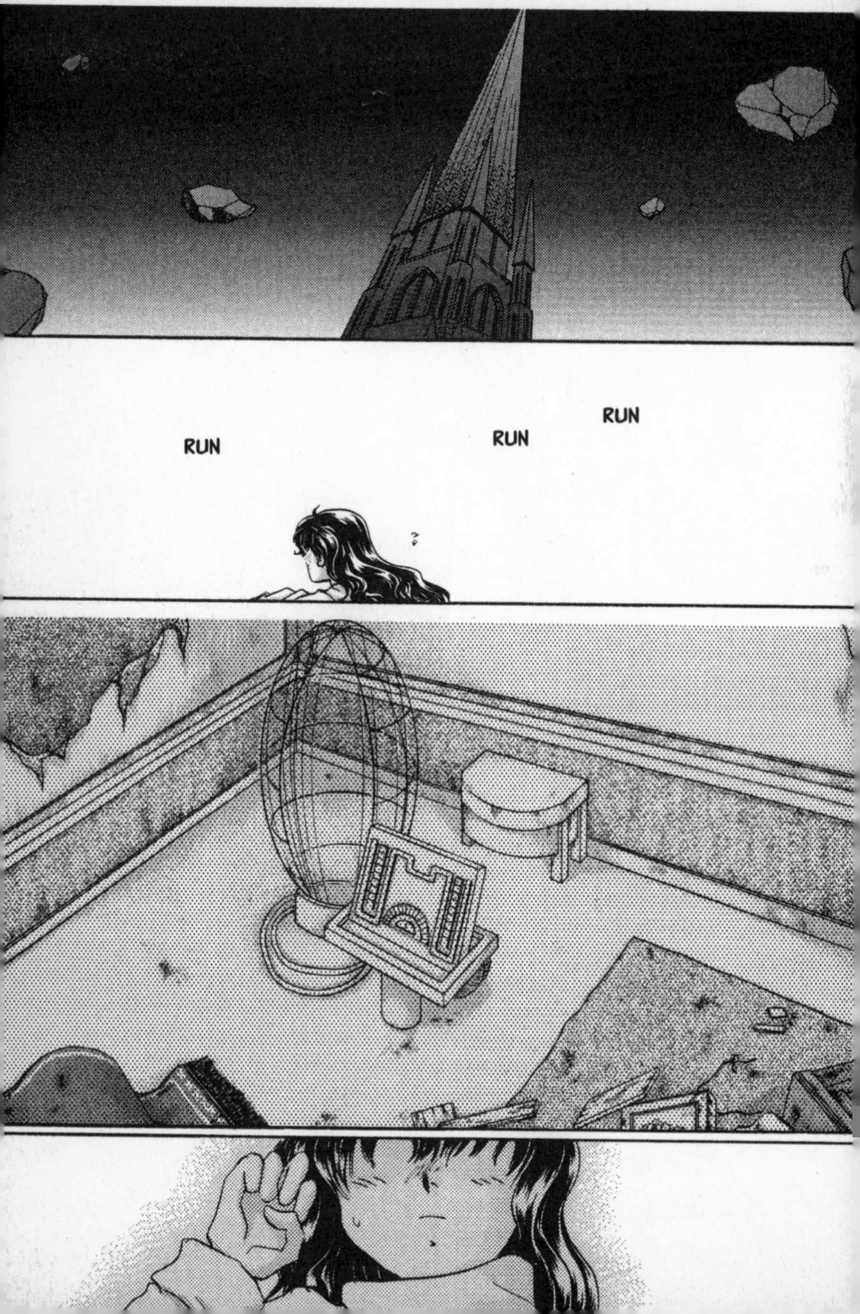
RUN
RUN
RUN

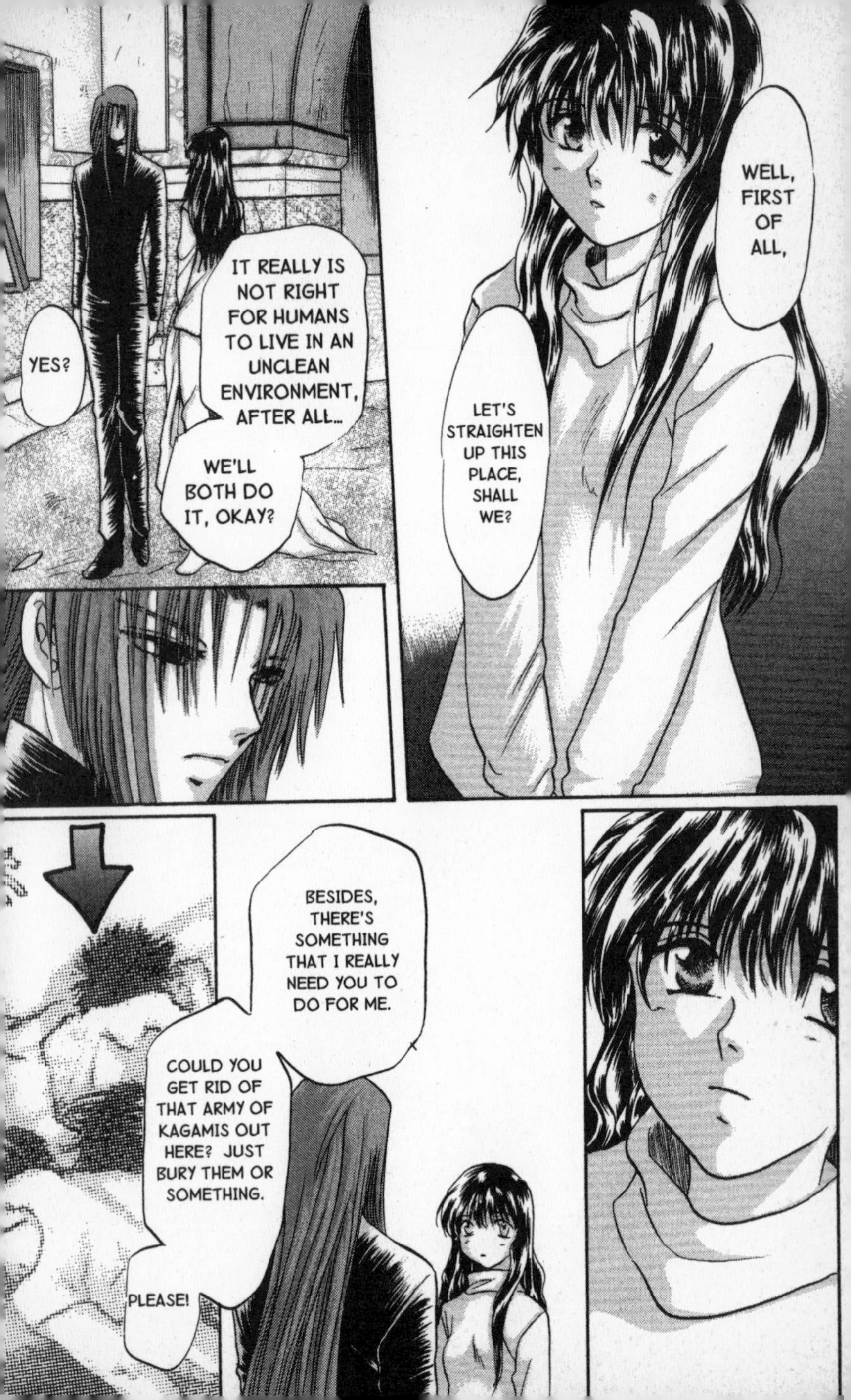
WELL, FIRST OF ALL,
LET'S STRAIGHTEN UP THIS PLACE, SHALL WE?
IT REALLY IS NOT RIGHT FOR HUMANS TO LIVE IN AN UNCLEAN ENVIRONMENT, AFTER ALL...
YES?
WE'LL BOTH DO IT, OKAY?
BESIDES, THERE'S SOMETHING THAT I REALLY NEED YOU TO DO FOR ME.
COULD YOU GET RID OF THAT ARMY OF KAGAMIS OUT HERE? JUST BURY THEM OR SOMETHING.
PLEASE!

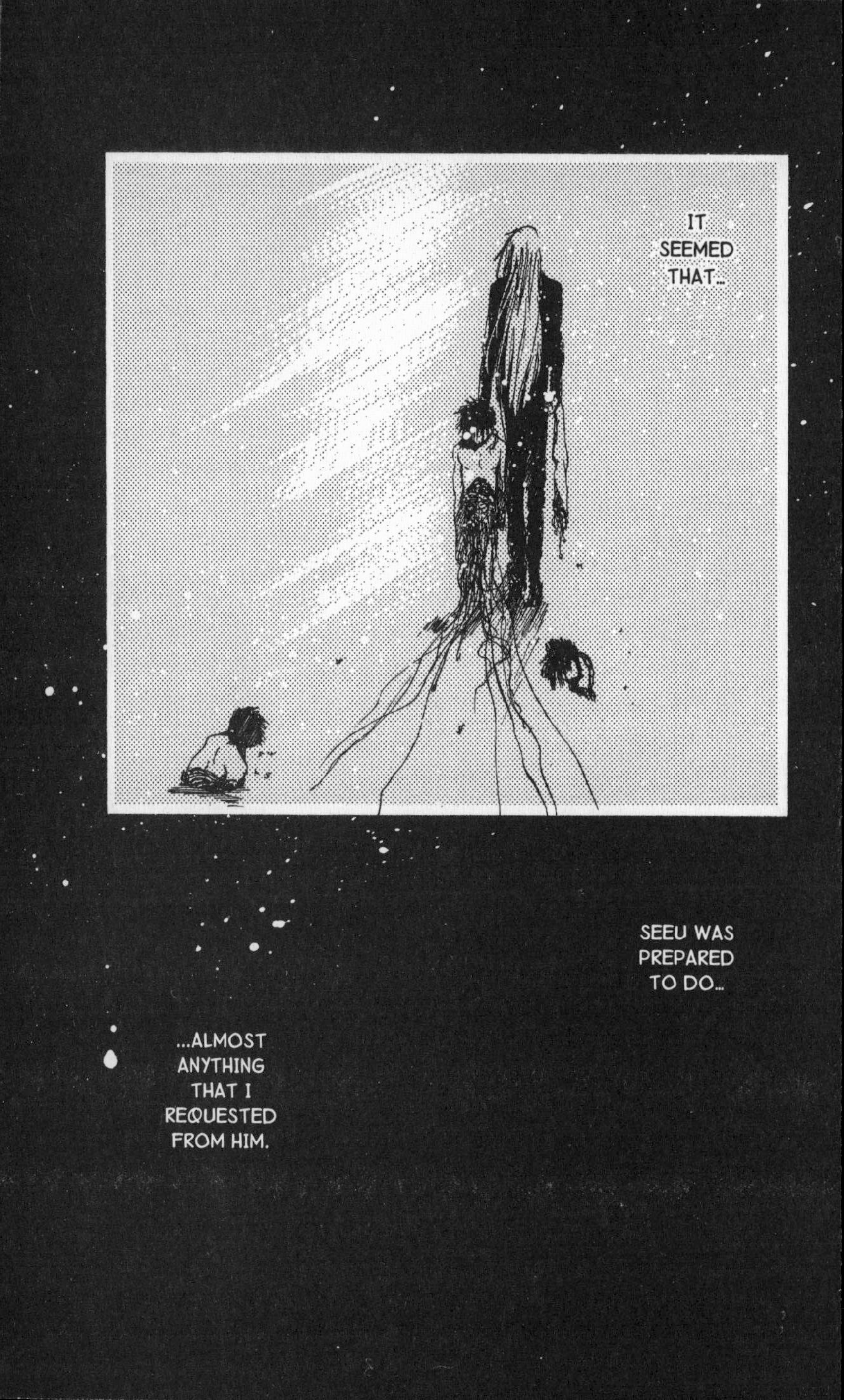
IT SEEMED THAT...
SEEU WAS PREPARED TO DO...
...ALMOST ANYTHING THAT I REQUESTED FROM HIM.

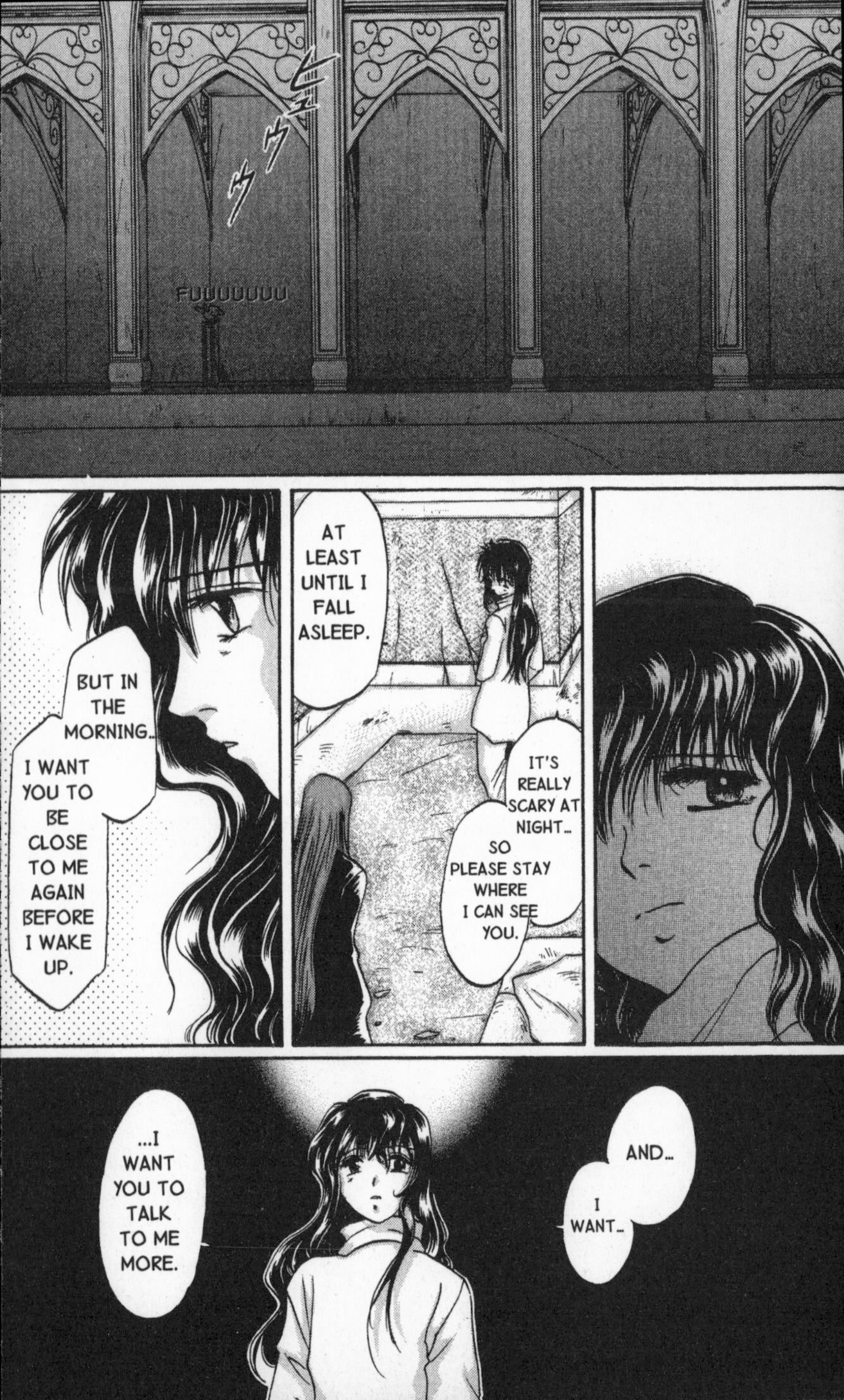
ヒュウウ
FUUUUUUU
IT'S REALLY SCARY AT NIGHT...
SO PLEASE STAY WHERE I CAN SEE YOU.
AT LEAST UNTIL I FALL ASLEEP.
BUT IN THE MORNING...
I WANT YOU TO BE CLOSE TO ME AGAIN BEFORE I WAKE UP.
AND...
I WANT...
...I WANT YOU TO TALK TO ME MORE.

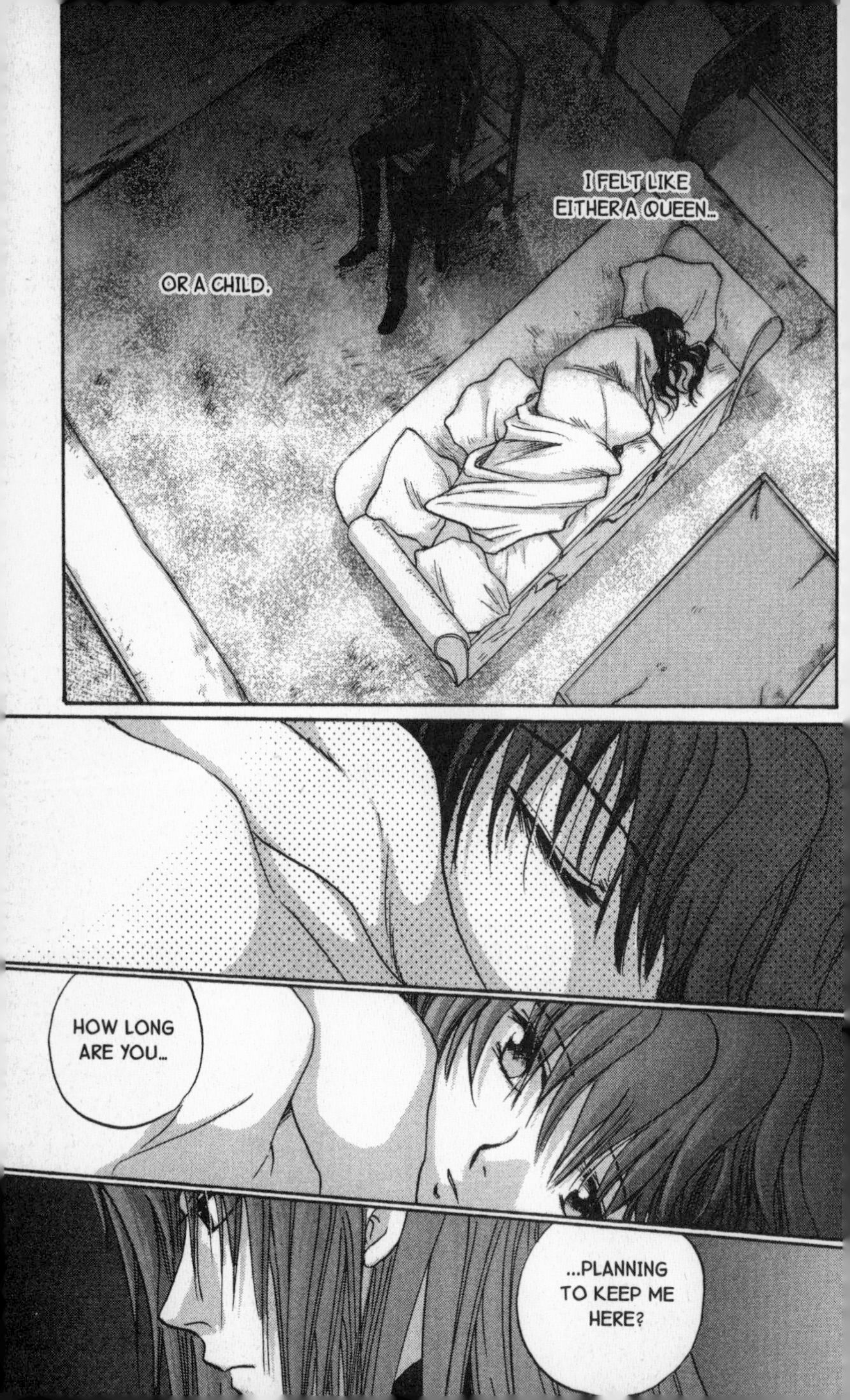
I FELT LIKE EITHER A QUEEN...
OR A CHILD.
HOW LONG ARE YOU...
...PLANNING TO KEEP ME HERE?

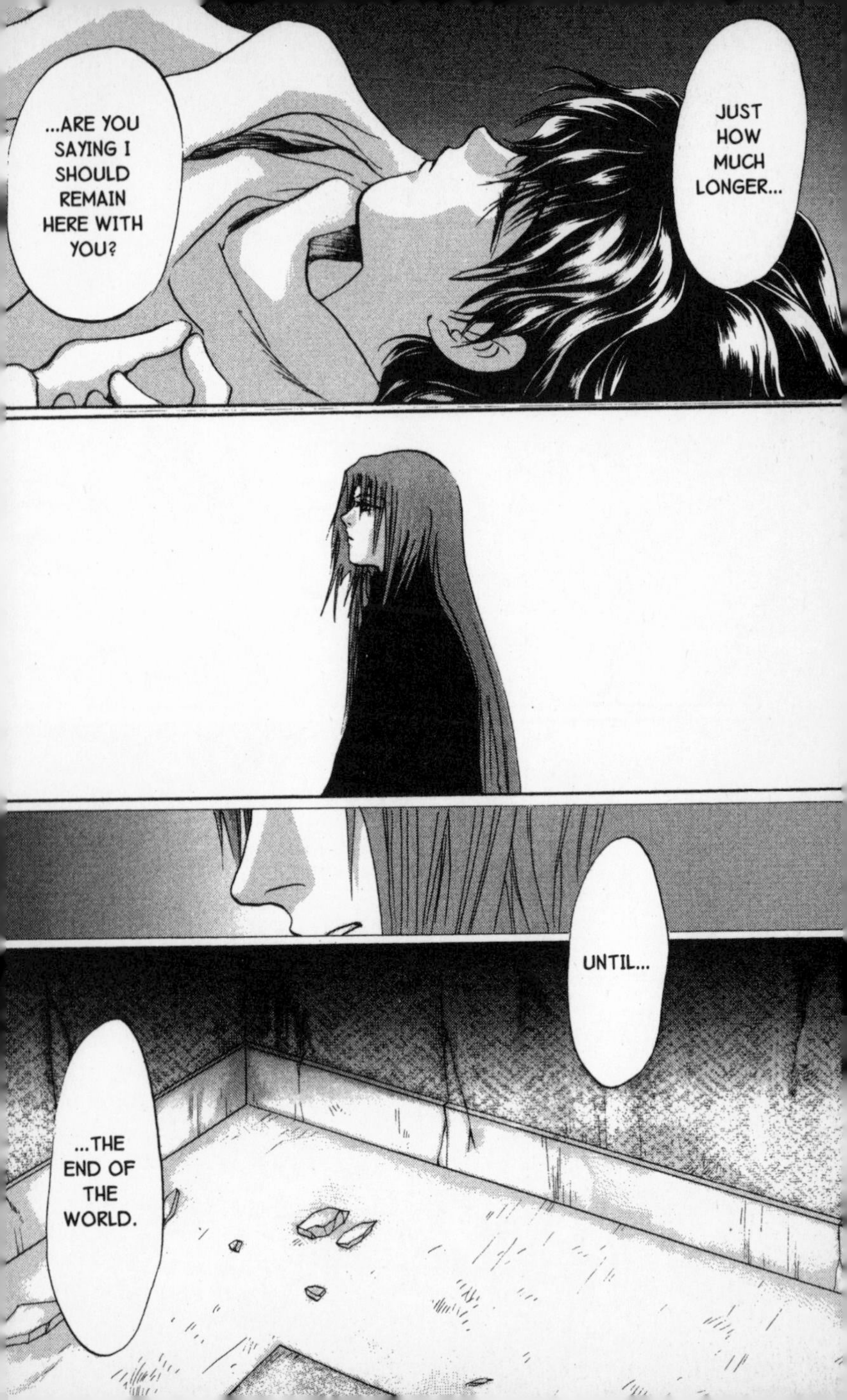
JUST HOW MUCH LONGER...
...ARE YOU SAYING I SHOULD REMAIN HERE WITH YOU?
UNTIL...
...THE END OF THE WORLD.

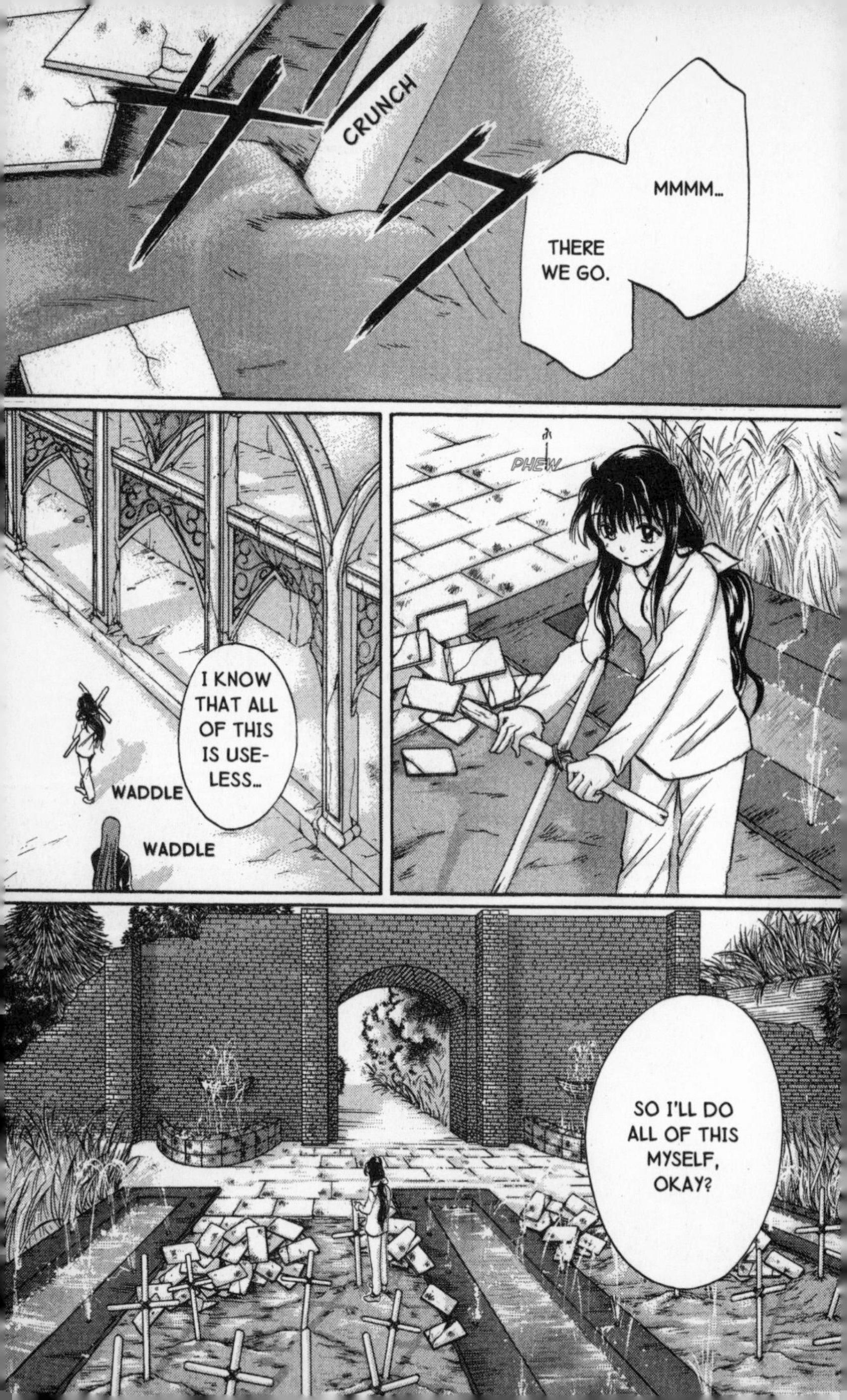
CRUNCH
MMMM...
THERE WE GO.
PHEW
I KNOW THAT ALL OF THIS IS USE-LESS...
WADDLE
WADDLE
SO I'LL DO ALL OF THIS MYSELF, OKAY?

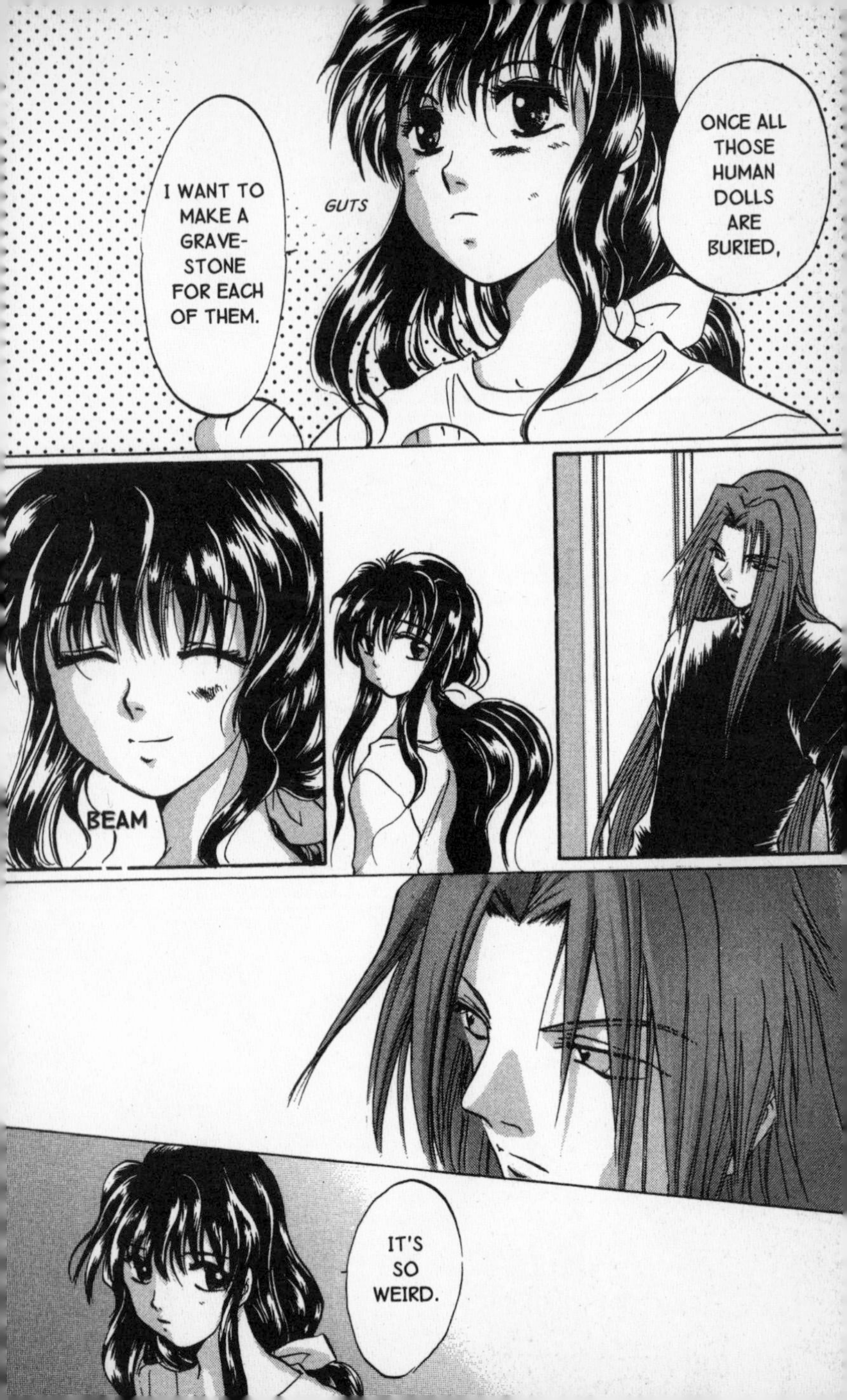
ONCE ALL THOSE HUMAN DOLLS ARE BURIED,
GUTS
I WANT TO MAKE A GRAVE-STONE FOR EACH OF THEM.
BEAM
IT'S SO WEIRD.

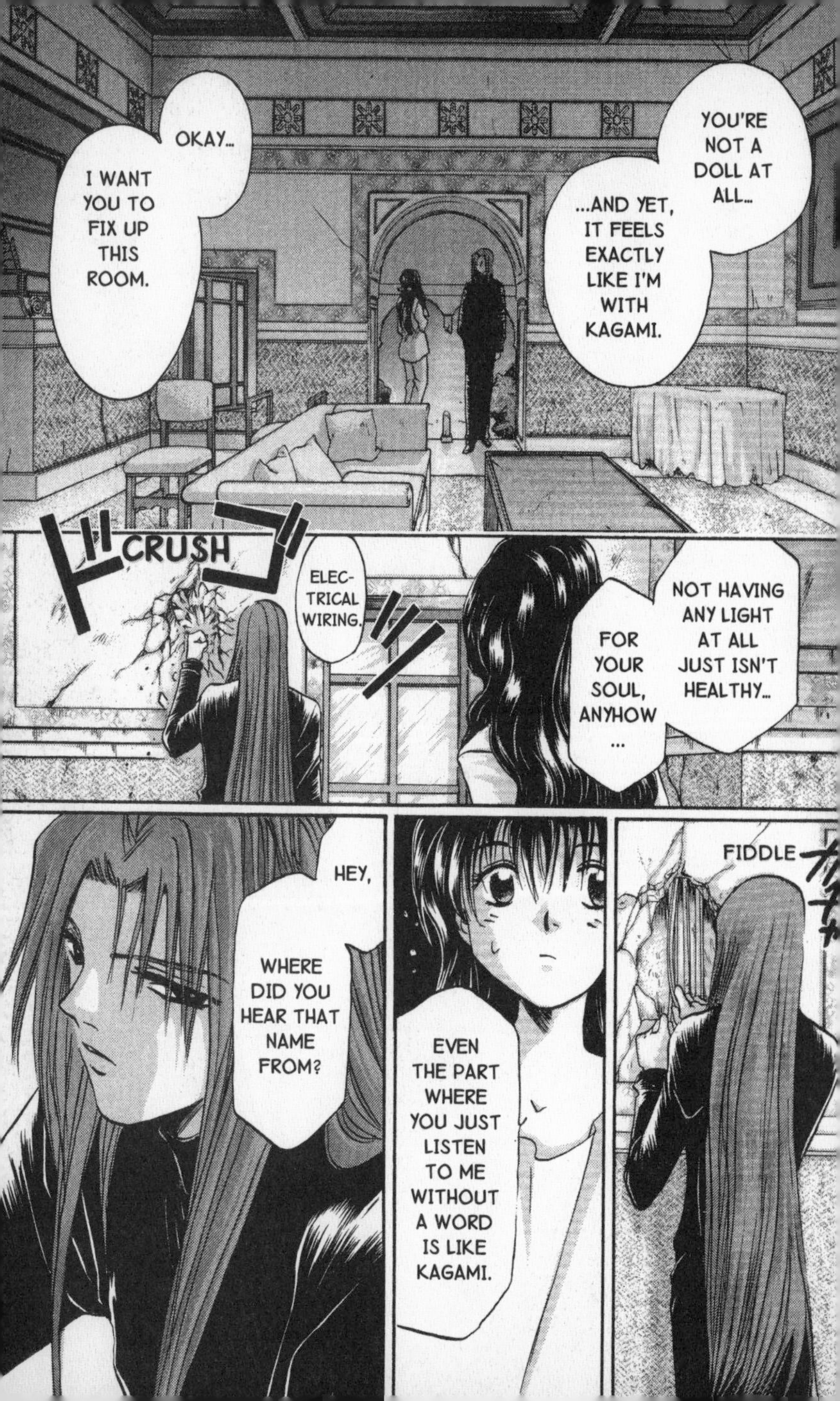
YOU'RE NOT A DOLL AT ALL...
...AND YET, IT FEELS EXACTLY LIKE I'M WITH KAGAMI.
OKAY...
I WANT YOU TO FIX UP THIS ROOM.
NOT HAVING ANY LIGHT AT ALL JUST ISN'T HEALTHY...
FOR YOUR SOUL, ANYHOW ...
ELEC-TRICAL WIRING.
CRUSH
FIDDLE
EVEN THE PART WHERE YOU JUST LISTEN TO ME WITHOUT A WORD IS LIKE KAGAMI.
HEY,
WHERE DID YOU HEAR THAT NAME FROM?

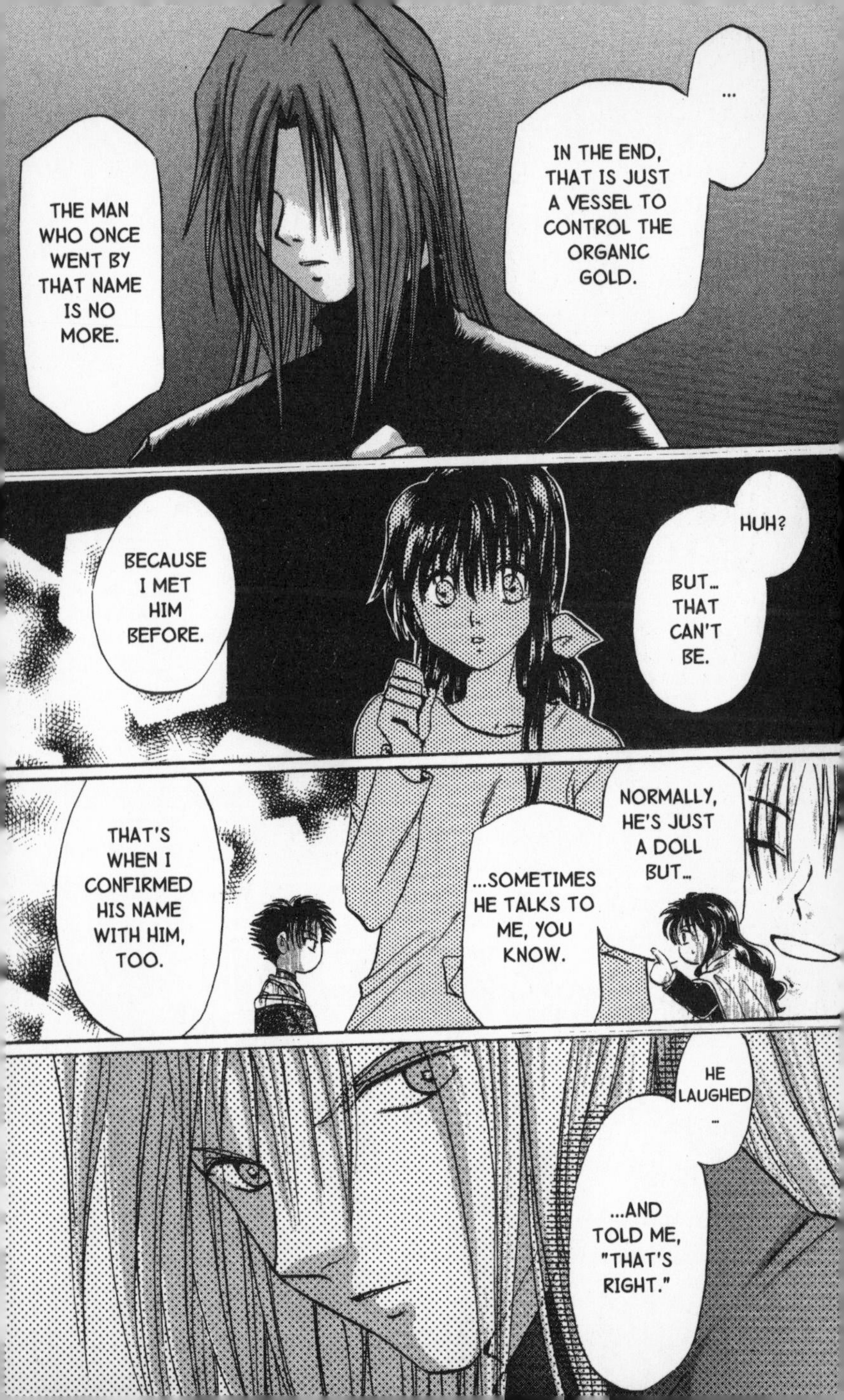
...
IN THE END, THAT IS JUST A VESSEL TO CONTROL THE ORGANIC GOLD.
THE MAN WHO ONCE WENT BY THAT NAME IS NO MORE.
HUH?
BUT... THAT CAN'T BE.
BECAUSE I MET HIM BEFORE.
NORMALLY, HE'S JUST A DOLL BUT...
...SOMETIMES HE TALKS TO ME, YOU KNOW.
THAT'S WHEN I CONFIRMED HIS NAME WITH HIM, TOO.
HE LAUGHED...
...AND TOLD ME, "THAT'S RIGHT."

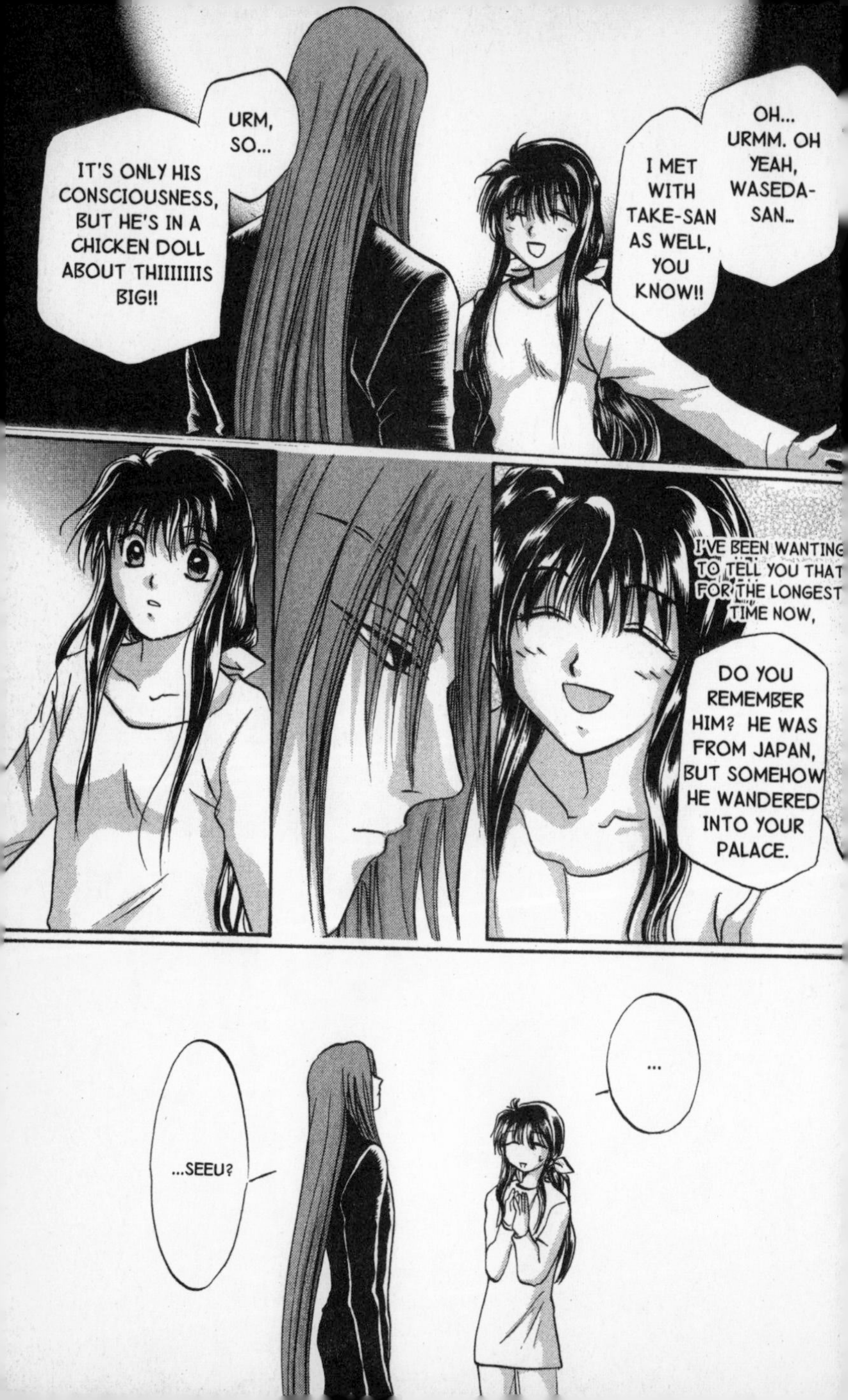
OH... URMM. OH YEAH, WASEDA-SAN...
I MET WITH TAKE-SAN AS WELL, YOU KNOW!!
URM, SO...
IT'S ONLY HIS CONSCIOUSNESS, BUT HE'S IN A CHICKEN DOLL ABOUT THIIIIIIIS BIG!!
I'VE BEEN WANTING TO TELL YOU THAT FOR THE LONGEST TIME NOW,
DO YOU REMEMBER HIM? HE WAS FROM JAPAN, BUT SOMEHOW HE WANDERED INTO YOUR PALACE.
...
...SEEU?

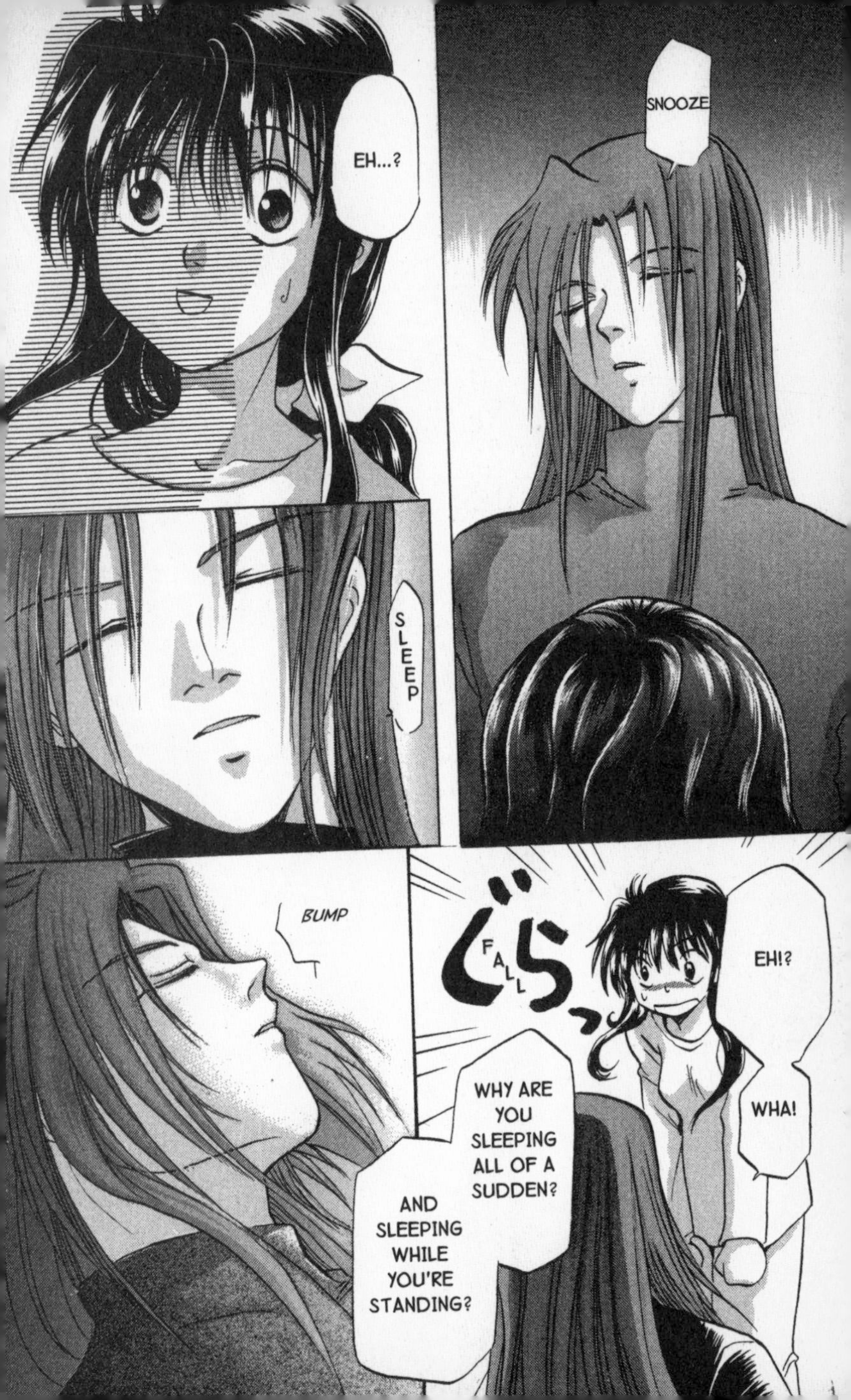
SNOOZE
EH...?
SLEEP
EHI!?
ぐらっ
FALL
WHA!
WHY ARE YOU SLEEPING ALL OF A SUDDEN?
AND SLEEPING WHILE YOU'RE STANDING?
BUMP

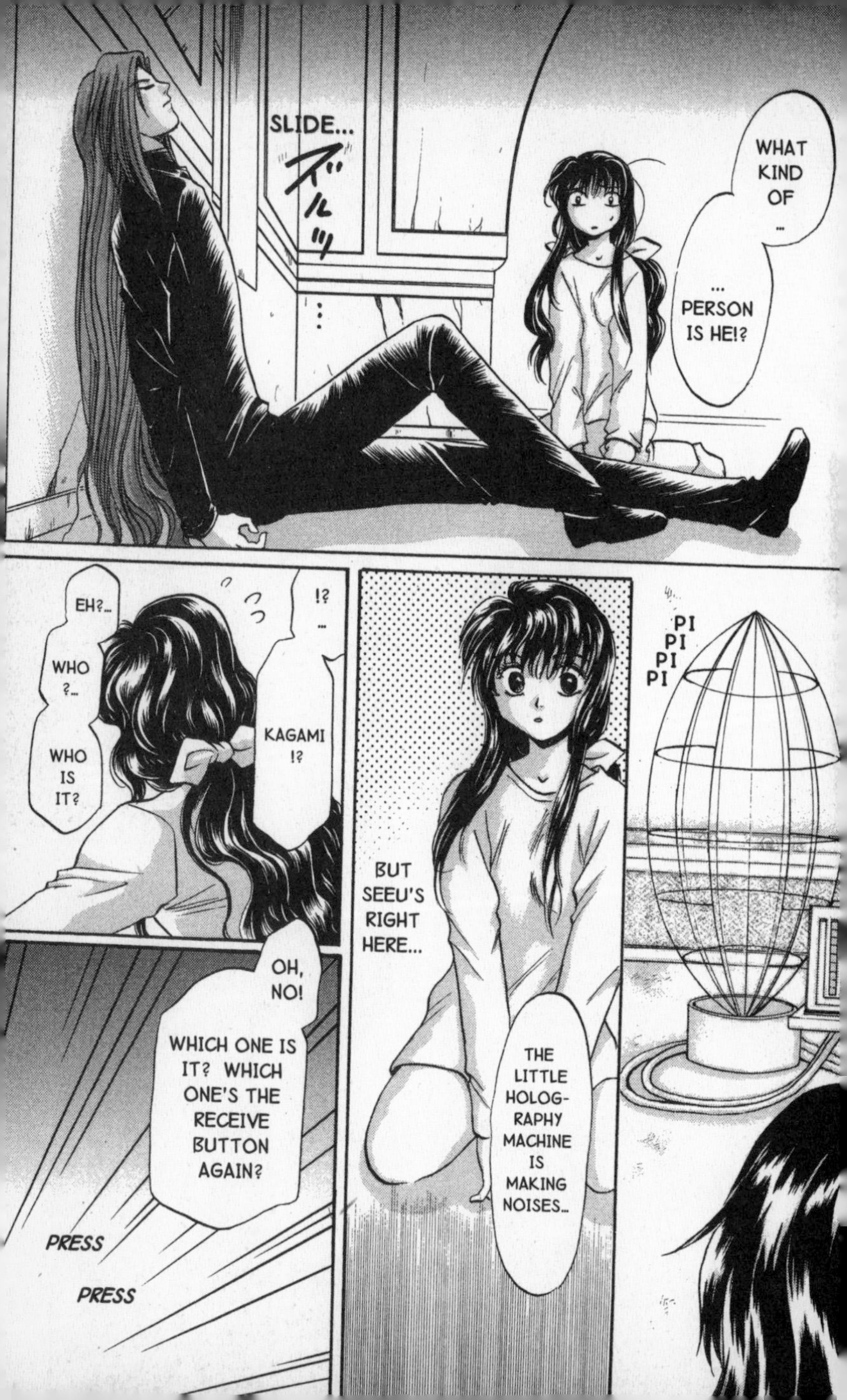

WHAT KIND OF ... ... PERSON IS HE!?
SLIDE...
ズルッ
...
PI PI PI PI
THE LITTLE HOLOG-RAPHY MACHINE IS MAKING NOISES..
BUT SEEU'S RIGHT HERE...
!? ...
KAGAMI !?
EH?... WHO ?...
WHO IS IT?
OH, NO!
WHICH ONE IS IT? WHICH ONE'S THE RECEIVE BUTTON AGAIN?
PRESS
PRESS

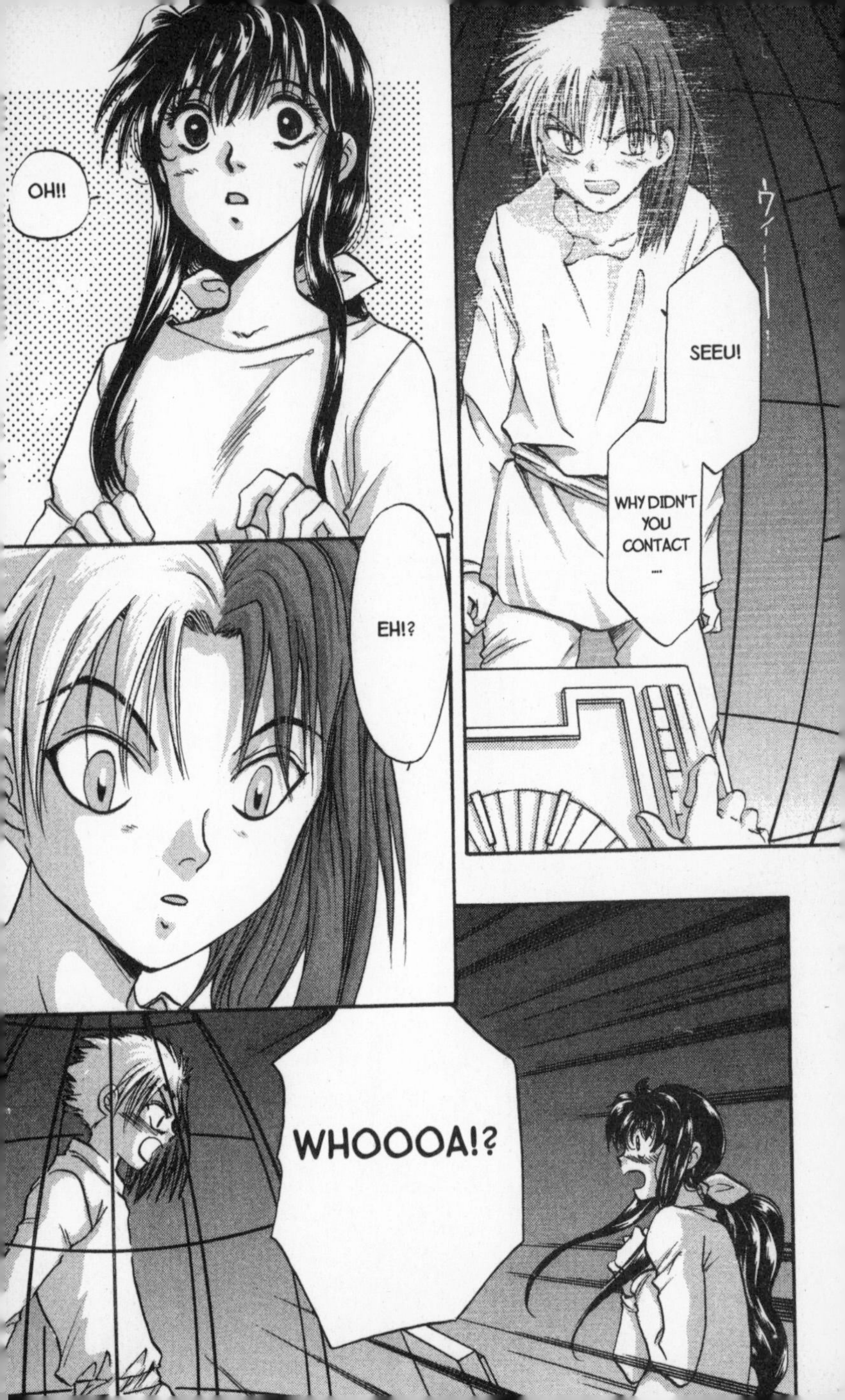
ウィー
SEEU!
WHY DIDN'T YOU CONTACT ...
OH!!
EH!?
WHOOOA!?

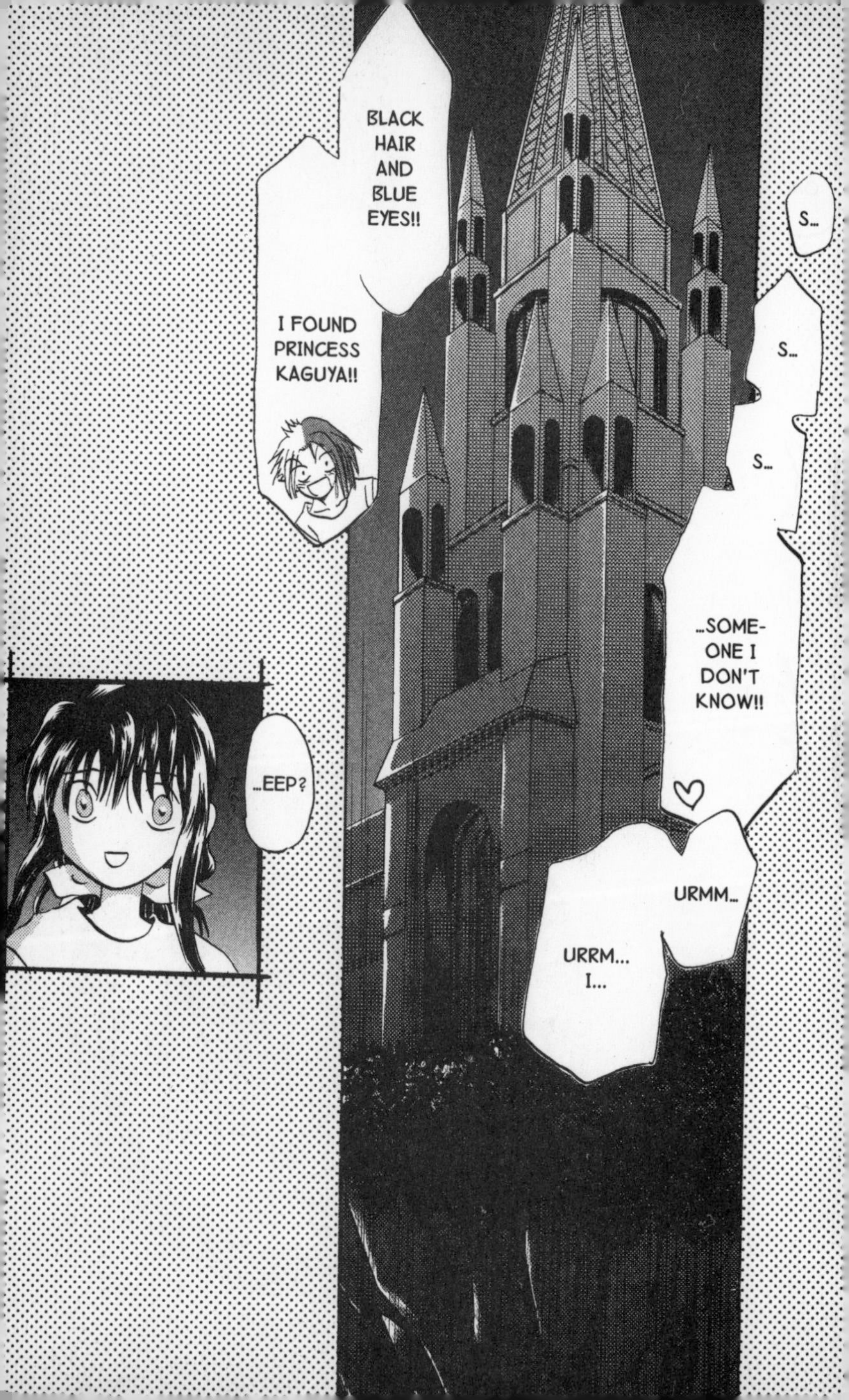
BLACK HAIR AND BLUE EYES!!
I FOUND PRINCESS KAGUYA!!
...EEP?
S...
S...
S...
...SOME-ONE I DON'T KNOW!!
URMM...
URRM... I...

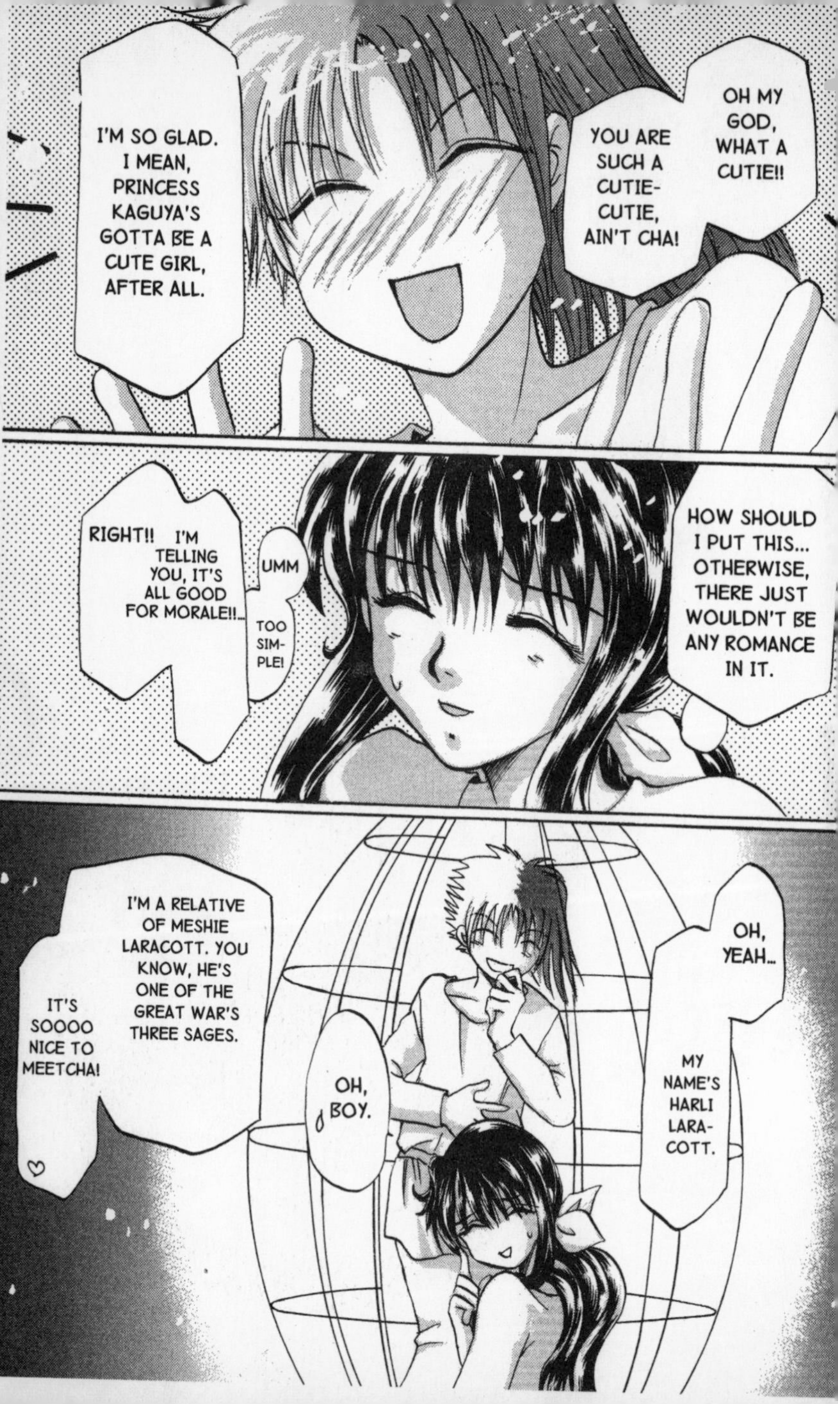
OH MY GOD, WHAT A CUTIE!!
YOU ARE SUCH A CUTIE-CUTIE, AIN'T CHA!
I'M SO GLAD. I MEAN, PRINCESS KAGUYA'S GOTTA BE A CUTE GIRL, AFTER ALL.
HOW SHOULD I PUT THIS... OTHERWISE, THERE JUST WOULDN'T BE ANY ROMANCE IN IT.
UMM
TOO SIMPLE!
RIGHT!! I'M TELLING YOU, IT'S ALL GOOD FOR MORALE!!
OH, YEAH...
MY NAME'S HARLI LARACOTT.
OH, BOY.
I'M A RELATIVE OF MESHIE LARACOTT. YOU KNOW, HE'S ONE OF THE GREAT WAR'S THREE SAGES.
IT'S SOOOO NICE TO MEETCHA!

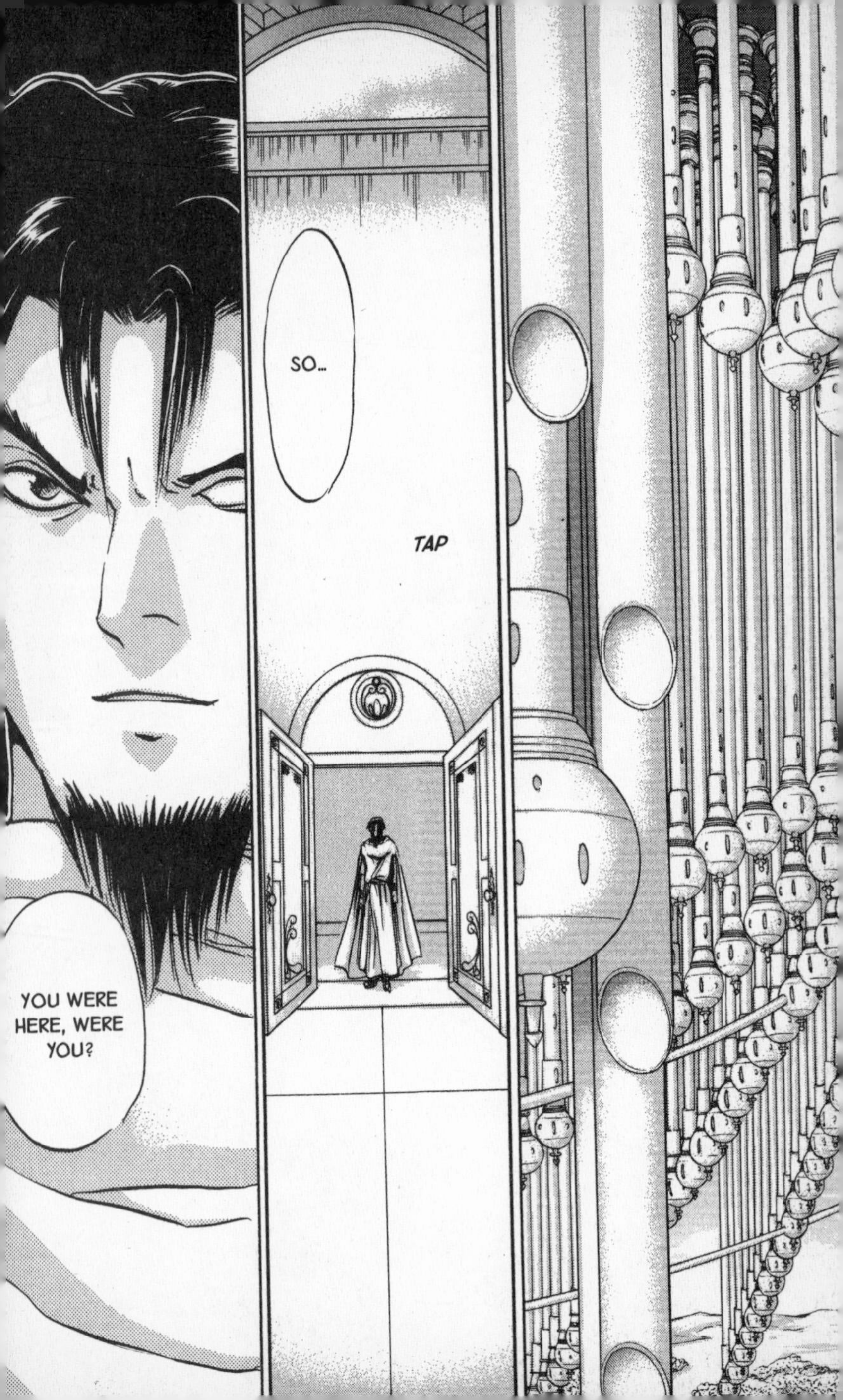
SO...
TAP
YOU WERE HERE, WERE YOU?

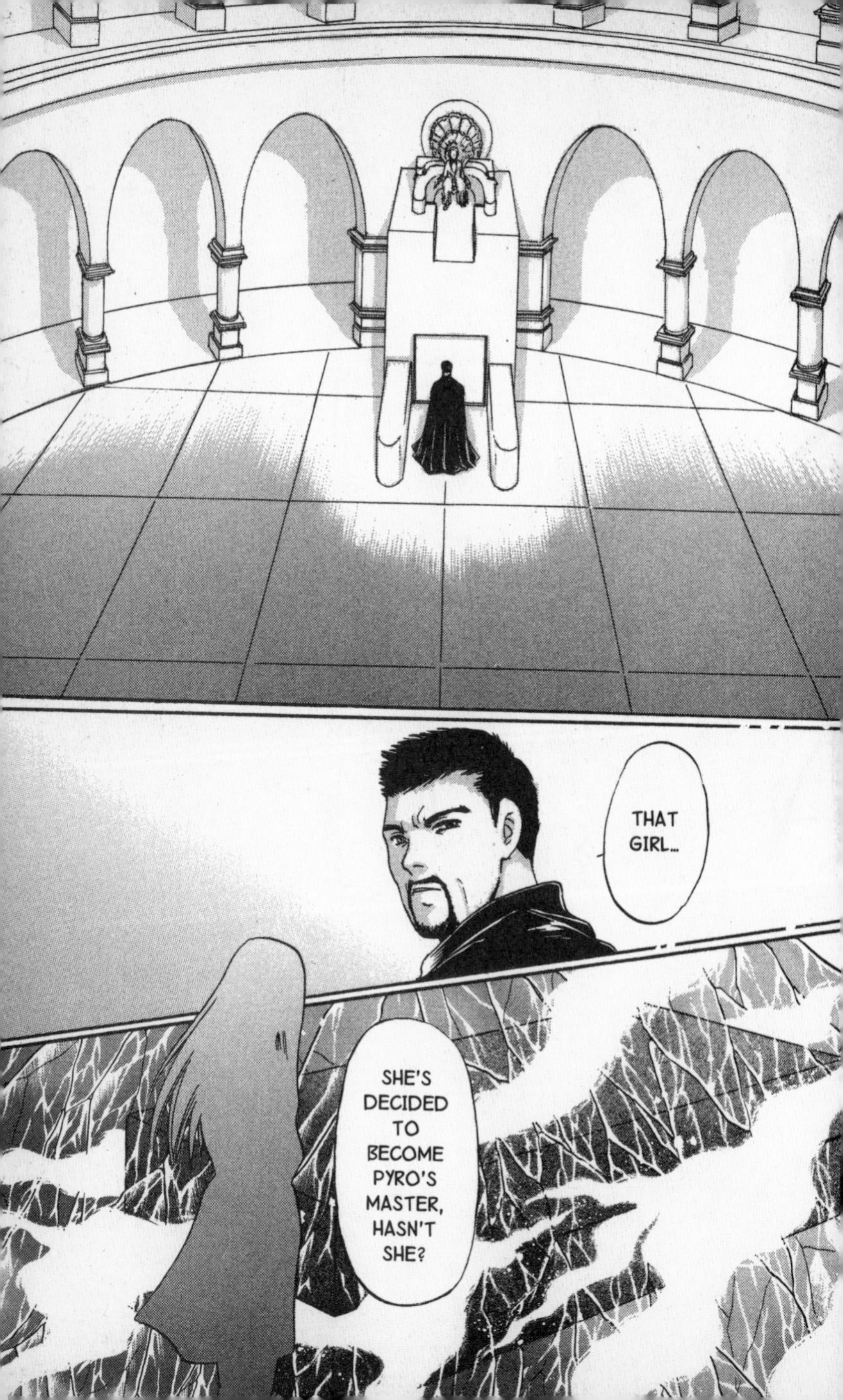
THAT GIRL...
SHE'S DECIDED TO BECOME PYRO'S MASTER, HASN'T SHE?

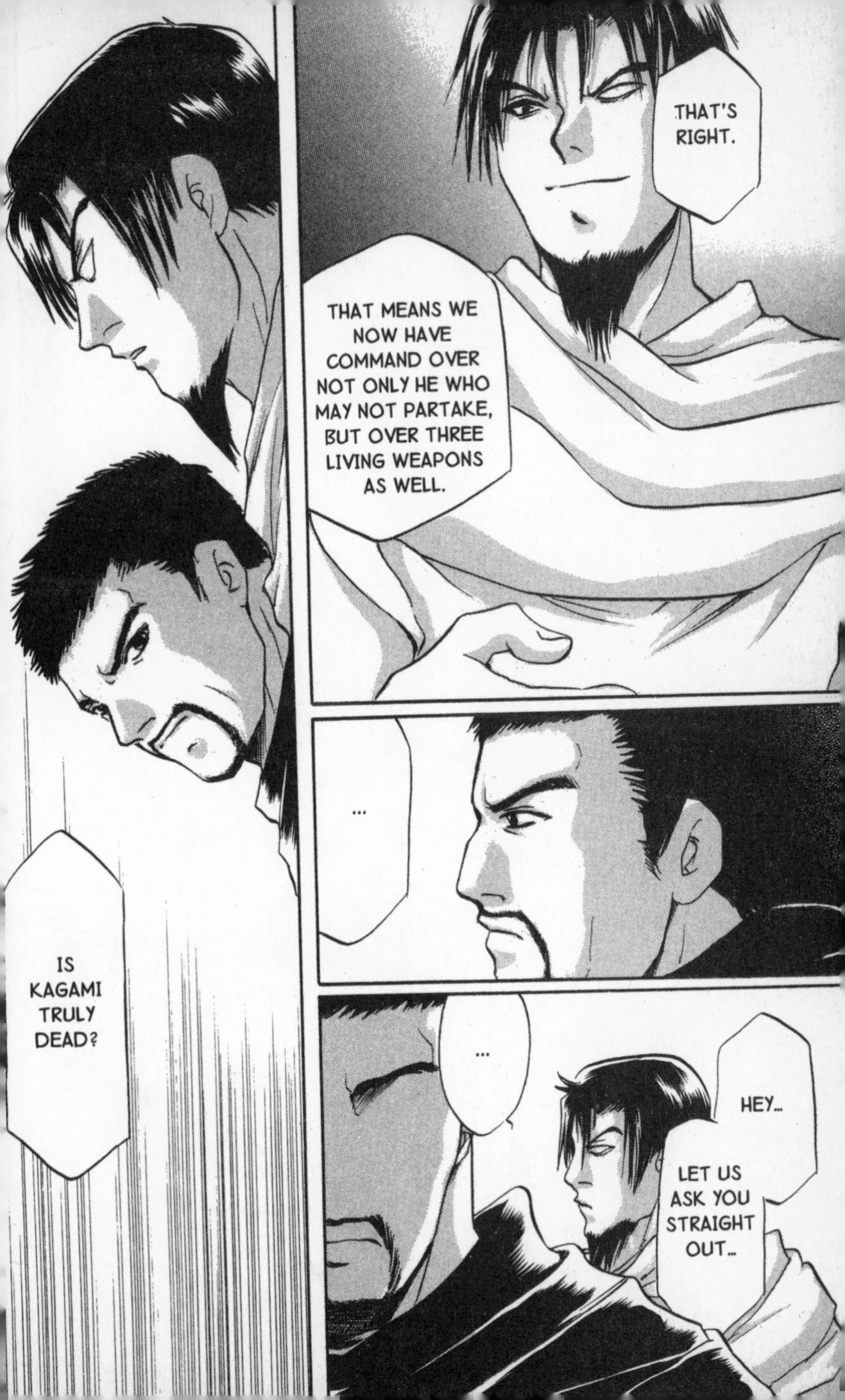
THAT'S RIGHT.
THAT MEANS WE NOW HAVE COMMAND OVER NOT ONLY HE WHO MAY NOT PARTAKE, BUT OVER THREE LIVING WEAPONS AS WELL.
...
...
HEY...
LET US ASK YOU STRAIGHT OUT...
IS KAGAMI TRULY DEAD?

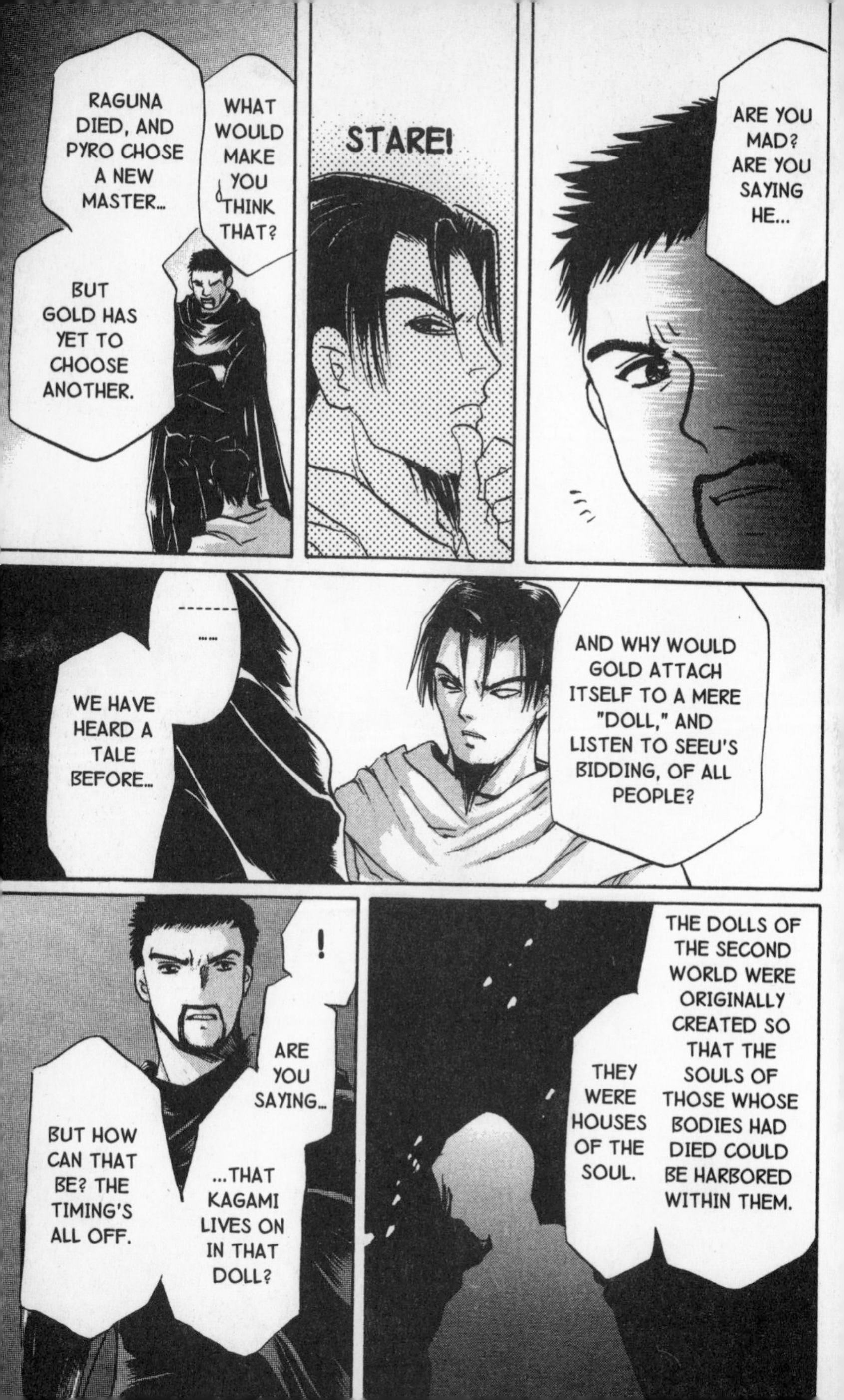
ARE YOU MAD? ARE YOU SAYING HE...
STARE!
WHAT WOULD MAKE YOU THINK THAT?
RAGUNA DIED, AND PYRO CHOSE A NEW MASTER...
BUT GOLD HAS YET TO CHOOSE ANOTHER.
AND WHY WOULD GOLD ATTACH ITSELF TO A MERE "DOLL," AND LISTEN TO SEEU'S BIDDING, OF ALL PEOPLE?
------ ......
WE HAVE HEARD A TALE BEFORE...
THE DOLLS OF THE SECOND WORLD WERE ORIGINALLY CREATED SO THAT THE SOULS OF THOSE WHOSE BODIES HAD DIED COULD BE HARBORED WITHIN THEM.
THEY WERE HOUSES OF THE SOUL.
!
ARE YOU SAYING...
...THAT KAGAMI LIVES ON IN THAT DOLL?
BUT HOW CAN THAT BE? THE TIMING'S ALL OFF.

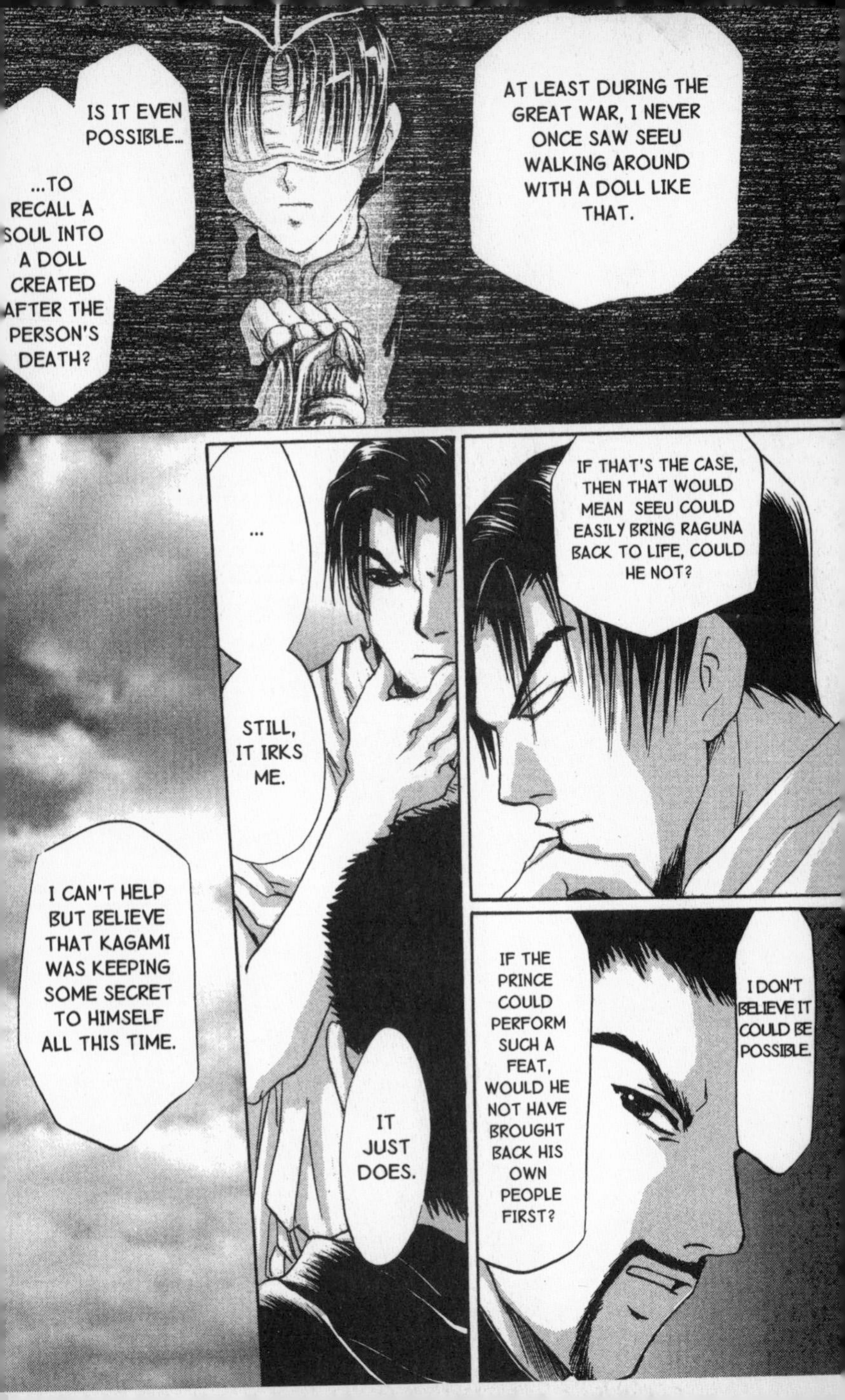

AT LEAST DURING THE GREAT WAR, I NEVER ONCE SAW SEEU WALKING AROUND WITH A DOLL LIKE THAT.
IS IT EVEN POSSIBLE...
...TO RECALL A SOUL INTO A DOLL CREATED AFTER THE PERSON'S DEATH?
IF THAT'S THE CASE, THEN THAT WOULD MEAN SEEU COULD EASILY BRING RAGUNA BACK TO LIFE, COULD HE NOT?
I DON'T BELIEVE IT COULD BE POSSIBLE.
IF THE PRINCE COULD PERFORM SUCH A FEAT, WOULD HE NOT HAVE BROUGHT BACK HIS OWN PEOPLE FIRST?
...
STILL, IT IRKS ME.
I CAN'T HELP BUT BELIEVE THAT KAGAMI WAS KEEPING SOME SECRET TO HIMSELF ALL THIS TIME.
IT JUST DOES.

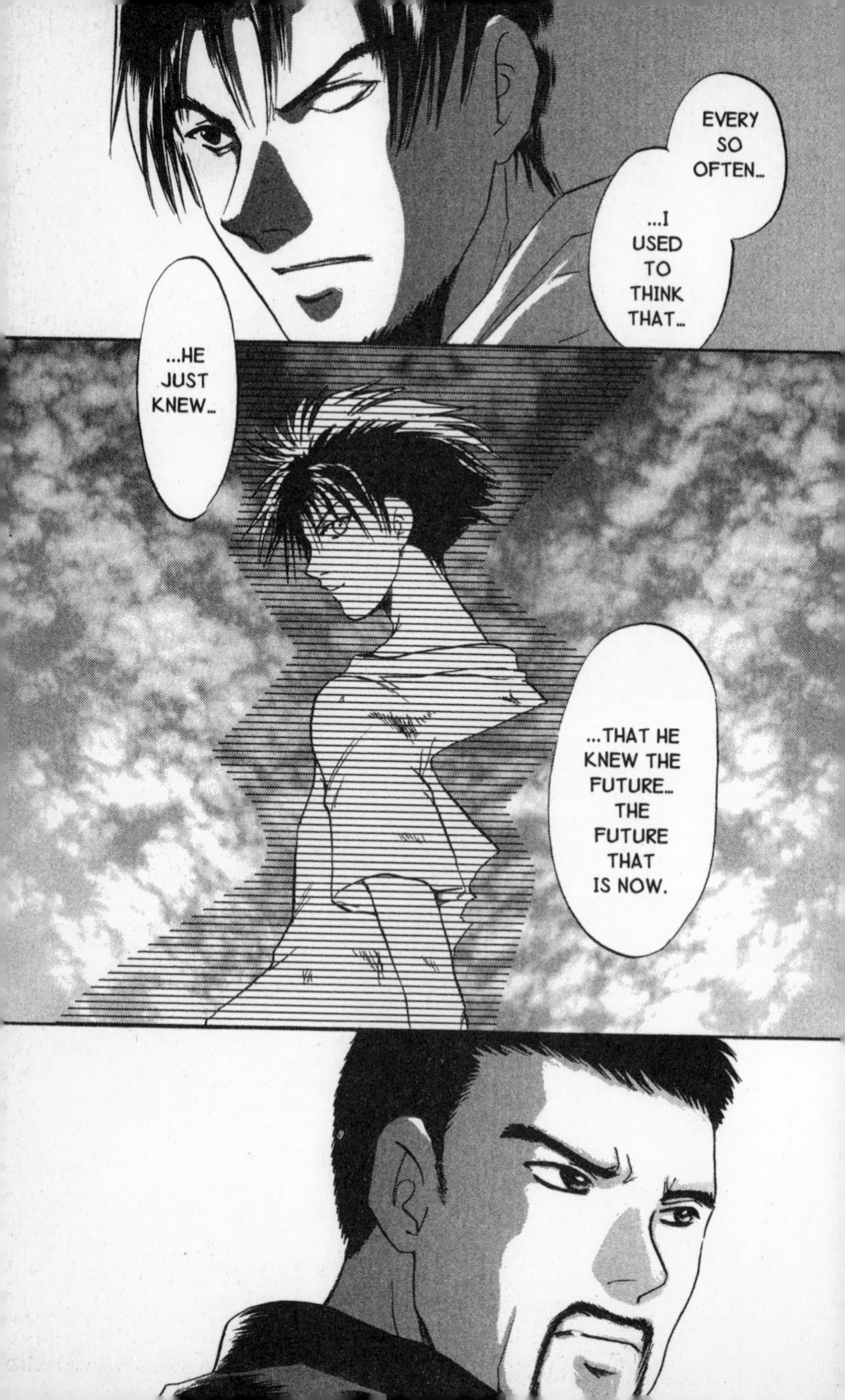
EVERY SO OFTEN...
...I USED TO THINK THAT...
...HE JUST KNEW...
...THAT HE KNEW THE FUTURE... THE FUTURE THAT IS NOW.

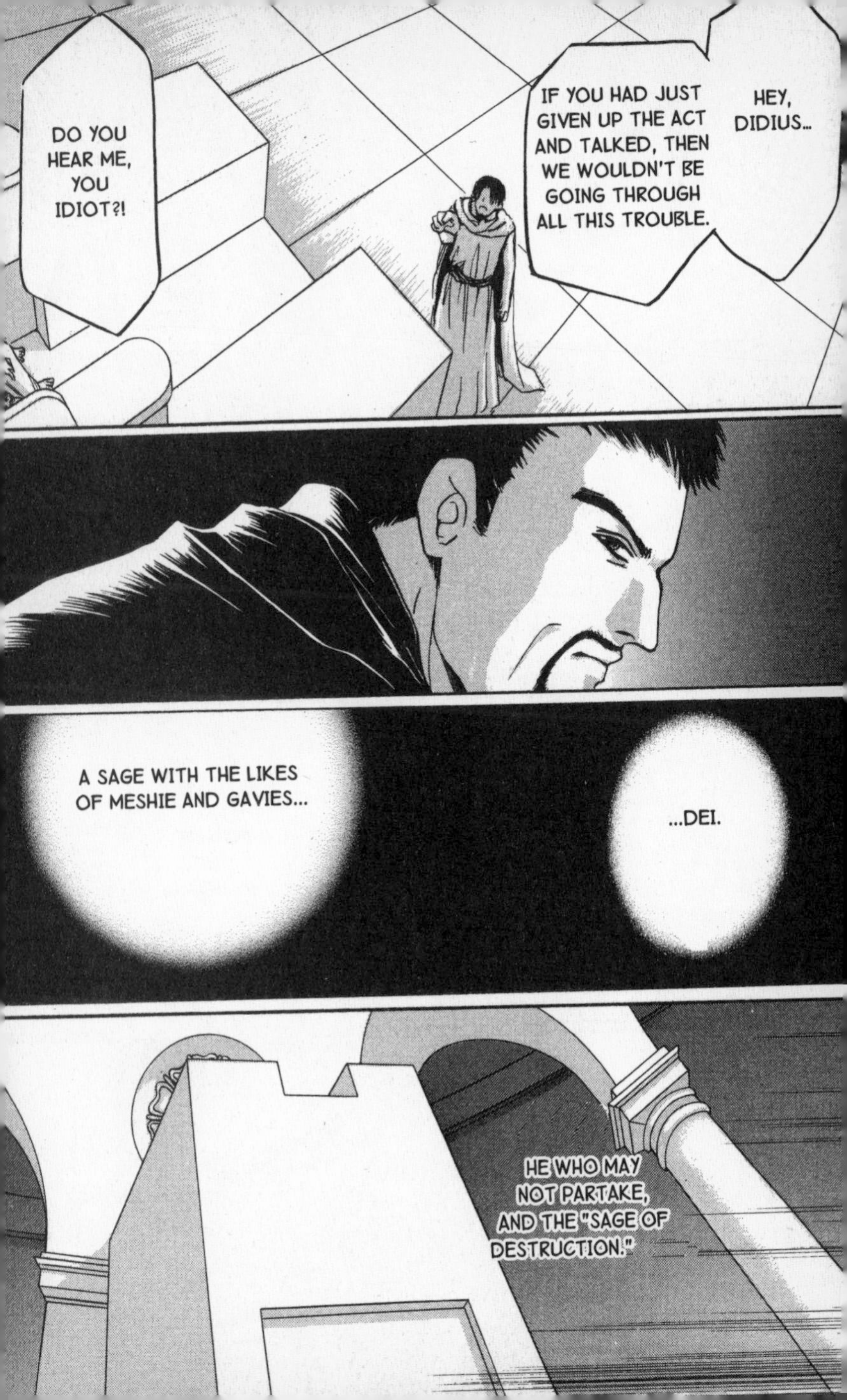
HEY, DIDIUS...
IF YOU HAD JUST GIVEN UP THE ACT AND TALKED, THEN WE WOULDN'T BE GOING THROUGH ALL THIS TROUBLE.
DO YOU HEAR ME, YOU IDIOT?!
...DEI.
A SAGE WITH THE LIKES OF MESHIE AND GAVIES...
HE WHO MAY NOT PARTAKE, AND THE "SAGE OF DESTRUCTION."

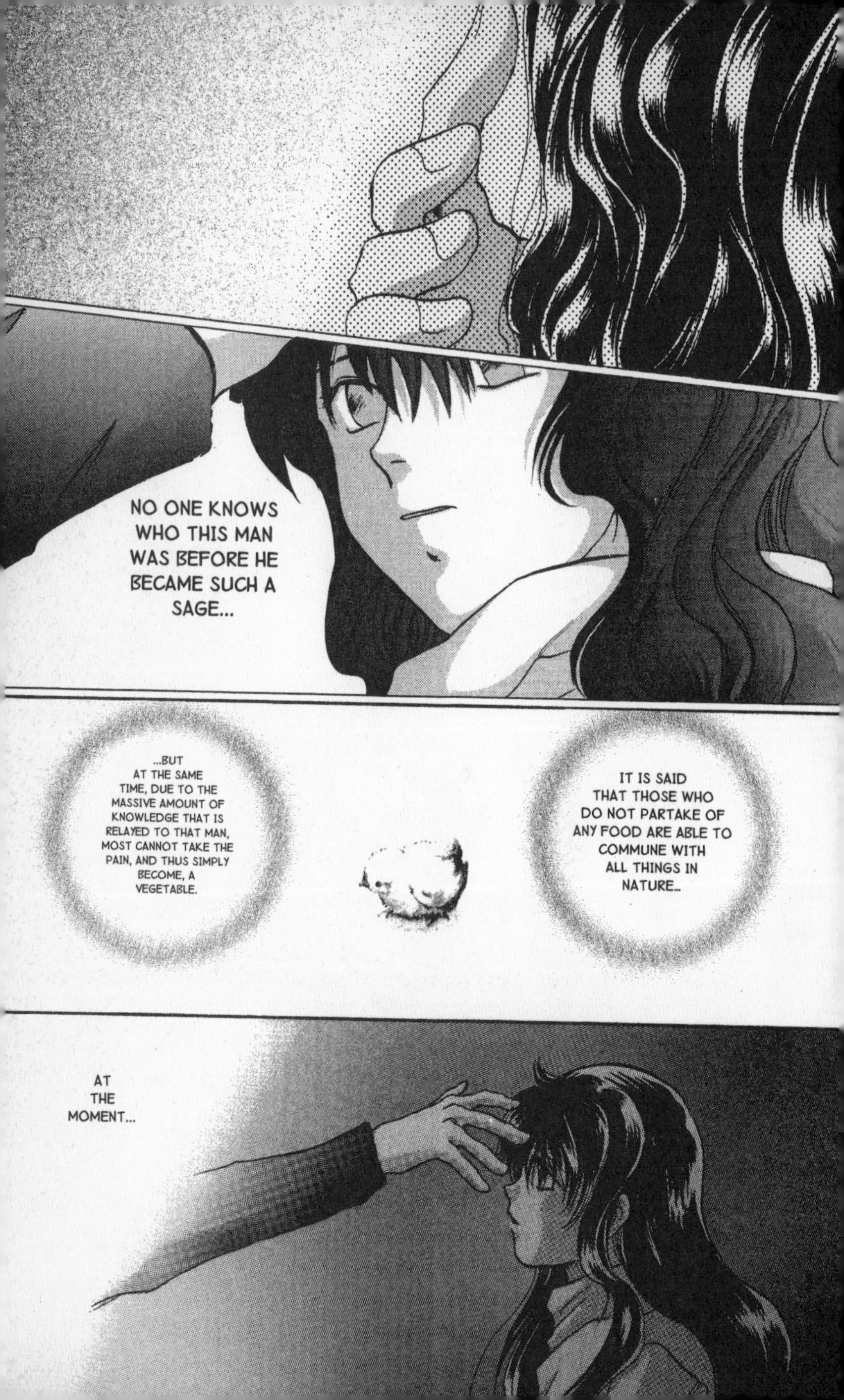
NO ONE KNOWS WHO THIS MAN WAS BEFORE HE BECAME SUCH A SAGE...
IT IS SAID THAT THOSE WHO DO NOT PARTAKE OF ANY FOOD ARE ABLE TO COMMUNE WITH ALL THINGS IN NATURE..
...BUT AT THE SAME TIME, DUE TO THE MASSIVE AMOUNT OF KNOWLEDGE THAT IS RELAYED TO THAT MAN, MOST CANNOT TAKE THE PAIN, AND THUS SIMPLY BECOME, A VEGETABLE.
AT THE MOMENT...

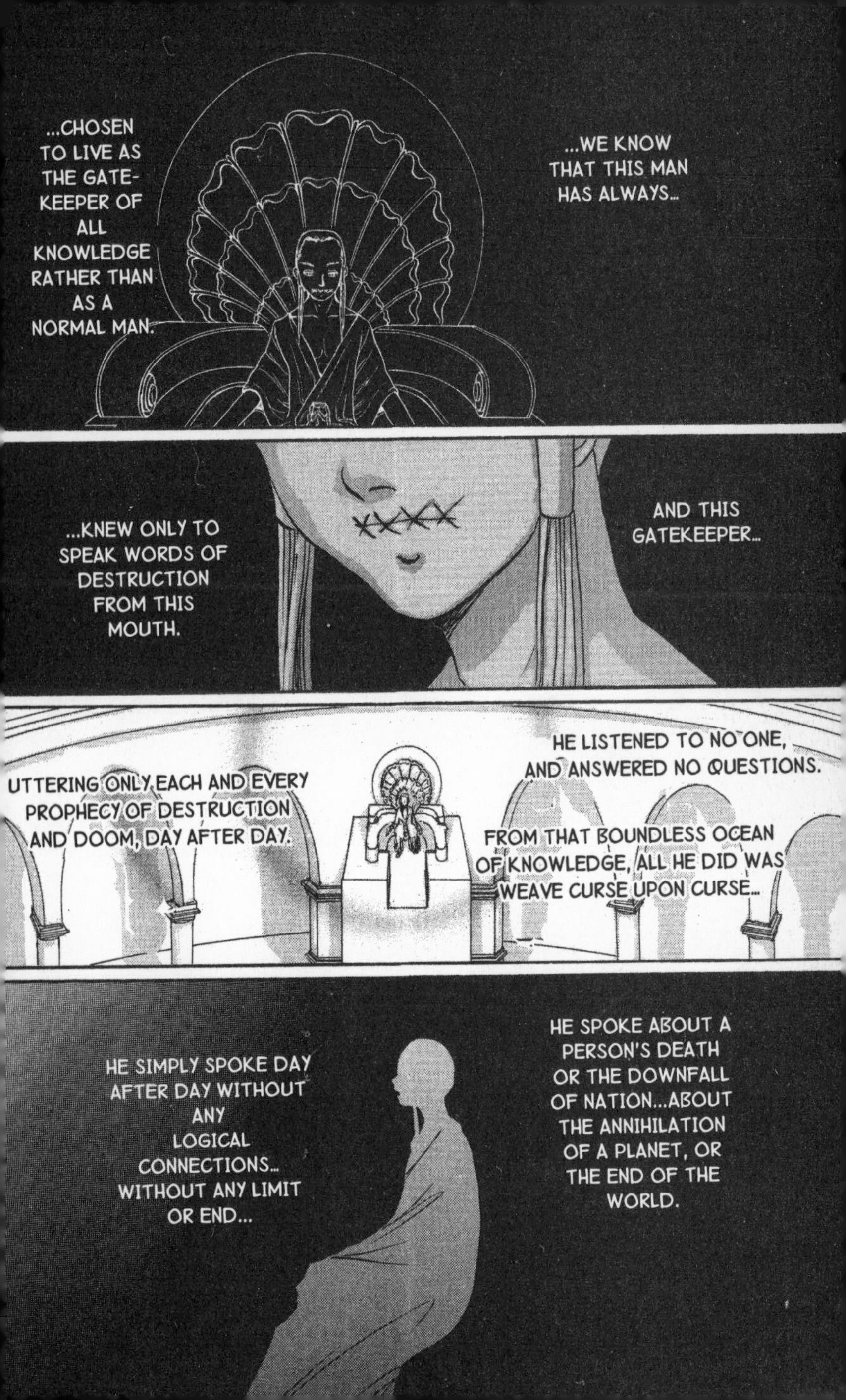
...WE KNOW THAT THIS MAN HAS ALWAYS...
...CHOSEN TO LIVE AS THE GATE-KEEPER OF ALL KNOWLEDGE RATHER THAN AS A NORMAL MAN.
AND THIS GATEKEEPER...
...KNEW ONLY TO SPEAK WORDS OF DESTRUCTION FROM THIS MOUTH.
HE LISTENED TO NO ONE, AND ANSWERED NO QUESTIONS.
FROM THAT BOUNDLESS OCEAN OF KNOWLEDGE, ALL HE DID WAS WEAVE CURSE UPON CURSE...
UTTERING ONLY EACH AND EVERY PROPHECY OF DESTRUCTION AND DOOM, DAY AFTER DAY.
HE SPOKE ABOUT A PERSON'S DEATH OR THE DOWNFALL OF NATION...ABOUT THE ANNIHILATION OF A PLANET, OR THE END OF THE WORLD.
HE SIMPLY SPOKE DAY AFTER DAY WITHOUT ANY LOGICAL CONNECTIONS... WITHOUT ANY LIMIT OR END...

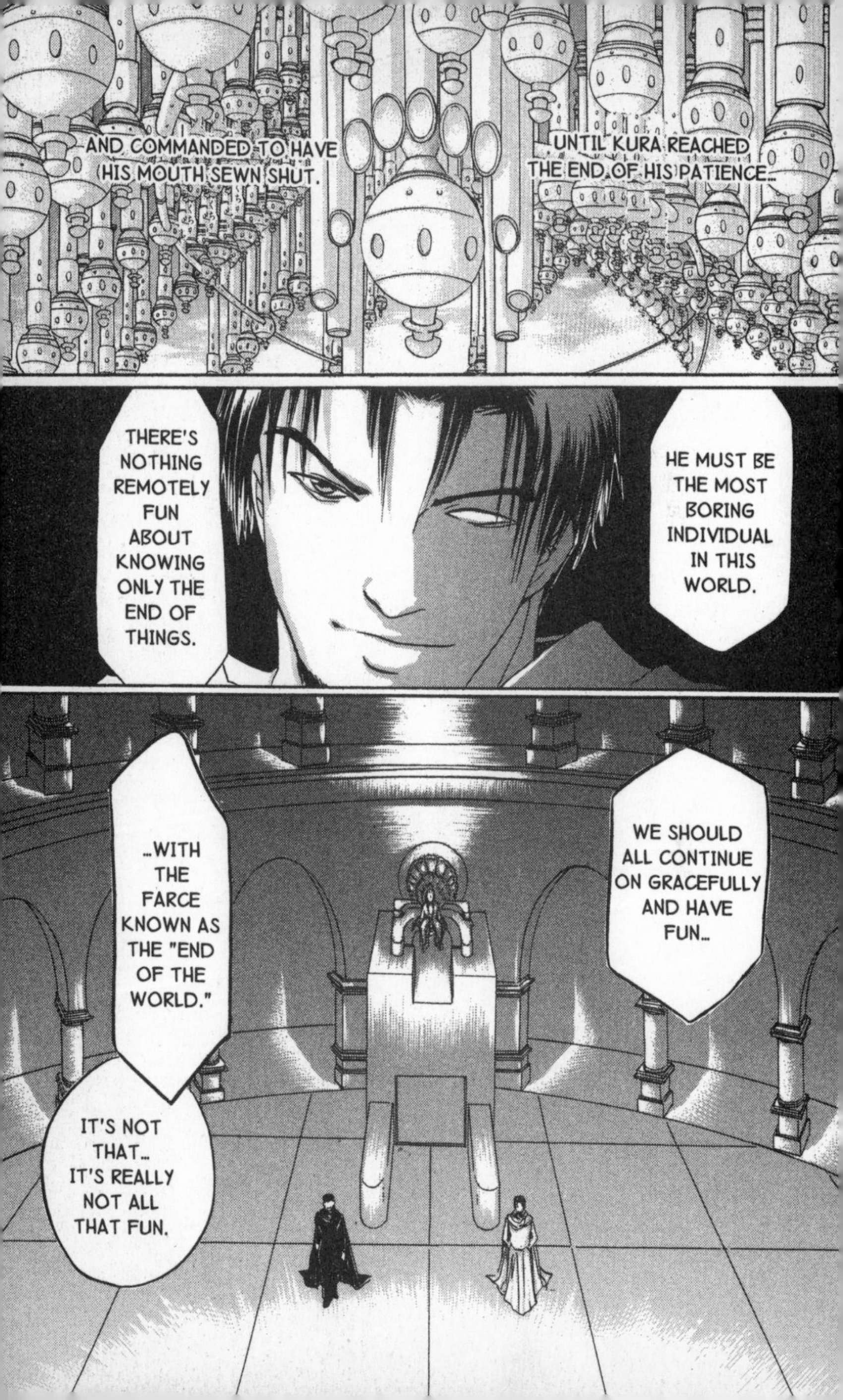
UNTIL KURA REACHED THE END OF HIS PATIENCE...
AND COMMANDED TO HAVE HIS MOUTH SEWN SHUT.
HE MUST BE THE MOST BORING INDIVIDUAL IN THIS WORLD.
THERE'S NOTHING REMOTELY FUN ABOUT KNOWING ONLY THE END OF THINGS.
WE SHOULD ALL CONTINUE ON GRACEFULLY AND HAVE FUN...
...WITH THE FARCE KNOWN AS THE "END OF THE WORLD."
IT'S NOT THAT... IT'S REALLY NOT ALL THAT FUN.

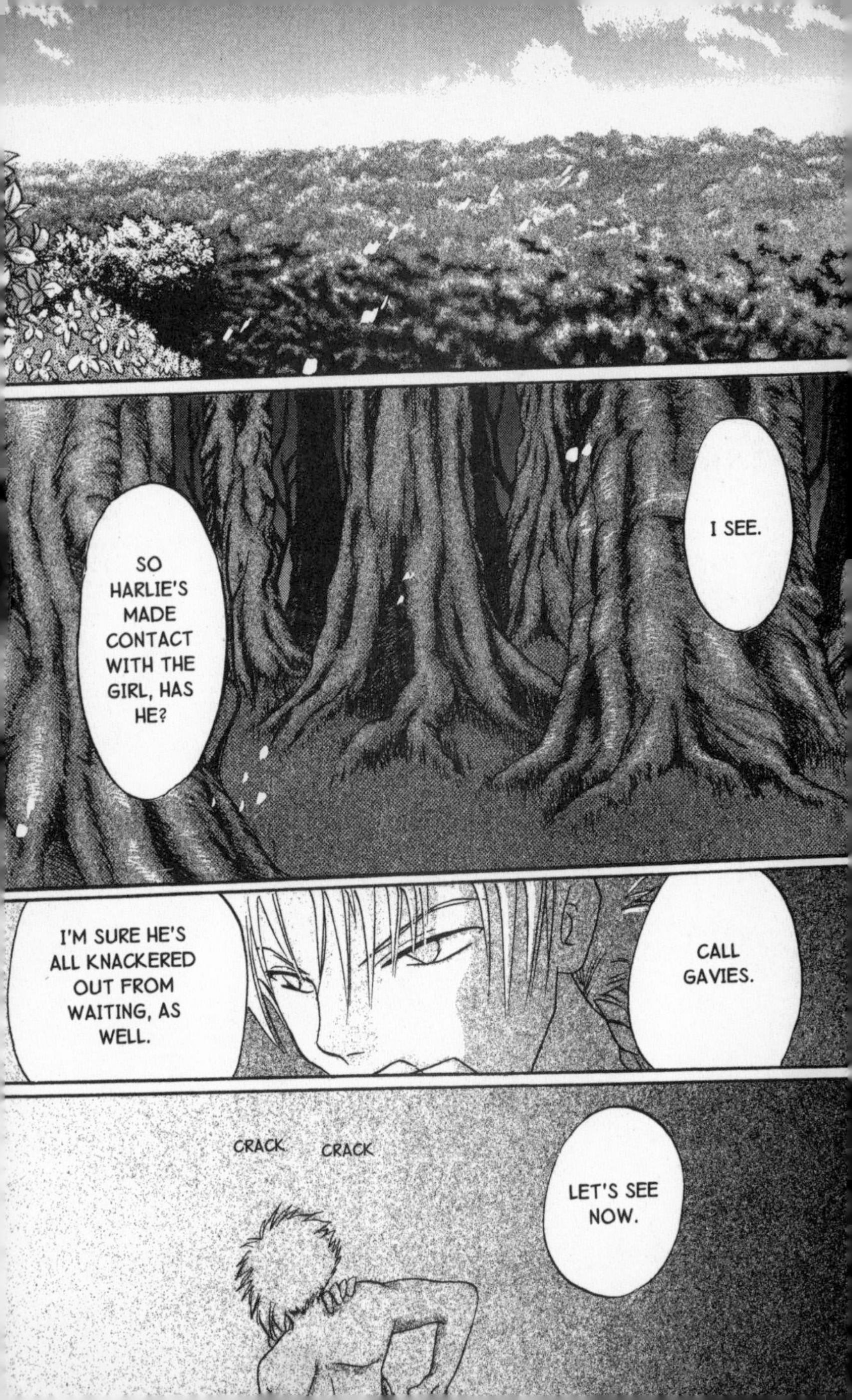
I SEE.
SO HARLIE'S MADE CONTACT WITH THE GIRL, HAS HE?
CALL GAVIES.
I'M SURE HE'S ALL KNACKERED OUT FROM WAITING, AS WELL.
LET'S SEE NOW.
CRACK
CRACK

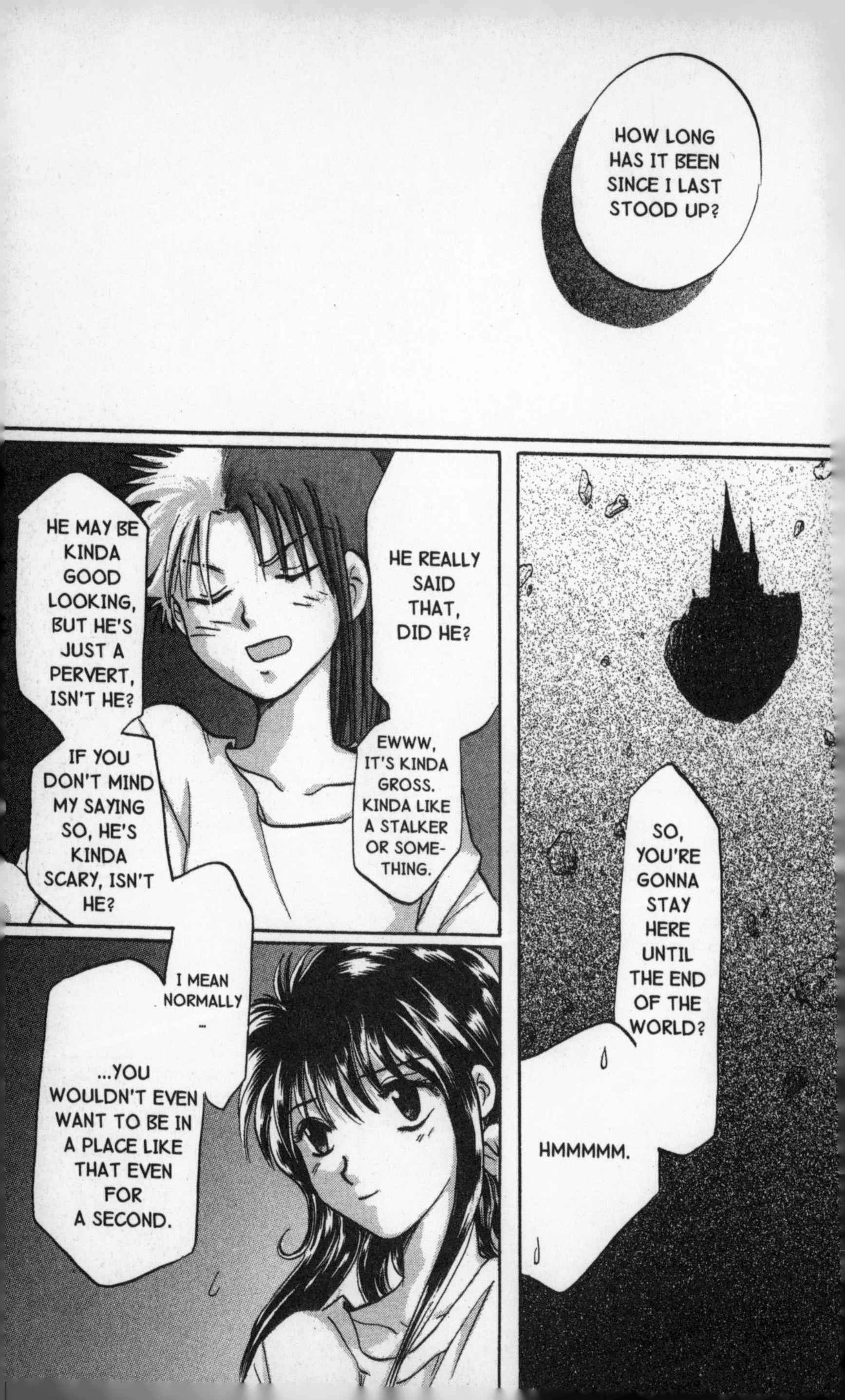
HOW LONG HAS IT BEEN SINCE I LAST STOOD UP?
SO, YOU'RE GONNA STAY HERE UNTIL THE END OF THE WORLD?
HMMMMM.
HE REALLY SAID THAT, DID HE?
EWWW, IT'S KINDA GROSS. KINDA LIKE A STALKER OR SOME-THING.
HE MAY BE KINDA GOOD LOOKING, BUT HE'S JUST A PERVERT, ISN'T HE?
IF YOU DON'T MIND MY SAYING SO, HE'S KINDA SCARY, ISN'T HE?
I MEAN NORMALLY ...
...YOU WOULDN'T EVEN WANT TO BE IN A PLACE LIKE THAT EVEN FOR A SECOND.

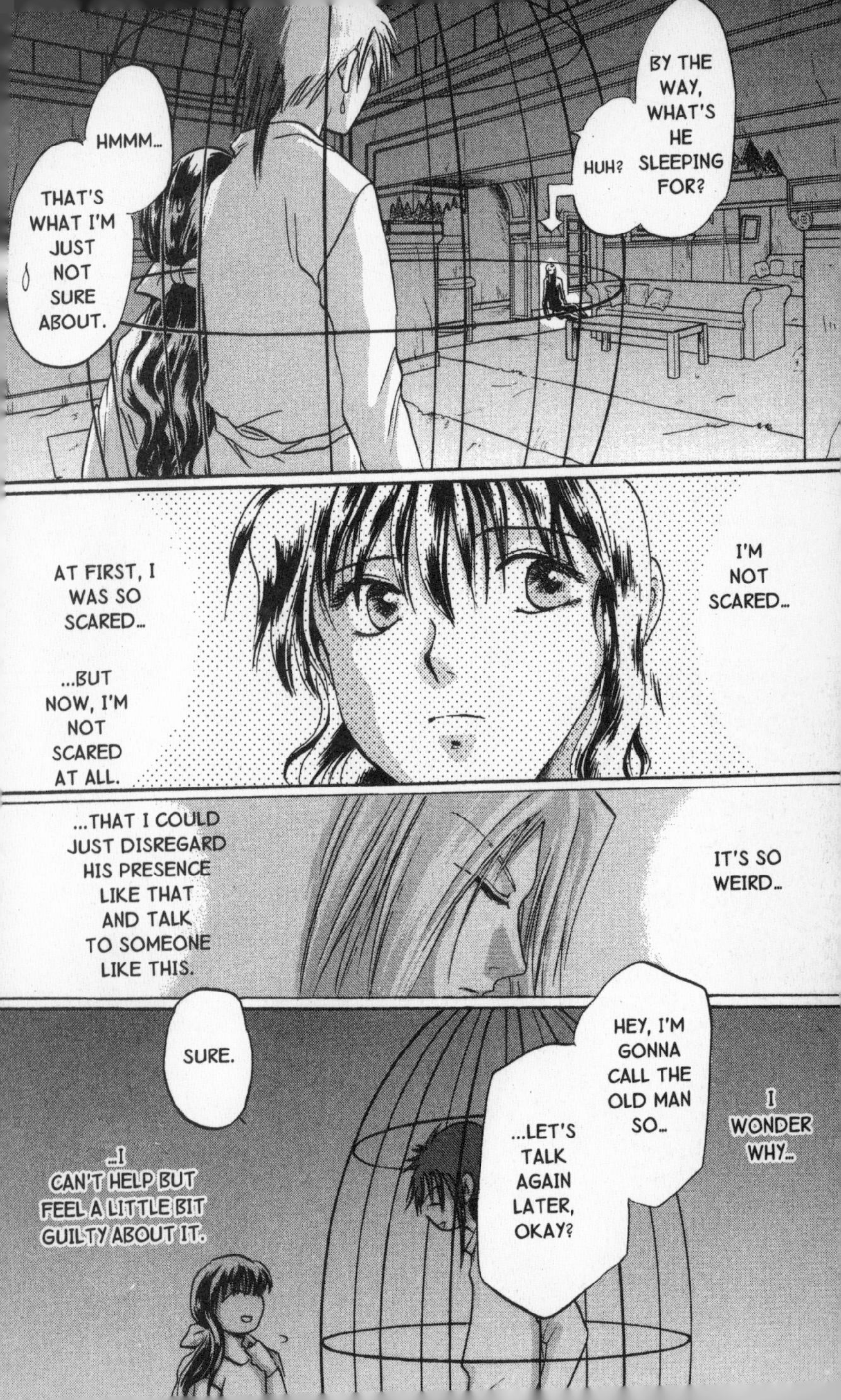
BY THE WAY, WHAT'S HE SLEEPING FOR?
HUH?
HMMM...
THAT'S WHAT I'M JUST NOT SURE ABOUT.
I'M NOT SCARED...
AT FIRST, I WAS SO SCARED...
...BUT NOW, I'M NOT SCARED AT ALL.
IT'S SO WEIRD...
...THAT I COULD JUST DISREGARD HIS PRESENCE LIKE THAT AND TALK TO SOMEONE LIKE THIS.
I WONDER WHY...
HEY, I'M GONNA CALL THE OLD MAN SO...
...LET'S TALK AGAIN LATER, OKAY?
SURE.
...I CAN'T HELP BUT FEEL A LITTLE BIT GUILTY ABOUT IT.

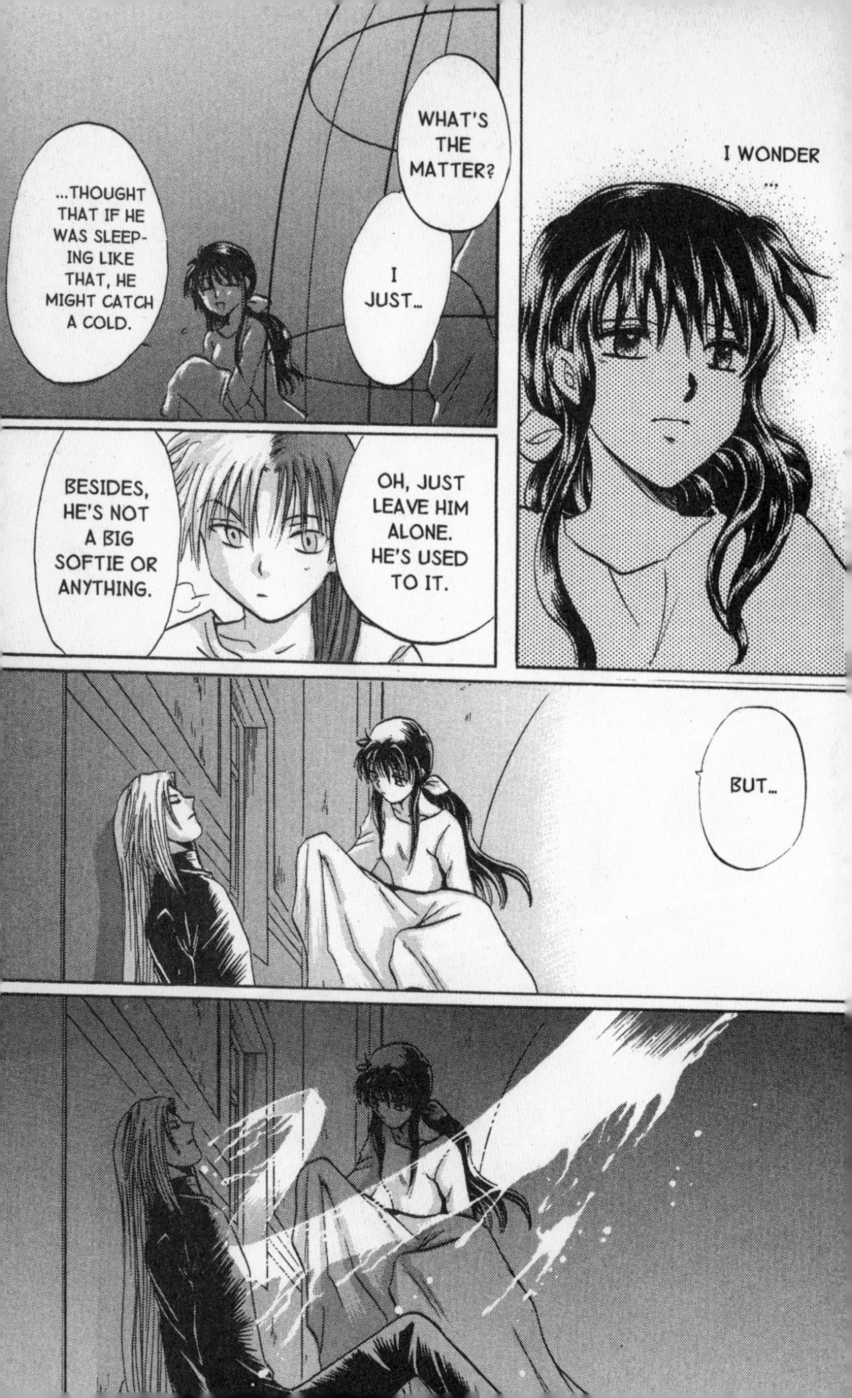
I WONDER ...
WHAT'S THE MATTER?
I JUST...
...THOUGHT THAT IF HE WAS SLEEPING LIKE THAT, HE MIGHT CATCH A COLD.
OH, JUST LEAVE HIM ALONE. HE'S USED TO IT.
BESIDES, HE'S NOT A BIG SOFTIE OR ANYTHING.
BUT...

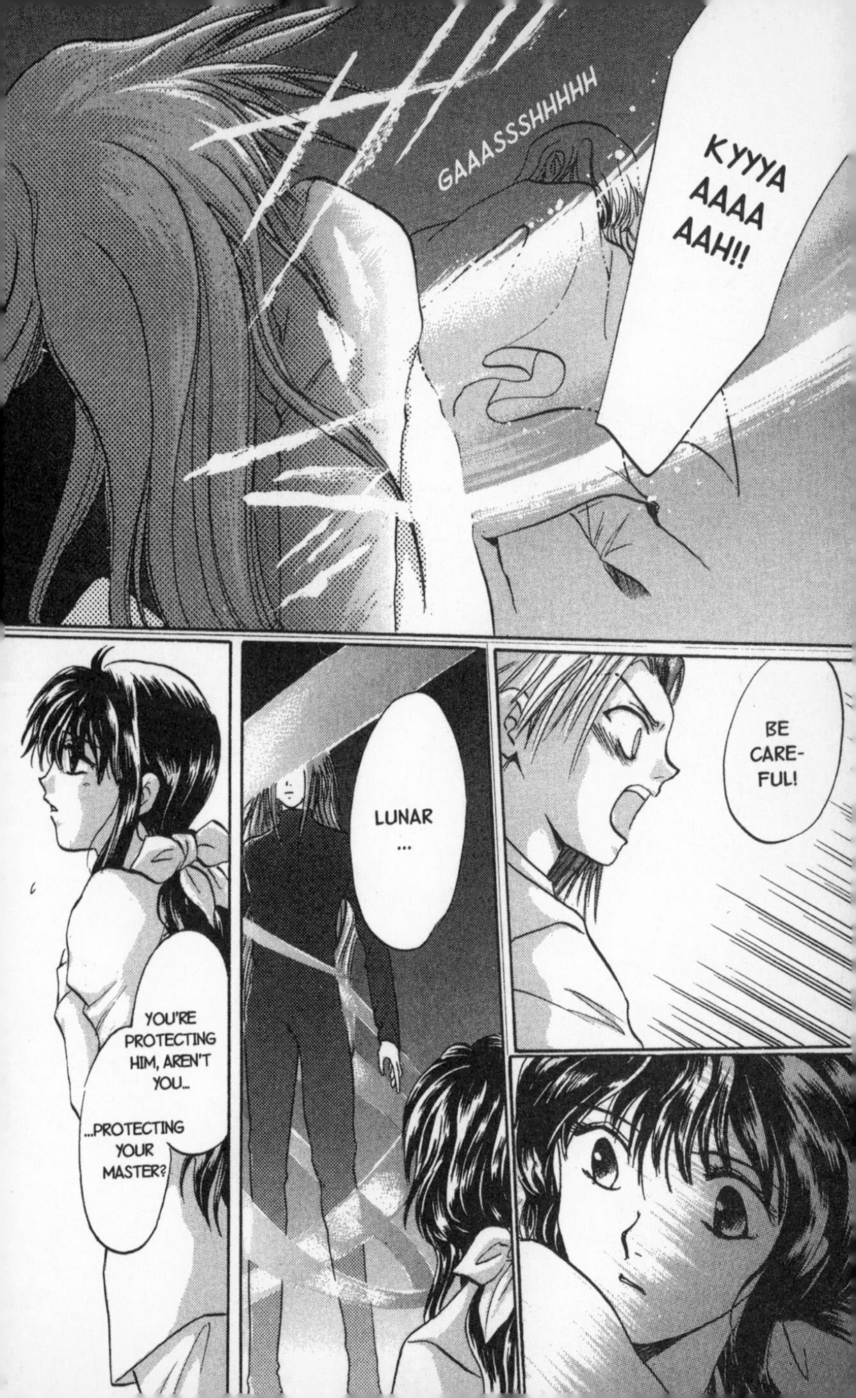
KYYYA AAAA AAH!!
GAAASSSHHHH
BE CARE-FUL!
LUNAR ...
YOU'RE PROTECTING HIM, AREN'T YOU...
...PROTECTING YOUR MASTER?

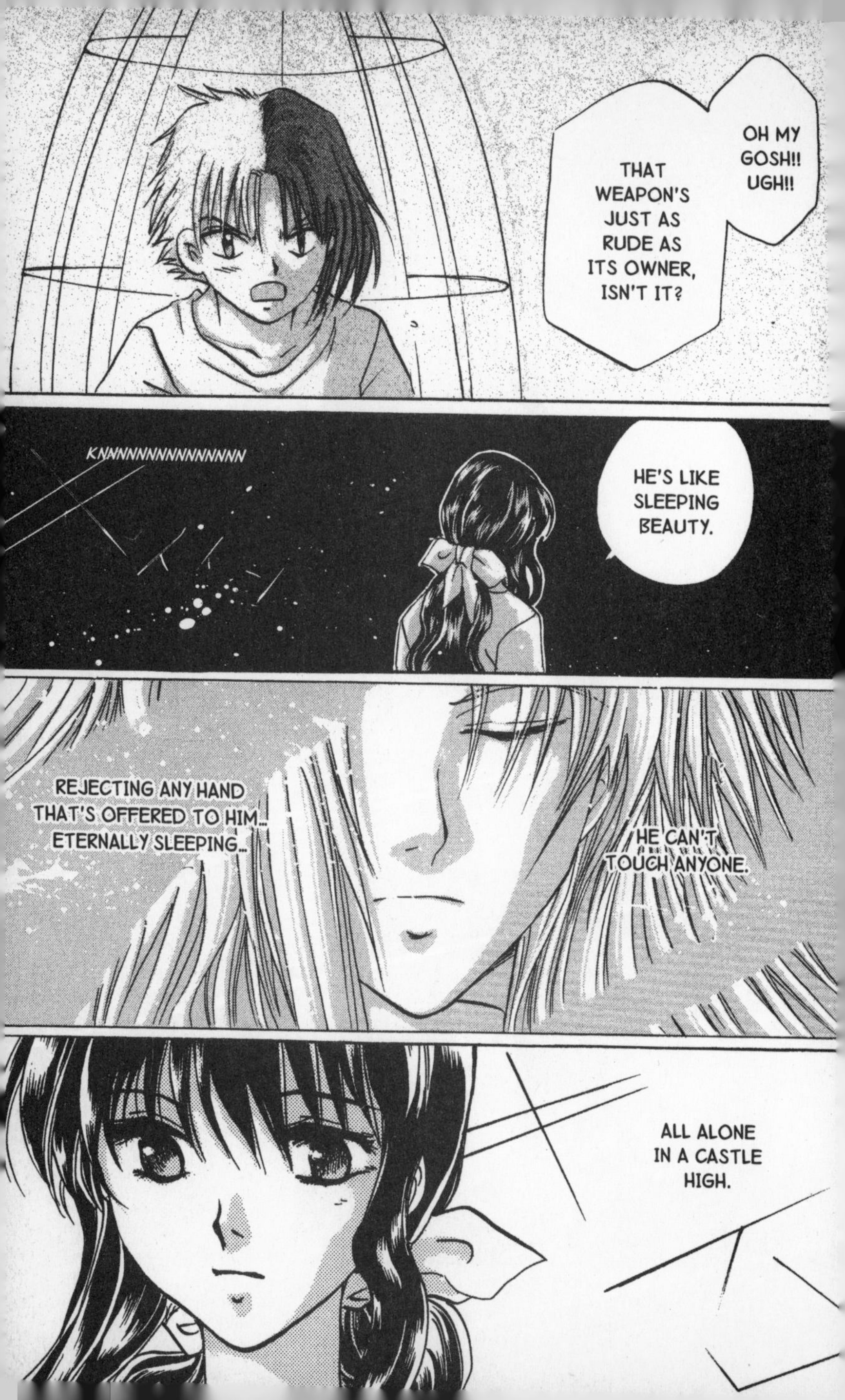
OH MY GOSH!! UGH!!
THAT WEAPON'S JUST AS RUDE AS ITS OWNER, ISN'T IT?
HE'S LIKE SLEEPING BEAUTY.
KNNNNNNNNNNNNNNN
HE CAN'T TOUCH ANYONE.
REJECTING ANY HAND THAT'S OFFERED TO HIM... ETERNALLY SLEEPING...
ALL ALONE IN A CASTLE HIGH.

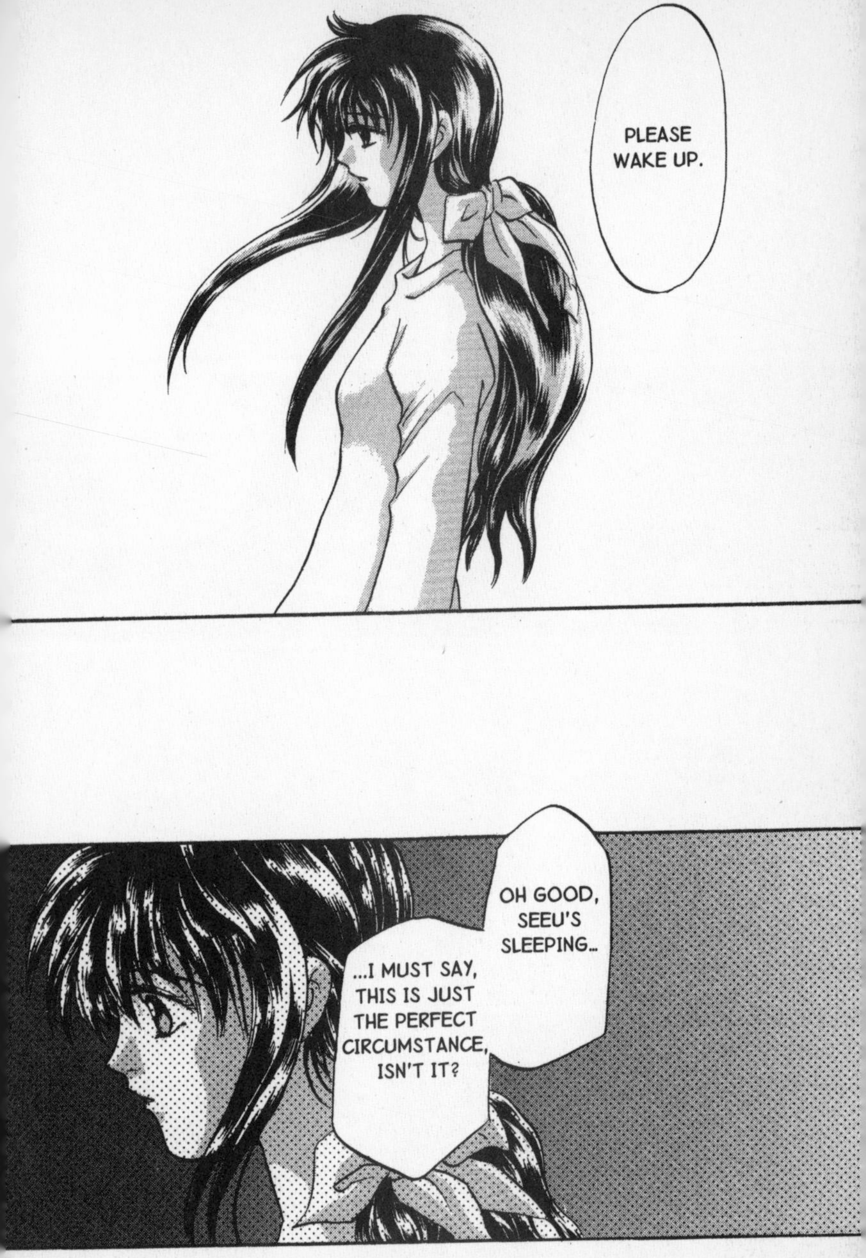
PLEASE WAKE UP.
OH GOOD, SEEU'S SLEEPING...
...I MUST SAY, THIS IS JUST THE PERFECT CIRCUMSTANCE, ISN'T IT?

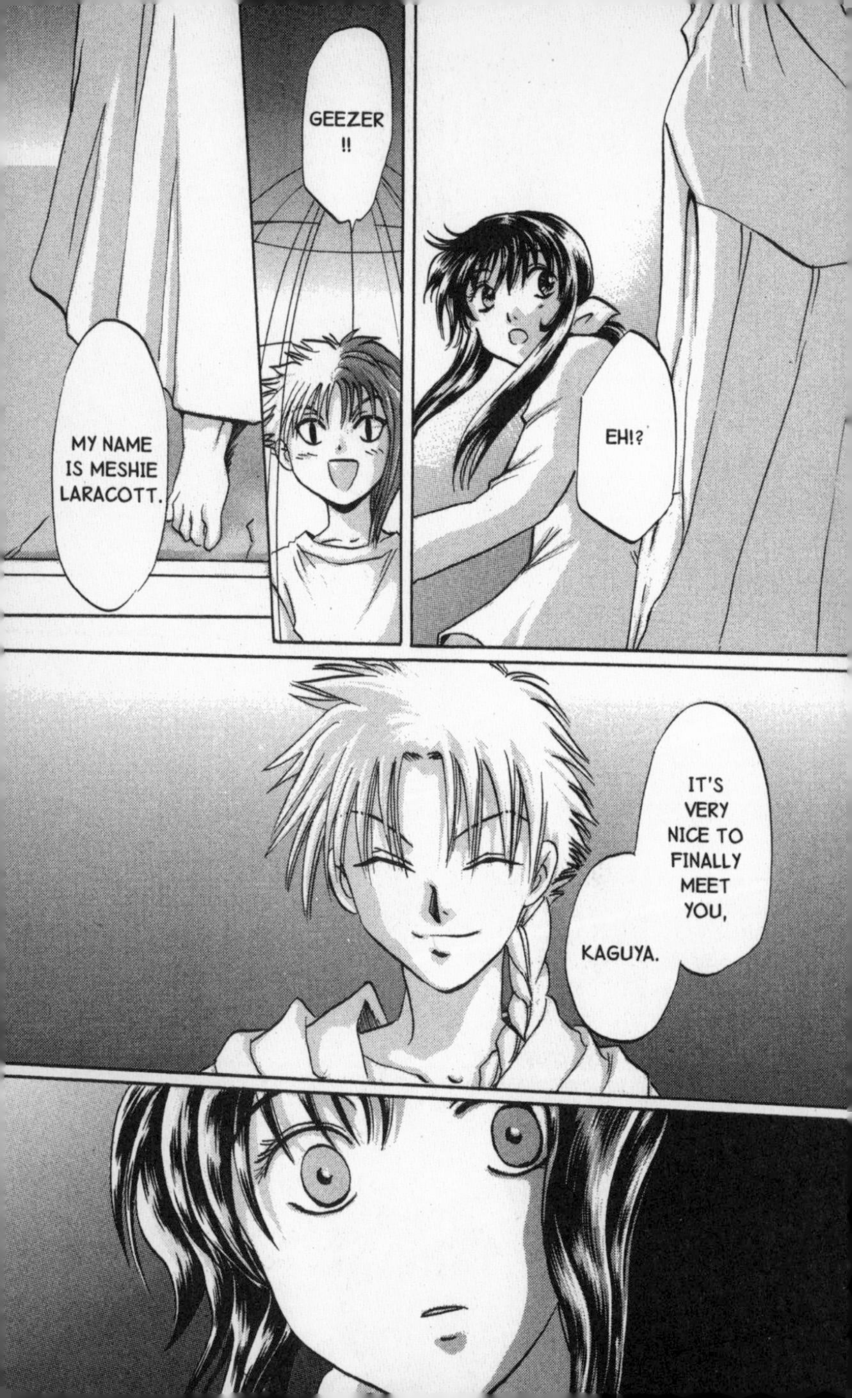
EH!?
GEEZER !!
MY NAME IS MESHIE LARACOTT.
IT'S VERY NICE TO FINALLY MEET YOU,
KAGUYA.

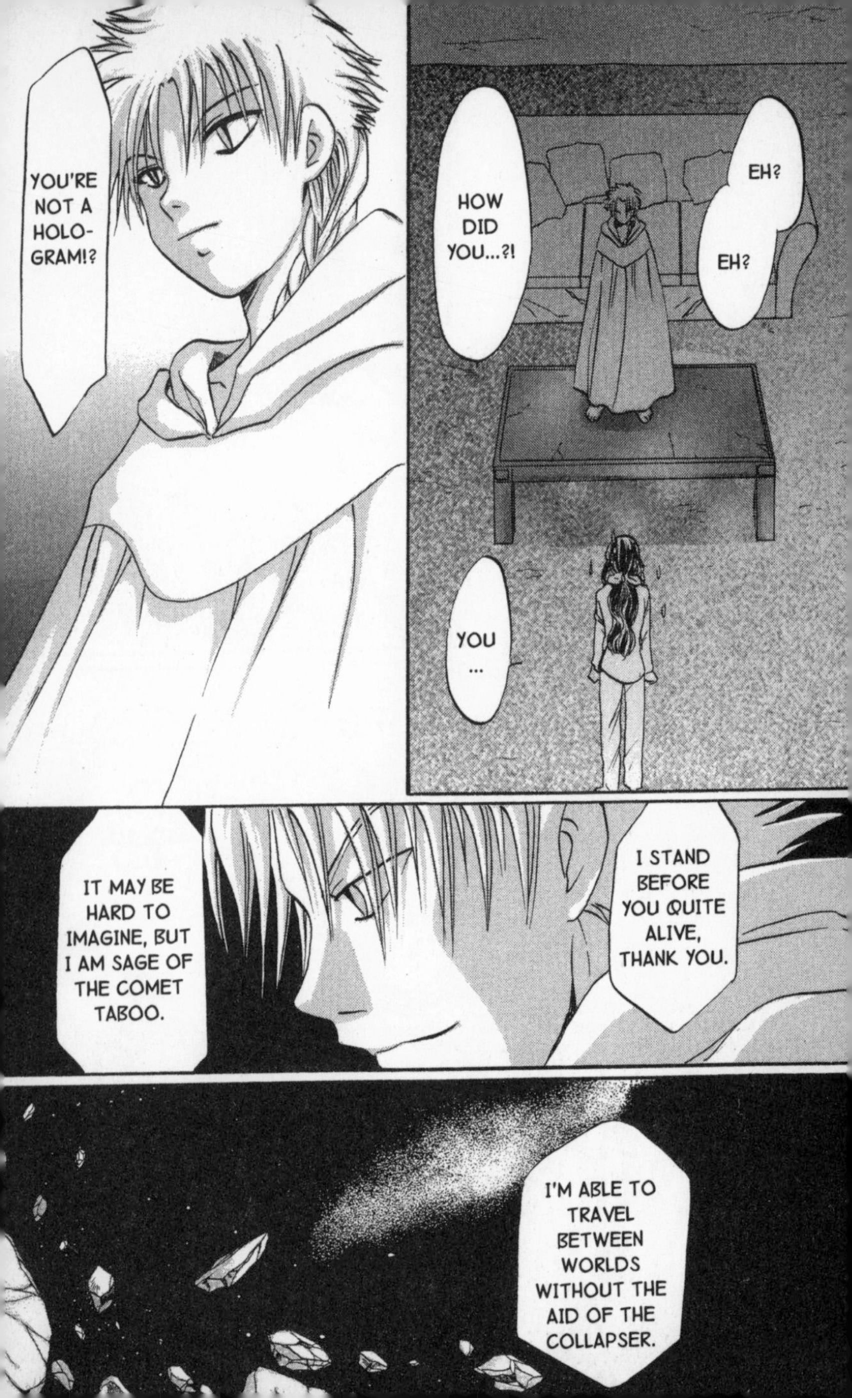
EH?
EH?
HOW DID YOU...?!
YOU ...
YOU'RE NOT A HOLO-GRAM!?
I STAND BEFORE YOU QUITE ALIVE, THANK YOU.
IT MAY BE HARD TO IMAGINE, BUT I AM SAGE OF THE COMET TABOO.
I'M ABLE TO TRAVEL BETWEEN WORLDS WITHOUT THE AID OF THE COLLAPSER.

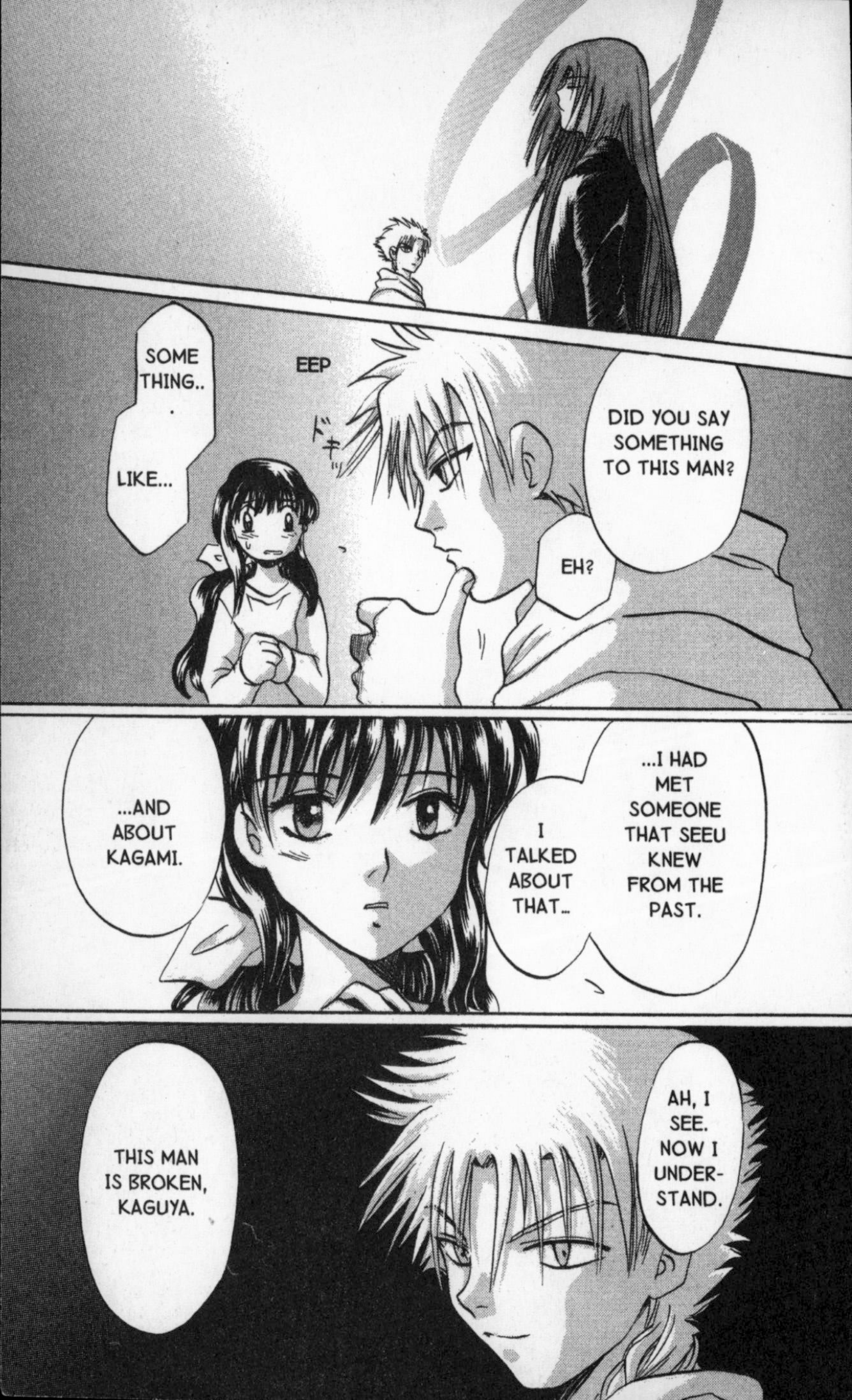
DID YOU SAY SOMETHING TO THIS MAN?
EH?
EEP
ドキッ
SOME THING.. . LIKE...
...I HAD MET SOMEONE THAT SEEU KNEW FROM THE PAST.
I TALKED ABOUT THAT..
...AND ABOUT KAGAMI.
AH, I SEE. NOW I UNDER-STAND.
THIS MAN IS BROKEN, KAGUYA.

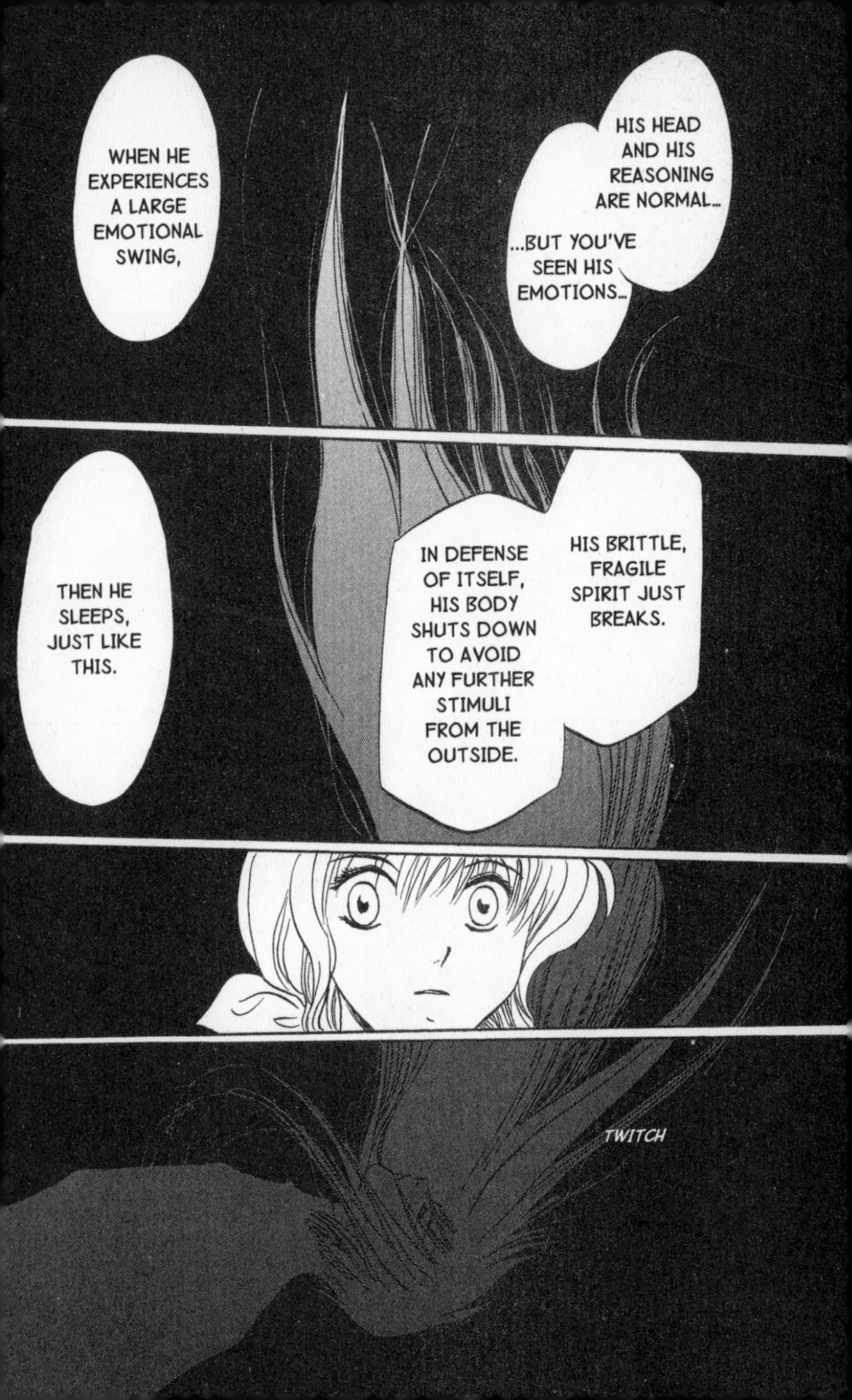
HIS HEAD AND HIS REASONING ARE NORMAL...
...BUT YOU'VE SEEN HIS EMOTIONS...
WHEN HE EXPERIENCES A LARGE EMOTIONAL SWING,
HIS BRITTLE, FRAGILE SPIRIT JUST BREAKS.
IN DEFENSE OF ITSELF, HIS BODY SHUTS DOWN TO AVOID ANY FURTHER STIMULI FROM THE OUTSIDE.
THEN HE SLEEPS, JUST LIKE THIS.
TWITCH

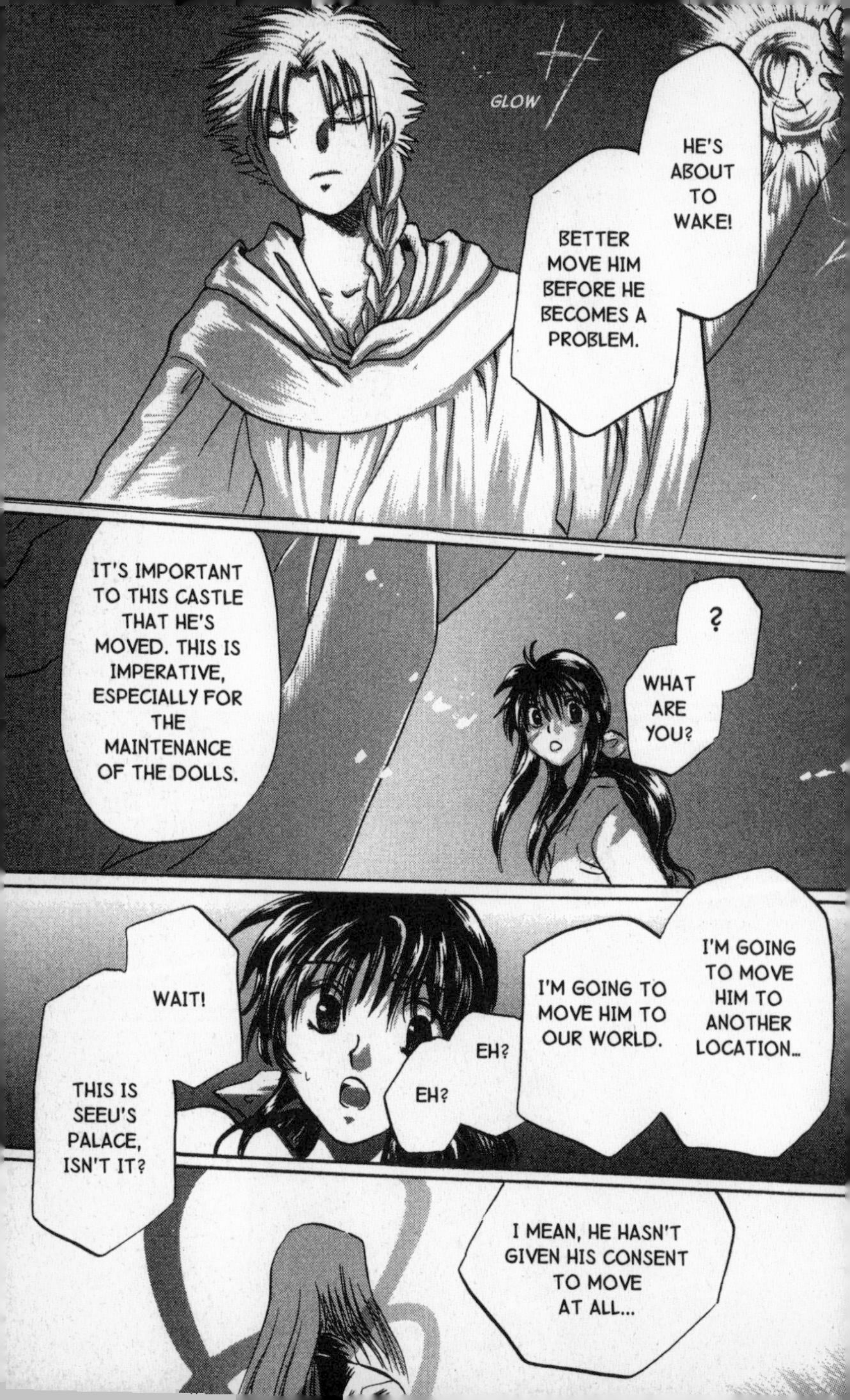
GLOW
HE'S ABOUT TO WAKE!
BETTER MOVE HIM BEFORE HE BECOMES A PROBLEM.
?
WHAT ARE YOU?
IT'S IMPORTANT TO THIS CASTLE THAT HE'S MOVED. THIS IS IMPERATIVE, ESPECIALLY FOR THE MAINTENANCE OF THE DOLLS.
I'M GOING TO MOVE HIM TO ANOTHER LOCATION...
I'M GOING TO MOVE HIM TO OUR WORLD.
EH?
EH?
WAIT!
THIS IS SEEU'S PALACE, ISN'T IT?
I MEAN, HE HASN'T GIVEN HIS CONSENT TO MOVE AT ALL...

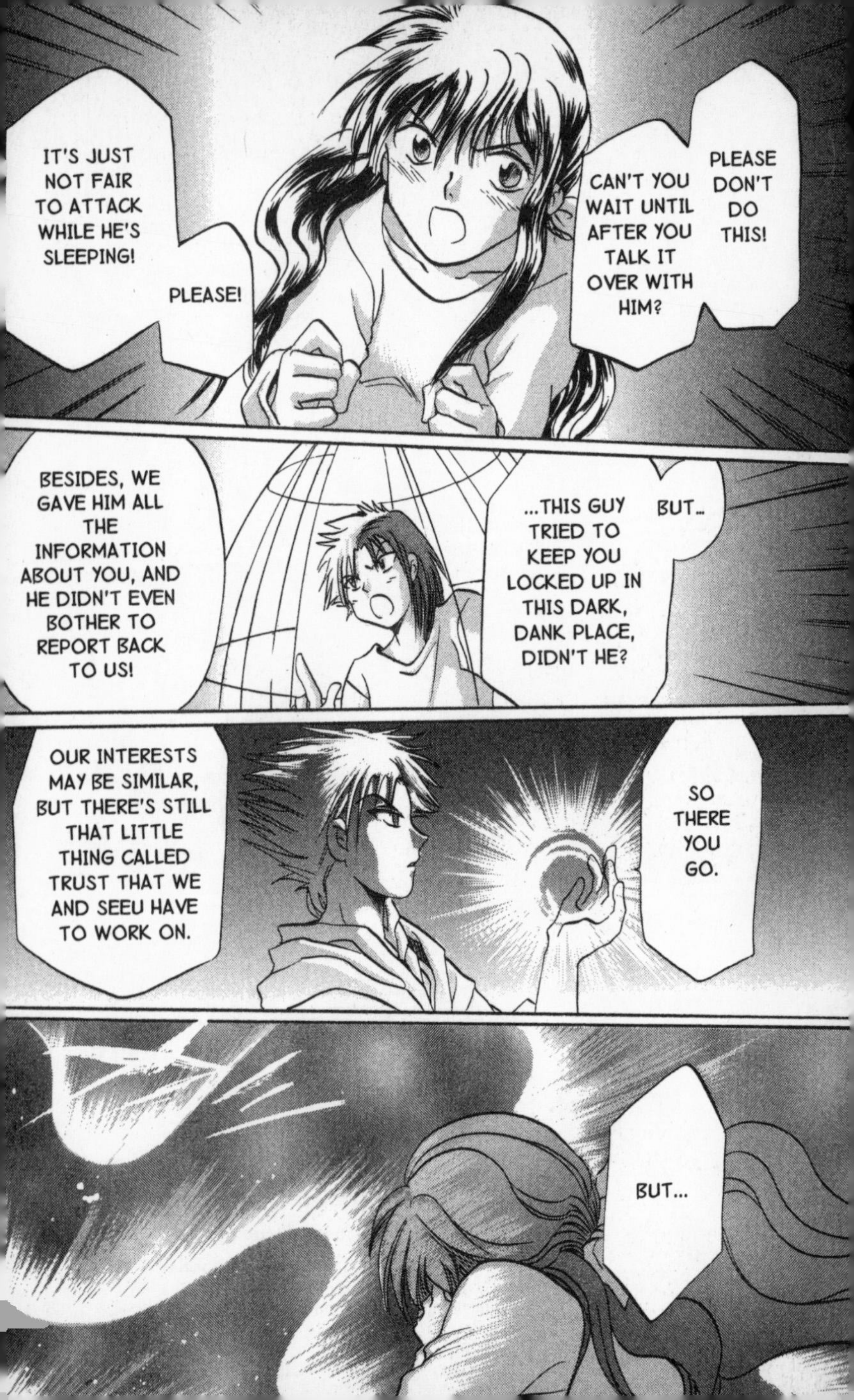
PLEASE DON'T DO THIS!
CAN'T YOU WAIT UNTIL AFTER YOU TALK IT OVER WITH HIM?
IT'S JUST NOT FAIR TO ATTACK WHILE HE'S SLEEPING!
PLEASE!
BUT...
...THIS GUY TRIED TO KEEP YOU LOCKED UP IN THIS DARK, DANK PLACE, DIDN'T HE?
BESIDES, WE GAVE HIM ALL THE INFORMATION ABOUT YOU, AND HE DIDN'T EVEN BOTHER TO REPORT BACK TO US!
SO THERE YOU GO.
OUR INTERESTS MAY BE SIMILAR, BUT THERE'S STILL THAT LITTLE THING CALLED TRUST THAT WE AND SEEU HAVE TO WORK ON.
BUT...

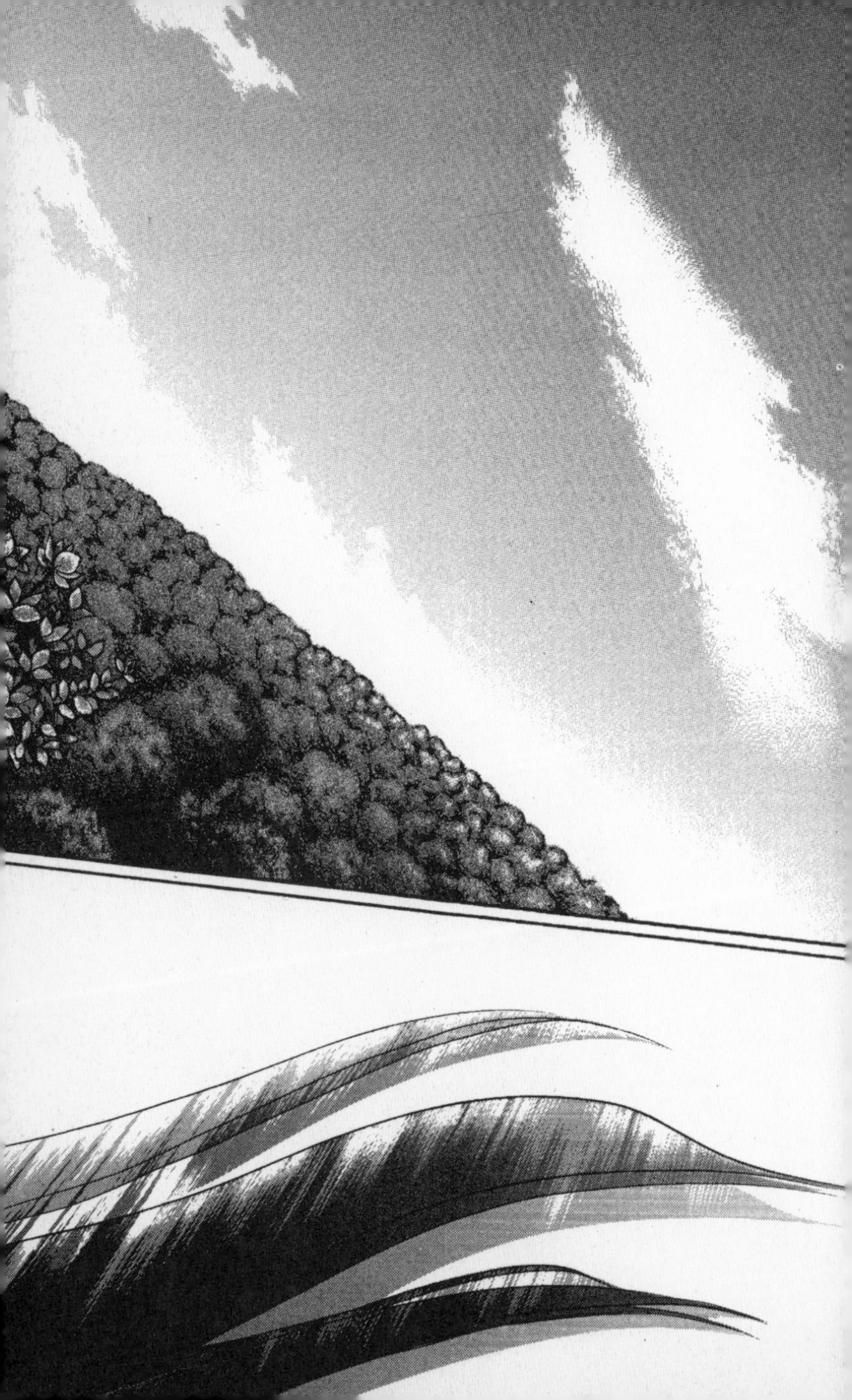

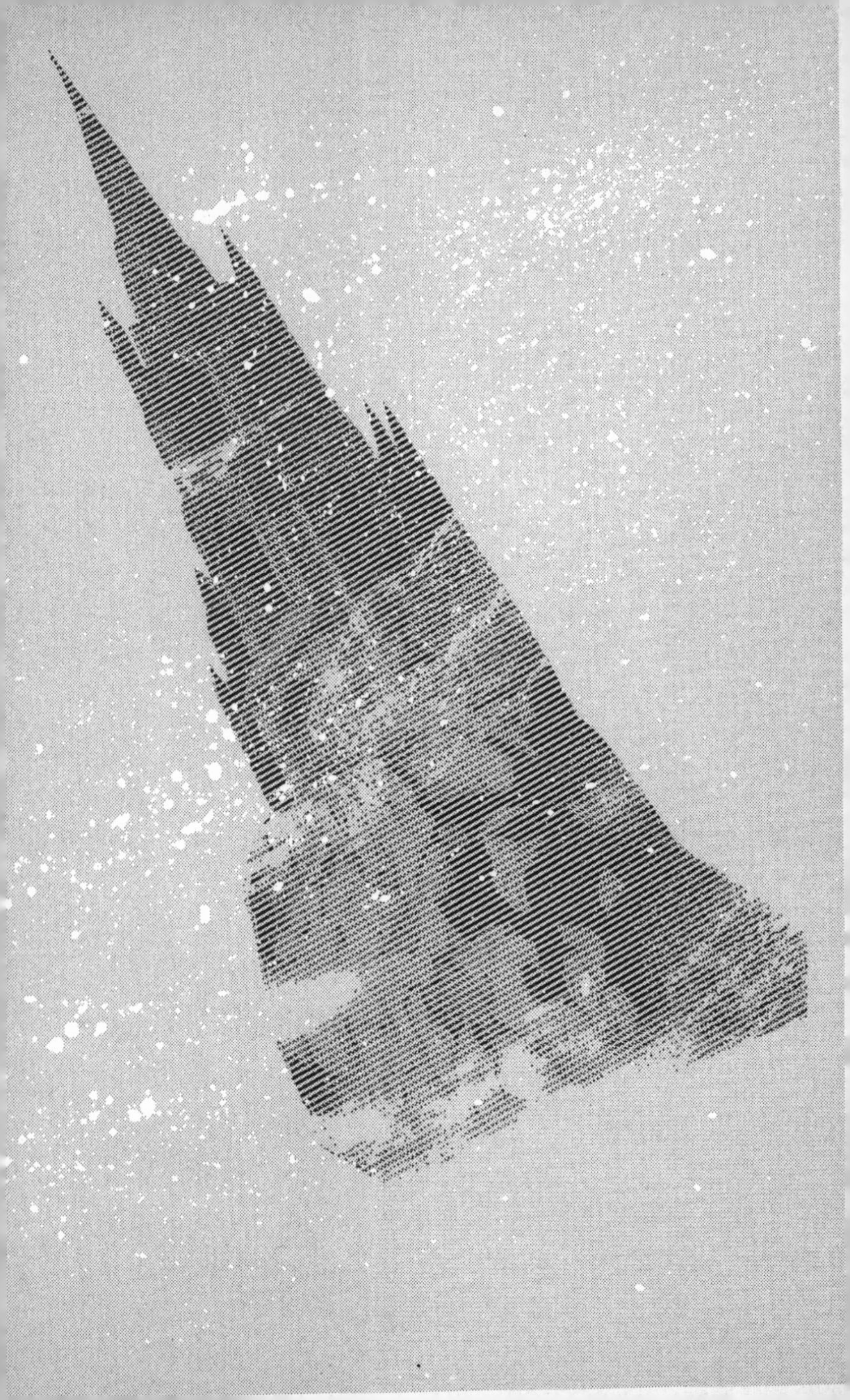

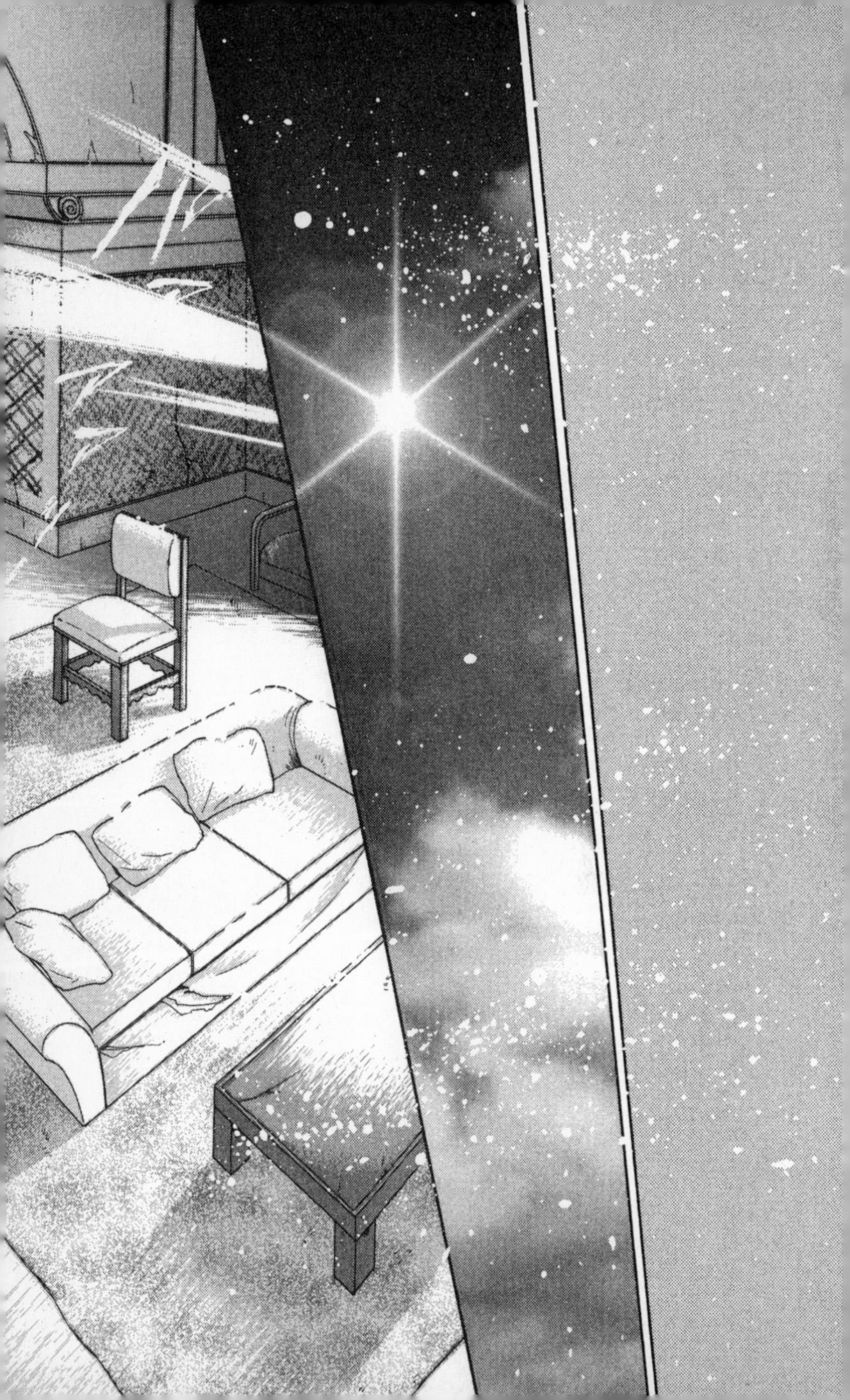

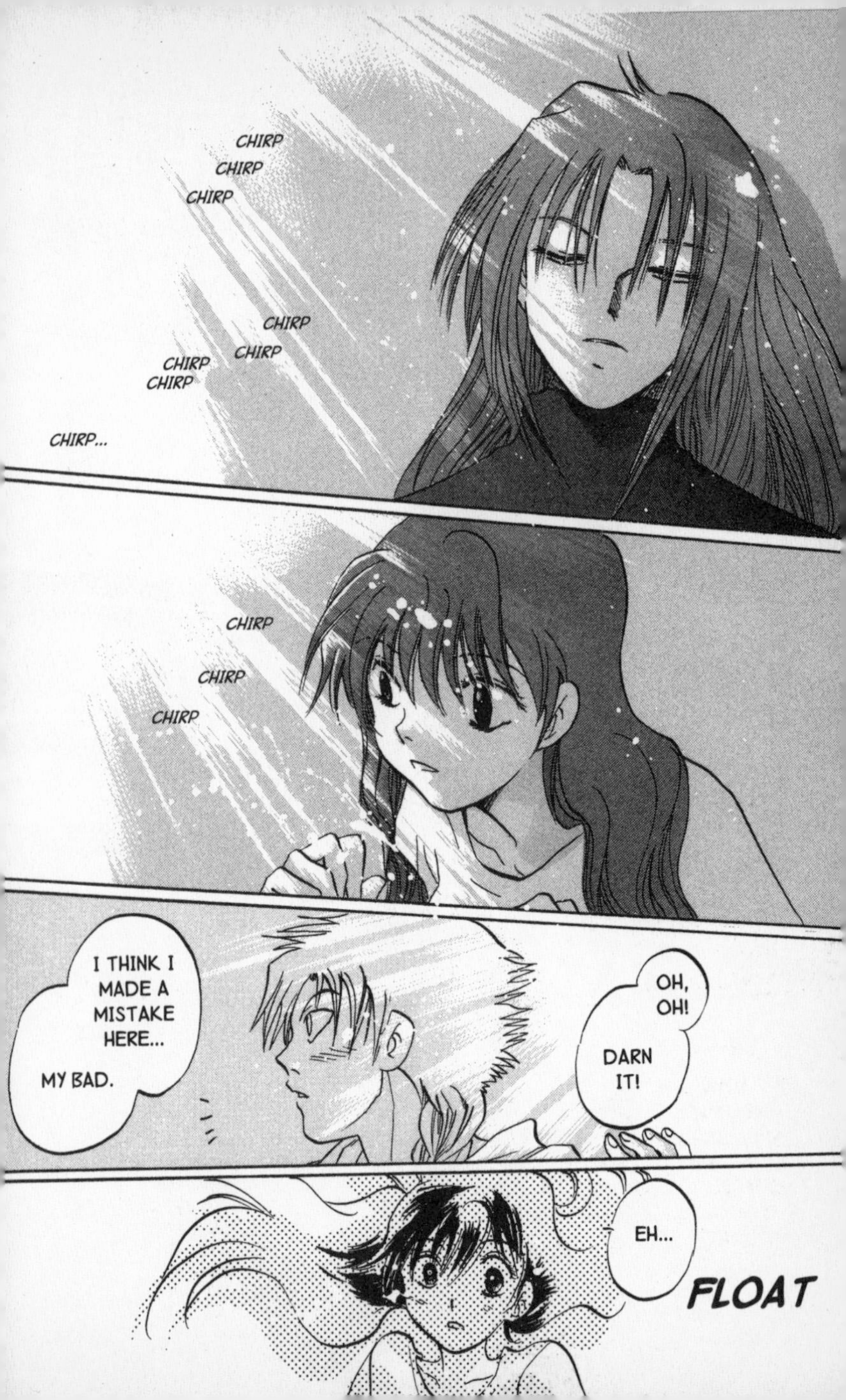
CHIRP
CHIRP
CHIRP
CHIRP
CHIRP
CHIRP
CHIRP
CHIRP...
CHIRP
CHIRP
CHIRP
OH, OH!
DARN IT!
I THINK I MADE A MISTAKE HERE...
MY BAD.
FLOAT
EH...

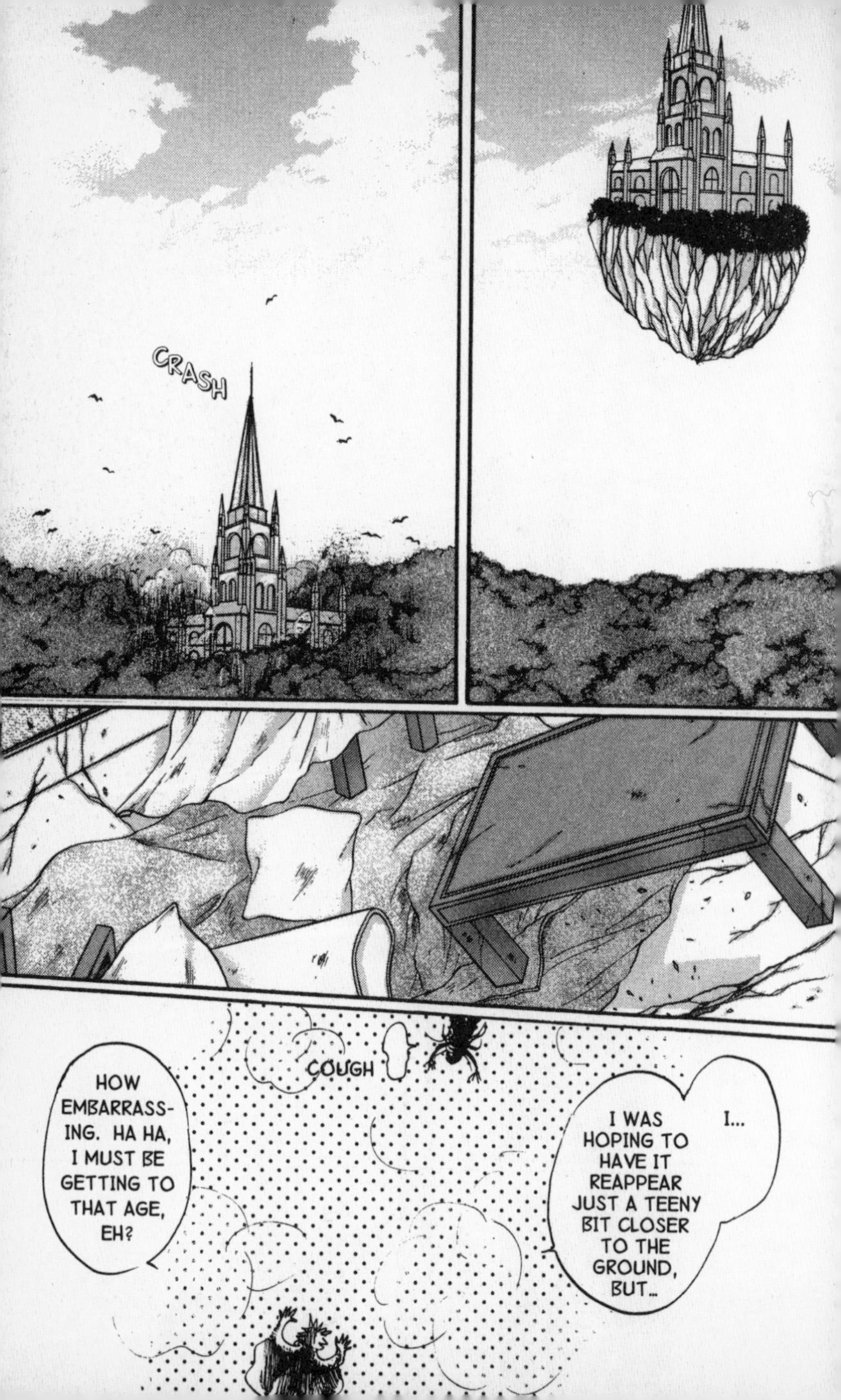
CRASH
I...
I WAS HOPING TO HAVE IT REAPPEAR JUST A TEENY BIT CLOSER TO THE GROUND, BUT...
COUGH
HOW EMBARRASS-ING. HA HA, I MUST BE GETTING TO THAT AGE, EH?

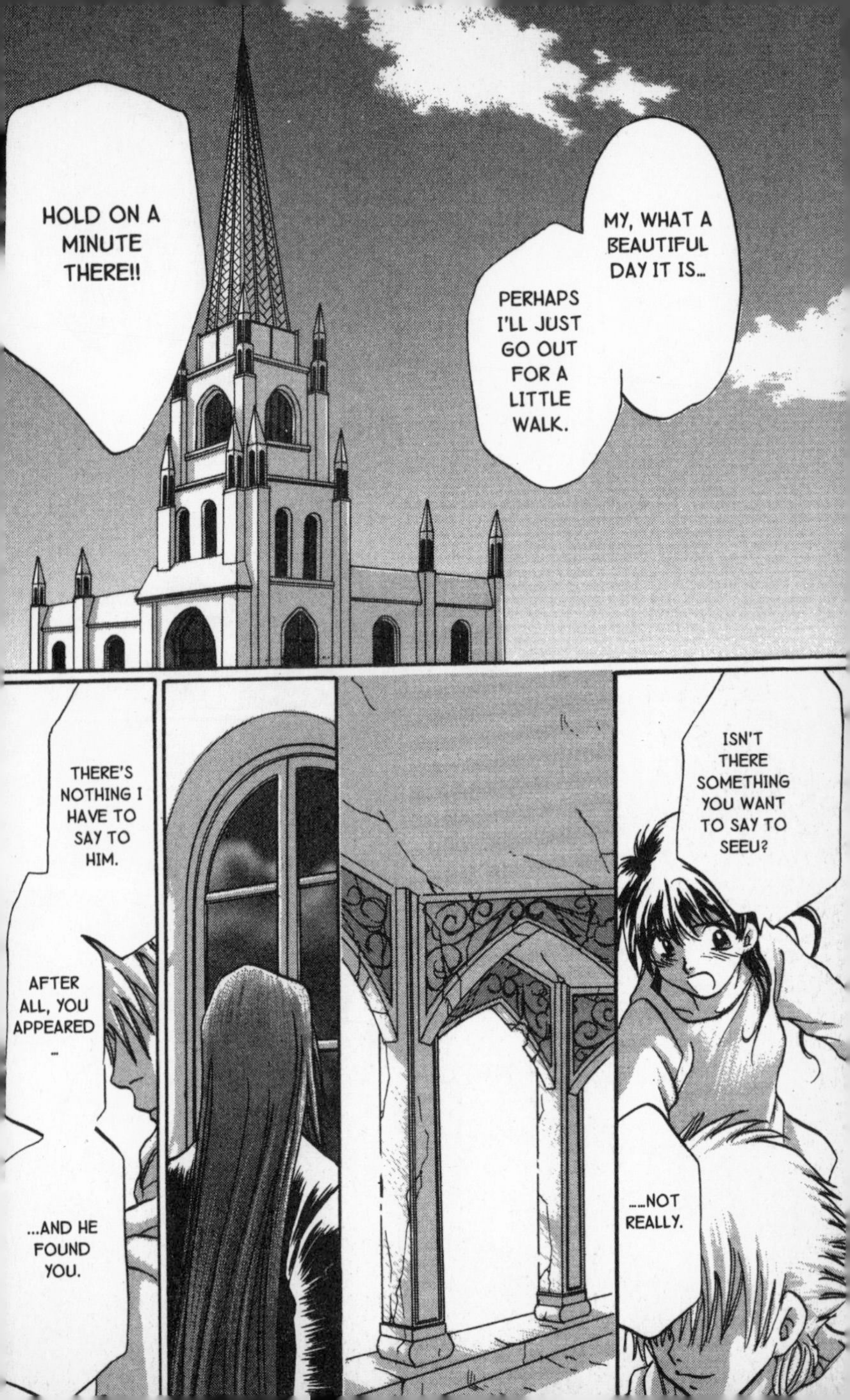
MY, WHAT A BEAUTIFUL DAY IT IS..
PERHAPS I'LL JUST GO OUT FOR A LITTLE WALK.
HOLD ON A MINUTE THERE!!
ISN'T THERE SOMETHING YOU WANT TO SAY TO SEEU?
.....NOT REALLY.
THERE'S NOTHING I HAVE TO SAY TO HIM.
AFTER ALL, YOU APPEARED ...
...AND HE FOUND YOU.

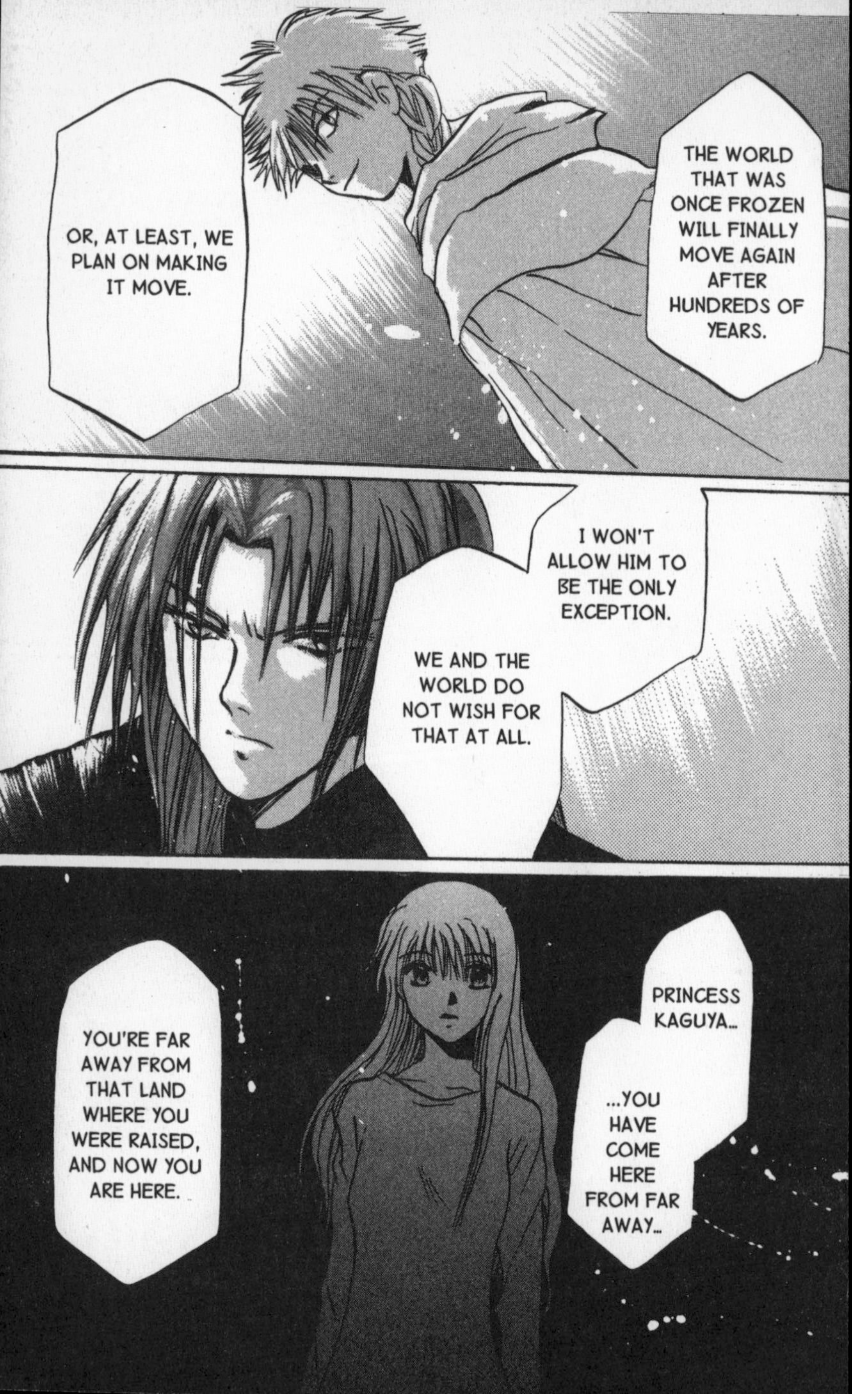
THE WORLD THAT WAS ONCE FROZEN WILL FINALLY MOVE AGAIN AFTER HUNDREDS OF YEARS.
OR, AT LEAST, WE PLAN ON MAKING IT MOVE.
I WON'T ALLOW HIM TO BE THE ONLY EXCEPTION.
WE AND THE WORLD DO NOT WISH FOR THAT AT ALL.
PRINCESS KAGUYA...
...YOU HAVE COME HERE FROM FAR AWAY...
YOU'RE FAR AWAY FROM THAT LAND WHERE YOU WERE RAISED, AND NOW YOU ARE HERE.

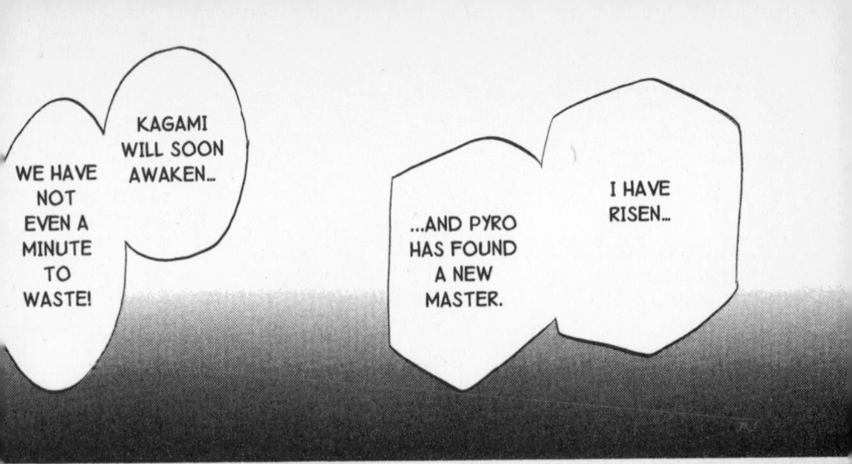
I HAVE RISEN...
...AND PYRO HAS FOUND A NEW MASTER.
KAGAMI WILL SOON AWAKEN...
WE HAVE NOT EVEN A MINUTE TO WASTE!
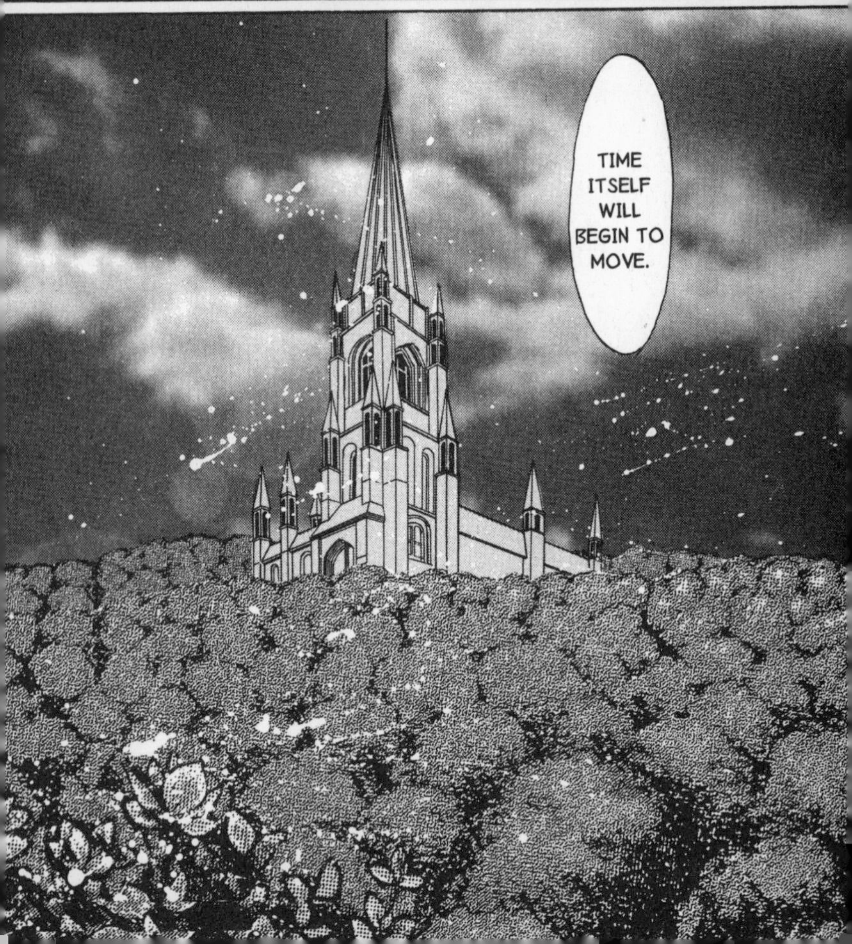
TIME ITSELF WILL BEGIN TO MOVE.

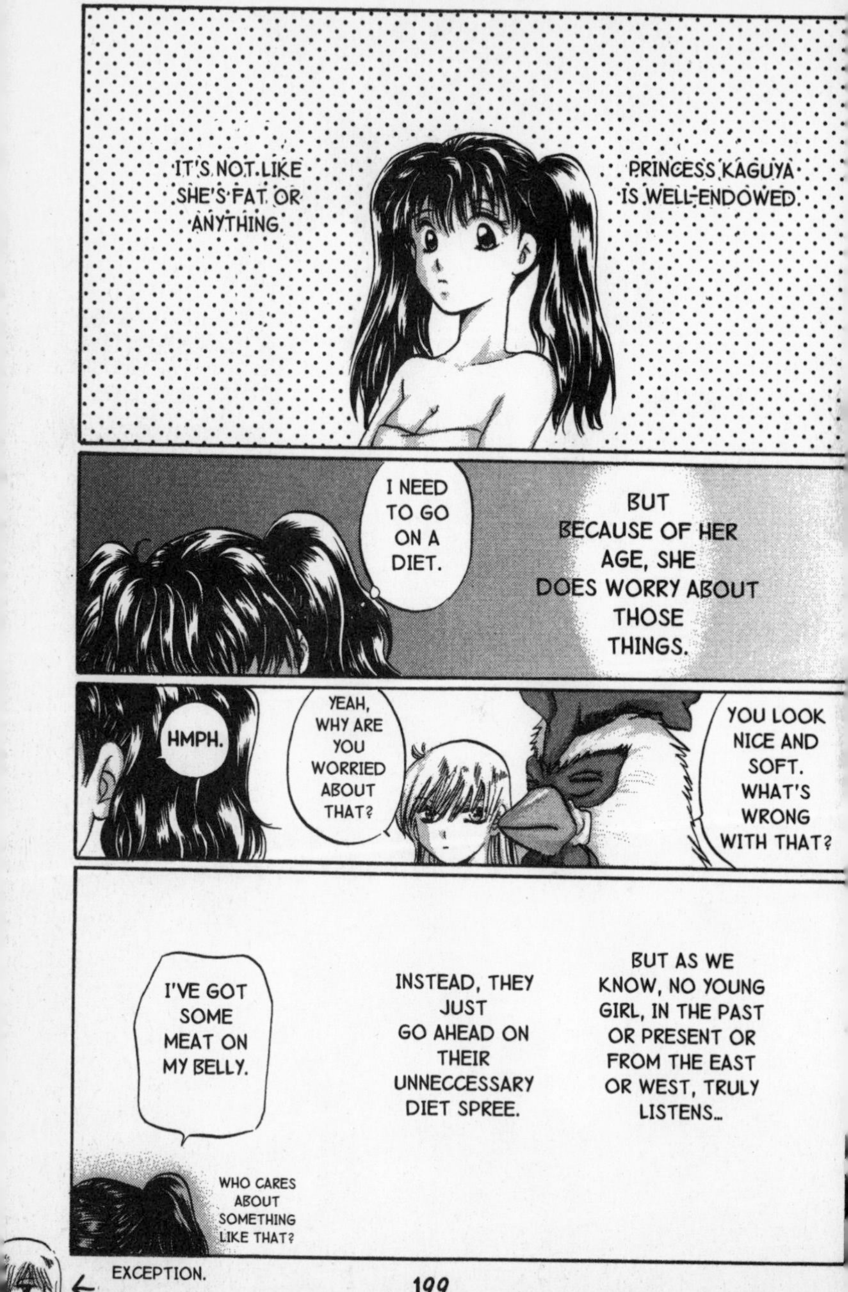
PRINCESS KAGUYA IS WELL-ENDOWED.
IT'S NOT LIKE SHE'S FAT OR ANYTHING.
BUT BECAUSE OF HER AGE, SHE DOES WORRY ABOUT THOSE THINGS.
I NEED TO GO ON A DIET.
YOU LOOK NICE AND SOFT. WHAT'S WRONG WITH THAT?
YEAH, WHY ARE YOU WORRIED ABOUT THAT?
HMPH.
BUT AS WE KNOW, NO YOUNG GIRL, IN THE PAST OR PRESENT OR FROM THE EAST OR WEST, TRULY LISTENS...
INSTEAD, THEY JUST GO AHEAD ON THEIR UNNECCESSARY DIET SPREE.
I'VE GOT SOME MEAT ON MY BELLY.
WHO CARES ABOUT SOMETHING LIKE THAT?
← EXCEPTION.

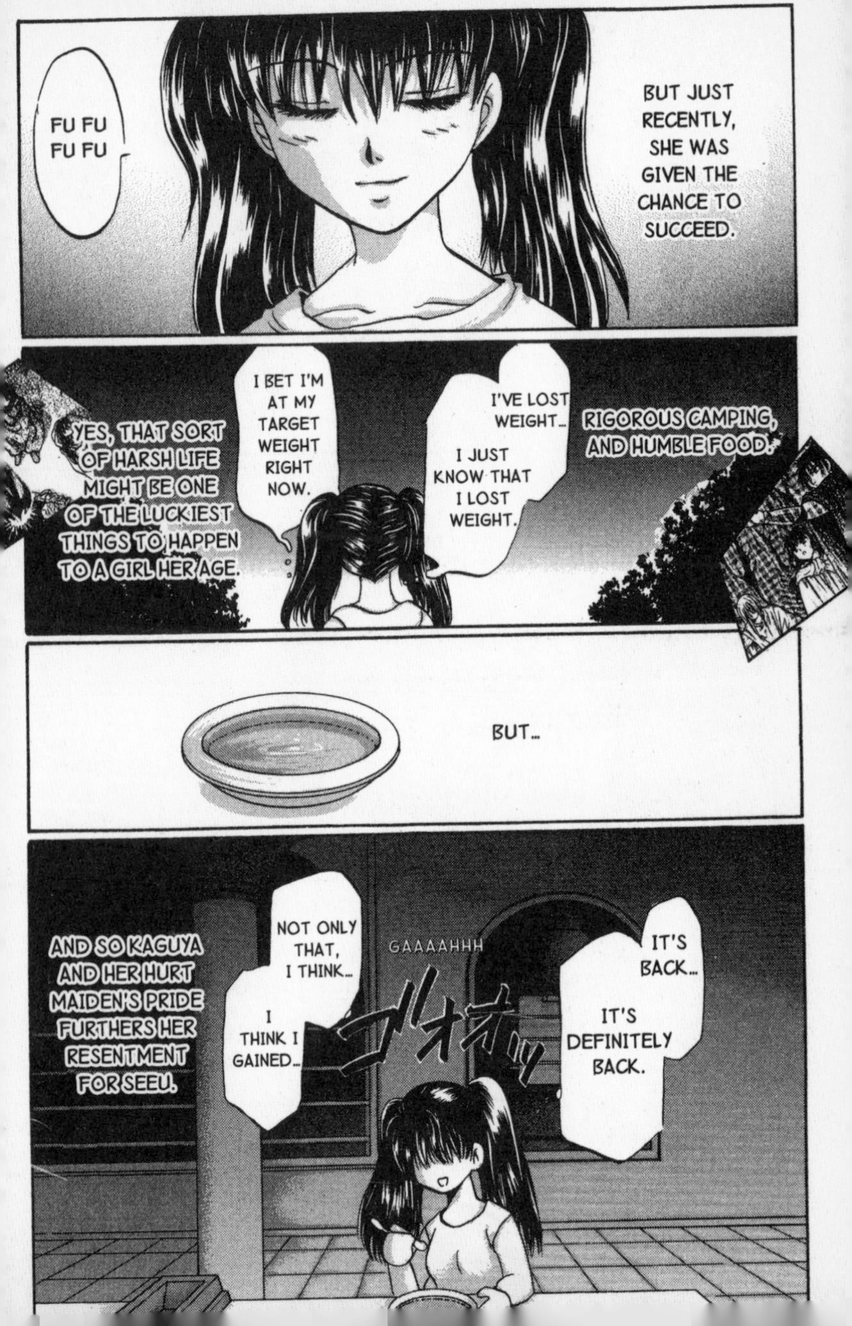
BUT JUST RECENTLY, SHE WAS GIVEN THE CHANCE TO SUCCEED.
FU FU FU FU
RIGOROUS CAMPING, AND HUMBLE FOOD.
I'VE LOST WEIGHT...
I JUST KNOW THAT I LOST WEIGHT.
I BET I'M AT MY TARGET WEIGHT RIGHT NOW.
YES, THAT SORT OF HARSH LIFE MIGHT BE ONE OF THE LUCKIEST THINGS TO HAPPEN TO A GIRL HER AGE.
BUT...
IT'S BACK...
IT'S DEFINITELY BACK.
GAAAAHHH
ゴオオッ
NOT ONLY THAT, I THINK...
I THINK I GAINED...
AND SO KAGUYA AND HER HURT MAIDEN'S PRIDE FURTHERS HER RESENTMENT FOR SEEU.

Planet Ladder 5
Coming in 2003

Will Kaguya ever be
able to save the
world and find her
way home?

Read about her
continuing
adventures
in Planet Ladder 5,
coming in 2003.

What's your favorite thing about
Kaguya and Planet Ladder?

Please send questions, comments, and
fan art to:
Julie Taylor, Senior Editor
TOKYOPOP
5900 Wilshire Blvd. Suite 2000
Los Angeles, CA 90036
editor@TOKYOPOP.com

Look for questions and responses to be
published in future volumes of Planet Ladder.

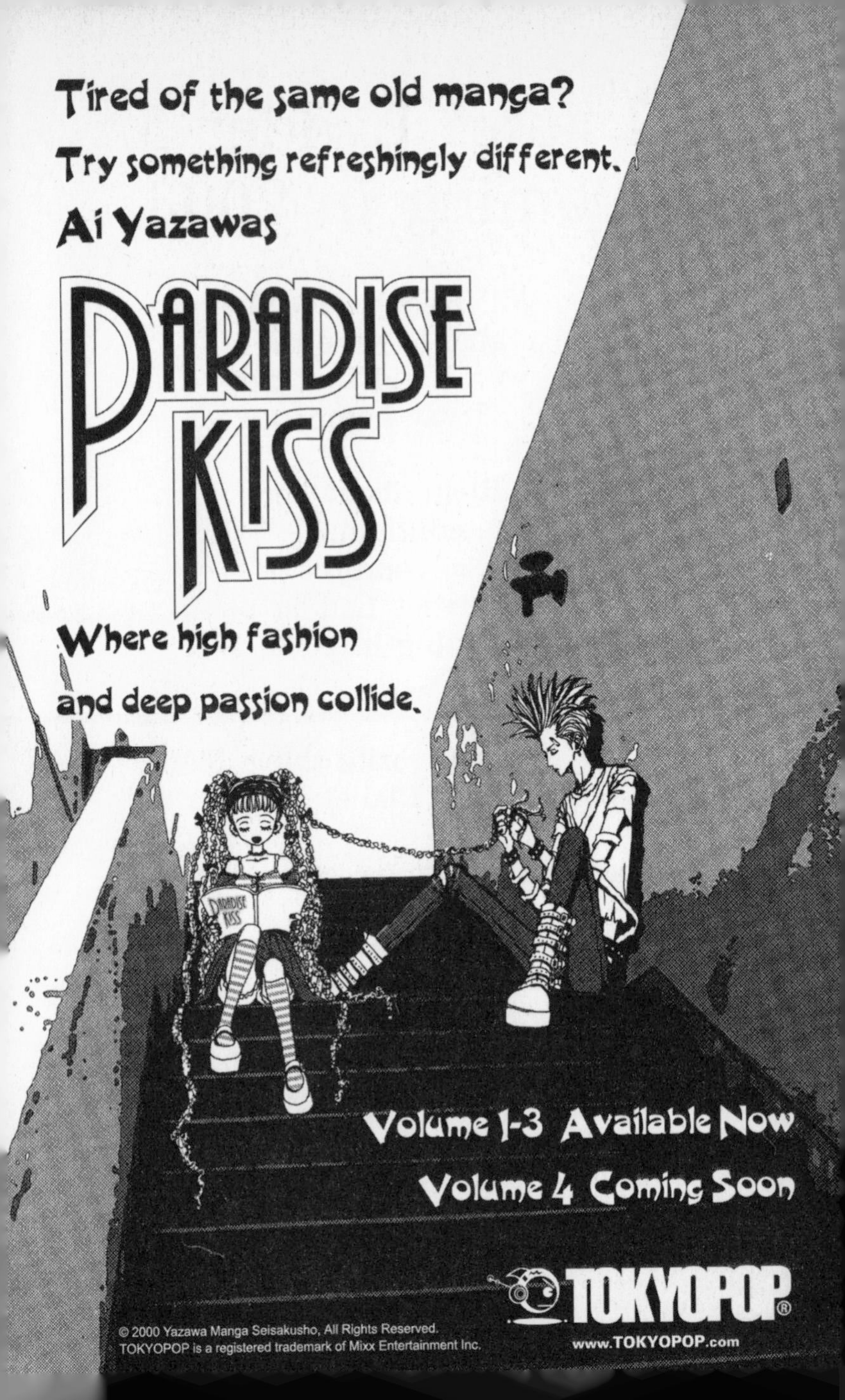
Tired of the same old manga?
Try something refreshingly different.
Ai Yazawas
PARADISE KISS
Where high fashion
and deep passion collide.
Volume 1-3 Available Now
Volume 4 Coming Soon
TOKYOPOP®
© 2000 Yazawa Manga Seisakusho, All Rights Reserved.
TOKYOPOP is a registered trademark of Mixx Entertainment Inc.
www.TOKYOPOP.com

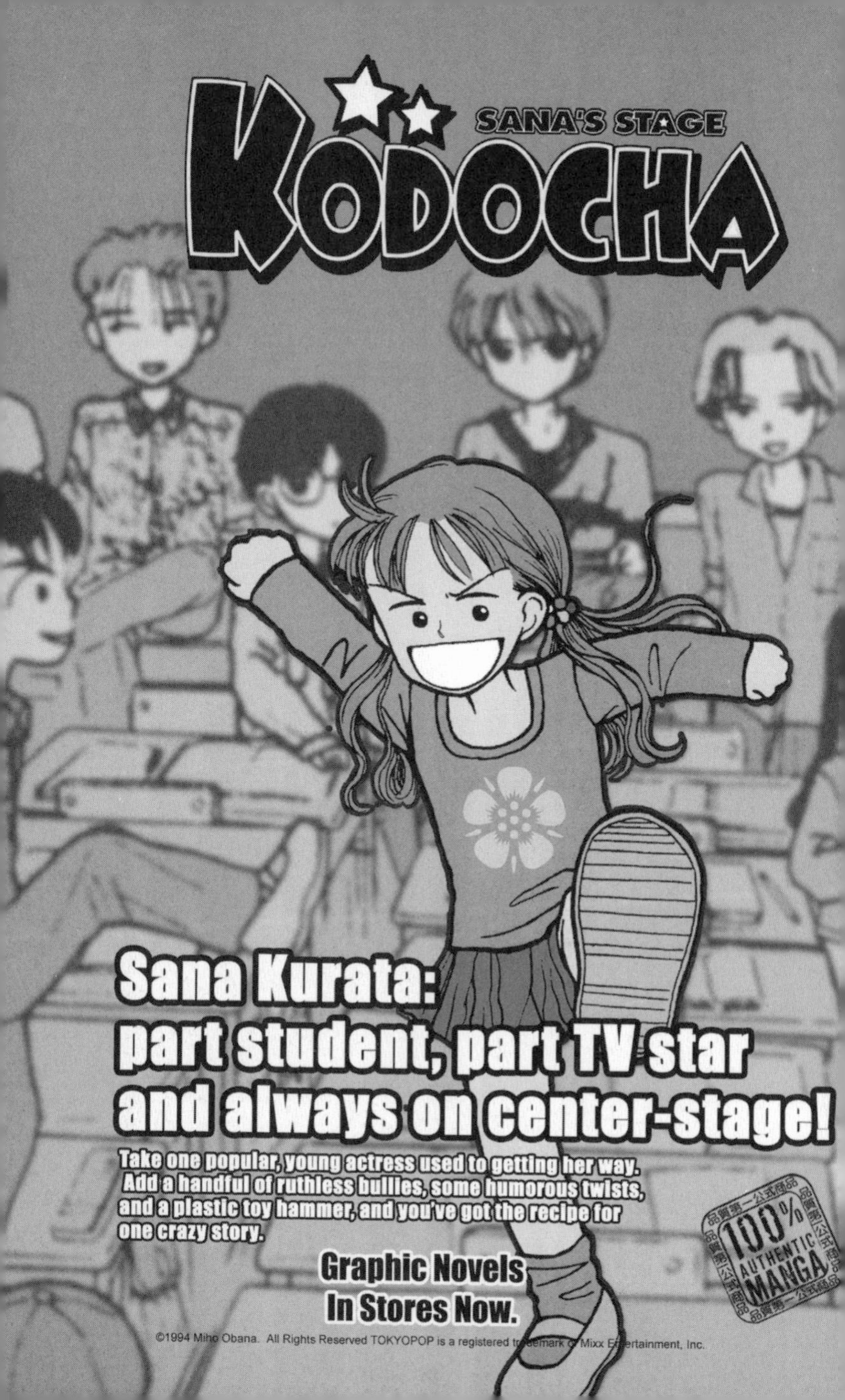
SANA'S STAGE
KODOCHA
Sana Kurata:
part student, part TV star
and always on center-stage!
Take one popular, young actress used to getting her way. Add a handful of ruthless bullies, some humorous twists, and a plastic toy hammer, and you've got the recipe for one crazy story.
Graphic Novels
In Stores Now.
100% AUTHENTIC MANGA
©1994 Miho Obana. All Rights Reserved TOKYOPOP is a registered trademark of Mixx Entertainment, Inc.

Miki's a love struck young girl and Yuu's the perfect guy.

There's just one minor complication in

Marmalade Boy

A tangled teen romance for the new millennium

"Marmalade Boy has a beguiling comedic charm...and the likable characters make for a delightful read."
- Andrew D. Arnold
Time.com

STOP!

This is the back of the book.
You wouldn't want to spoil a great ending!

This book is printed "manga-style," in the authentic Japanese right-to-left format. Since none of the artwork has been flipped or altered, readers get to experience the story just as the creator intended. You've been asking for it, so TOKYOPOP® delivered: authentic, hot-off-the-press, and far more fun!

DIRECTIONS

If this is your first time reading manga-style, here's a quick guide to help you understand how it works.

It's easy... just start in the top right panel and follow the numbers. Have fun, and look for more 100% authentic manga from TOKYOPOP®!